Hermeneutics and Psychological Theory

HERMENEUTICS

AND

PSYCHOLOGICAL THEORY:

Interpretive Perspectives on Personality, Psychotherapy, and Psychopathology

EDITED BY
Stanley B. Messer,
Louis A. Sass, and
Robert L. Woolfolk

RUTGERS UNIVERSITY PRESS

New Brunswick and London

Second paperback printing 1990

Copyright © 1988 by Rutgers, The State University

All rights reserved

Manufactured in the United States of America

Library of Congress Cataloging-in-Publication Data

Hermeneutics and psychological theory.

  Based on a symposium held in 1985 and sponsored
by the Graduate School of Applied and Professional
Psychology of Rutgers University.
  Includes bibliographies and index.
  1. Personality—Congresses.   2. Psychology,
Pathological—Congresses.   3. Psychotherapy—
Congresses.   4. Psychoanalytic interpretation—
Congresses.   I. Messer, Stanley B.   II. Sass, Louis
Arnorsson.   III. Woolfolk, Robert L.   IV. Rutgers
University. Graduate School of Applied and Professional
Psychology. [DNLM: 1. Personality—congresses.
2. Psychoanalytic Interpretation—congresses.
3. Psychoanalytic Theory—congresses.   4. Psycho-
pathology—congresses.   5. Psychotherapy—congresses.
WM 460.7 H553 1985]
BF698.H46 1988   150'.1   87-23521
ISBN 0-8135-1291-3
ISBN 0-8135-1292-1 (pbk.)

British Cataloging-in-Publication information available

To
Doris and Harry Evin
Jane D. Woolfolk

Contents

Empirical Perspectives

ONTOLOGICAL HERMENEUTICS

CRITIQUE OF IDEOLOGY

Preface

The social sciences in North America are currently in a state of ferment, with traditional objectivist approaches being questioned in a variety of ways. The limits and disadvantages of a narrowly defined scientific approach have been noted increasingly by scholars in fields such as anthropology, sociology, and political science. Many of these social scientists propose an "interpretive" or "hermeneutic" approach that emphasizes the difference between the data of the natural sciences and those of the human or social sciences—where the objects studied are subjects, embedded in cultural practices, who think, construe, understand, misunderstand, and interpret, as well as reflect on the meanings they produce. In elaborating this distinction, such social scientists have drawn on the work of various philosophers critical of scientism.

With some notable exceptions, psychology has been relatively impervious to these developments. As a discipline psychology deliberately separated itself from philosophy at the turn of the century and has been dominated ever since by a self-conscious effort to model itself on the natural sciences. The present volume is an attempt to lead the discipline of psychology more fully into these current intellectual debates. It does so by bringing together philosophers, psychologists, and other social scientists to discuss fundamentals of psychological method and theory.

How are we to define "hermeneutics," and what is its relevance for psychology? We have adopted a rather broad usage of the term—'hermeneutics" as a rubric covering a disparate assortment of alternatives to, and critiques of, scientism in the understanding of human beings. One of these approaches emphasizes methodological alternatives to the natural sciences. Here, "hermeneutics" is understood as an art or science of interpretation specially adapted to the human domain. Unlike objectivist social science, "methodological hermeneutics" does not strive for decontextualized facts, but emphasizes meanings as experienced by individuals whose activities are rooted in given sociohistorical settings. The hermeneutic approach insists upon the inseparability of fact and value, detail and context, and observation and theory. It seeks less to generate universal laws than to understand the specific case in its historical and cultural context. Methodological hermeneutics utilizes qualitative description, analogical understanding, and narrative modes of exposition. It deemphasizes quantification and controlled experimentation, and does not seek a neutral, objective vocabulary with which to characterize social phenomena. Part One of this volume, "Methodological Issues," is divided into two sections: first, theoretical explorations of hermeneutic method as applied to psychology and psychoanalysis; second, articles that integrate empirical methods with hermeneutic perspectives, or that criticize hermeneutics from an empirical standpoint.

A second approach, known as "ontological hermeneutics" (covered in Part Two of this volume), is not primarily concerned with the role of interpretation in scientific method, but with its central role in the constitution of human existence itself. This approach accepts the claim made by hermeneutic thinkers like Heidegger and Gadamer that our fundamental mode of being-in-the-world is that of creatures who understand and interpret. To comprehend what it is to be human, therefore, we must seek to understand as fully as possible what understanding itself is about. Ontological hermeneutics takes the position that there is no knowledge free of presuppositions. Human knowing is always interpretive, and interpretation always takes place within an at-best dimly perceived horizon of bodily activities, symbol systems, and cultural practices and institutions. Thus, the ontological perspective calls into question the Cartesian world view and philosophical anthropology, with its subject-viewing-object picture of knowledge acquisition and its notion of a decontextualized subject recording neutral, objective facts.

A third branch, "critical hermeneutics" (covered in Part Three), incorporates certain key insights of both methodological and ontological hermeneutics, but has a different intellectual goal: that of revealing the moral and ideological underpinnings of intellectual practices and social institutions, in order to foster emancipation from arbitrary forms of cultural and political domination. This is exemplified by the work of Habermas, who follows the tradition of Critical Theory (initiated by the Frankfurt School) in bringing Freudian and Marxist perspectives to bear on the social sciences.

These three facets of hermeneutics—methodological, ontological and critical—define the three parts of this volume, which is based on a symposium held at Rutgers University. The symposium grew out of the editors' shared dissatisfaction with the current overvaluation of a scientistic and positivistic attitude within psychology, and an appreciation of the role of the humanities, especially philosophy and literature, in psychological discourse. We invited several distinguished philosophers and social scientists to address some aspect of this topic and to comment on one of the other papers, which they read in advance. The symposium was characterized by vigorous debate and discussion, both among the speakers and with the audience. After the symposium, we encouraged the authors to clarify their papers where necessary, to expand on their commentaries, and to offer a rejoinder to the commentaries on their papers. In this way we have tried to preserve the excitement of live dialogue and debate while avoiding the disadvantages of publishing conference proceedings in the raw. One paper (by Louis Sass), not delivered at the conference, was added in order to elucidate the often misunderstood relationship of ontological hermeneutics to humanism in psychology (psychology's "third force").

The book begins with an introductory overview of the fundamental ideas of hermeneutics. Here we sketch the historical and intellectual background necessary to understand three major areas of hermeneutic endeavour as we have defined them—methodology, ontology, and critique of ideology—and to place each of the individual chapters within its appropriate intellectual context.

In addition to illustrating an aspect of hermeneutic thinking, the papers all address issues of current importance in one or more areas of psychology, including personality (e.g., Gergen, Kovel, Sass, Taylor), psychotherapy (Fox Keller and Flax, Maddi, Spence), psychopathology (Bernstein, Dreyfus and Wakefield), and methodology (Grünbaum, Meichenbaum). A wide variety of theoretical approaches are also represented or discussed, including psychoanalysis (Bernstein, Fox Keller and Flax, Grünbaum, Spence), cognitive-behaviorism (Meichenbaum), existentialism (Maddi), hermeneutic phenomenology (Dreyfus and Wakefield, Sass), Marxism (Kovel), social constructionism (Gergen), and the history of ideas (Taylor).

Planning the symposium and book were major undertakings that could not have been accomplished without the help of several people, and we would like to express our gratitude to them. Donald Peterson, former Dean of the Graduate School of Applied and Professional Psychology, encouraged us to launch this endeavor and aided us along the way with his enthusiasm and astute editorial advice. Nathaniel

Pallone, previously Academic Vice President of Rutgers University and Chair of the Rutgers University Press Council, generously offered the support and facilities of the university, and lent his personal interest and commitment to this project. Charles Guignon provided thoughtful comments on an earlier draft of this volume. Charlotte Schulman did a superb job of handling a host of administrative matters and in seeing that all went smoothly during the conference. The symposium was made possible by a grant from the Humanities Grant Program of the New Jersey Department of Higher Education. We are thankful that the administrators of that program perceived the importance of fostering dialogue between philosophy and psychology.

Stanley B. Messer
Louis A. Sass
Robert L. Woolfolk

New Brunswick, N.J.
April 1990

Contributors

RICHARD J. BERNSTEIN is Vera List Professor of Philosophy at the Graduate Faculty, New School for Social Research. His interest is in contemporary social and political philosophy, especially the interrelations of Anglo-American and Continental philosophy. His books include *Praxis and Action, The Restructuring of Social and Political Theory, Beyond Objectivism and Relativism,* and *Philosophical Profiles.*

HUBERT L. DREYFUS is Professor of Philosophy at the University of California at Berkeley. He works in the phenomenological tradition, applying the philosophical techniques and insights of this school to contemporary concerns. His books include: *What Computers Can't Do: The Limits of Artificial Intelligence; Michael Foucault: Beyond Structuralism and Hermeneutics* (with Paul Rabinow); and *Mind over Machine* (with Stuart Dreyfus).

JANE FLAX, a political theorist and psychotherapist, is Associate Professor of Political Science at Howard University. Her interests are in feminist theory, psychoanalysis, epistemology, and contemporary philosophy. She is currently completing a book, *Freud's Children?: Psychoanalysis and Feminism in the Postmodern West.*

EVELYN FOX KELLER is Professor of Rhetoric and Women's Studies at the University of California, Berkeley. She is the author of numerous articles on molecular biology, theoretical physics, mathematical biology, and the history, philosophy, and sociology of science. Her books include *A Feeling for the Organism: The Life and Work of Barbara McClintock* and *Reflections on Gender and Science.*

KENNETH J. GERGEN is Professor of Psychology at Swarthmore College. His special interests are in the nature of psychological discourse, microsocial theories of human action, and scientific metatheory in postmodern perspective. He is the author of *Toward*

Transformation of Social Knowledge and the co-editor of *Historical Social Psychology, The Social Construction of the Person,* and *Metapsychology: The Analysis of Psychological Theory.*

ADOLF GRÜNBAUM is Andrew Mellon Professor of Philosophy, Research Professor of Psychiatry, and Chairman of the Center for Philosophy of Science at the University of Pittsburgh. He has written extensively on the philosophical foundations both of the natural sciences and of psychoanalysis. His best-known books are *Philosophical Problems of Space and Time* and *The Foundations of Psychoanalysis: A Philosophical Critique.*

JOEL KOVEL, a psychiatrist and psychoanalyst, is Alger Hiss Professor of Social Studies at Bard College. He recently held a fellowship of the John Simon Guggenheim Foundation. His most recent books are *The Age of Desire* and *Against the State of Nuclear Terror.* A forthcoming book, *History and Spirit,* concerns the themes discussed in his essay in this collection.

SALVATORE R. MADDI is Director of the Program in Social Ecology at the University of California, Irvine. He has written on personality, psychopathology, creativity, stress management, and psychotherapy, as well as on empirical and conceptual aspects of existential psychology. He is the author of *Personality Theories: A Comparative Analysis* and *The Hardy Executive: Health under Stress,* among other books.

DONALD MEICHENBAUM is Professor of Psychology at the University of Waterloo in Ontario, Canada. He has written extensively on cognitive behavior therapy, pain, and stress management. He is the author or co-editor of several books, including *Cognitive Behavior Modification* and *Coping with Stress.*

STANLEY B. MESSER is Professor of Clinical Psychology in the Graduate School of Applied and Professional Psychology at Rutgers University. He has conducted empirical research on cognitive style and psychotherapy outcome, and his conceptual papers have examined the values, visions of reality, and ways of knowing inherent in different psychological theories and therapies. He is co-editor of, and contributor to, the book *Psychoanalytic Therapy and Behavior Therapy: Is Integration Possible?*

LOUIS A. SASS is Associate Professor of Clinical Psychology at the Graduate School of Applied and Professional Psychology, Rutgers University. He has written on the philosophical foundations of psychoanalysis and the social sciences, and on the etiology and phenomenology of schizophreniform illnesses. Currently, he is completing one book on Wittgenstein and the Schreber case and another concerning experience and expression in schizophrenia and in modernism and postmodernism.

DONALD P. SPENCE is Professor of Psychiatry at the Robert Wood Johnson Medical School. He is interested in the relation between clinical evidence and psychoanalytic theory and the ways in which traditional methods of reporting cases interfere with clear views of the evidence. He is the author of *Narrative Truth and Historical Truth* and a critical study of psychoanalytic theory entitled *The Freudian Metaphor*.

CHARLES TAYLOR is Professor of Philosophy and Political Science at McGill University. He has written extensively on the philosophy of psychology, hermeneutic theory, and political philosophy. His books include *The Explanation of Behavior*, *Hegel*, two volumes of *Philosophical Papers*, and, most recently, *Sources of the Self: The Making of the Modern Identity*.

JEROME WAKEFIELD is Assistant Professor at the Columbia University School of Social Work. Trained as a philosopher and as a psychotherapist, his main interest is in the philosophical foundations of clinical theory. He is currently working on two books, one on *Freud and Intentionality*, the other a critique of recent conceptualizations of sexual disorder, tentatively titled *The Myth of Sexual Harmony*.

ROBERT L. WOOLFOLK is Professor of Psychology at Rutgers University. He has conducted empirical research on psychological stress, skilled motor performance, and the effects of psychotherapy and has written on the philosophical and sociocultural foundations of psychology and psychotherapy. He is the co-author of *Stress, Sanity, and Survival* and co-editor of *Principles and Practice of Stress Management*.

Hermeneutics and
Psychological Theory

Chapter 1

Introduction to Hermeneutics

ROBERT L. WOOLFOLK,
LOUIS A. SASS, and
STANLEY B. MESSER

This volume brings hermeneutic perspectives to bear upon psychological theory, especially that related to clinical psychology, psychiatry, and the practice of psychotherapy. The term *hermeneutics* recently has begun to appear in a variety of discussions within psychology, psychoanalysis, and the social sciences at large—where it has been given various definitions, some broad and some narrow. Our characterization of hermeneutics is that of a family of related approaches that have developed as a corrective to scientism—the modern proclivity to view the natural sciences as models for all forms of inquiry. This opposition to the domination of intellectual and cultural activity by standards and practices extrapolated from the "successful" sciences is the common thread that unites very diverse bodies of thought. Thus, within our account hermeneutics is a broad rubric that encompasses the views of thinkers who have attempted to provide cultural, philosophical, or methodological alternatives to the quantification, naturalism, objectivism, ahistoricism, and technicism that have increasingly come to dominate the modern *Weltanschauung*.

Hermeneutics defies straightforward and concise definition. One negative definition is perhaps best stated in relation to positivism: the philosophical view which holds that genuine knowledge is scientific and that no procedures other than those utilized by the natural sciences can determine truth. Questions that science cannot answer are deemed unanswerable. Positivism may be thought of as a counterpoint to hermeneutic thought, and one aim that unites such dissimilar thinkers as Wilhelm Dilthey, Hans-Georg Gadamer, and Jürgen Habermas is that of countering the misappropriation of natural science models to various spheres of investigation. Much hermeneutic thought seeks to criticize the position that the methods and criteria of the natural sciences are normative for all forms of intellectual activity and that an ahistorical, objective, empirical account of science is sufficient.

Hermeneutic thinkers, however, vary widely in the nature of their individual projects. Whereas Dilthey aimed to devise humanistic methods for the social sciences, Gadamer, Habermas, and Martin Heidegger have been interested in criticizing those aspects of modernity represented by scientism, by the supplanting of moral theory, practical knowledge, and political wisdom by technocratic expertise, and by the denigration of the epistemological status of ethics and aesthetics. Gadamer (1975b) describes the mission of hermeneutic philosophy as follows:

> I think, then, that the chief task of philosophy is ... to defend practical and political reason against the domination of technology based on science. That is the point of philosophical hermeneutics. It corrects the peculiar falsehood of modern consciousness: the idolatry of scientific method and of the anonymous authority of the sciences and it vindicates again the noblest task of the citizen — decision-making according to one's own responsibility — instead of conceding that task to the expert. (p. 316)

Habermas has commented on the replacement of the practical by the technical. He has argued that in modern society, forms of life derived from technology, e.g., means-ends expertise and the technical administration of society, have superseded those "practical" (in the Aristotelian sense) folkways that sought the cultivation of character and the deliberation of societal goals. The replacement of "politics" (in the ancient sense) by social engineering is one symptom of this social transformation. This elimination of the distinction between the practical and the technical reflects "not the sundering of an ethical situation but the repression of 'ethics' as a category of life" (Habermas, 1970, p. 112).

Affirmative definitions of hermeneutics require differentiation.

Our formulation partitions the hermeneutic world into three areas: methodological hermeneutics, ontological hermeneutics, and critical hermeneutics. *Methodological hermeneutics* refers to those approaches whose specific aim is to reform, broaden, and humanize the social sciences. Often writers in this tradition assume, as did Dilthey, that appropriate methods for the human sciences will diverge from those of the natural sciences. *Ontological hermeneutics* refers to the philosophy of understanding that begins in the writings of Heidegger. Ontological hermeneutics employs phenomenological methods, views understanding as a fundamental mode of being-in-the-world, and, through an exploration of the nature of interpretation, seeks truths that are foundational for and clarifying of the nature of all inquiry, including science. Writers in this group also aim at the recovery of a kind of philosophic and cultural sensibility that has been nullified by those forms of philosophy that make epistemology their primary concern. *Critical hermeneutics* refers to work that seeks to expose and criticize ideological underpinnings of all social practices, including political and scientific activity. It attempts, in particular, to reveal sources of domination and coercion that prevent open discourse, the free exercise of reason, and the enhancement of possibilities for human self-determination.

The spirit that gives rise to hermeneutics is found in G.W.F. Hegel's (1931) critique of Kantian epistemology that is developed in his *Phenomenology of Mind.* In this work Hegel fashions a metacritical prototype for hermeneutical inquiry—one that has been adopted by Heidegger, Gadamer, and Habermas. The argument is straightforward: any critique of knowledge itself presupposes knowledge or, at the very least, a framework within which knowledge is constituted (cf. Kortian, 1980). For example, the Kantian project itself, which purported to establish a set of apodictic criteria by which all knowledge claims could be evaluated, was based upon a tacit picture of the epistemological arena and an ontology that comprised a mental subject receiving sense impressions emanating from physical objects. Hegel's argument applies to any epistemology that seeks to identify some ultimate foundation for knowledge. A clear and monumental implication of Hegel's analysis is that all epistemology since Descartes is grievously flawed. This kind of Hegelian metacritical argument can be used with devastating effect against the philosophy of such British empiricists as John Locke, George Berkeley, and David Hume, as Charles Taylor and Alan Montefiore (1980) have shown. An examination of the Hegelian argument not only entails a critique of empiricist-associationist philosophy, but also brings to light subsequent hermeneutic criticisms of the philosophical underpinnings of much modern psychology.

The aims of traditional epistemology were to provide a basis for determining the origins, structure, and validity of all knowledge. Many philosophers have viewed epistemology as a necessary first step in conducting other forms of philosophical inquiry. Their thesis is that if we can establish what counts as knowledge and what standards can be used to evaluate truth claims, then we have formed essential guidelines for other branches of inquiry, and we have developed a framework within which the assertions of any form of intellectual activity can be assessed. The empiricist program based its epistemology on the primacy of "experience," conceived as "impressions" or "sense data." The empiricists believed that, as a self-evident starting point, epistemology could begin with pure experience, unburdened by any metaphysical baggage, and therefore uncompromised in its objectives. The thrust of Hegel's metacritical argument, however, is that this initial notion of "experience" is constituted by an implicit ontology, which itself is assumed by the position and never subjected to critical scrutiny. Taylor and Montefiore (1980) have stated this view simply:

[the assumptions of empiricism] were based on some insufficiently articulated view of the subject's position in the world, a subject conceived as a mind somehow affected by the action of objects in contact with the sense organs belonging to the body with which this mind was in some way linked. 'Impressions' were taken to constitute the most basic elements of experience. We could know them for what they were independently of any other knowledge or assumptions. (p. 5)

But this view is laden with assumptions of its own. An atomistic conception of knowledge is assumed. Perception is construed as a passive process. The viability of taking visual perception as prototypical for all knowledge acquisition is presupposed. Hegel's argument goes on to assert the inevitability of some implicit assumed foundation for any theory of knowledge, and, hence, the lack of viability of the entire modern epistemological enterprise.

Much hermeneutic philosophy, e.g., that of Heidegger or Gadamer, is antifoundational in the sense that no ultimate grounding of knowledge outside of history and culture is considered possible. Therefore, critical examination of science as a mode of inquiry is not countenanced as a means of developing some superior methodology that will yield certainty in other spheres of knowledge. Even those hermeneutic writers with foundationalist leanings—e.g., Habermas —demand that identifiable tacit presuppositions of any body of knowledge claims be made explicit and be subjected to criticism.

Consonant with their Hegelian-inspired attack on foundationalist epistemology, hermeneneutic philosophers have criticized and attempted to reformulate the correspondence theory of truth that has dominated Western philosophy since Plato's metaphor of the cave. The correspondence theory identifies truth with a concordance or matching between a physical state of affairs on the one hand and its mental representation or verbal description on the other. Within the confines of the correspondence theory of truth, the predicate "true" can refer only to a situation in which there is isomorphism between some physical state of affairs and the mental state or language structure that mirrors or represents it. In their attempts to criticize and revise this theory of truth, Heidegger, Paul Ricoeur, and Habermas show great affinity with the later Wittgenstein and various writers from the ordinary language tradition such as Richard Rorty. In the pages that follow we delineate some variations on these hermeneutic themes.

HERMENEUTICS AS A METHODOLOGY FOR THE SOCIAL SCIENCES

Methodological hermeneutics begins with the work of Friedrich Schleiermacher (Palmer, 1969) and the appropriation of his insights by Wilhelm Dilthey. It was Schleiermacher who, in his writing on the interpretation of ancient texts, proposed that the typical philological methods of his time failed to reveal the deeper structure of understanding present in literary works of prior ages. Such fundamental understanding was to be derived from an understanding of the sociocultural context in which the work was created and an examination of any factor that gave rise to and made meaningful the author's productions. In particular, understanding the original intentions of the author was considered to be the *sine qua non* of valid textual interpretation.

Schleiermacher gave the first description of the now famous "hermeneutic circle" (Palmer, 1969). Because understanding inevitably involves reference to that which is already known, it operates in a circular, dialectical fashion. Consider the meaning of a sentence, for example. The sentence derives its meaning from the individual words it comprises, but our interpretation of word meanings within a sentence is also governed by their relations within the sentence and the meaning of the sentence as a whole. Thus interpretation occurs within a circle in which parts are always interpreted within some understanding of the whole, which in turn is understood by coming to understand constituent parts. The hermeneutic circle describes the contextual nature of knowledge. A "fact" does not stand on its own independent from its context or its interpreter, but rather is partially constituted by them. A fact can be evaluated only in relation to the larger structure of theory or argument of which it is a part. At the same time, this larger structure is dependent on its individual parts, as well as on other related information. In explicating the circle of understanding, we move back and forth between part and whole. As a modern hermeneuticist (Geertz, 1973) has put it, this involves "a continuous dialectical tacking between the most local of local detail and the most global of global structure in such a way as to bring both into view simultaneously" (p. 239).

Dilthey was impelled by what he viewed as fundamental mistakes in the positivism of Auguste Comte and John Stuart Mill. Although sympathetic to the aim of achieving objectivity in the human sciences, he was opposed to the atomism and associationism at the root of positivism. Dilthey was influenced by Immanuel Kant's project and, in fact, viewed his own efforts as an attempt to produce a Kantian critique of historical reason, to identify the conditions that made reliable knowledge in the human sciences possible. He, however, radically diverged from Kant in that he could not accept the Kantian idea that one area of knowledge, the physical sciences, is normative for inquiry. Nor could he accept the concept of a transhistorical system of categories that organizes and makes social knowledge possible. "Our understanding of life is only a constant approximation; that life reveals quite different sides to us according to the point of view from which we consider its course in time is due to the nature of both understanding and life" (Dilthey, 1961, p. 109). Because its subject matter consists of meanings and signifiers as opposed to nonintentional events, the human sphere is different from the domain explained by the physical sciences. There is no transcendental ground beyond history and culture from which to render human life in purely objective terms.

At the center of Dilthey's work is an all-encompassing, irreducible concept of "life", which is known from within and which cannot be further analyzed into more fundamental constituent parts (Dilthey, 1961). Dilthey adopted from Johann Gustav Droysen the *Erklären-Verstehen* (explanation-understanding) distinction. For him, understanding (as opposed to explanation) possesses the fullness of life and encompasses lived human experience. Science may "explain" nature but only can "understand" human beings. Though holding that the methods of the social sciences cannot yield the objectivity and certitude of the natural sciences, he did believe that empirical, intersubjectively agreed-upon conclusions can be reached and should be actively sought.

As a means of achieving *Verstehen*, Dilthey advocated a transpositon of the consciousness of the interpreter into the culture and historical epoch that produced the object of interpretation. To grasp in its fullness the "life" contained in historical and social events he believed that a kind of empathic reliving *(Nacherleben)* was required. In his early work Dilthey placed great emphasis upon plumbing and reconstructing the psychological states and intentions of historical figures. In his later work, however, this psychological, introspective emphasis began to be replaced by a distinctly Hegelian approach. He utilized Hegel's concept of objective mind to refer to linguistic expressions that reveal and make objective the inner workings of the mind (Guignon, 1983). Thus an interpreter's grasping of subjectivity and intentionality proceeds through an examination of writings and other objects that form the cultural matrix within which the work was created. This allows for a reconstruction of the meanings inherent in a given sociohistorical situation.

From a Diltheyan hermeneutic perspective, if we seek to understand rather than explain life, then our social science must employ radically different methods from those utilized in the natural sciences. This assertion of a fundamental methodological difference between the *Geisteswissenschaften* and the *Naturwissenschaften* is characteristic of much social thought influenced by hermeneutics. According to such hermeneuticists as Charles Taylor and Rom Harré, the fundamental data of the social sciences are meanings, intentions, plans, goals, and purposes. Human life is inescapabably enmeshed in a web of meaning. Since the meanings that attach to our construals and conduct are integral elements of thought and action, they cannot be removed from our explanations without irretrievably losing the essence of these phenomena. Metatheories such as behaviorism that seek to emulate the physical sciences by ruling out of bounds any meanings or purposes that attach to behavior are wrong-headed, from this point of view, because they eliminate the very essence of that which they seek to render and explain.

Methodological hermeneutics recently has become a controversial topic within psychoanalysis. One contemporary hermeneutic trend within the psychoanalytic literature, exemplified by the work of Roy Schafer and Donald Spence, emphasizes the role of narrative form (versus scientific objectification) in psychoanalytic understanding. Narrative accounts, as opposed to exteroceptively framed scientific laws, are hermeneutic in the sense that they incorporate the phenomenology of the actor, the meaning-laden character of social behavior, and the contextual nature of knowing. The narrative mode also incorporates human intentions and goals, and describes the significance that conduct has for human agents. It allows for the use of connotative as well as denotative meanings in its forms of description and often employs metaphor, simile, and other rhetorical devices. A narrative account sums up the meaning of the chain of events with which it deals in the manner of a satisfying and intelligible story, i.e., by lending coherence and shape to the events described therein.

Several psychoanalytically-informed writers view the narrative form of truth as implicit in and central to the notion of fact in psychoanalysis. Writing on Freud as a hermeneuticist, Ricoeur (1981) has proposed the metaphor of the person as text. In his view psychoanalytic accounts require a certain narrative unfolding that produces coherence and unity in the description of lives. Schafer (1981) sees the analysand as engaged in a narrative performance, which changes as the analytic work progresses. In the course of formulating interpretations, the analyst is viewed by Schafer as "engaging in acts of retelling" or of "narrative revision." Schafer describes the analyst as using the past to make the present more intelligible to the patient—intelligible within a narrative structure characterized by coherence, continuity, and credibility. Rather than simply comprising a set of historical facts that are linked meaningfully, the psychoanalytic narrative can be said, in part, to be constitutive of the facts themselves such that putative "facts" of the patient's life history do not qualify as psychoanalytic facts when they are presented initially by the analysand. Only after they have been "systematically retold by the analyst" are such facts constituted. This relation of part and whole in psychoanalytic narrative is reminiscent of Schleiermacher's conception of the hermeneutic circle.

Spence (1982) has argued that the psychoanalyst is not so much an archaeologist unearthing significant moments of the patient's veritable history—as more objectivist accounts contend—as he or she is an artist or writer lending form and coherence to the fragments of memory, fantasy, and association that the patient has produced. Spence argues that we cannot recapture some veridical, objective occurrence of the original happening or trauma in the way that traditional psychoanalysis has claimed. What we discover in psychoanalysis are not pieces of personal history so much as meanings, filtered through memory and through language—that is, through the conversation of analyst and patient. What makes a particular narrative or story therapeutic is its aesthetic quality or appeal, and its pragmatic ability to persuade.

In their contributions to this volume, two psychologists who have been influenced by hermeneutic philosophy, Spence and Kenneth Gergen, attempt to develop and refine the methodological implications of a hermeneutic point of view by raising criticisms of explanatory strategies often associated with hermeneutic approaches. Spence warns of the ease with which psychoanalysts can find potentially spurious patterns in their patients' associations. In his view a hermeneutic position might encourage excessive credulity in psychoanalytic interpreters and lead them to assume more order in psychic life than may exist. It is far better, Spence argues, to begin with a know-nothing or random view of the world, but to link this with a hermeneutic attitude toward the text. That is, one should use the standard hermeneutic methods of interpretation to generate hypotheses, but then one must subject these to relentlessly skeptical criticism. The analyst should be suspicious of all findings, whether they emanate from empirical studies or arise from within the context of psychotherapy. In a related endeavor, Gergen, who takes what he terms a "social constructionist" position, identifies difficulties with a metaphor widely employed in hermeneutic writings: that of person as text to be read and interpreted. Chief among these difficulties is involvement in the several dualisms: inner-outer, manifest-latent, subject-object, signifiant-signifié. He illustrates how the meaning of such a "text"—in this case a two-person interchange—keeps shifting, depending on both the context and the vantage point ("the forestructure of understanding") of the "reader." Gergen notes, also, the difficulty of validating the occurrence of inner events (the goal of early Diltheyan hermeneutics), particularly if they are viewed as residing in some fixed state in the mind. Instead, he prefers the social metaphor of "the dance" which emphasizes the continuous movement of the partners, their forms of relatedness, and the meanings these entail.

Adolf Grünbaum attacks that cornerstone of the hermeneutic reconstruction of psychoanalysis—the contention of such writers as George Klein, Schafer, and Ricoeur that reasons rather than causes are appropriate to clinical explanation in psychoanalysis. Such hermeneutically-inclined writers have argued that explanation by reasons is believed to be logically incompatible with the kind of causal explanation found in the natural sciences. Such a position recapitulates the bifurcation of the *Naturwissenschaften* and *Geisteswissenschaften* found in Dilthey and advocated by such contemporaries as Taylor, Harré, Alan Gauld, and John Shotter. Grünbaum argues, by contrast, that the reason-cause dichotomy is spurious and rests on misunderstandings of the logic of scientific explanation. He upholds the proposition (also advanced by both John Searle [1983] and Donald Davidson [1980]) that intentional phenomena can and do function as species of causes. Explanations that rely upon reasons, in his view, do not imply acausality and are not fundamentally different in kind from other kinds of causal explanations.

Two empirically-oriented psychologists represented in this volume, Salvatore Maddi and Donald Meichenbaum, suggest that many of the hermeneuticists' concerns about the sterility and inappropriateness of empirical research in psychology are misplaced. Maddi's contribution describes his program for operationalizing and gathering data on constructs derived from the writings of such existentialist philosophers as Søren Kierkegaard and Jean-Paul Sartre. His approach allows for the empirical exploration of how such slippery, nonbehavioristic notions as "commitment," "alienation," and "authenticity" operate to influence people's lives. Similarly, Donald Meichenbaum contends that experimental, cognitive, and clinical psychology have already assimilated much of the critique found in methodological hermeneutics and have modified their practices accordingly. He reminds us that the behavioristic psychology that drew the scorn and criticism of teleologically-inclined social theorists no longer exists. Meichenbaum suggests that in the age of the "cognitive revolution" the data of contemporary psychology are those very meanings that had been neglected by behavioristic empirical social science, and he argues that the paradigms of cognitive psychology are ideally suited for the study of purposive action. Furthermore, he advances the thesis that interpretation itself is expeditiously investigated by empirical methods. He also stipulates the contextual character of psychological knowledge, as well as the theory-laden nature of observation.

Both Meichenbaum and Grünbaum are intent on debunking several of the claims of methodological hermeneutics. Meichenbaum's focus is on altering the dust-bowl empiricism stereotype of experimental psychology. Grünbaum's effort is to dissect and discredit the logic and scholarship of those who advocate a hermeneutic revision of psychoanalysis. Both Meichenbaum and Grünbaum argue that there is methodological overlap between the social and natural sciences. Each asserts the need for the social sciences to study meanings and purposes, but insists that no methodological revolution is required to assimilate these intentional phenomena.

ONTOLOGICAL HERMENEUTICS

Dilthey's "life" philosophy, which was part of his project to establish an epistemological basis for inquiry within the human sciences, ironically served as the point of departure for a radically different enterprise that was to repudiate Dilthey's use of hermeneutics. Ontological hermeneutics—an approach represented in this volume by the papers of Taylor, of Louis Sass, and of Hubert Dreyfus and Jerome Wakefield—finds its first expression in the work of Heidegger. In *Being and Time*, Heidegger attacked Dilthey's view that hermeneutics is one among a variety of methods. In Heidegger's philosophy hermeneutics is constitutive of human being *(Dasein)*. "The phenomenology of Dasein is *hermeneutic* in the primordial signification of this word" (Heidegger, 1962, p. 62). Or as Charles Guignon (1983) has put it:

In our everyday lives we grasp entities in terms of a tacit understanding of what it is to be, and we are constantly driven to make that understanding explicit and revise it on the basis of passing encounters and collisions. The hermeneutic approach to fundamental ontology, far from being a technique for uncovering meanings in an alien text, is just a more rigorous and explicit version of the kind of movement toward clarity and depth which makes up life itself. (p. 71)

The relation of ontological hermeneutics to methodological issues in the social sciences is often misunderstood. In fact, neither Heidegger's ontological hermeneutics nor the work of his successor, Gadamer, claimed to offer a methodology for the social sciences:

> We want neither to replace the sciences nor to reform them. On the other hand, we want to participate in the preparation of a decision; the decision: Is science the measure of knowledge, or is there a knowledge in which the ground and limit of science and thus its genuine effectiveness are determined ... we stand outside the sciences, and the knowledge for which our question strives is neither better nor worse but totally different. (Heidegger, 1967, p. 10)

Though Gadamer does analyze the social sciences extensively in the course of his various writings, his aim is not the reformation of scientific understanding, but rather the elucidation of the ontological relation of "methodical" (method-driven) knowledge to the Heideggerian preunderstanding. Gadamer seeks to explicate the relation of the social sciences to other forms of knowing and participation in life, to show their hermeneutic foundation, and to illustrate their historical nature. Gadamer, himself, is quite articulate on the aims of his work vis-à-vis the social sciences: "The hermeneutics which is here developed is not a methodology of the human sciences, but the quest for an understanding of what the human sciences are in truth beyond their methodical self-consciousness and what connects them with the whole of our experience of the world" (quoted in Bubner, 1981, pp. 53–54). And also: "Hermeneutic reflection cannot seek to change anything in it [science]. But in that it makes transparent the pre-understanding which guides science at any time it can expose new dimensions of the question and thereby indirectly serve methodical work" (quoted in Bubner, 1981, p. 54).

In the course of his existential analytic of Dasein, Heidegger (1962) advanced the thesis that scientific activity takes place within a context of preunderstanding that derives from a certain situatedness in the life-world and from participation in various activities that include practical dealings with tools and implements. Such practical dealings and understandings are achieved in the course of various customary, everyday transactions with the environment. These occur within a taken-for-granted cultural and historical background that consists of practices, habits, and skills, but cannot be spelled out explicitly and comprehensively because it is so pervasive that we cannot make it an object of inquiry. This is the lived-world of what Heidegger called "Everydayness."

Heidegger argued that the fundamental mode of human existence — that on the basis of which all other modes must be understood — is not detached knowing but rather, engaged activity. In his view other modes of experience, like the disinterested contemplation of the scientist or the phenomenologist, are preceded, both temporally and logically, by everyday situations of involvement with the world. Thus, for Heidegger everydayness is not just a possible mode of existence; it is a primordial foundation from which other modes derive. And, according to him, a careful, unprejudiced investigation of a typical everyday situation of activity shows the untenability of certain philosophical assumptions that have pervaded Western philosophy at least since the time of Descartes, and have persisted, albeit in disguised form, in the transcendental (as opposed to hermeneutic) phenomenology of the philosopher Husserl. One of Heidegger's standard illustrations of everydayness is the situation of a carpenter hammering a nail.

For Heidegger, the paradigmatic object in the human world is something like the carpenter's hammer — that is, not a mere physical thing or a sensation or an idea contemplated from a position of scientific or philosophical detachment (as the empiricist philosophers would have it), but a tool that is used. Such a tool seems to occupy a kind of middle realm that defies the traditional Cartesian and Platonic polarities. That is, it cannot be equated with either the "subject" or the "object" of Cartesian philosophy, nor with the "quality" or "substance" of Platonic philosophy. Such objects of equipment are termed by Heidegger, *ready-to-hand*. An entirely different ontology is involved here. An object of equipment that is ready-to-hand is the locus of both subject and object, self and world, quality and substance. Thus, a hammer is not a "hammer" by virtue of some objective characteristics that it has "in itself," apart from its place in the human world. Nor is its quality of "hammerness" something that comes from some subjective inner space and gets "projected" onto a material or sensory substrate. Thus, in Heidegger's account both the subject-object distinction and the distinction between quality (or meaning) and substance (be it material or sensory) turns out to be misleading. In the lifeworld of engaged human activity, according to Heidegger, the hammer's "hammerness" is experienced as out there in the world, inseparable from the substance it imbues, and the external world is "always already" imbued with human purpose and meaning. The ready-to-hand mode is contrasted with another form that Heidegger calls *present-at-hand*. An object that is present-at-hand is not in a unified, integrated, field-like relation with a subject, but rather corresponds to the isolated perceptual object that is studied by a detached, uninvolved observer.

Just as the unity of subject and object is crucial to readiness-to-hand, so too is the quality of complete interrelatedness. Heidegger emphasizes that a particular item of equipment can never be understood in isolation from other objects that are ready-to-hand, since it only exists as such in a purpose-imbued context of other equipment and their respective uses. Thus, Heidegger emphasizes that the objects in one's world are not separate entities but constituents of a unified field, a field that is itself constituted by the essential unity of subject and object: A hammer is what it is because it fills a slot in the "equipmental context" of the human lifeworld.

In Heidegger's view, then, human being (Dasein) involves what might be called an implicitly sensed "ground," "horizon," or "clearing," which is the context or totality within which experience occurs. This horizon, which undercuts the Cartesian opposition of subject and object, is in a sense the most important aspect of human existence, for it is the very condition or possibility of anything at all appearing or being known. Moreover, it is the only place where the being of either "man" or "world" is disclosed.

The Heideggerian view of human existence is, at its deepest level, opposite to that of the early Dilthey, who took for granted the essential self-transparency or intelligibility of consciousness. In the Heideggerian view, the conscious experience of another person or culture cannot be ascertained in any objective sense. The horizonal character of Dasein makes it impossible to retain faith in the transparency and certitude of phenomenological description. Dasein can know its own being only in an approximate, tentative, and indirect way—not by taking its own ordinary self-understanding at face value, nor through some quasi-scientific method of direct intuition with access to certain and foundational data. For on this view experience is a kind of text-analogue that needs to be interpreted

(hence, Heidegger's is a hermeneutic phenomenology), an intrinsically obscure object with which one must adopt an approximate and
metaphoric, rather than quasi-scientific mode of description.

Heidegger also emphasizes the shared and public nature of the
contexts of significance that mediate human awareness. To a great
extent, it is the customs, institutions, and language of a given culture,
not the idiosyncratic perspectives of isolated individuals, that channel and constitute human experience. Thus, even the nature of our
own self-interpretations or self-understandings are largely determined by the possibilities laid open by a shared world of social
practices and institutions. In the view of ontological hermeneuticists
like Gadamer or Charles Taylor, we are constituted by our self-
interpretations; but, for the most part, these interpretations are not
freely chosen or consciously recognized, since they are so deeply
embedded in culture, history, and bodily being, and since they are so
pervasive as to be nearly invisible. One implication of this is that
self-understanding cannot be obtained by studying individual subjectivity alone; it requires an understanding of culture, of language and
of history: "In fact, history does not belong to us, but we belong to
it," writes Gadamer. "Long before we understand ourselves through
the process of self-examination, we understand ourselves in a self-
evident way in the family, society and state in which we live: ... The
self-awareness of the individual is only a flickering in the closed
circuits of historical life" (Gadamer, 1975a, p. 245).

The title of Gadamer's major work, *Truth and Method*, is suggestive of his project, the contrasting of an ontological form of truth
with that found in the sciences and presupposed in Kant, Husserl,
and much 20th-century Anglo-American philosophy, and, hence, in
contemporary psychology as well. His analyses of play and art lead to
a concept of truth that has little to do with the correspondence of the
propositional content of sentences with observables. As was his
teacher, Heidegger, Gadamer is critical of the traditional (Cartesian)
conception of knowing as the confrontation of a knowing and
controlling subject with an external object. In place of this subject-
object dichotomy with its premise of detached, objectified knowledge, he offers a vision of knowing based on the phenomenology of
game-playing—a situation in which game and player seem to merge
with each other. The players of a game play the game, but do not
completely determine or create the game. One's play and, hence,
one's actual existence as a player are, in part, constituted by all the

various features of the game. In some sense the player is also played by the game.

By extending his phenomenology of play to art and literature, Gadamer seeks to recover and expand upon a more ancient view of aesthetic experience in which such experience is accorded more epistemological status than it receives in modern subjectivist accounts. Gadamer criticizes the Kantian view that removes art from the realm of knowledge and accords to it only the function of providing pleasure through the apprehension of the beautiful. According to Gadamer art can convey knowledge—not the theoretical knowledge that science contains, but practical, moral knowledge. Science involves an objective stance on the part of the observer, whereas in art there is a giving over of oneself to the work of art. Gadamer contends, "What one experiences in a work of art and what one is directed towards is rather how true it is, i.e., to what extent one knows and recognizes something and oneself" (1975a, p. 102). The subject and the work of art coparticipate in a "fusion of horizons" in which the meaning of the interpretation of the work and the self-definitions of the interpreter are involved in a kind of dialectic of mutual influence.

Gadamer begins with the Heideggerian assumption that all knowledge has an inescapably hermeneutic character in the sense that it ultimately derives from the fundamental human activity—interpretation. Since what is known is always known by a knower situated within history and society, interpretation is always conditioned and influenced by the tradition and the horizon of understanding within which one operates. For Gadamer, therefore, there is no overcoming of our prejudices or sociohistorical vantage point, and no technique can secure an absolute objectivity in interpretation. In fact, Gadamer contrasts technique and method with the path to truth. For Gadamer, to seek absolute objectivity in interpretation is to misunderstand the hermeneutic enterprise. Tradition and history are not barriers to understanding, rather they are indispensible to it. And because the sociohistorical context constantly changes, as well as does our vantage point within it, there can never be final or absolutely certain interpretations. Understanding, and especially understanding through language, is a primary form of being-in-the-world. Human beings not only come to know through the hermeneutic process, but are formed and constituted by it. This process of self-formation and self-understanding can never be final or complete.

One of Gadamer's main concerns is the criticism of what he has called "the prejudice against prejudice"—the conviction, stemming from the scientism of the Enlightenment, that the ideals of truth and liberation demand a bringing-to-light of all unexamined beliefs and assumptions. As we have seen, the Heideggerian conception of the horizons of understanding suggests that any such attempt would be impossible. If what has been called the hermeneutic circle is a valid characterization of the conditions of all knowing, then prejudices or kinds of foreknowledge are always present and always required as devices that organize and orient perception. This is why Gadamer can make the paradoxical-sounding claim that, far from isolating us from the new, "prejudices are biases of our openness to the world" (Gadamer, 1976, p. 9). Any attempt to dispense with prejudices would lead not to their eradication but to their deeper concealment.

Although ontological hermeneutics does not have as one of its aims the development of a methodology for the social sciences, this does not mean that its insights have no relevance for the human studies. One straightforward implication of the ontological hermeneutic view is that human subjectivity cannot be understood as a concatenation of what logical positivists have called "atomic facts" —that is, of isolable and fully specifiable events that either do or do not exist in a determinate fashion (or exist to a specifiable degree). It is, rather, an interweaving texture of only partially specifiable themes that exist at various levels of implicit and explicit awareness, often merging imperceptibly with one another. Ontological hermeneuticists have argued that the former notion involves a mistaken and misleading importation into the realm of subjectivity of a certain atomistic conception of the physical universe; by means of what Gadamer has called an "objectivist subjectivism," experiences come to be treated as if they were inner objects. In his comment on Meichenbaum's paper, which he criticizes from a Heideggerian perspective, Wakefield makes just such an argument: he points out that Meichenbaum's argument fails to take into account an impor-tant version of the distinctiveness thesis—i.e., the ontological her-meneutic notion that human meaning is different from physical reality because of its inherent ambiguity and contextuality. (Inciden-tally, what Wakefield in his comment calls the phenomenological view is what we are calling ontological hermeneutics or hermeneutic phenomenology.)

In his contribution to this volume, Sass presents an overview and analysis of the concept of human nature (the philosophical anthropology) that is at the core of the ontological hermeneutics of Heidegger, Gadamer, and Ricoeur. In doing this Sass expands on a number of the points discussed above. Also, he contrasts the ontological hermeneutic position with the views of Dilthey, Husserl, and Sartre, and with the philosophical anthropology that is implicit in the third force or humanistic psychology in America. Sass concludes by considering the implications of ontological hermeneutics for our notions of interpersonal communication and understanding and of authenticity, and for the conduct of psychotherapy.

In their chapter in this volume, Dreyfus and Wakefield argue for a conception of psychopathology based on the Heideggerian notion of the "clearing." In their view the traditional Freudian approach to the unconscious is epistemological and has strong affinities with Husserl's thought, with its objectivist subjectivism. Thus, the traditional Freudian approach is a depth psychology that conceives of psychopathology as involving repressed mental contents or representations. Dreyfus and Wakefield argue for the importance of adding to this a breadth psychology that incorporates the insights of the ontological hermeneutic position. In such an approach, that which is unconscious would not be understood in its entirety as having the character of an object in a clearing. In certain important cases, it would be understood as having the qualities of a clearing itself, i.e., it is something that exists everywhere and nowhere, like a theme imbuing all conscious experiences without itself necessarily existing as a specifiable mental content either in the conscious or the unconscious mind.

Charles Taylor's study of the self in this volume takes seriously Heidegger's and Gadamer's insistence on the constituting role of language and culture. Instead of treating the self as if it were a timeless element of human experience, he investigates certain notions of selfhood that have developed in the last several centuries of Western thought, notions that emphasize processes of self-control and self-exploration and that downplay the role of external sources of meaning and value. Taylor argues that these notions, given especially clear expression in the writings of thinkers such as Descartes and Montaigne, have played a significant role in constituting modern civilization and its characteristic modes of experience.

Gadamer's ontological hermeneutics has provoked criticism and charges of relativism from several writers who identify more closely with the tradition of methodological hermeneutics. Emilio Betti (1980) has attacked both Gadamer and Heidegger as "destructive critics of objectivity" who would "plunge hermeneutics into a standardless morass of relativity" (p. 79). In a vein similar to that of Dilthey, Betti sees the data of interpretation as objectifications of mind in which the interpreter must identify the meanings, intentions, and significances that formed them. Another criticism of Gadamer's work has come from the writings of E. D. Hirsch (1967). Claiming that what is ultimately at stake is the capability of any humanistic discipline to assert that it has achieved genuine knowledge, Hirsch has echoed the methodological aims of Dilthey—to achieve objective, valid interpretations of cultural phenomena. As contrasted with the Gadamerian fusion of horizons—which is predicated upon the impossibility of any nonparticipatory, ahistorical vantage point from which to evaluate the intentions of the creators of social products—both Hirsch and Betti believe that enough distancing from historical objects is possible to allow for an objective social science, albeit one that does not rely on verification in the manner of natural sciences. Unlike Gadamer, Hirsch believes that we can objectively distinguish what a literary text meant to its author from what it means to us, a distinction difficult to make within the Gadamerian ontology. Although he grants that these interpretations can never achieve absolute certainty, Hirsch argues that this failing does not mean that the validity claims of interpretations cannot be evaluated. In fact, he contends that to claim validity for an interpretation requires that we be prepared to assert its superiority over rival claims, which also necessitates the assumption that some correct understanding is possible. In the case of literary texts, Hirsch identifies these "correct" understandings with the original intentions of the author. The logic of interpretation, however, is seen as a logic of argumentation, dialogue, or probability, rather than a logic of verification.

A more sympathetic criticism of Gadamerian hermeneutics is found in the work of Ricoeur (1981), who contends that hermeneutics is the proper method for the social sciences but that ontological hermeneutics leaves little role for the social sciences in the discovery of truth. He contends that an important task for hermeneutics is that of providing standards for choosing among different interpretations and also attempts to analyze the explanation-understanding dichotomy in a way that allows for transcending it.

In the present volume Richard Bernstein argues that interpretation is not arbitrary, even though there are no definitive standards, criteria, or rules by which interpretations can be evaluated as true or false, better or worse. Interpretations can be supported by appeal to reasons and evidence. Despite the lack of an absolute foundation for adjudicating the validity claims of interpretations, Bernstein claims that there is nevertheless "a logic of argumentation, an elaborate 'choreography of critique' involved in the moves and countermoves of analyzing and evaluating an interpretation".

CRITICAL HERMENEUTICS

Habermas's work is properly viewed as an outgrowth of the work on Critical Theory begun by members of the Institute of Social Research established in Frankfurt in 1923. The best known of these "Frankfurt School" thinkers were Max Horkheimer, Theodor Adorno, and Herbert Marcuse. The Frankfurt School advanced Critical Theory as an alternative to the positivistic social science that purports to be value free and politically neutral. Very much in the Marxist tradition, the aim of a critical social theory is not exclusively to understand the world but also to change it so as to further human emancipation. "The [critical] theoretician and his specific object are seen as forming a dynamic unity with the oppressed class, so that his presentation of societal contradictions is not merely an expression of the concrete historical situation but also a force to stimulate change" (Horkheimer, 1972, p. 215). Both by refusing to view culture as reducible to economics and by employing psychoanalysis to elucidate the relationship between individual and society, however, Critical Theory produced a revision of classical Marxism. It also offered a rather searching critique of modernity that sought to analyze and transform both contemporary patterns of intellectual activity and modern social institutions. Special emphasis was placed upon tracing the connections between the increasing rationalization (in the Weberian sense) of the relations of social life in a technically managed society and contemporary forms of intellectual and social fragmentation and alienation.

The work of Habermas emanates from the base of Marxism and Critical Theory. Although it shares many of the features and aims of both methodological hermeneutics and ontological hermeneutics, it has many distinctive aspects. True to his Marxist roots, Habermas views knowledge as produced and influenced by social and economic factors. Central to his thesis is the contention that epistemology is possible only as social theory. One aspect of Habermas's project is the identification of the putative ideological underpinnings of the intellectual disciplines. This has led to his assertion that institutionalized forms of thought are based on what he terms *cognitive interests*, which function to regulate inquiry by influencing metatheory, methodology, and the categorical schemes. These cognitive or "knowledge-constitutive" interests themselves have a "quasi-transcendental status," in that Habermas claims for them a kind of universality that transcends history and culture, while recognizing, at the same time, that those categories that describe and organize the ideological underpinnings of knowledge partially flow from a particular socio-historical context.

> "Cognitive interest" is therefore a peculiar category, which conforms as little to the distinction between the empirical and the transcendental or factual and symbolic determinations as to that between motivation and cognition. For knowledge is neither a mere instrument of an organism's adaptation to a changing environment nor the act of a true rational being removed from the context of life in contemplation. (Habermas, 1971, p. 197)

The three primary cognitive interests are the technical, the practical, and the emancipatory. Habermas also has a tripartite typology of knowledge with three disciplinary categories, each corresponding to one of those cognitive interests. Thus the *empirical-analytic* disciplines (the natural sciences) are underlain by a technical interest directed toward control over natural phenomena. Unlike the natural sciences with their empirical testing procedures, the *historical-hermeneutic* sciences gain knowledge within a different methodological framework. Access to the facts is provided by the understanding of meaning, not direct observation of neutral facts. The verification of lawlike hypotheses in empirical-analytic sciences has its counterpart here in the interpretation of texts. Thus, hermeneutic procedures determine the validity of theories and propositions advanced within the cultural sciences. These disciplines are shaped by a practical interest that serves to elucidate the conditions that underlie communication and social interaction. Historical-hermeneutic sciences thus serve to promote intersubjective understanding, those shared cultural meanings that are the prerequisites for social consensus on the practical dimensions of life. In his distinction between the empirical-analytic and historical-hermeneutic sciences, Habermas recreates the bifurcation of the natural and human sciences found in Dilthey. There exists, however, a third sphere of intellectual activity, which Habermas terms *empirical-critical*. The empirical-critical sciences are guided by an emancipatory interest and are distinguished by their capacity to reflect critically upon their own ideological foundations. Habermas uses his own critique of ideology and Freud's psychoanalysis as examples of this form of thought. "The critiques which Marx developed as a theory of society and Freud as metapsychology are distinguished precisely by incorporating in their consciousness an interest which directs knowledge, an interest in emancipation going beyond the technical and the practical interest of knowledge" (Habermas, 1973, p. 9). The self-reflection found in psychoanalysis is seen as prototypical, in that identifying and analyzing the patient's repressions putatively enables the liberation of the patient from the constraints and distortion of psychic barriers. Habermas views such critical sciences as forms of a depth hermeneutic that reveals sources of domination and distortion in communication.

Language and communication occupy a central role in Habermas's writings. In contradistinction to Heidegger and Gadamer, who are antifoundationalists, Habermas proposes that knowledge and practice are ultimately grounded in what he contends is the teleology implicit in the nature and use of language. He argues that the successful exchange of "speech acts" (communication) necessarily makes claims to validity and presupposes a community of speakers intent on finding truth. The process of critical self-reflection with its goal of emancipation emerges as a kind of fundamental property of human practice.

> The human interest in autonomy and responsibility [emancipation] is not mere fancy, for it can be apprehended a priori. What raises us out of nature is the only thing whose nature we can know: *language* ... Our first sentence expresses unequivocally the intention of universal and unconstrained consensus ... the only ideas we possess a priori in the sense of the philosophical tradition. (Habermas, 1971, p. 314)

Thus, for Habermas the use of language presupposes the ideal of free and uncoerced discussion. This "ideal speech situation" is the somewhat utopian arena in which validity claims are evaluated free from constraint and distortion. A rational consensus under such conditions is what passes for Habermas's theory of truth. The truth is that upon which agents agree in the course of ideal speech.

In the present volume the offerings by Joel Kovel and by Evelyn Fox Keller and Jane Flax are closest to the approach of critical hermeneutics. Both chapters aim to uncover ideological dimensions that underlie intellectual trends or social practices in order to show how unacknowledged interests, power relations, or value commitments actually shape the activity or belief system in question. Each is informed by the Hegelian-Marxist perspective that views knowledge and sociohistorical factors as inextricably related. Kovel seeks to subject the notion of human nature to analysis and critique. In so doing he argues both for its indispensibility and for its susceptibility to carry repressive ideological baggage. The result is a meditation on humanity and its capacities for domination and emancipation. Fox Keller and Flax have produced a critique of the current view of science, emphasizing the ways in which it has been deeply influenced by male gender-related attributes such as the valorization of autonomy and objectivity, and the tendency to emphasize power relationships. They go on to present a feminist critique of psychoanalysis that illustrates how implicit and explicit masculine ideological perceptions permeate psychoanalytic theory and practice.

In the preceding discussion we have delineated the main currents of hermeneutic thought with the aim not only of introducing a series of contributions but also of providing a background that will increase the intelligibility of hermeneutic thought and clarify its relation to psychology. The relationship between certain varieties of hermeneutics and psychological theory, however, are perhaps less than self-evident. The writings of such thinkers as Heidegger and Gadamer are abstruse and their aims are different from those of individuals such as Dilthey and Ricoeur, who attempt to address directly the methodological concerns of social scientists. There appear, however, to be enough common threads that run through the entire fabric of hermeneutics that may enable us to derive some very general suggestions for the conduct of psychologists in their roles as theorists and researchers.

Perhaps the most radical implication of a hermeneutic outlook for psychology is the attitude it fosters toward the nature of evidence, data, and empirical investigations. Most contemporary psychology researchers write as if they believe themselves to be accumulating neutral, objective facts in a value free, transhistorical, epistemological arena. From a hermeneutic perspective, such an approach ignores the extent to which such facts are inextricably interwoven with theory, with the researcher's biases, with the choice of language used to describe the terms employed, and with sociocultural and historical influences—all of which preclude the notion of facts existing apart from the interpretative process. This is not to say that traditional psychological data-gathering approaches are without value in the study of personality, psychopathology, and psychotherapy. It does say, however, that such methods have no epistemic pedigree that renders them superior to other methods, including clinical case analysis, phenomenological description, anthropological field studies, metaphorical comparisons, narrative forms, and literary studies. Adumbrating as it does the multiple social, historical, cultural, and philosophical dimensions that affect and are influenced by psychological theory, a hermeneutic approach tends to favor interdisciplinary pluralism. Dialogue among disciplines is necessary to promote the sophistication required to comprehend the complexity of the contextual features that complicate, but at the same time enrich, psychological inquiry.

REFERENCES

Betti, E. Hermeneutics as the general methodology of the Geistes wissenschaften. In J. Bleicher (Ed.), *Hermeneutics: Hermeneutics as philosophy, method and critique*. London: Routledge & Kegan Paul, 1980.

Bubner, R. *Modern German philosophy*. Cambridge: Cambridge University Press, 1981.

Davidson, D. *Essays on actions and events*. New York: Oxford University Press, 1980.

Dilthey, W. *Meaning in history: W. Dilthey's thoughts on history and society* H. P. Rickman, ed. London: George Allen & Unwin, Ltd., 1961).

Gadamer, H. G. *Truth and method*, trans. G. Burden & J. Cumming. New York: Seabury Press, 1975. (a)

Gadamer, H. G. Hermeneutics and social science. *Cultural Hermeneutics*, 1975, 2, 307–316. (b)

Gadamer, H. G. *Philosophical hermeneutics*, ed. and trans. D. E. Linge. Berkeley: University of California Press, 1976.

Geertz, C. *The interpretation of cultures*. New York: Basic Books, 1973.

Guignon, C. *Heidegger and the problem of knowledge*. Indianapolis: Hackett, 1983.

Habermas, J. *Toward a rational society*. Boston: Beacon Press, 1970.

Habermas, J. *Knowledge and human interests*, trans. J. J. Shapiro. Boston: Beacon Press, 1971.

Habermas, J. *Theory and practice*, trans. J. Viertel. Boston: Beacon Press, 1973.

Hegel, G. W. F. *The phenomenology of mind*, trans. J. B. Baillie. New York: Macmillan, 1931.

Heidegger, M. *Being and time*, trans. J. Macquarrie & E. Robinson. New York: Harper & Row, 1962.

Heidegger, M. *What is a thing?*, trans. W. B. Barton & V. Deutsch. Chicago: Henry Regnery, 1967.

Hirsch, E. D. *Validity in interpretation*. New Haven: Yale University Press, 1967.

Horkheimer, M. *Critical theory: Selected essays*, trans. M. J. O'Connell. New York: Herder & Herder, 1972.

Kortian, G. *Metacritique*. Cambridge: Cambridge University Press, 1980.

Palmer, R. E. *Hermeneutics: Interpretation theory in Schleiermacher, Dilthey, Heidegger, and Gadamer*. Evanston, Ill.: Northwestern University Press, 1969.

Ricoeur, P. *Hermeneutics and the human sciences*, ed. and trans. J. B. Thompson. Cambridge: Cambridge University Press, 1981.

Schafer, R. *Narrative actions in psychoanalysis*. Worcester, Mass.: Clark University Press, 1981.

Searle, J. R. *Intentionality*. Cambridge: Cambridge University Press, 1983.

Spence, D. *Narrative truth and historical truth: Meaning and interpretation in psychoanalysis*. New York: W. W. Norton, 1982.

Taylor, C., & Montefiore, A. From an analytical perspective. In G. Kortian, *Metacritique*. Cambridge: Cambridge University Press, 1980.

METHODOLOGICAL ISSUES

Chapter 2

If Persons Are Texts

KENNETH J. GERGEN

For those concerned with problems of human understanding, the metaphor of persons as texts has become widely heralded in recent years. For the psychological sciences it has been a particularly welcome addition to our implements of understanding. From roughly the 1930s to the 1960s, mainstream psychology was enamored with the possibility of viewing humans as somewhat more complex forms of the laboratory animal. Work with rats, dogs, and pigeons was simply a preliminary exercise to gaining stimulus control over human action.[1] The image of the laboratory animal, constrained and predictable, largely guided the construction of laboratories for research on human behavior. This metaphor of the laboratory animal later gave way to that of the machine. The mind operates like a complex machine, it was (and is) believed, responding in systematic ways to environmental inputs much as an engine will respond to inputs of gasoline, oil, and water. It is this metaphor of mind as machine that is played out today in the cognitive sciences. The mind has become a form of computer—not even a particularly good one at that—and it is the scientist's task to understand both its hard and software functions. Cognitive theories of human deficit (depression, stress, and the like) owe much of their rhetorical power to the pervading metaphor of mind as computer.

Within this context the newly emerging metaphor of the person as text stands in marked and refreshing contrast. The metaphor seems to restore a dignity to the human being that is largely lost when considered merely animal- or machine-like. Texts are, after all, human artifacts, aesthetically rendered, standing at the apex of human development. And the vision of the text suggests that beneath the human exterior lies a richly elaborated, subtly patterned, and fundamentally passionate set of impulses. The study of human action thus holds the promise of a fascinating odyssey into a foreign land, where surprises are possible at every turn and from whence one may return edified not only about the subject in question, but about oneself, if not the whole of humankind. If persons are texts, inquiry into human action becomes an honorable and intriguing quest into the unknown.

The concept of persons as texts has also enabled those in the clinical domain to link their pursuits with developments in the philosophy of social science more generally and to hermeneutic study in particular. Since the 19th-century attempt to separate the Geisteswissenschaften from the Naturwissenschaften, thinkers have sought means of differentiating the methods of understanding human action from those of understanding natural events. Dilthey's method of *Verstehen* was perhaps the most compelling candidate of the early era. However, the viability of the concept suffered under the combined weight of empiricist philosophy of science and the behavioral movement in psychology. The further development of psychological testing and the appearance of such works as Meehl's *Actuarial versus clinical prediction* further suggested that the clinical attempt to probe the depths of human experience would soon give way to technology. Attempts to explicate a unique process of understanding human action became largely moribund.

Within recent years, however, both empiricist metatheory and the behavioral orientation have withered.[2] Many philosophers of social science have returned to the task of understanding human understanding. From this work the widely accepted conclusion has been reached that human action cannot be understood without reference to its underlying intentions. Regardless of the accuracy and sophistication of one's measures, the observations are without meaning or interest until they are linked to the actor's intention (Peters, 1958). Such conclusions made it apparent that the lynchpin of the social sciences was the process of interpretation (Taylor, 1971). Until intentions were rendered accessible, human activity remained opaque. At the same time, the one significant and relevant tradition of scholarship that had not succumbed to the empiricist rise to power

was that of hermeneutics. This tradition, concerned with the interpretation of texts—biblical, literary, judicial, and otherwise
—offered a rich repository of thought on the task of interpreting
human intention. For those in the clinical domains, there were now
new and sophisticated allies. With person as text, the problem of
clinical interpretation could be revisited. It is to this union that we
largely owe the contemporary renaissance in the exploration of the
clinical relationship.

I myself have been much intrigued with extending the intellectual
and practical implications of the metaphor of persons as texts. I have
been absorbed with the possibility that people's lives are constructed
around pervading literary figures or tropes. In the same way that
scientific theories are typically guided by or derived from root
metaphors, so may people's lives be dominated by views of themselves as the archetypical hero, Earth Mother, or knave. And in the
same way that theories of human development are dependent on
narrative forms deeply embedded in our literary traditions, so are the
stories we tell about ourselves—to others and to ourselves—with
important ramifications (Gergen & Gergen, 1986).

Yet, as the metaphor of person as text has played itself out, I have
also come to find substantial limitations. I have been moved to
serious reconsideration of both intellectual and moral moment. It is
to these limitations that this chapter will initially be addressed. This
does not mean that I wish to see a return to the empiricist view of
knowledge and a behavioral orientation to clinical understanding. On
the contrary. As we lay out the problems inherent in the metaphor of
person as text, we can begin to glimpse the possibility for a significant
alternative to understanding human meaning. It is this relational
orientation to understanding that will be outlined in the closing
section of the paper.

THE IMPASSE OF INNER KNOWLEDGE

The contemporary concept of the text is at least as old as the
hermeneutic tradition itself. It is essentially a dualistic conception,
making a significant distinction between a primary domain of intentionality or meaning, and a secondary domain of the intentions as
publicly manifest—meaning within the inner realm of the mind and
its expression within the objective text. For the early 16th-century

scholar, the biblical knowledge of the text *qua* text was only a means to a much nobler end—namely, knowledge of God's will. Biblical texts were the emanations of an agent far removed—akin to the messages delivered by Hermes, the messenger of the gods. Hermes himself is but a low and insignificant figure in comparison to the profound powers he represented. It is this dualistic conception of the text—with an insignificant surface and a profound depth—that continues to inform our contemporary undertakings. We read poetry to ascertain its deeper insights into human nature; we discuss novels and plays not in themselves but in terms of the deeper truths they may reveal; we make fundamental distinctions between the manifest and the latent content, the symptom and the unconscious source, the signifiant and the signifiee, the surface and the deep structure, and so on. Human understanding is achieved, we believe, when we successfully penetrate the surface and ascertain its source.

Yet, if we do embrace this dualistic conception of the text, precisely how is the process of human understanding to proceed? How are we to grasp the essential leanings or to gain intimacy with another? What possibilities are there for human knowledge on the level of daily life, within the therapeutic encounter, or within the halls of science? Let us explore a single incident and work our way toward more general conclusions. The incident is one I have used previously for a different audience, but it has a certain saccharine charm that recommends its repetition in the present context.

We may begin with a simple dilemma: If I see my good friends Ross and Laura approach each other at a social gathering, and Ross reaches out and momentarily touches Laura's hair, precisely what have I observed? What action has occurred before me? How am I to interpret it? What does the action suggest about their relationship and the manner in which I should regard it if I wish to retain their friendship? Such dilemmas of interpretation are frequent; one might even conjecture that they are as numerous as there are discriminable social actions. And such dilemmas must be solved, it would appear, in order for us to carry on effective interpersonal relations. How then, do we normally solve the essential problem of behavioral interpretation?

The problem is an especially vexing one, for it would appear that the action in itself can tell us little. We know only that Ross has engaged in a series of actions that might be described as "touching Laura's hair." Yet this level of description is virtually uninformative. What does it mean to engage in such an action? Of what interpersonal or theoretical significance is the behavior? This information is not contained in the action itself. Perhaps the most compelling solution to this dilemma lies in the employment of contextual indicators. We may locate the meaning of a given action by placing it within the context of its antecedents and its consequences—its past and future within the relationship itself and the culture more generally. Let us first consider in this case the *retrospective context*, those events believed to define the action but occurring prior to it. For example, if Ross informed me the week before that he was madly in love with Laura, this information would solve my dilemma. I could confidently view his action as a signal of affection or attraction. If in later interaction with Ross I were to treat it as such, and not as a signal of derision, Ross and I would presumably continue to maintain a smooth and umproblematic friendship.

We must expand the retrospective context. Ross's announcement of the previous week may not be the only contextual constituent. Suppose I also learned from Laura several days ago that she told Ross she didn't really believe he was a warm and affectionate sort of person. At this point we may doubt the initial conclusion that the act was a signal of affection. Rather, we might consider the possibility that it was an attempt on Ross's part to demonstrate that he is an affectionate person after all. In effect, the action is not quite so much an affectionate one as an act of self-presentation, or personal identification. Yet, consider the nasty bit of gossip to which I was just exposed: a mutual friend indicates that the lovers have recently had a serious quarrel in which Laura accused Ross of being a prime egotist who believes he can have any woman he likes. Laura has told him she wants nothing more to do with him; he is vulgar, insensitive, and aggressive. With this new information, we may wish to interpret the action. Perhaps it was an act of derision on Ross's part after all. Perhaps he was saying with this action that in fact he could have any woman he wanted, and that Laura would soon be his in spite of her abuse. Thus, to relate effectively with Ross at this point, it would be appropriate to treat the act as one of derision as opposed to attraction or self-presentation.

Yet, can one be so certain, after all, that derision is the proper interpretation of the action? Perhaps Ross was badly hurt by Laura's words and was making one last attempt to express his affection or to demonstrate finally that he was a most affectionate kind of person. More information is necessary before Ross's behavior can be interpreted with confidence. So far we have attended only to information based on the retrospective context. For additional information we must turn to the *emergent context*, that is, to relevant, defining events that follow the action in question. For example, we immediately observe Laura smile and take Ross's hand. This reaction now relieves our doubts. Laura had clearly been touched by Ross's gesture and feels contrite over the scolding she has administered. The stroking of the hair was a profound expression of affection after all. Or was it? Several minutes later, when we see Ross talking briefly with a friend, we notice that his posture and facial expressions are those of a man who is very proud of himself. Perhaps the gesture was, after all, not so affectionate in itself, but his attempt at successful self-presentation. He is now quite pleased with himself because he has apparently succeeded in convincing Laura of his open expressiveness. But the evidence is not yet complete. The following day we learn that Laura subsequently asked Ross if she could borrow his car to run an errand, and once the car was in her possession, she scraped its entire right hand side against a stone wall and thereupon abandoned the vehicle. At last, the mystery is solved. Laura saw that the stroking action was one of derision, yet treated it as an effective gesture in winning her love. This she did in order to gain Ross's confidence, wereupon she borrowed the car in order to damage it and thus avenge the callous action.

A month later Ross and Laura are spied walking arm in arm. . . .

Let us now collect several major propositions that may be derived from this turgid saga.

1.   The interpretation of any given action is subject to infinite revision. As we are exposed to events from both retrospective and emergent contexts, our manner of interpreting the present action is continuously modified. Theoretically, this process is without limit. First, the range of past indicators is without evident bounds, for we must be prepared to account not only for all events in the lives of the individuals in question but also for all those events within the cultural history that shape current meanings. For example, in the case of Ross's life, if we learned that his feelings of affection were often fleeting, we might have been less inclined to view the action in question as one of affection. With respect to the culture more generally, if we learned that public touching between opposite sex pairs was a culturally sanctioned signal of ownership or possession, we might hesitate in accepting the event as proof of affection.

It is also apparent that the relevance of one's life events or events within the cultural history may wax or wane according to our present manner of determining intelligibility. For example, events in Ross's early childhood may be viewed by the psychoanalytic theorist as relevant to the proper identification of the action in question (e.g., it could be a reaction formation growing from the Oedipal period and expressing the opposite from the apparent emotion). However, the same early childhood events might not be viewed as relevant by one who is unschooled in this particular system of intelligibility.

The emergent context is similarly without anchor point. The present action is subject to continuous redefinition as further events take place. As we saw, the final action cited (that of the couple walking happily together) appeared to throw the "ultimate definition" once again into jeopardy. Yet, this latter event itself should scarcely be considered final. Nor are the future actions relevant to the interpretation only those uniting the two individuals. Any further action on the part of any person may, if one possesses an appropriate system of intelligibility, be employed to reconstruct the meaning of the act in question. For example, if in the light of later social history we learned that this historical period was one of great superficiality in emotional expression, we might retrospectively discount the sincerity of Ross's action: perhaps it was simply a matter of artificial stylistics. We see, then, that the interpretation of any given action is effectively open-ended.

2.   The anchor point for any given interpretation is not fundamentally empirical, but relies on a network of interdependent and continuously modifiable interpretations. This second proposition amplifies the first. As we see, there is no obvious way in which one can satisfactorily interpret any given action in itself. The action in question does not furnish any empirical touchstone for proper interpretation. One is thus forced to consider the context of events both preceding and following the action. Yet, to extend the analysis, we find that these events are also in need of interpretation, and one must search the ever-unfolding context of events in order to determine their meaning as well. For example, we were moved to interpret the stroking of Laura's hair as an expression of affection when we took into account Ross's previous declaration of love. Yet, the declaration itself is in need of interpretation. We must be certain that it is a declaration of affection rather than an attempt on his part to convince us of her ardor, for example, rather than an attempt at self-conviction, a whimsical gesture, an act of self-deception, or any number of other reasonable competitors. In order to determine which of the interpretations is valid, we are again driven outward to

consider the ever-unfolding context of events within which his declaration is embedded.

Of course, events within these contexts are equally subject to the interpretative dilemma. Thus, we find that the single, critical interpretation is not fundamentally tied to any single set of observables; rather, the interpretation rests on a potentially immense array of interdependent interpretations. Further, any given interpretation is continuously subject to modification in light of a continuously altering context, and any event occurring within the array may wax and wane in its relevance as intelligibility systems evolve over time. Thus the contextual array cannot be viewed as static but as in continuous and reverberating motion.

3. Any given action may be subject to multiple interpretations, no one of which is objectively superior. Our third proposition extends the logic implied in our arguments thus far. In the initial example, we took the perspective of a single observer of a given action. However, this perspective is hardly sacrosanct and could be replaced by a wide number of competitors. Each competitor might differ in (1) what counts as or constitutes an event, (2) the range of events to which he or she is exposed, and (3) the system of intelligibility used to make sense of the present action. Given the ultimate lack of an empirical touchstone on which to rest any given interpretation, one cannot easily argue for the superior validity of one conclusion as opposed to another.

One may contest this view on two grounds. First, it could be countered that an explanation based on multiple contextual inputs is superior to one that rests only upon a few. Yet, on closer inspection this view fails to be convincing. At the outset, as the number of events believed relevant to a given interpretation increases in number, one does not move unproblematically toward clarity of account. Rather, it would appear, one might anticipate increasing doubt in any given account. As increasing numbers of events are considered, their contexts of interpretation appraised, and multiple interpretations are encountered in the behavioral reports of others, so confidence in any given interpretation might well be eroded. Thus, the most informed account of any given action might be no account at all. Although silence is philosophically defensible in this case, it does not enable us to solve the essential dilemma of interpretation. A second problem in seeking salvation through multiple indicators resides in the earlier argument that the number and range of events considered relevant to any interpretation may vary from one individual to another: events that one observer views as particularly relevant to a given act, a second observer may see as insignificant. For example, many people would dispute the relevance of early childhood events to the proper definition of their adult actions. One person's attempt to increase the number of contextual inputs may be another person's exercise in inanity. Finally, since any given event may be subject to multiple interpretations, it should be possible for an observer to justify any given interpretation by reference to virtually any earlier contextual event. Once one has fixed on a given interpretation, increasing the number of events lends no additional strength to the interpretation. It merely demonstrates the conceptual agility of the observer in generating a veneer of consistency among interpretations.

The most powerful challenge to the argument for equivalidity of interpretation might be based on the claim that the actor's position is superior to any other. The actor, it can be argued, knows more about his or her own life history and about the internal state (intentions, motives, needs) giving rise to his or her actions. Actors essentially know what they are about, and if asked for a candid account in the present case, Ross could furnish the correct interpretation. Yet, when more fully considered, this rebuttal too is found to be unwarranted. First we find that it cannot be sustained on grounds that the actor knows more about his or her life history than does another. This would be to argue that the actor's account of his or her action benefits from taking into account a wider context of relevant events. Yet, as we have just seen, increasing the range of events bearing on a given interpretation in no way increases its validity. In effect, as Ross considered more carefully the full complexity of his preceding life experiences, his cultural, historical, and genetic heritage, and so on, his attempt to identify his motives might only be rendered the more problematic.

More fundamental, however, is the problem of identifying internal states such as intentions, motives, and dispositions. Our analysis thus far has not revealed a means of objectively anchoring the interpretation of overt action. The problem is exacerbated manifoldly as we move to the covert level. In particular, we find ourselves without an intelligible explanation of how it is one might determine the accuracy of his or her identification of a psychological state. Several momentous problems confront the aspirant in this case. Three of these may be briefly considered.

1.   Process in search of itself. We commonly speak of our intentions, emotions, needs, and so on as if they were readily accessible to

experience. Yet, if we examine the supposition that we may experience internal states it is found that we rapidly approach the border of incredulity. Such a conclusion would entail a concept of mind in which psychological process would be capable of turning reflexively upon itself and identifying its own states. Rather than a single stream of consciousness, one would be forced into a mental dualism in which one level of consciousness acted as a sensing and/or recording device and a second process furnished the stuff to be sensed and recorded. Yet how are we to extricate the subject from the object, or the sensing agent from the object of experience? How is it that consciousness can be aware of itself? Such a dualism is sufficiently awkward that one is invited to consider how such a peculiar construction might have acquired such broad credibility. It seems most plausible in this case that the assumption of "internal perception" is a reconstructed form of the traditional metaphor for "external perception." The latter view is based on a subject-object dichotomy: A subject apprehending the character of the external object. The present model of internal perception appears to represent a projection of this view into the covert world. We implicitly presume the functioning of an "inner eye." Yet, unlike the case of external perception we are unable to identify the sensing device and to differentiate it from the object of perception. Until an intelligible account can be rendered of internal perception, it seems unwise to rely on this assumption to rescue us from the shoals of relativity in interpretation.

2. Internal perception as self-biased. If one can perform the theoretical circumlocution necessary to justify an internal dualism, one faces a second problem of no lesser magnitude. Specifically, if both the sensing process and the sensed data are constituents of the same psychological structure, what safeguards (if any) can be placed over misperception? How can we be certain that no other psychological influences act so as to occlude the object of perception? In particular, could the entities one hoped to identify not themselves hinder or distort the very task of identification itself? Freudian theory indeed posits just the kind of psychological processes that would obscure those entities (states, drives, intentions) one hoped to ascertain. On what grounds can one argue that internal processes do not operate in this way? If one's consciousness is controlled in such a manner, the attempt to answer the interpretive question by self-observation would be futile.

3. The constructed properties of psychological states. A third difficulty emerges when one inquires into the properties of mental

states that would enable them to be identified. What is the size, shape, color, sound, or smell, for example, of an intention, a thought, a motive, a desire, a need, or a hope? Even the question seems ill conceived. Given the paucity in the existing language for describing or characterizing internal states, one begins to confront the possibility that the language of the mind is less a mirror of mental states than it is product of the broader conceptual systems of the culture. Mental state terms appear to be derivatives of cultural conventions of intelligibility rather than characterization of a separate ontological realm. Such a conclusion is supported by much anthropological inquiry into mental concepts within other cultures and historical climes (Heelas & Locke, 1981; Kessen, 1979; Shweder & Bourne, 1982). Such study reveals markedly different "ontologies of mind" as one moves from one cultural or historical sphere to another. Charles Taylor's contribution to the present volume represents an additional contribution to such understanding. If the vocabulary of mental states was determined or constrained by the natural characteristics of such states themselves, such variations would scarcely be anticipated.

Over the years there have been numerous attempts to surmount the problem of relativity in interpretation. As we saw, there was Dilthey's attempt in the late 19th century to develop the method of *Verstehen*, through which one might project oneself into the experiences of another. Although severely criticized as a method of acquiring knowledge, something approximating the method was later to be advocated by the historical theorist, R. G. Collingwood (1946). As he proposed, knowledge of earlier historical periods was to be achieved by projecting oneself into the early context. Without penetrating the intentional systems of the past, indeed, history could not be properly written. However, neither Dilthey nor Collingwood could furnish an account of how one could determine whether accuracy of mental projection had been achieved. There have since been the attempts of Emilio Betti (1962) to develop formal canons of interpretation, and by Hirsch (1967) to develop an empirical means of testing hypotheses about the "object directedness" of the speaker. Both of these attempts have come under attack and have largely been abandoned by contemporary hermeneuticists. Not only has it been difficult to realize in practice their formalisms of hermeneutic interpretation, indeed the formalisms resist the sort of interpretation that would enable one to determine whether or not their intention was being fulfilled.

Gadamer's *Truth and method* contains promises of the potential for valid intersubjectivity. Yet, perhaps the major concept to emerge from Gadamer's analysis is that of the horizon of understanding. This concept, to which we shall return shortly, lends itself rather forcefully to relativist and historicist conclusions. Gadamer's "failure" to furnish standards of valid interpretation hardly escaped Habermas's attention in his critique of Gadamer (Habermas, 1970). Tentatively, and with complex alterations in certitude, Paul Ricoeur (1976) has argued that it is possible for the interpreter to distance him- or herself from the biasing foreconceptions of understanding. Yet, he is unable to demonstrate how the processes of determining the text's underlying structure can proceed without such bias. Within recent years perhaps the strongest voice for transparency in interpretation has been that of Habermas (1979). Habermas attempts to lay out a set of ideal speech conditions (such as the absence of domination in relations) that will enable undistorted communication to occur. Yet the grounds upon which validity in understanding rests in this case remains unclear. Further, Habermas inadvertently favors in his analysis the possessor of the greatest rhetorical skills. Such individuals (presumably well educated) would inevitably win out in the attempt to reach rational consensus in a democratic community.

These comments are, of course, appallingly brief and volumes could be (and have been) written to explicate the problems inherent in these analyses (Bleicher, 1980; Palmer, 1969). The main point is that standing in the present era, we find ourselves with no viable account of validity in interpretation. We stand without a compelling promise that knowledge of the other is possible. And, if the logic of my preceeding example is correct, there is little reason to suppose that such an account will be forthcoming. Richard Bernstein (chapter 4, this volume) does maintain that we can transcend relativism in interpretation. Yet, he eschews the possibility of formalized rules of procedure and rests his case on a "hard and messy sorting out of issues." A more elaborate rationale seems to be required to secure the case. And why should we anticipate the emergence of such an elaborated rationale? After all, we have at our disposal only a domain of public discourse. We imagine there is a domain of private discourse to which this must be attached. Yet, we possess access neither to the private discourse itself nor to the rules by which it is translated into the public domain. It follows that any attempt to translate (or understand) must be based on an analytic as opposed to a synthetic procedure. That is, readings or translations can only be rendered true by definition—by virtue of circularity rather than verification.

We would face a similar problem if we assumed that all cloud formations were symbols of God's thoughts. Such thoughts could be read if we could but crack the code of how God's thoughts were transformed into nimbus as opposed to cirrus clouds, to thunderstorms and tornadoes. If such presumptions were made what hope would we have of discovering through our observations the impulses of God? All readings would inevitably be the result first, of an imaginary vernacular of the Holy One (e.g., God is a being who "wishes," "desires," "wills"), and second, an imaginary set of translation rules (e.g., when God is angry the sky is dark). Once developed, such vehicles would indeed render God's thoughts transparent. However they would do so only by virtue of the imaginary system of definitions constructed to carry out the task. If there is no inner voice to which one can gain access, then all attempts to interpret the "inner" by virtue of the "outer" must be inherently circular.

THE ORIGINS OF THE "GHOST IN THE TEXT"

One is moved at this juncture to ask why the dualistic conception of the text is so compelling. Why is it so easy to believe in a meaning behind the words, impulses behind action? What gives rise to the virtually immutable belief in underlying intentions? Let me propose a possible answer to the riddle. One of the major uses of language in social interchange is that of signaling. Linguistic terms can be rapidly and effectively deployed as a means of designating the presence or absence of various objects, entities, or states of affairs. To be told that "it is raining," "your socks are mismatched," or "your house is on fire" is to be signaled of conditions that may require readjustment in one's action. Such utterances refer to events external to or independent of the language itself, and their utility as signals depends importantly on the human capacity to master the relationship between the arrangement of sounds and an array of other events. It may be ventured that the flexibility and discriminative capacity of the language make it an ideal medium for signaling within the sphere of ongoing relations and that this process makes an essential contribution to the survival of the species.

In human affairs one of the most prominent candidates for discursive signaling is human action itself. It is frequently useful to make verbal reference to the kinds of activity (e.g., fighting, helping, loving, eating) in which people are engaged. Yet, in spite of the utility of the process it is beset with profound difficulty. As described more fully elsewhere (Gergen, 1982), words as arrangements of discrete sounds may optimally be associated with (or used to signal) events with stable, spatiotemporal patterning. If the patterns to be signaled are in continuous, nonrepeatable motion the signaling process is subverted. Not only is the spatiotemporal boundary of the indexed event highly ambiguous, but since the event itself is nonrecurring it would be difficult to acquire knowledge over time of its relationship to any particular word. Knowledge would essentially be momentary and disposable. To illustrate, there is an extensive and reliable vocabulary for signaling or talking about kinds of chairs (e.g., stuffed, rocker, Ames, director's). The vocabulary is useful and seldom is one mistaken, as the classes of objects denoted by the terms are stable across time and space. Yet, we have a relatively impoverished vocabulary for speaking of ocean waves and candle flames. In the latter cases it is difficult at the outset to discern where one event is terminated and another begins. In addition, such a vocabulary would have limited utility, as the recurrence of any particular wave or candle form would seldom occur.

There is good reason to believe that with respect to the process of signaling, human action is more like ocean waves and candle flames than chairs. The body is in continuous, multiplex motion, and seldom is the precise pattern repeated over time. As a result there are relatively few terms in the language that refer to the spatiotemporal configuration of the body itself. We can speak of the body as erect or prone, in motion or motionless. However, we can scarcely speak of the velocity and direction of the combined array of moving bodily parts. In effect, such linguistic characterizations of the body in motion are rendered problematic by the arduous nature of the task. An overwhelming effort would be required to develop such a vocabulary, and its utility would be severely delimited.

How, then, is the pragmatic problem of reference to be solved in the case of human action? It would appear that a solution is reached in two steps. First, words are employed to signal not the spatiotemporal particulars of bodily movements themselves, but the accomplishments or endpoints that the movements are achieving (have achieved, will achieve). For example, when we say that a person has helped another, we essentially refer to what the action accomplished.

The descriptive term tells us virtually nothing of the overt movements of the actor's body. If the same movements were to bring pain to another, we might say of the actor that he or she was hurting another. Yet, to use the endpoint of movement as the basis for one's signaling does not fully solve the problem of accounting for the actor's conduct. It is not specifically the achievement or result of action that is at issue. The problem is to index what the actor is doing, not what is accomplished by the actions. It is not the state of being helped or hurt that one is attempting to signal in the present case, but the conduct of the actor. To solve this problem, the language of person description reinstates the result of action as its aim. What is achieved is said to be the aim, attempt, tendency, disposition, or intention of the person. It is the person who intends to help or harm. In this sense person descriptors essentially index not the concrete behavior of actors but their dispositional states (Taylor, 1964).

For present purposes the most important result of this solution to the pragmatic problem of referring to or signaling about human action is the establishment of an inventory of internal dispositions. In order to account for human action we must speak as if people possess motives, needs, drives, intentions, wants, preferences, attitudes, dispositions, and the like—all terms that reinstate at the internal level what persons appear to accomplish in their behavior. Such dispositional terms may designate an immense range of endpoints; one may be motivated to achieve pleasure, approval, wealth, peace, and so on. The list of possibilities may be extended indefinitely. And, as we speak of people's motives for these ends, such dispositional terms are objectified. That is, they fall into the same position *vis-à-vis* the language as do real world events. In the same way one speaks of chairs or salt shakers, one speaks of intentions to help or hinder. In the same way we assume that the former words index a world independent of the words themselves, we also come to presume a world of mental dispositions. The result is a reified language of psychological events.

To summarize, in the attempt to solve the pragmatic problem of referring to or signaling about human activity in the sphere of daily relations, a language of psychological dispositions (intentionality) is born. Such a language seems to be necessitated by the human incapacity to cement linguistic integers to the proteanlike activity of the human body. As this language of dispositions is expanded and reified, the inner realm of psychology becomes an accepted reality, part of the common sense world of daily relations.

THE IMPASSE OF READER CONSTRUCTION

Thus far we have seen that the metaphor of the text places us in a position from which neither reading, intimacy, nor self-knowledge is possible. If persons are texts they must be viewed as isolated social atoms who can neither know nor understand each other. Further, they cannot comprehend their own actions; such actions lie beyond the boundary of objective interpretation. Such conclusions are not only dolorous, but unfortunate in their implications for social life. They hold little promise for intimacy, for genuine contact, for authenticity—or indeed for any profound form of human relatedness. Before exploring an alternative perspective, a second aspect of the textual metaphor must be touched upon. Specifically, it may be asked, if persons are texts then who are the readers? The metaphor itself is all inclusive on this account; it suggests that all persons are embodied texts manifesting symbolic indications of an intentional world. Yet, if people are only texts, then we have no account of the critical task of reading. People must then be more than texts; the metaphor is fundamentally incomplete.

It is the reader who, within the past decade of literary theory, has almost fully displaced the text as the center of concern. This shift in concern is not unrelated to the problematics of truth standards in interpretation; if texts themselves place no powerful constraints over the range of interpretations to be made of them, then one is invited to turn to alternative sources of interpretation. The reader stands as the most obvious alternative. Gadamer (1976) was well aware of this possibility, as captured in his concept of horizons of understanding. As Gadamer proposed (following Heidegger), we approach each text with an historically situated array of foreconceptions. Understanding cannot proceed except in its terms. However, because of their overarching concern with criteria of validity it is not the hermeneuticists who have brought Gadamer's argument to the conclusion it invites. Rather, this move is left to literary theorists in general and to deconstructionists in particular.

Consider first a series of influential essays by Stanley Fish (1980). As Fish proposes in literary interpretation, the "interpreting entity [or agent], endowed with purposes and concerns, is by virtue of its very operation, determining what counts as the facts to be observed" (p. 8). Concern with "reader effects," as they are often called (see Suleiman & Crosman, 1980), reaches its epitome in deconstructionist writings. In the hands of Derrida, deMan, and other deconstructionists, the rendering of the literary critic (reader, philosopher, therapist, or scientist, by analogy) is guided by all-consuming literary devices, figures, or tropes. Such figures dominate interpretation to the exclusion of the text itself. Text and author are thereby deconstructed. Often, as well, the critic or philosopher manages unwittingly to deconstruct his or her own rendering in the very process. And to speak of this process is itself an autonomous literary effort and deserving of its own demolition.

To demonstrate, the psychoanalyst who purports to develop an understanding of a patient typically commits him- or herself to a particular metaphor of the mind—namely, one dominated by conflicting forces. This commitment precedes the confrontation of the particular case to be considered. When the analysand is subsequently confronted, he or she simply acts as a trigger for the analyst's exercising of the rules for elaborating the metaphor. The analysand is simply an excuse for the analyst to engage in a particular literary form, and the analysand is thereby deconstructed as an entity to be understood. Possibly the analyst will also employ a second order metaphor, one that will serve to reveal his or her artifice and thereby deconstruct the rendering as well.[3]

We now find ourselves at yet another unhappy juncture. The view that persons are texts left us with a seeming impasse with regard to either communication or genuine relatedness. When we extend the metaphor to include the reader, we again find that human understanding is impossible. In the process of reading, both the text and its author are obliterated. The individual again falls back into isolation, unable to know, and unable to communicate. Not only do we find ourselves to be social atoms, but each is hermetically sealed from the other. We are invited by such an analysis to each pursue our own individual ends; for after all, others cannot know us nor we, them. There is little left but privatized self-seeking.

TOWARD MEANING AS RELATIONAL FORM

At this point, both for intellectual and moral reasons, one is inclined to abandon the metaphor of person as text; required is an alternative means of understanding the process of human interpretation and the character of human understanding and knowledge more generally. Clarity and confidence in such an alternative can scarcely be generated at this juncture. However, I do think there are significant precursors for such an account and a slowly emerging consciousness of its major contours. The seeds were planted in the writings of Wittgenstein and J. L. Austin. Intimations may be found in some of Bateson's later writings and in the works of those who shared his wholistic perspective. Strands are contained as well in some of Harry Stack Sullivan's writings and, in certain respects, are being amplified in contemporary theories of family therapy and organizational theory. Let me attempt, for present purposes, to bring several critical assumptions into clearer perspective, particularly as they relate to the problem of human interpretation.

First, while accepting the fact that accounts of individual action must be premised on intentional or dispositional language, let us not be tempted to reify the terms of intention themselves. We have been too quick to assume that the language of person description represents the process of human understanding. Thus, let us consider abandoning the assumption that understanding is achieved when we penetrate the veil of the exterior. Rather, let us confront each others' actions directly. Let us consider the possibility that human actions are what they are and not an array of cryptic indicators of yet some other ontological realm. It further seems permissible to admit that others' words (and their performance more generally) are of significant consequence to our actions. That is, we are not self-contained monads, as implied by an extension of the deconstructionist account. Rather, when others speak of their happiness, their sorrow, their anger, and so on, and when their arms are clasped about themselves rather than about us, it makes a difference to our subsequent actions.

Now, let us extend the implications of our first two propositions —that forms of action are what they are, not symbols or emanations, and that people are responsive to others' words and actions. Specifically, we can shift from an emphasis on the text and its reader, or the single action and reaction, to more extended patterns of interdependence. Each of my actions is not only a reply to yours, but is simultaneously an action to which you will reply. In this sense my conduct is neither a response nor a stimulus, but an integer in an extended pattern of which both of us are a part. Or to put it another way, the two of us (and the numbers could be expanded) together achieve a pattern of relationship. The jointly achieved pattern is not decomposable into the fragmentary units that make it up any more than a Jackson Pollock painting could be reduced to the variety of colors by which it is constituted.

Given these three moves, what is to be said about the so-called meaning of words, gestures, and other actions, and the cognate problem of human interpretation? First, we find that the meaning of a word is not to be found in its underlying intention or locked deeply within the unconscious. Rather, the meanings of words, gestures, or actions are realized within the unfolding patterns of relationship. The problem is thus not to look inward to an interior region for the meaning of a word or action, but outward into the continuously expanding horizon of the relationship. Let me attempt the case in a more concrete form.

We speak of persons as having aggressive motives, altruistic inclinations, playful intentions, and so on, as if these were properties of individual selves. However, if my arm is raised above my head there is little that may be said about me as an individual. I am merely a spatiotemporal configuration locked in an otherwise meaningless pose. In contrast, if another person were before me, crouching and grimacing, suddenly it is possible to speak of me as aggressive, oppressive, or ruthless. If the other were a child standing on tiptoes, arms outstretched, his ball lodged in a tree above my head, it would be possible to characterize my pose as helpful or paternal. Additional configurations of the other might yield the conclusion that I was playful, obedient, protective, or proud. Note that my action is the same in all circumstances; yet, there is little that may be said of me—to characterize myself—until the relational context is articulated. Similarly, the other person's movements have little bearing on our language of understanding until they are seen within the context of my own. In effect, what we acquire as individualized characteristics—our aggressiveness, playfulness, altruism, and the like—are primarily products of the joint configuration. They are derivatives of more wholistic units. Intelligibility is thus an outcome of ongoing relational pattern.

What are we to make of human understanding or knowledge from the relational perspective? Here we are again invited to abandon the traditional view of the reader, who works alone and isolated to achieve understanding. Rather, understanding from the present perspective is essentially a social achievement—a derivative of persons in an ongoing relationship. When two persons successfully coordinate their actions to bring off a romantic relationship, a conversation, or even the mutual bidding of goodbye, it may be said that understanding has occurred. The same might also apply to combat and domination. When participants coordinate their actions in such a way that a culturally intelligible pattern is achieved, we may speak of the emergence of understanding along with Ryle (1949)—knowledge is a "knowing how" rather than a "knowing that"—only in this case the knowing how is a collective achievement. In this context the question of accuracy is obviated. One is not attempting to determine the correspondence between intention and interpretation. Rather, we may view the spoken word (in this case) much as an invitation to dance. If the dancers succeed in coordinating their actions, understanding has been achieved. Understanding is not contained within me, or within you, but is that which we generate together in our form of relatedness.

Let me illustrate this relational orientation to human understanding with a report of preliminary inquiry into the nature of mental predicates. We have just seen that the simple movement of my hand raised above my head is itself meaningless and acquires significance only in terms of another's actions. In the same way, the announcement "I am angry" is the utterance of an idiot until it is understood within an unfolding context of relationship. It cannot be said to just anyone at random; the utterance must be embedded in an historical sequence of events—both preceding and following—in order to be rendered sensible. Given these two moves, the first, which exteriorizes so-called mental events such as emotion, and the second, which places such performances into relational context, we are prepared for the third. This is to recenter our attention on the unfolding pattern of which the single emotional performance is a part. That is, we may bring into the center of our theoretical interest the relational pattern of which the performance of a given individual is merely a component.

Consider the concept of depression. Normally depression is thought to be a private, neurologically-based event. If one announces that he or she is depressed, we treat the communication as if it were a report on the status of a strange, exotic land. Yet, if we presume that expressions of depression are first, public, and second, constitutive of relationships, we need not ask whether the person is giving an accurate portrayal of his or her inner realm or whether we are interpreting the words correctly and can begin to ask about the nature of the relationships in which they figure. For example, we have confronted research participants with vignettes in which a friend tells them that he or she is depressed. We then ask the participants about their probable replies to such an expression. As it happens, one cannot respond to such announcements of depression in just any random fashion. You can't easily say, "Oh, that's nice," or, "It is a lovely day at that," without risking rebuff. Rather, as our participants showed us, there are only a limited set of discursive moves that may be made. Primarily, one is limited to some form of sympathy, inquiry, indifference, or irritation. Now we begin to see the possibility for four different units of relationship, each beginning with a particular emotional performance on the part of person A followed by an appropriate reply by person B.

However, these are only the beginning of what may be termed *relational scenarios*, that is, sets of interdependent moves that make up given relational units. We now ask our research participants how person A would reply if he or she expressed depression, and person B replied with one of the four different reactions. Each of these combinations yields a still further array of reactions. Rather than examining the full range of possible scenarios produced by this iteration and several iterations following, let me simply summarize one of the major scenarios that is revealed as one continues to carry the exercise forward. This particular scenario may be called *relation affirming*. It is composed of A's expression of depression, B's reply of sympathy, A's further elaboration of the reason for the depression, B's further sympathy, A's further elaboration, B's advice or encouragement, and finally A's expression of gratitude. At this point the relational unit is generally considered terminated. That is, one is free at this point to select an alternative scenario—talking about plans for the weekend, secret dreams, and so on. As it seems, the entire scenario has been generally affirming of a friendship between the two participants.

Elucidating a number of these major scenarios is only the first important step of our present research. We are also attempting to locate these scenarios within broader sequences of relationship—viewing them as components of still larger units. For example, the relation-affirming scenario just described may typically be located within a larger scenario of a friendship relation. Without this subscenario that affirms the relation, one could not in modern society be said to be properly carrying out a friendship. In contrast, the depression as relation-affirming scenario would not typically be a subpart of a more general competitive or hostile relationship. We are also attempting to explore not only the embedding of scenarios, but the relationship of such scenario forms to each other. If A and B are involved in a certain range of relational scenarios, what are the implications for the kinds of relational patterns they are permitted with C? These are among the many questions we are now attempting to ask—not only with terms of emotion but other mental predicates (such as memory and thought) as well.

Briefly, what do such findings say about the therapeutic relationship? It seems to me that they invite an approach radically different from that embodied in depth analysis. Rather than exploring the unknown world of the interior, one moves to the level of client-therapist relationship. Recent inquiry in this domain has insightfully centered on the mutual construction of reality within such encounters (Cronen, Pearce, & Tomm, 1985; Spence, 1982). However, the present analysis invites an enhancement of such sensitivity. When a client reports depression, for example, what form of "dance" is the therapist being invited to join? Are the achieved patterns the client has developed in other relationships likely to be manifest? Can the therapist help to develop new dances or relational forms that are more beneficial to the client? In this sense the therapist is not attempting to "get to the bottom" of the case or to "plumb the inner depths," but to make manifest the patterns of interchange that are invited by the client's actions, to explore their viability, and to develop means of altering or expanding the repertoire of potentials.

In conclusion, the present paper places under critical consideration the metaphor of person as text. It is this metaphor from which the major questions of traditional hermeneutic analysis have been drawn. It is such inquiry—largely concerned with the process and validity of interpretation—that also informs much recent thinking within the clinical domain. However, as the present analysis attempts to demonstrate, the metaphor of person as text draws the analyst into two conceptual impasses from which escape seems doubtful. No viable account can be given as to how valid inference from external manifestation to the inner region of intent or motive can occur; and there is little means of demonstrating how texts can resist absorption into the reader's forestructure of understanding. Thus, the metaphor of person as text favors the conclusion that valid communication, correct interpretation, and genuine intimacy are all beyond human reach. A preliminary sketch is then furnished of an alternative means of understanding the interpretive process. This relational account views the interpretive process not as the act of the single individual attempting to locate the inner region of the other, but as a process of mutual collaboration. The metaphor of the dance or the game replaces that of the text. Questions of validity are replaced by queries into the forms of relatedness into which our verbal expressions (among others) fall, and into their implications and alternatives.

NOTES

1. For a more extended treatment of metaphor in psychological theory, see Gergen (in press).

2. An account of this interdependent determination of theory and metatheory is contained in Gergen (1985).

3. Spence's important work, *Narrative Truth and Historical Truth*, parallels these analyses in its attempt to demonstrate that the truth generated in the psychoanalytic encounter is essentially a product of aesthetic and linguistic demands rather than a reflection of historical actuality. As Sass and Woolfolk (in press) discern, however, there is an implicit commitment in the work to the empiricist assumption that there are indeed "uncontaminated" experiences to which the narrative reconstruction could be compared. This latter assumption is also apparent in Spence's contribution to the present volume.

REFERENCES

Betti, E. Hermeneutics as the general methodology of the *Geisteswissenschaften*, trans. in J. Bleicher, *Contemporary hermeneutics* (1980). London: Routledge & Kegan Paul, 1962.

Bleicher, J. *Contemporary hermeneutics*. London: Routledge & Kegan Paul, 1980.

Collingwood, R. G. *The idea of history*. Oxford: Clarendon Press, 1946.

Cronen, V., Pearce, W. B., & Tomm, K. A dialectical view of personal change. In K. J. Gergen & K. E. Davis (Eds.), *The social construction of the person*. New York: Springer-Verlag, 1985.

Fish, S. *Is there a text in this class?* Cambridge, Mass.: Harvard University Press, 1980.

Gadamer, H. G. *Philosophical hermeneutics*, trans. D. E. Linge. Berkeley: University of California Press, 1976.

Gergen, K. J. *Toward transformation in social knowledge*. New York: Springer-Verlag, 1982.

Gergen, K. J. Social psychology and the phoenix of unreality. In S. Koch & D. Leary (Eds.), *A century of psychology as a science*. New York: McGraw Hill, 1985.

Gergen, K. J. Metaphors of the social world. In D. Leary, (Ed.), *Metaphors in the history of psychology*. Cambridge: Cambridge University Press, in press.

Gergen, K. J. & Gergen, M. M. Narrative form and the construction of psychological science. In T. R. Sarbin (Ed.), *Narrative psychology: The storied nature of human conduct*. New York: Praeger, 1986.

Habermas, J. Toward a theory of communicative competence. *Inquiry*, 1970, *13*, 360–375.

Habermas, J. *Communication and the evolution of society*. Boston: Beacon Press, 1979.

Heelas, P., & Lock, A. *Indigenous psychologies*. London: Academic, 1981.

Hirsch, E. D. *Validity in interpretation*. New Haven, Conn.: Yale University Press, 1967.

Kessen, W. The American child and other cultural conventions. *American Psychologist*, 1979, *56*, 815–821.

Meehl, P. J. *Clinical vs. statistical prediction*. Minneapolis: University of Minnesota Press, 1954.

Palmer, R. E. *Hermeneutics*. Evanston, Ill.: Northwestern University Press, 1969.

Peters, R. S. *The concept of motivation*. London: Routledge & Kegan Paul, 1958.

Ricoeur, P. *Interpretation theory: Discourse and the surplus of meaning*. Fort Worth: The Texas Christian University Press, 1976.

Ryle, G. *The concept of mind*. London: Hutchinson, 1949.

Sass, L. A., & Woolfolk, R. Psychoanalysis and the hermeneutic turn. *Journal of the American Psychoanalytic Association*, in press.

Shweder, R. A., & Bourne, E. Does the concept of the person vary cross-culturally? In A. J. Marsella & G. White (Eds.), *Cultural conceptions of mental health and therapy*. Boston: Reidel, 1982.

Spence, D. P. *Narrative truth and historical truth*. New York: W. W. Norton, 1982.

Suleiman, S. R., & Crosman, I. *The reader in the text*. Princeton, N. J.: Princeton University Press, 1980.

Taylor, C. *The explanation of behavior*. London: Routledge & Kegan Paul, 1964.

Taylor, C. Interpretation and the sciences of man. *The Review of Metaphysics*, 1971, *25*, No. 1.

Wittgenstein, Empiricism, and the Question of the "Inner": Commentary on Kenneth Gergen

CHARLES TAYLOR

I agree with much in Kenneth Gergen's lively and well-argued paper—all except the essential thesis, I fear. Certainly he has shown the limitations of the metaphor that treats people as texts. If the hermeneutical position stood or fell on the strength of this originating metaphor, it would be in a bad way indeed.

More fundamentally, I think that Gergen's incorporation of Wittgensteinian insights into the epistemology of our action- and intention-terms is extremely important and valuable. In fact, much of our thought about the verification of psychological attributions, both in science and in everyday life, has suffered from a neglect of this basic truth, that many of our actions only can be the actions they are because they occur within "relational scenarios." And these relational patterns in turn are only possible because we share a certain language of action, feeling, sensibility. Virtually all the possible descriptions of Ross's behavior in the story that Gergen outlines are only possible descriptions within one or other scenario of a love "duet" (or perhaps love/hate duet) that he plays out with Laura. For a lone agent, or one who didn't stand in any kind of relations of intimacy to those around him, these descriptions would be literally inapplicable. They would make no sense.

This was perhaps the great contribution of the late Wittgenstein, to show us what the conditions of intelligibility were of our actions, thoughts, feelings, or "mental states," events we were previously tempted to envisage as understandable on their own, standing perhaps in causal relations to others, but still the objects of a possible atomist science. But an action, feeling, or thought is what it is only in virtue of its having a certain meaning; hence the conditions of the intelligibility of the meaning are the conditions of existence for the action, or feeling. Once one takes this point, one is prized forever out of the inner space that was so dear to our empiricist forbears. For so many of the things we do and experience have their essential conditions of intelligibility in what surrounds them, in the story in which they are embedded. Ross's gesture is just an unremarkable example among countless others.

So far, so agreed. I am only saying much less well what Gergen expresses so clearly and eloquently in his paper. But here comes the disagreement. I don't see how this important truth we derive from Wittgenstein engages with the issue of validity in interpretation. The two seem to me to be on different levels. The issue raised by the Ross/Laura story is simply: What really was Ross doing? Reading Wittgenstein will cure us forever of the temptation to think that there is an answer to this question that is buried deep in some inner space within Ross; that if we just had the right kind of probe—either psychoanalytic, or perhaps even neurophysiological—we could go in there and find out, disregarding completely the surrounding context.

Reading Gadamer may cure us of the fixed idea that there can only be one valid answer to this question. We may come to see that different observers may be asking rather different questions about this event; that the issue as it appears to us in our society (and Gergen's alternatives offer a familiar range in which most of us can find ourselves) may be quite strange to other people who have a quite different ethic and way of life and who would see other issues as significant. Just think how the questions we ask of this sort of gesture have been transformed by the rise of contemporary feminism. We now wonder about what this gesture says about Ross as a man who either respects or is contemptuous of women, either is open to them or stereotypes them. Previous generations may have been oblivious to this issue, wouldn't have been placing Ross's gesture in this dimension at all.

And just being around human beings for a decade or two must have cured us of the temptation to think that there must be an unambivalent answer, that there can't be important questions to which both opposed answers may be true. He may both respect her and have contempt for her. Moreover, he may not be living this ambivalence as a self-aware conflict, but the whole issue may still be muddled and unresolved, even unfocused in his mind.

But when all this is said, we still haven't disposed of the problem of the valid interpretation. Questions still arise to which we seek answers about what someone really thinks or feels or wants. Does our relationship mean as much to you as to me? Are you deep down angry at me? Can you ever forgive me for what I did 10 years ago? These are questions we can't help asking of each other, not as psychologists or sociologists, but in the course of living our lives. One could say that we live our lives on the basis of one or other answer to questions of this kind. That is why being uncertain about them can be so upsetting and unsettling. An epistemological theory that tries to tell us that there isn't a genuine question here, or that the answer is up to the observer or the interlocutor to supply, is just not credible.

Of course, you can only be in one or other of the states I'm concerned with because you already stand in some relationship to me because we are linked in the same story. As Gergen so well puts it: "The announcement 'I am angry' is the utterance of an idiot until it is understood within the unfolding context of relationship." But this doesn't empty the issue of whether you are angry of its meaning. It's precisely because of the relationship within which we both stand that it has such tremendous importance for me. And we must allow that you may be ambivalent, both angry and forgiving, struggling between the two, or alternatively one or the other. Yes, but then this is the description I'm looking for, the one I'm going to have to live with and around. A declaration of ambivalence is also an answer to my question.

The question of interpretation is still there, still inescapable, even after we have taken the full Wittgensteinian point. This latter is not a way out of this question with all its difficulty and epistemological embarrassments. What it does do for us is enable us to put the question differently, to see it in its context. But it remains unavoidable. What makes it so is not some questionable theory we might have invented to get a handle on action, some language of dispositions that we have devised to help "solve the pragmatic problem of referring to or signaling about human activity in the sphere of daily relations." Rather it is the way we live our lives and build our relations. There being some answers in this domain is a precondition of our having any human stories to talk about.

But true as I think this point to be, I recognize that it still doesn't do entire justice to Gergen's thesis here. For is it not often the case that faced with a question of this kind, we end up elaborating a clear answer between us? My initial question is whether you are angry, or still hold a grudge. But this being a question becomes itself a major event in our ongoing relationship. The way it comes up or fails to come up colors the relationship. If it does come up, then the answer is not simply something we register. Finding it out may require a self-clarification on your part, one that you carry out partly in conversation with me, and in the course of this conversation how you feel will also characteristically develop and change. You may be brought to formulate for yourself your resentment of me, and that may fuel this resentment; or in luckier cases help you to get over it, or any of a host of other possibilities.

Finding here is inseparable from changing. And that brings us to one of the basic tenets of the hermeneutical view, that human beings are partly constituted by the self-interpretations they accept, that there is no answer to how things are with us that is quite independent of our interpretations.

But this still doesn't mean that the issue of the valid interpretation has been made to disappear. Finding and becoming are intertwined. But one misunderstands the whole process if one just collapses the first into the second. As I get you to articulate why you resent me, perhaps in the process intensifying your hard feelings in the first phase, I may be able to answer the story you're now unfolding with my own version of events. Perhaps I can convince you that there's another way of seeing things, one in which I am not as culpable, not as insensitive and uncaring as you were portraying me. Perhaps if things go very well, you might lose your resentment. Then the whole thing will fit into a certain story for us, the story of an original wound and your smoldering feelings and our talking it out to a new understanding. But all this "negotiating" of the final scenario is not at all incompatible with their being a fact of the matter, how you felt. On the contrary, it presupposes it. We now agree that you felt smoldering and not fully self-admitted resentment over what I did back then. We further agree that now you're over that. These are taken as truths of interpretation by both of us. There is no other way of thinking of them that will make sense of our lives.

But if the "truth of interpretation" emerges out of the "negotiation," then is it not factitious? Not at all. The basic constraint with which we live is that not just any interpretation was possible. In this respect my term *negotiation* may mislead. It's not that anything we can settle for would be true. If one of us were so eager to please the other that they were willing to swallow any story to get peace, that would be a reason to distrust the conclusions we arrived at. People who do cave in like this are always hiding the fact from themselves and bitterly resent the imputation. That's because the transcendental condition of this negotiation, the founding assumption under which it proceeds, is that there are answers to these questions about how people feel, what they want or think, what they meant by that gesture, and so on.

But it might be thought that all this is beside the point. Ken Gergen wouldn't perhaps deny that we normally proceed on this assumption. He might say that this is just another manifestation of our habit of reifying our motivational states in order to get a handle on the evanescent flow of human action. It is within the circle of illusion that science is trying to escape. So harping on the way we proceed in life is nothing to the issue.

But to profer this answer would be to make a fundamental mistake. Here we come to a crux of the whole argument and a basic parting of the ways in our philosophical procedure. To some people it might make sense to speak in this way. But it seems to me that our entire philosophical discourse hangs in the air once we turn to take this step. Once we have established our best possible account of the questions we have to take seriously in order actually to live our lives, once we have clarified, in other words, what the ontological assumptions are that we can't help making in practice as we go about the business of living, where in heaven or earth could the epistemological arguments come from that should convince us that we are wrong? What considerations could possibly trump the best self-understanding of what is inseparable from and indispensable in practice?

There was a time when at least some philosophers would confidently answer this challenge with the single term *science*. Their belief was that science would tell us what the real structure of human consciousness or behavior was, quite independently of our self-understanding. Phenomenology could be quite ignored. But this hope seems based on a gigantic *petitio principii*. How would we ever know that a given theory offered a good or valid explanation of our knowing, or thinking, or feeling, unless it accounted for these things as we actually live them? What else are we trying to account for? An explanation of some process that was quite unrelated to our lived experience of, say, suffering misunderstanding and then clearing it up, would be an account of something else than misunderstanding and its overcoming. It would be changing the subject.[1]

In fact, the great strength of Wittgenstein's reflections in his later work comes from just this. He shows again and again that whatever the "official" empiricist theory says about mental contents, or the meanings of words, we don't actually live our lives that way. We don't treat pain as something in a private inner space. And we don't use our psychological language just to portray what goes on in this space. He makes us see that we are imposing an alien interpretive grid on language, thought, and feeling; and once we see this, this grid loses its credentials. The only justification for this empiricist theory would have been that it actually captures the lived experience of thinking, feeling, and talking—which was, of course, the claim of the original founders of the tradition. Once we see that it fails to do so, it has no more recourse.

The reflections I am offering here are, I believe, in the same spirit. Nothing can trump the best account of what we have to presuppose in order to get on with the business of living.

In sum, my crucial difference from Gergen comes in what we respectively draw from Wittgenstein. Where he sees a single issue, I see two. The old empiricist idea of mental states as "inner," as having the nature they have independent of their embedding in an interpersonal story, ought to have been laid to rest forever by Wittgenstein's later work. But this is quite independent from the issue whether one can speak of "the meaning of Ross's gesture" as something to be discovered, as something about which true and untrue descriptions can be offered. Indeed, there is even a valid use for the image of inwardness, and there are occasions when we can talk of someone's "deep" feelings, or "inner" thoughts.

But one musn't confuse the two senses of inner, the old empiricist one and the perfectly valid image we invoke in our self-explanations. The first was defined by the notion of first-person privileged access. The Cartesian or empiricist inner was a domain that is directly accessible in principle only to the agent him/herself. Others have to make shaky inferences about it from "external" signs. Inwardness as a category of ordinary self-understanding in our civilization isn't like this at all. One of the reasons I may describe some of my feelings as 'deep' is my difficulty in contacting them, in making them palpable and perspicuous. But this is as much a difficulty I have in being clear about my own feelings as it is a puzzle for you. And I will often overcome this, if I do, in the course of an extended conversation with you, in which I try to make sense of my feelings in a way that both of us together can find convincing—rather like in the conversation I mentioned above, I get you to agree with me on a new reading of the events that triggered your resentment. Depth and inwardness here are quite unconnected to privileged access. This whole Cartesian-inspired idea is a red herring.

But Gergen doesn't seem to be taking this into account when he says, e.g., "The metaphor of person as text favours the conclusion that valid communication, correct interpretation, and genuine intimacy are all beyond reach." Of course, there is lots wrong with the image of the text, as I said above. But insofar as we mean just minimally by it, that what people do has a "meaning", which is often not clear on the face of it, then it doesn't need to lead us astray. Unless, that is, we in turn interpret this notion of 'deeper' meaning in the terms of the old empiricist theory and think of it as hidden in some space that by its very nature is inaccessible to the "outside" observer. Then, indeed, we can no longer make sense of our human experiences of communication and intimacy, as Gergen says.

But we have no reason to make this elision. Perhaps in making it we are still too much in the grip of the old epistemology. It is still colonizing our metaphors for the human condition, preventing us from seeing what 'depth' means in our modern cultural experience. The liberating effect of Wittgenstein's later work, as of that of Heidegger, can be to remove this distorting prism. Undoubtedly Ken Gergen and I are in agreement on this. Where we part company is in the lessons we draw from this work. He may think I have not yet fully assimilated it. But I for my part think that he hasn't yet gone all the way along the path it beckons.

NOTE

1. This is what seems to me to be wrong with Quine's project of "Epistemology Naturalized" (in *Ontological Relativity and other Essays*, New York: Columbia University Press, 1969). He permits himself statements like the following: "What to count as observation now can be settled in terms of the stimulation of sensory receptors, let consciousness fall where it may" (p. 69). As though we could ever identify something as an observation quite independent from our experience of observing.

Rejoinder to Charles Taylor

KENNETH J. GERGEN

Because of Charles Taylor's pivotal contributions to the interpretative turn in the social sciences, it is gratifying to find critical points of agreement in our views. This accord is particularly useful in lodging a position counter to the dualist view of psychological knowledge and its implications both for hermeneutics and empiricist accounts of science more generally. Rather than perserverating on these matters, however, I wish to turn to what appears to be the major issue that separates us. It is a matter deserving of further exploration.

In my view Taylor has responded to the radical relativity of interpretation suggested in my paper with a passionate and compelling plea for authenticity. My analysis suggests that the search for validity in interpretation has no objective crucible, datum, or set of criteria against which one interpretation may be claimed superior to another. As Taylor sensitively discerns, if this view is sustained, then all claims to interpretation—of both self and others—are rendered suspect. Further, in demeaning the activity of claiming meaning in action, one simultaneously abandons hope of authenticity. Only the unsophisticated and unreflective would then believe in the sincere expression of friendship, love, compassion, or anger. Those who were aware of the ungrounded character of interpretation would be apprised of the ontological emptiness of such expressions. The expressions may appear to reflect friendship, love, and the like, but in light of our more scrutinizing analysis, we now realize that knowledge of what we are truly expressing is beyond our grasp. Indeed, the entire assumption of "true expression" is found deeply flawed. In effect, once the apple of interpretive relativity has been tasted, human action seems to be reduced to so many stances, gestures, or "as ifs." Justifiably, Taylor wishes to hold fast to authenticity in action.

Yet, what I fail to find in Taylor's analysis is the kind of account of the interpretive process that would rescue the concept of authenticity from its precarious position. We are told that even after the problem of valid interpretation has been disposed, we still seek answers about what people feel or want. We are told that these are genuine and important questions to people; having answers is a precondition of our having human stories to talk about; and these interpretations are self-constituting. All these points are compelling; however, in their present form they seem more indicative of the profound degree to which we are immersed within our cultural conventions than they are a conceptual justification for these commitments. It is as if to say we must hold fast not because our commitments are well founded so much as they are dear. The argument is then advanced that once we have made our commitments to a given account, to ontological assumptions, to various lifeways, there are no epistemic arguments that could dislodge us. More broadly, any attempt to explain our lives that did not employ the languages embedded within life practices themselves would simply be "off the mark." This, too, may be accurate, but more of a practical consideration as opposed to a conceptual justification. Further, such argument would not appear to leave us in an auspicious resting place. For if we valorize common sense understanding in these ways, then it appears we must resign ourselves to an endless recapitulation of existing cultural forms. By implication, such arguments admonish one for challenging the common sense conventions that rationalize the various forms of oppression, exploitation, and dehumanization of which the world has grown so accustomed. And, although I agree with Taylor that the sciences cannot furnish us with objectively accurate interpretations of human action, I believe there is a critical role for the sciences to play in hammering out unsettling and emancipatory forms of discourse. All that is dear is not necessarily just.

Is there a safe passage to be located between the deconstruction of mental talk, on the one side, and the loss of innocence on the other? I believe there is, and it is suggested by the relational alternative to human understanding sketched in the latter part of my offering. There I proposed that we abandon the assumption of meaning as lying within single individuals—analysands, authors, or consociates

—and consider it a fully collaborative outcome, embedded within and generated by ongoing relationships. Expressions of friendship, love, anger, are not viewed as reflections of yet another psychological world, nor are they viewed as the attempts of one isolated individual to penetrate the subjectivity of another. Rather, such expressions are manifestations of various forms of relationship. They may or may not be permitted to stand unchallenged depending not on their veracity but on the extent to which they are congenial with the form of relatedness emerging at the time. Their implications are subject to infinite revision, not because of their truth value but because their pragmatic effects may be deleterious to the emerging forms of relatedness.

This approach does not demand that we view "expressions of our mental life" as mere postures. On the contrary, the acts themselves are inherently and inescapably innocent. That is, at the moment of action they are what they are, not indexes or readings of yet something else. Whether such actions become otherwise interpreted depends on the character of our interdependency. Such expressions are thus akin to existential leaps into a mutually generated faith. In each action the character of our existence together is at the foundry. No mere game, tactic, mask, or facade here; even that which we call pretense is a committed action. The question of whether human action is authentic or contrived fails to be relevant at this level. To ask such questions is to focus wrongly on the veracity of the make-believe world created by the language and not the actuality of the interchange itself. So there is, as Taylor proposes, "a valid use for the image of inwardness," and "occasions where we can talk of someone's deep feelings." However, let us not reify the referents of such words, but rather, attend to the ways in which these statements constitute and reshape our lives together. If we set out to build a house together there is little need to ask whether the movement of my hands with nail and mortar are true or valid; they are as they are, and depending on your relationship with them we may or may not achieve shelter. If one is embarked upon a love affair, there is little need to inquire into the internal source of expressions of adoration —whether they are somehow true. The nature of the relationship in which such expressions are embedded may be of utmost importance to the participants. However, to seek carefully into the inner meaning of loving "expressions" is to launch yet another form of relationship—one of potential doubt and alienation. To ask of the lover what he/she is truly about is to lose the invitation.

Chapter 3

Tough and Tender-minded Hermeneutics

DONALD P. SPENCE

It is now some 26 years since C. P. Snow divided the world into two cultures and tried to convince us that one side represented the hope of the future whereas the other—the literary culture—could best be described as a collection of "natural Luddites" who were incapable of understanding the Industrial Revolution and were even unhappy that trains ran on Sunday. Pure science, although impoverished in a number of ways (scientists, Snow claimed, almost never read a book), was clearly superior in the sense that it really was a culture, its members could communicate with each other, a higher proportion of them had overcome the disadvantages of coming from poor families (so said Snow, 1959), and best of all, in a phrase that Leavis never let him forget, best of all they had "the future in their bones."

The classification was particularly influential in this country where we have no tradition of Geisteswissenshaft, and its influence far outstripped its truth value (the original lecture went through 11 printings). Whatever the merits of Snow's outburst, it helped significantly to polarize the two cultures and give them the de facto appearance of being members of two quite distinct species. And even though there have been a number of well-reasoned rebuttals (the one by F. R. Leavis [1962] is the best known), the catch phrase "two cultures" has remained in our vocabulary and has established its own kind of currency.

I think the present debate about whether psychoanalysis is a science or some form of hermeneutics is, at bottom, an extension of Snow's two-culture argument in more modern dress. Just as his original dichotomy was suspect and open to many of the criticisms that Leavis leveled against it, so I will argue that the current argument is beside the point and neglects the main issue in favor of something more fashionable and faddish. Hermeneutics, of course, was not mentioned in Snow's original critique, but if he were alive today he would, without doubt, have listed the hermeneutic approach as a key aspect of his softer culture and another reason to give it low marks. Even without Snow on the scene to give this argument a further push, we find the attacks on hermeneutics follow very clearly from his tradition. Grünbaum, for example, in his discussion of the philosophical foundations of psychoanalysis, finds hermeneutics to be akin to shamanism; argues that in the hands of such spokesmen as Habermas and Ricoeur it amounts to a "scientophobic" method of analysis; that in the hands of these critics, it searches for explanations in terms of reasons, not causes; and that overall, the hermeneutic approach contains "multiple ontological and epistemic blunders" and is based on a "profound misunderstanding of the very content and methods of the natural sciences" (1984, p. 1). Clearly, it belongs among C. P. Snow's less-favored nations.

In a similar vein, Marshall Edelson, in his recent book (1984), makes an argument for the scientific development of psychoanalytic theory and contrasts this possibility with attempts such as mine to try out a more hermeneutic reading. In current psychoanalytic discussions the battle lines are clearly drawn (Blight has asked whether "psychoanalysis must retreat to hermeneutics"), and the polarity is clear: either psychoanalysis is a science—and therefore respectable and destined for a long and fruitful life—or it is something hermeneutic, in which case it deserves its present state of suffering and should look forward to all kinds of grief. If it does not have the future in its bones, to use Snow's phrase, perhaps it will disappear before the century is out.

If science is the patron saint of all clear-thinking scholars, then hermeneutics is the enemy, a kind of medieval witch who dabbles in sorcery and who threatens to take us back to the Dark Ages of alchemy and the transmutation of elements. In similar fashion identities have become either/or; once you are stained with the hermeneutic brush, you are always suspect; once suspected as being sympathetic, even if not a recognized member of a recognized hermeneutic cell, you are always in jeopardy, and no amount of recantation can ever clear the air.

For a more reasoned perspective, and one that gets away from C. P. Snow's two cultures, let me quote from a recent paper by Manicas and Secord:

> Put in simple terms [they write] the insight of the hermeneutic perspective is this: If our aim is to explain behavior as it occurs in ordinary life there is no escaping the ordinary description of behavior and experience. Certainly causal mechanisms and structures discovered by experimental psychology or other sciences apply to such behavior, but by themselves they do not provide sufficient explanation, and they certainly do not enable us to dispense with ordinary language and to substitute a pure scientific language of behavior. We hasten to add that the reverse cannot be done either: Ordinary language cannot substitute for the language of causal mechanisms and structures. (1983, p. 410)

They go on to raise the question of what is the character of hermeneutic science, and by joining those two words in a single sentence they have clearly tried to put Snow behind them. Why hermeneutic? Because a simple positivism is no longer sufficient: "It is by now commonplace that there is no such thing as a non-interpreted 'given' that can serve as the foundation of knowledge" (ibid.). The new science, at the same time, must have public, critical, and systematic standing. The public aspect deserves particular attention: "Hermeneutic inquiry as a science would be constrained by the systematic, public demands of establishing the evidential credibility of its accounts" (p. 411). This is a particular problem in psychoanalytic explanations, and I will come back to this point later.

What is not discussed, however, is the kind of world view necessary to make this new science work, and to that problem I wish to devote the bulk of this paper. I will consider two extreme positions. First is the assumption that the world is a partly random collection of happenings held together by a certain number of general principles. Few, if any, of these general laws are accessible to immediate observation. Thus, a clear-eyed, honest, and truthful description of everyday events—especially people events—would admit to more randomness than we like to assume. I will call this the Know-Nothing world view; it is clearly the most conservative of all possible outlooks and is one of the factors that has contributed to the power and scope of the experimental method. By contrast, at the other extreme is the assumption that an underlying lawfulness pervades our existence, and this view has taken various forms over the centuries. In the Middle Ages it came under the label of "the Hand of God"; in modern-day modes of thought, it becomes the accepted psychoanalytic assumption about clinical behavior and serves as our central approach to patients. However nonsensical or disconnected their superficial behavior, however unrelated the pieces of their life story, if we listen carefully enough and long enough, we will find an underlying pattern, a deep-seated lawfulness that will explain everything. This view is best captured in Freud's metaphor of analysis as a kind of archaeology.

You are all acquainted with the Know-Nothing position from your courses in research method. If, in the course of my research, I have collected response measures from two experimental conditions on two matched samples and if I can establish a significant difference between these two sets of values, I am only permitted to say that the null hypothesis has been disproved. In other words I have identified an exception to the general rule that God plays dice with the universe; I have established a regularity that goes against the world view that all is chaos. Statistics may tell me that such a difference could only occur by chance 5% or 1% of the time, but statistics will not tell me what caused the difference or whether it really supports my hypothesis or only appears to. Replication can support the idea that I have established a true difference, and I am allowed to combine the probabilities of n independent tests to arrive at an overall estimate of the nonchance likelihood; but in the long run, all I have really established is that the difference or differences would not have occurred by chance.

The Know-Nothing position as described here has much in common with the realist view of science set forth by Bhaskar (1975) and more recently by Manicas and Secord (1983). Their position assumes that there is "no pre-interpreted 'given' and that the test of truth cannot be 'correspondence.' Epistemologically, there can be nothing *known* to which our ideas [sentences, theories] can correspond" (p. 401). They go so far as to argue that only one science is grounded on specific causal regularities, and that science is celestial mechanics. And even there we presuppose theoretical and explanatory properties that probably do not exist in the real world (see p. 404).

This null position, this assumption of a random universe in which

apparent difference is most likely the result of artifact or coincidence
—this null position is extraordinarily hard to teach, and once taught,
all but impossible to adopt as an article of faith. It demands relentless
suspicion of all possible contaminating conditions, a near-paranoid
attitude that doubts all findings until they are replicated. In the
context of this world view, talk is cheap but largely meaningless, and
true explanation becomes the exception rather than the rule. In the
face of a possible explanation, whether or not it is supported by
hypothesis, the rule of parsimony always holds sway: it may be
simpler to assume that the difference is a matter of chance than to
assume that it is a true difference that reflects an underlying cause.

One reason this position is so hard to maintain is that it flies in the
face of the way we lead our lives. We could hardly last a day if we kept
saying that Yes, the sheep is black but only on this side; if we did not
impute motives to others in light of past experience and in the
absence of any certain knowledge; and if we did not continually try to
read beyond surface appearance to make a guess at the underlying
cause. The simple art of conversation is a clear example of this kind
of inductive and deductive leap. Your choice of vocabulary and syntax
will never quite match mine; as a result the meanings that seem to
emerge from your sentences, or from my parsing of your
nonsentences, will always be somewhat ambiguous or irrelevant or
even opaque. Nevertheless, I continue the conversation with the faith
that we can mutually inform one another; that unclarities will
gradually be resolved; that what seems on the surface to be a series of
nonsequiturs will gradually resolve themselves into a clear message
to which I can respond. A Know-Nothing world view would very
quickly destroy this enterprise, and encounters with certain kinds of
paranoid or obsessive patients founder because they do not give us
the benefit of the doubt; the first sign of contradiction breaks off the
engagement.

One of the unsung merits of the Know-Nothing position is its
influence on the context of discovery. If I make no assumptions about
lawfulness or preexisting pattern, then the pattern that does emerge
—the pattern that I generate inductively from a series of nonchance
differences—is more likely to be something truly new and different.
Thus a strict adoption of the null hypothesis allows me to see the
world in a truly new manner. Although chance may favor prepared
minds, as Claude Bernard has told us, a truly nonchance finding may
stand out because it is strikingly new and different, and that is the
way nature forces us to change the course of our thinking. It goes

without saying that the opposite world view tends to perpetuate the same old mythology. What is wrong with most psychoanalytic research—and this includes both clinical and experimental varieties —is that it poses as discovery but, in reality, is only interested in confirmation. So long as we assume that patterns are waiting to be discovered, we will tend to assume that we know their form and content; we are thus engaged in pseudo-confirmation and, ultimately, in pseudo-science.

Where the Know-Nothing world view is clearly at odds with our general approach to life, the opposite position—that everything has meaning—would seem to be a natural outgrowth of the way we lead our lives. Freud's search for a connected story in the patient's past is only a more sophisticated version of our own attempts to build a continuous narrative from each of our encounters. Freud's fascination with repetition and his attempts to show parallels in dreams and behavior must resonate with our folk beliefs in the significance of things that happen over and over again.

Freud's concept of the Unconscious is a central part of this lawful world view because it gives us a method for supplying pattern and continuity to almost any piece of behavior. Faced by gaps or perturbations in the conscious record—a slip of the tongue, for example, an unexplained piece of forgetting, or the emergence of an out-of-context tic—Freud found it convenient to suggest that these symptoms could be defined as manifestations of the dynamic Unconscious. The dream is apparently meaningless because it is the outgrowth of unconscious activity; once we penetrate the censorship and restore the latent content, we can read the dream as we might read a book. The central mission of the Dora Case was to show how each dream, apparently a meaningless interruption in the patient's account, could be analyzed and rewritten in light of the patient's associations and then inserted back into the original context to generate a story that was, in Freud's language, "intelligible, consistent, and unbroken."

But the world view of underlying order goes beyond specific aspects of the theory; it supplies the underlying approach that the clinician takes towards his reality. Charles Brenner, a spokesman for the orthodox psychoanalytic position, tells us, "If the unconscious cause or causes can be discovered, then *all* apparent discontinuities disappear and the causal sequence becomes clear" (1955, p. 14; my italics). Freud, in his famous jigsaw puzzle analogy, compares the solution of a puzzling symptom to the solution of a puzzle. "If one succeeds in arranging the confused heap of fragments, each of which bears upon it an unintelligible piece of drawing, so that the picture acquires a meaning, so that there is no gap anywhere in the design and so that the whole fits into the frame—if all these conditions are fulfilled, then one knows that one has solved the puzzle and that there is no alternative solution" (Freud, 1923, p. 116).

Notice that this approach to the evidence must assume that there is an underlying pattern waiting to be discovered. This is clearly the case with a real jigsaw puzzle or any other man-made artifact that has come apart and is waiting to be reassembled. But to take this position about the natural world is to make a substantial leap of faith for which there is no very strong body of evidence. And if I were to take the opposite position—that the world is a collection of random happenings—then I would draw quite a different conclusion from Freud's heap of fragments. If they do seem to generate a meaningful picture, I would only be suspicious that this picture was somehow being imposed on the evidence—the very presence of meaningfulness would be cause for alarm, just as we know that whenever we see a straight line or a right angle in nature, we are discovering something man-made.

Let me spell out some of the more insidious implications of the second world view. If lawfulness is always assumed, then it follows that a failure to find it—in a dream, for example, a patient's life story, or a transcript of a session—is only evidence for the fact that we have not looked far enough or listened in the right attitude or found just the right way to translate the patient's key phrases. If the pattern is always there, waiting to be discovered, then the failure to find it puts the burden on us to look harder. Apparent discontinuities are seen as a misreading of the evidence and are almost never identified as the true state of affairs. If pattern is only waiting to be discovered, the search must continue, and since the dimensions of this search go far back into the past and deep into the unconscious, the search space can never be exhausted.

A second consequence bears on the criteria for pattern match. If a pattern is always waiting to be discovered, then almost any pattern finds ready acceptance because we are not asking the question about pattern vs. no pattern, but only, which pattern has appeared? I think this deep-seated faith in patterning explains the general readiness of clinicians to accept almost any explanation; it also explains the virtual absence of alternative explanation because the task is to find some kind of lawfulness, and almost any kind will do. On the other hand, if randomness is the ground condition, then any pattern is an exception to the rule and needs careful justification. Taking the null position, I would be much more likely to ask for alternatives, to search for ways of choosing among alternatives, and for including alternative explanations in my explanatory account. And finally, I would be readier to reject all solutions as violating the law of parsimony and conclude, finally, that no pattern really exists. This is a position that is never taken by a practicing clinician—at least, never taken in print.

What makes the nonrandom assumption so hard to disconfirm is, in the last analysis, the standing of the Unconscious. You can see how a deep-seated belief in unconscious motivation and unconscious determination conflicts directly with the null hypothesis that chaos is everywhere. If the Unconscious truly does exist, then there is always the potential for explaining all apparent discontinuities in behavior. If the Unconscious is always at work, then there is no such thing as a random act or a piece of behavior that "doesn't make sense"; the limitation lies only in our understanding. Much the same kind of argument was made in the Middle Ages to deal with disbelievers. If the ways of God seemed inscrutable or baffling or perverse, the problem lay with us, the sinners, and in our lack of faith; what was apparently random on the surface stemmed only from a misguided reading of the natural order, a reading very possibly inspired by the Devil. But the underlying order was never in doubt.

Resting explanation on the Hand of God was finally seen—in the late Middle Ages—to be an empty exercise because everything could be explained, and it was in part the dissatisfaction with this mode of explanation that led to the development of the experimental method —and to the null hypothesis. I am going to argue that much the same problem holds with the present-day concept of the Unconscious. What was originally intended as a working hypothesis (Freud, 1914) that could be used to further our understanding of the clinical material and whose nature could be clarified by a careful reading of this material has been reified into a concept whose standing is beyond question and whose significance has increased in direct proportion to its inaccessibility. As its significance has increased, direct knowledge has diminished. Legitimized as an axiom, it has been largely screened off from study, and a careful review of current conceptions would probably show little advance over Freud's (1915) model. We have little more precise knowledge, at the present time, of the workings of the primary process, of the rules and conditions of transformation, or of what might be called the half-life of the typical unconscious fantasy, than we did in 1915.

I would argue, further, that the belief in the Unconscious is perhaps the critical reason that clinicians in particular accept the view of a nonrandom universe. This view, furthermore, can never be challenged because the Unconscious, as defined in the orthodox theory, is essentially prescientific. There is no chance for disconfirmation because of the two assumptions that, first, the Unconscious is internally inconsistent—"exempt from mutual contradiction" is Freud's language—and second, the Unconscious is "alive and capable of development." Given these two axioms, I can never show that what you called the Unconscious is not what I would call it because you can simply say that your description referred to time t and my description to time t_1. Or you could say that each of us has only a partial view and given the law of mutual contradiction, there is no reason to expect consistency.

Because it is prescientific and nonfalsifiable, the Unconscious as a concept provides only pseudo-explanation and does not advance our clinical knowledge. Every time fresh pieces of the Unconscious are used to explain a particular clinical occurrence, we are simply restating Freud's original hypothesis of unconscious motivation. But these discoveries are usually misinterpreted as something much more important—they are seen as validations of orthodox theory. And this is where the mischief comes in. Because, of course, they are no more validations of psychoanalysis than a cure at Lourdes is proof of the Hand of God.

What does all this have to do with hermeneutics? Simply this: If the hermeneutic approach—and I will define this more precisely in a minute—is coupled with a belief in a nonrandom universe, then we have the worst of both worlds. Given the sheer richness of the physical world, it is ridiculously easy to find patterns once we look for them; and if we assume that a pattern is waiting to be discovered, the hermeneutic method only adds more grist for the mill. Weak pattern matches are immediately elaborated into causal structures of surprising subtlety and narrative appeal; chance overlaps are invested with unshakable significance; and we are simply at the mercy of the infinite universe, what Hannah Arendt calls the "sheer entertainment value of its views, sounds, and smells" (1977, p. 20). The hermeneutic method cannot protect us against this kind of pseudo-significance; when grounded in the assumption of a patterned universe, it can only do more harm than good. But the fault, I would argue, lies in the grounding, not in the hermeneutics.

Now consider the other point of view. If the hermeneutic approach is coupled with a belief in a random universe, then we are protected against weak pattern matches. We have the benefits of a general skepticism coupled with the infinite richness of the hermeneutic data base. If pattern is the exception rather than the rule, then every pattern match must meet some kind of parsimony test; and although the richness of the observed world and all of its construed meanings may add to the plausibility of a pattern, it does not necessarily blind us to its problematic status. What is more, we can draw on the greater richness provided by the hermeneutic approach to make certain kinds of convergent checks; the greater size of the data base makes replication more possible. And finally, if we practice a disciplined hermeneutics, we can stay with surface, or near-surface meanings and never have to take refuge in what is unconscious and therefore nonfalsifiable.

For examples of the first position—of an undisciplined hermeneutics coupled with a firm belief in nonrandomness—we do not have to turn farther than Freud's fragment of a study in hysteria—the Dora Case (1905). His aim there was to tell a story that was "intelligent, consistent, and unbroken," and it was his assumption, as we have seen, that this story already existed and only waited to be discovered, much the way Michaelangelo's *David* lay waiting in the marble, only waiting to be revealed. Guided by the belief in underlying pattern, Freud is quick to take seriously any evidence for nonrandom behavior, and thus we find him fascinated by the fact that Dora's pseudo-appendicitis occurred exactly nine months after her meeting with Herr K. by the lake. He finds this interval "sufficiently characteristic" to conclude that the meeting with Herr K. precipitated the attack of appendicitis—or pseudo-appendicitis—which "thus enabled the patient ... to realize a phantasy of *childbirth*" (Freud, 1905, p. 103). This explanation is offered without question or comment, and no other possibility is offered.

What other explanations might be found? If we were operating from a more conservative (null) position, we would like to be convinced, beyond all possible doubt, that the attack did not occur for quite different reasons, and that the nine-month interval was not merely coincidentally the same as the time for a normal pregnancy. If, for example, a pregnancy fantasy had actually been stimulated by the meeting with Herr K., we might expect to see other signs that supported this hypothesis—attacks of morning sickness, for example, early in term; accounts of specific food preferences; swelling in the breasts; and so forth. Convergent evidence of this kind would add significantly to our conviction that a particular hysterical fantasy had been triggered by the kiss and that this fantasy had led to the delusion that Dora had become pregnant. Hysterical pregnancies of this kind have been documented and under the right conditions have brought the patient to the door of the delivery room and sometimes beyond, fooling even the most knowledgeable obstetrician. You can imagine how much convergent data could be found in such a situation.

The point I want to make is that because Freud was convinced that patterns lay just beneath the surface waiting to be discovered, he was more than ready to draw a strong conclusion from rather weak evidence. The patient's story as initially told is compared to "an unnavigable river whose stream is at one moment choked by masses of rock and at another, divided and lost among shallows and sandbanks ... The connections—even the ostensible ones—are for the most part incoherent, and the sequence of different events is uncertain." But a continuous flow is assumed, something that links beginning with end, and even though the river may at times go underground or be lost behind bushes, its presence is knowable and findable. Only a few links are necessary to establish the overall connection.

This kind of pattern finding comes out of a longstanding Romantic tradition that flourished during the 19th century, particularly in literature. Listen to the beginning of a Sherlock Holmes adventure:

> It had been a close, rainy day in October ... Finding that Holmes was too absorbed for conversation, I had tossed aside the barren paper and, leaning back in my chair, I fell into a brown study. Suddenly my companion's voice broke in upon my thoughts.
>
> "You are right, Watson," said he. "It does seem a very preposterous way of settling a dispute."
>
> "Most preposterous!" I exclaimed, and then, suddenly realizing how he had echoed the innermost thought of my soul, I sat up in my chair and stared at him in blank amazement.

Here is a prime specimen of pattern-finding at its best, and Holmes goes on to explain how it is done.

"After throwing down your paper, which was the action which drew my attention to you, you sat for half a minute with a vacant expression. Then your eyes fixed themselves upon your newly framed picture of General Gordon, and I saw by the alteration in your face that a train of thought had been started. But it did not lead very far. Your eyes turned across to the unframed portrait of Henry Ward Beecher, which stands upon the top of your books ... Your face was thoughtful. You were recalling the incidents of Beecher's career ... You could not do this without thinking of the ... Civil War ... [When] I observed that your lips set, your eyes sparkled, and your hands clenched, I was positive that you were indeed thinking of the gallantry which was shown by both sides in that desperate struggle. But then, again, your face grew sadder; you shook your head. You were dwelling upon the sadness and horror and useless waste of life. Your hand stole towards your old wound, and a smile quivered on your lips ... At this point I agreed with you that it was preposterous, and was glad to find that all my deductions had been correct." ("The Resident Patient." From *The Complete Sherlock Holmes*, vol. 1, pp. 423–424)

Holmes's deductions are confirmed by the fact that they exactly match the thoughts that were running through Watson's mind, thoughts that leave behind revealing clues in the expression on his face and the direction of his gaze. In story after story, the master-mind Holmes attests to the idea that nature can be read like any other book so long as one pays attention to the smallest detail and is careful to organize his observations in the most logical fashion. Inspector Dupin, in the *Murders on the Rue Morgue*, shows a similar ability —he also broke in on a chain of associations in a most remarkable manner—and Henry James was fond of referring to the figure in the carpet that the practiced eye might discern. If nature was a book, we could learn to read it; the patterns, if not immediately obvious, are waiting all around us to be discovered; and truth is simply a matter of finding the pattern. Freud extended the model to include psychic reality and the discovery of patterns in the Unconscious. The logic had become much more complicated because he no longer believed in the transparency of motives, a crucial assumption for Holmes, but the search for pattern continued along with the belief in a set of givens out there, waiting to be discovered.

To my mind, the search for the singular solution bears a striking correspondence to the Romantic legend of Sherlock Holmes. We are charmed by Holmes's adventures, but we do not really believe that a train of thought can be followed by the expressions on a man's face or the direction of his gaze; no one is quite that transparent any more (or ever was). In the same way, we are charmed by Freud's attempts to uncover the form and content of Dora's unconscious fantasies and attempt an excavation of her mind, but the charm wears thin if we no longer believe in the metaphor. What is lacking is real conviction; the proper explanation, as I see it, must lead to replicated persuasion, just as a work of art leads to replicated aesthetic experience. In other words the convincing explanation should produce an aesthetic experience of conviction without the additional suspension of disbelief.

Speaking in this mode, I am, of course, falling back on the Know-Nothing view of the world which holds that there are few if any givens out there against which our stories can be checked; as a result we must give up the correspondence theory of truth. How, then, do we arrive at firm conclusions? One of the most persuasive answers has come from Habermas in his belief that truth is arrived at through dialogue and argumentation leading to consensus. Theory statements, he would claim, are true not because they perfectly describe the world, but because they achieve better and better interpretations of it, interpretations sharpened by argument and discussion. In the words of Mary Hesse: "Theoretical science is part of the human goal of reflective and intersubjective self-understanding, which embraces the hermeneutic and critical sciences as well as the empirical, and involves norms and value judgments as well as empirically constituted facts" (1982, p. 105). And the dialogue is never final—always open to new evidence and new ways of combining the evidence.

The dialogic nature of truth-seeking puts a special premium on public discussion, and here is another point where we must break with psychoanalytic tradition. Freud was not interested in what I have called replicated persuasion, and early in his career, he argued that if the reader was not inclined to agree with his formulation, then additional data would scarcely change his mind (Freud, 1912). Some privacy was needed to protect the patient's identity; some to protect the analyst's fallibility; but the tradition has grown far beyond these two restrictions and, as a result, we have few if any case presentations today that match the disclosures of Freud's classic five. Appeals to authority have replaced appeals to the evidence, and acceptance of an interpretation or a conclusion usually reduces to agreement on faith. This is particularly true when the Unconscious is invoked because, by definition, the Unconscious can never be made available for public examination. Appeals to the Unconscious simply close off discussion because they end any possible chance for dialogue.

In the tough-minded hermeneutics that is grounded in the Know-Nothing tradition, argument must necessarily remain on the surface and be sufficiently transparent to allow for dedicated public involvement. Second, there must be public criteria for success or failure of any particular line of reasoning; arguments cannot be settled, as is usually the case, by appeals to authority. Third, there must always be the possibility for free assent to the argument—the chance to reach what Habermas calls an "uncompelled" conclusion. The overall aim has been well summarized by Geuss (1981): "If an unrestricted community of rational agents investigate a state of affairs, under conditions of complete freedom and eventually reach a stable consensus, the judgment which expresses that consensus is the 'objective truth' about that state of affairs" (p. 72). We have left the correspondence theory far beyond. We no longer claim a match to what is in the person's mind (as in Sherlock Holmes) or in his unconscious or in his past (as in Freud); all that is being offered is a line of reasoning that has no obvious loopholes and that leads to replicated persuasion.

Let me illustrate this approach with a careful analysis of a clinical vignette (Kanzer, 1981). At least two lines of argument seem to follow from these data: one is pursued by the author (who is under the impression that his view is the only view), and the other can be gleaned from other pieces of the material. I will try to compare the two lines of reasoning and show how it is possible to use other parts of the case to make checks of the internal validity of the argument; this step is possible because of the density of the clinical material. One of the benefits of the hermeneutic method is that it allows us to take advantage of this density.

As the author develops his argument, you will see that he relies heavily on the assumption that a cancellation is always resented; that all encounters are invested with some aspect of the transference; and, third, that a negation can always be interpreted to mean the opposite. By the use of words like *all* and *always*, I wish to emphasize the strong nature of these laws and the extent to which the analyst/author tries to normalize the relationship to the patient and turn it into a nomothetic encounter. This leads to an important point: The very attempt to "scientize" the encounter generates the most significant misunderstanding. In other words assumptions of lawfulness interfere with a clear reading of the material.

I begin by describing the analyst's stance. Here are his words:

> With the analyst's unswervingly neutral stance and single interpretation, so close to the ego level that it was almost a confrontation, maximum leeway could be given to the flow of associations and the patient's own independent self-observation to direct the course of the session. The trend was almost entirely devoted to conflicts over separation from the analyst and wishes for union with him that he fought off ... This was indeed a "good analytic hour ... " (1981, p. 84)

Here is how the hour begins:

> *After a three-day official holiday weekend during which the analyst canceled the usual Monday session, the patient, a man in his mid-forties who was well advanced in treatment, returned and began by speaking glowingly of the fine parties he had attended (the analyst silently considered it likely that he was being told that the patient got along very well without the session).*

We may be surprised by that inference—was that in the material? We note, further, that it was not checked with the patient; it remains an assumption. We suspect that this reading of the patient's first remark may have more to do with the analyst's need to compare treatment with parties, and that in the patient's mind, it may simply be a statement of recent events, made perhaps in an effort to bring the analyst up to date.

> *Then he casually mentioned his somewhat belated arrival (which might not otherwise have attracted attention). "You will think it is a resistance," he remarked sarcastically, "but it was nothing of the kind."*

How late? How casual? How sarcastic? Once again, an appeal is being made to the authority of the analyst and we have no alternative but to accept it. But it is also possible that the supposedly casual tone of this remark is something attributed to it by the analyst. This interpretation would be in keeping with the line of thought that the sessions are not valued as highly by the patient as they ought to be: he speaks glowingly of the weekend parties but barely mentions being late to a session.

In his remark about resistance, the patient has turned the tables —now it is he who is attributing thoughts to the analyst. We are taken aback by the boldness of his denial and remember Freud's position on negation—what is claimed not true very often is, and the stronger the denial, the more likely we can believe the opposite. On the other hand, a spade is sometimes a spade and nothing more. The analyst might have clarified the matter by commenting on the denial, but he chose to remain silent.

> *He had hailed a taxi that would have gotten him to the office on time. However, the traffic light changed just before the cab reached him, and someone else got in instead. He was so annoyed that he 'yelled "Fuck you!" after the cab driver, an expression of profanity very unlike him.*

Why the outburst? We are told that it was uncharacteristic, and thus we have reason to assume that the patient had his heart set on getting the cab. Again, why? One possibility is that if he wasn't late, he wouldn't have to talk about it—but why not? Because he would be forced to explain why? Because the patient was the kind of person who liked to be in charge of his life? By this reading, the "Fuck you" was more a reaction to loss of control than to the analytic situation.

> *A brief pause (pause 1) ensued, followed by laughter as the patient repeated "Fuck you!"—this time clearly directed to the analyst. His anger was relieved by the opportunity to "cuss out" the analyst, for whom the cabbie had been a displaced object in the first place, and also by his own display of insight—that the cab driver who had passed him by also replaced the analyst who had canceled a session.*

We wonder, first, how the second "Fuck you" was expressed, and what made the analyst think he was the target. Did the patient turn his head or perhaps sit up—or merely say it again? Here again, we have no choice but to accept the facts as stated (notice how different they are from the usual kind of data). Second, we are left in doubt as to the source of the alleged "insight." If no more was said than is presented here, then the connection between cabbie and analyst lies entirely in the mind of the analyst who chooses, on the evidence of the second "Fuck you," to attribute it to the patient. If the so-called insight did indeed originate with the analyst, then we are more than ever skeptical that the second "Fuck you" was in fact directed toward the analyst. Once again, we are aware that this mode of analysis by comparison—weekend versus analytic hour and cabbie versus analyst—originates with the analyst, and up to this point, no explicit comparison or contrast has been made by the patient. Both of these contrasts, or presumed displacements, may have some truth to them, but they are largely hypotheses and unsupported by direct evidence.

> The obscenity, after the brief pause regulated by the funda-mental rule, had served as a switch word to shift the chain of associations from the cab driver to the analyst and from a day residue in the outer world to the analytic scene. After this brief intermission he returned to his weekend experiences and de-clared that he and his wife had decided to accompany their son to the opening of his college and help him get settled. He might lose an analytic session, but the son was more important.

For the first time, the patient makes a comparison between the analysis and something else—in this case taking care of his son and getting him settled. But the analyst hears this comparison somewhat differently.

> After another brief pause (pause 2), it was the analyst who broke the silence and injected his first and only interpretation of that session. The theme of losing a session was still continu-ing and was obviously very charged with feeling, he asserted. The decision to accompany the son to college showed that he, unlike the analyst, was a good father and at the same time returned the affront of the analyst in dropping his own session.

To my mind this interpretation represents a serious misreading of the material. The analyst is not being punished by the trip to college; all the patient is saying is that he can't be in two places at the same time. Second, there is no evidence that the patient was upset by the Monday cancellation, and third, the analyst had just concluded that the patient preferred parties to analysis.

What theme does the patient seem to be pursuing that is being missed? At the most basic level, we are being told a story of events in his own life and plans for the future. These may have a bearing on the transference, but this hypothesis is only one of many and can hardly, in fairness, be imposed on the material in the way we have seen. We have clear indications of how the analyst sees the material, but we are much more in doubt as to the patient's reading. But if we are in doubt, the analyst is not; we have already come across such phrases as "considered it likely that ..."; "this time clearly directed to the analyst"; "the cab driver ... replaced the analyst"; and the final interpretation, that the decision to take the son to college was an indication that he was a good father and the analyst was not. The claim to certainty in each of these assertions seems to vary in inverse proportion to the amount of evidence available.

What is more serious, the transference scenario being proposed by the analyst makes it all the more difficult to follow other lines of reasoning. Consider the sequence thus far. Thoughts of weekend parties are followed by thoughts of being slightly late and by the claim that being late is not a resistance, even though the analyst will think it is. We begin to see the grounds for the patient's concern; whether or not his lateness had a meaning, he has come to expect that it will be interpreted as something bearing on the transference, and if present evidence is a representative sample, these interpretations are often lacking in persuasion. Failing to get the cab gives the analyst another opportunity to make this kind of comment, and the original curse at the cabbie may have indicated the depth of the patient's feeling over this possibility. Thus the issue is not the question of displacing feelings about the analyst onto other parts of his life—the cab driver and his son, for example—but rather, the question of being given a fair hearing and the opportunity to show that in some cases, appearances do not necessarily conceal something deeper.

> *The patient was furious, his anger coming to the surface again, not least of all because the analyst had made the interpretation. "Who are you that I should care about missing that session?" he stormed. "I wouldn't have believed it," he added more ruefully, indicating that he was believing it.*

Why is the patient angry? Because the interpretation is correct? Or because the interpretation is wrong? Is the patient angry at being accused of something that is not true, and in an atmosphere where protestation—"I wouldn't have believed it"—is treated as its opposite? In such an atmosphere, needless to say, there is no room for persuasion, much less analysis—denial is immediately treated as confession.

Suppose we assume that the patient is correct and that the statement "I wouldn't have believed it" means what it says. One reading of this statement is that the analyst has gone beyond the bounds of reasonable expectation in claiming significance for the Monday cancellation. Not only does the interpretation seem ungrounded in the material but it was apparently uttered in a manner that underlined the speaker's assurance that it was true; argument by authority once again, and the patient is the loser.

> He paused again (pause 3), and then reflected more tranquilly, "My father, I suppose." Having solved the puzzle, he was again silent (pause 4) and drifted off, as the analyst supposed, into a regressive line of thought that unexpectedly brought to the fore a memory from childhood. This time it was the word "father" that served as the switch word to a new line of thought. "My father was distant, like you," he began. "We never really had a conversation. The closest we ever got was in a shower."

Is the analyst, by virtue of his insensitivity and dogmatic manner, bringing to mind a father who is similarly insensitive and overbearing? There is an obvious irony in the complaint that patient and father never had a conversation; this description could also be applied to the analysis. Thus the memory of the father and the material associated with him may be a comment on the management of the transference; heard in this light, it is a reaction to the truth value of the interpretation (about missing the session) and to the chances for a real dialogue.

But exactly why does the father stand for the analyst? Not because of his fatherly attributes, it would appear, not because he is caring and sensitive, but because of his inability to listen, to engage in a dialogue, and share a point of view. But this possibility is never explored because the analyst sees the situation in quite a different light.

It seems more and more likely that the analyst's particular reading of this material was set in motion before the hour even started. The rule of cancellation leading to resentment defines the pattern to be discovered. Reasoning that this pattern was about to unfold, it then became possible to find "evidence" for it in each of the patient's comments: the weekend party, the trip to college, and the several outbursts of anger.

If all patients resent all cancellations whatever the cause, then this line of thinking would be unremarkable. But of course this is not the case. Not all cancellations are resented—some, perhaps during a phase of negative transference, are even welcomed—and it is by no means clear that an interruption because of a holiday is necessarily seen as a cancellation in the first place. But if the rule is not inviolate, then there is no inevitable pattern waiting out there to be discovered. Instead, we are faced with a more complicated situation: some of the patient's reactions may represent transference displacements and some may not, and the pattern, if it exists, must be put together in the course of a hermeneutic investigation—if possible, a shared dialogue with the patient. By the same token, some of the figures discussed may represent stand-ins for the analyst, but there is no Supreme Law that a given person always has a given meaning. Here again, the pattern, if it exists, must be discovered from scratch. And the possibility must be considered that no pattern exists at all. But this heretical possibility would never be considered if the analyst belongs to the pattern-finding school. As noted earlier, once it is assumed that a pattern exists, then no amount of ambiguous evidence or nonconfirming testimony can do anything to influence the argument. The patient, in this situation, is in an impossible, no-win situation. What is more serious, whatever patterns actually exist can never be seen in their proper light because they are always being deconstructed in favor of the standard pattern prescribed by clinical experience. There is no little irony in the analyst's statement that, given his clinical experience, he did not need to rely on empathy.

Can hermeneutics resolve some of these issues? To my mind there is no other way, and it is for that reason that psychoanalysis is preeminently a hermeneutic discipline. Trying to be "scientific" is what gets the analyst into trouble. To move from an idiographic to a more nomothetic approach is exactly what the analyst was trying (unsuccessfully) to do. Only a Know-Nothing hermeneutics is capable of taking the position that we have no idea what patterns, if any, are present and that their discovery can only result from a series of small decisions that are always checked against other parts of the material and with the patient himself. The patient, of course, is not always right; but then neither is he always wrong. Only a Know-Nothing hermeneutics is capable of extracting maximum meaning from the clinical material because it is the very absence of a priori patterns that allows us to look at each piece of meaning in the largest number of ways and to come to considered decisions after rather than before the fact. Only a Know-Nothing hermeneutics can take the position that everything in this vignette may be unrelated to everything else, and that even the most modest assertion of cause and effect must be flavored with skepticism and held in abeyance until we are impressed—over and over again—by converging lines of thought.

How do we start? Not enough has been written about the special kind of hermeneutic logic that allows us to look intensively at a clinical specimen and detect the underlying intermixture of pattern and randomness. Freud dropped many hints in his five case studies, and if we examine them inductively, we can begin to assemble a list of rules. Let me give you a sample:

1. Contiguity often signals cause—particularly when we have evidence that the patient is in an altered state of consciousness and his associations are truly free. This rule may also apply to the report of a dream; again, it is important that the account comes as close as possible to a veridical report and that secondary revision has not brought about too much logical rearrangement in the interests of making sense. The contiguity rule allows us to find a possible relation between apparently disconnected pieces of material, but is obviously no more than a working hypothesis; it is certainly nothing like a Law.

2. Form often masquerades as content, and vice versa. The way something is said often informs us as to its content, and any given content may be repeated in a variety of nonverbal methods. This is one of Freud's most important discoveries and a careful application of this rule allows us to discover many patterns lying beneath the surface. For example, suppose the analyst provided an extra session at no extra cost and the patient began that session with a revealing dream; we might say that the first gift is being returned by the second.

3. Important themes are presented in many different versions. This might be called the canon principle—the same melody is presented in a series of different voices and these are more or less difficult to recognize, depending on the amount of transformation. It takes no great talent to hear the original melody when it is transposed up or down an octave, but repeating it a second higher may go unnoticed. The same rule applies to clinical material, and much of the uncertainty over the clinical vignette just presented stems from the analyst's reading of presumed transpositions. Does the curse at the cab driver,

for example, repeat (and therefore represent) the battle with the analyst, or should it be seen as an unrelated incident?

4. Repetition is often a form of remembering, without the patient being aware that the past is informing the present. This kind of remembering stands in contrast to the usual form where a special mode of awareness is attached to the recall of information. But as Freud made clear, the mode may be in error; under these conditions —screen memories, for example—the sense of recall has nothing to do with the past. The opposite distortion occurs in the case of repetition: the past is revived without an awareness of remembering.

5. Surface disorder frequently masks underlying regularity. This rule is perhaps the central theme of hermeneutic listening, but it should be used as a working hypothesis, subject to falsification. Because there are conditions, not well documented, in which surface disorder mirrors underlying chaos, and this possibility is almost never discussed in the traditional clinical literature.

I have listed a sample of what might be called hermeneutic turns that can be applied to a clinical episode in an effort to extract meanings that are not obviously on the surface. Each of these rules contains a certain degree of truth, but their standing is far from lawful, and they are best used against the assumption that the world is essentially a random collection of happenings that now and then reveals a piece of a pattern. But as we have seen, there is a world of difference between pattern finding and pattern making, and only the former can qualify as useful.

REFERENCES

Arendt, H. *The life of the mind. Thinking* (Vol. 1). New York: Harcourt, Brace, Jovanovich, 1977.

Bhaskar, R. *A realist theory of science.* Leeds, England: Leeds Books, 1975.

Brenner, C. *An elementary textbook of psychoanalysis.* New York: International Universities Press, 1955.

Conan Doyle, A. *The complete Sherlock Holmes* (Vol. 1). New York: Doubleday, n.d.

Edelson, M. *Hypothesis and evidence in psychoanalysis.* Chicago and London: University of Chicago Press, 1984.

Freud, S. Fragment of an analysis of a case of hysteria. S.E., 1905, Vol. 7.

Freud, S. Recommendations to physicians practicing psychoanalysis. S.E., 1912, Vol. 12.

Freud, S. On narcissism. S.E., 1914, Vol. 14.

Freud, S. Remarks on the theory and practice of dream interpretation. S.E., 1923, Vol. 19.

Geuss, R. *The idea of a critical theory*. Cambridge: Cambridge University Press, 1981.

Grünbaum, A. *The foundations of psychoanalysis*. Berkeley: University of California Press, 1984.

Hesse, M. Science and objectivity. In J. B. Thompson & D. Held (Eds.), *Habermas: Critical debates*. London: Macmillan, 1982.

Kanzer, M. Freud's "analytic pact": The standard therapeutic alliance. *Journal of the American Psychoanalytic Association*, 1981, *29*, 69–87.

Leavis, F. R. *Two cultures? The significance of C. P. Snow*. London: Chatto & Windus, Ltd, 1962.

Manicas, P. T., & Secord, P. F. Implications for psychology of the new philosophy of science. *American Psychologist*, 1983, *38*, 399–413.

Snow, C. P. *The two cultures*. Cambridge: Cambridge University Press, 1959.

The Ubiquity of Interpretation: Commentary on Donald P. Spence

DONALD MEICHENBAUM

After reading Donald Spence's thoughtful analysis, especially his description of Freud's analysis of Dora's pseudo-appendicitis and Kanzer's analysis of his patient's behavior, I am reminded of a recent incident that occurred to a colleague of mine. He was at work in a psychiatric setting and received an urgent phone call from his cleaning lady. Having a clinical set that came from engaging in psychotherapy all morning, he responded with alarm when his cleaning lady announced with some concern, "I have no future!" She indicated that she had searched everywhere but felt it was hopeless. She simply couldn't continue if she had "no future." "What can I do? I need your help," she insisted!

Upon hearing this the psychotherapist immediately reminded himself of the multiple clinical signs that had been all too evident. Now that he thought about it, he recalled her recent depressed manner. She had failed to convey her usual cheerful goodbye that morning. Her being late must also be related. Oh, would she do something dangerous? What about the new white rug he had put down throughout the house? Was it too late? She sounded desperate.

As the conversation between them continued, it began to dawn on the therapist that his cleaning lady was referring to the cleaning product "Future," which she needed to work on the floors.

How many times do we misinterpret? How often do we infuse our clients' behavior with surplus meaning? How frequently do psychological practitioners and others make the types of errors that Freud and Kanzer made with their patients?

We are all in the business of interpretation, imputing motives, reading beyond the surface meaning, looking for and creating patterns. In some basic way each of us, as a professional or lay person, is conducting hermeneutic inquiry. Spence's paper reminds us of the nature of the hermeneutic inquiry in which we engage in both our clinical practice and scientific endeavors. Our preconceptions influence what behavior we choose to interpret and how we interpret it.

Although C. P. Snow viewed both the literary and scientific cultures as separate, the hermeneutic movement makes us aware that they share a common basis in searching for meaning, in using interpretation to understand phenomena. Events are not merely "out there" to be revealed, but rather our (pre)conceptions influence the very nature of what is revealed. This is particularly relevant when it comes to understanding the multifaceted nature of human behavior.

One wonders what the field of psychological inquiry would be like today if Sigmund Freud had been more cognizant of his confirmatory biases as reflected in his analysis of Dora's pseudo-appendicitis. As Spence appropriately notes, Freud's belief "that patterns lay just beneath the surface, waiting to be discovered" led him to draw strong conclusions often from rather weak data. Like Freud, and like my colleague who mistook his cleaning lady's request as a reflection of despair and depression, we all too often confuse pattern finding with pattern making. The hermeneutic mode of inquiry, as I try to show in my paper, sensitizes us to our penchant for slipping from the role of pattern finder into the role of pattern maker. We often deceive ourselves into thinking, as do our clients, that we merely discover patterns. The field is indebted to Donald Spence for reminding us of the extent to which we construct and create rather than discover patterns in human behavior.

Chapter 4

Interpretation and Its Discontents: The Choreography of Critique

RICHARD J. BERNSTEIN

From 1900 onward, in a series of essays ... that ... fill twenty-three volumes ... Freud created the masterwork of the century, a psychology that counsels mothers and fathers, lovers and haters, sick and less sick, the arts and sciences, that unriddles —to use Emerson's prophetic catalogue of subjects considered inexplicable in his day—"language, sleep, madness, dreams, beasts, sex." Freud's doctrine, created piecemeal and fortunately never integrated into one systematic statement, has changed the course of Western intellectual history.

So begins Philip Rieff's masterful study, *Freud: The Mind of the Moralist* (1979). Rieff's judgment that Freud's doctrine "has changed the course of Western intellectual history"—although contestable and controversial—is, I believe, essentially correct. And more than that, it would be difficult to name another intellectual figure of our century whose "doctrine"—whether we consider it rightly interpreted or brutally misinterpreted—has so deeply influenced (for better or worse) the ways in which we think about ourselves and others, act, and even describe our most intimate feelings, emotions, and anxieties. From the very beginning of his career, Freud, Freudianism, and the "new science" of psychoanalysis have met with skepticism, suspicion, and resistance. But also with seductive fascination, and, at times, with quasi-religious fervor. One can conceive of writing an intellectual history of the 20th century as a narrative of the vicissitudes of reactions, silences, interpretations, and reinterpretations of Freud. Over and over again Freud has been condemned as a charlatan, a false prophet who mesmerizes. Freudianism has been pronounced to be the mythology, superstition, the alchemy of our time—lacking any serious empirical confirmation despite the self-serving aura of scientific rhetoric that surrounds it. Although it has been a repetitive, almost obsessive, refrain that psychoanalysis is a sham or pseudo-science, it continues to fascinate and to be a source of interminable analysis and interpretation. Freud has even been celebrated as the sublime prose/poet of our time (Bloom, 1982). What is at once intriguing and disconcerting are the multifarious, conflicting interpretations of Freud—their confusing and Babel-like profusion (see Jacques Derrida's discussion of Babel in Derrida, 1985). Imagine the thought experiment that at some future date all of Freud's texts were to be destroyed without a trace—except for the texts of his commentators and interpreters. Would we even be able to reconstruct a coherent common primary source for all those secondary works that speak of "Freud"? I doubt it.

There was something prophetic about Freud's assigning the date 1900 to his masterpiece, *Traumdeutung* (even though it actually appeared in 1899), for the 20th century might be labeled "The Age of Interpretation." In virtually every domain of cultural discourse, including the range of natural and human sciences, thinkers following the most diverse pathways have been drawn to reflection on the character, scope, varieties, strategies, and tactics of interpretation (and anti-interpretation). There are philosophers like Heidegger and Gadamer who claim that what is most fundamental about human beings is that we are beings who are "always already" engaged in the happening of understanding and interpretation. But for all the concern with interpretation and the varied attempts to characterize what is distinctive about interpretive processes, this discourse has been plagued by discontents and anxieties.

Bertold Brecht spoke of the need for crude or vulgar thinking, *plumpes Denken*, and there are crude questions that haunt all the talk about interpretation. How are we to discriminate a "true" from a "false" interpretation? How are we to distinguish "better" from "worse" interpretations? For those who think it is now passé to distinguish the true from the false, the better from the worse, they still cannot escape the question of discerning when an interpretation

is arbitrary, idiosyncratic, blindly willful, or merely "subjective"
—in the pejorative sense of this much abused term. Freud becomes a
test case for this *plumpes Denken*. Not only is he always interpreting
—from minute and seemingly innocuous details to global claims
about religion, culture, and civilization—but the most sympathetic
readers of Freud experience at times the apparent arbitrariness and
perversity, albeit brilliant ingeniousness of some of his interpretations. When this is acknowledged there will be those who want to
distinguish between Freud's blindnesses and his insights. But this
does not solve the problem; rather it emphasizes what is troubling.
What are the standards and/or criteria for sorting out "legitimate"
from pseudo-interpretations? What does (should) "legitimate" mean
when applied to an interpretation?

The problem here is not limited to questioning Freud's conception
and tactics of interpretation. It resonates throughout most of modern
philosophy and more generally, modern thought. Descartes, who has
become the target for so much contemporary criticism—or, in this
context, we might say the father-figure who is to be overthrown and
"murdered"—did raise the question that still does (and ought to)
haunt us. Suppose one brackets the talk of indubitability and foundations, we must recognize that he was asking a simple, straightforward, inescapable question. How are we to discriminate between
those opinions that are nothing but blind prejudices from cognitive
claims that can be legitimately warranted? No philosopher, no
thinker can ignore some version of this question, even if one thinks it
cannot be answered. After all the criticism of a tradition that spans
Descartes, empiricism, the Enlightenment, and 20th-century positivism, we must honor the tradition for keeping alive this crude
question. To put the issue in a slightly different way, the challenge
this tradition poses to anyone who wants to speak of interpretation is
that in the final analysis this question cannot be avoided. You may try
to escape it, but like the "return of the repressed" it will stubbornly
and insistently impose itself. Freud knew this. It is to his great credit
that he was constantly aware of the need to face the thorny issues in
evaluating competing and conflicting interpretations. This feature of
his argumentation cannot be passed off as scientific rhetoric or a
scientistic misunderstanding of what he was doing.

I do not believe it is possible to state once and for all, in a rigorous,
determinate, and nonvacuous manner, what are or ought to be the
standards, criteria, or rules by which interpretations can be
epistemically evaluated. In this respect I categorically reject one of

the deepest aspirations of the modern epistemological tradition as a deceptive illusion. But I also do not believe what many have claimed to be a consequence of, or to be entailed by this rejection, namely, that if there is no permanent legitimate and legitimizing matrix of cognitive evaluation, then one must ultimately concede that interpretations are based on assumptions, beliefs, and norms that are epistemically arbitrary. In short, the language games of interpretation are entrapped in a self-defeating relativism. Nobody wants to deny that some interpretations—despite their plausibility, authority, and persuasiveness—are not only mistaken but rest on arbitrary claims. It is the stronger, more pernicious, thesis that I want to combat: that if we cannot specify, even *in principle* (the favorite escape clause of philosophers) clear, determinate criteria for the cognitive evaluation of competing interpretations, then we can never judge whether they are arbitrary and/or "merely subjective" (see Bernstein, 1983). There is no way to prove my thesis in any conclusive fashion. Rather, what is required is to show that there is a rationale, a logic of argumentation and counter argumentation involved in advancing and critically evaluating specific interpretations. To show this, to reveal the elaborate choreography of critique, one must be hermeneutically sensitive to the specificity of details in the relevant contexts (and even to clarify what is a relevant context). Of course, it is always open to the skeptic to object that even if one succeeds in showing this in several instances, this is not sufficient to illuminate or draw conclusions about other interpretations. I share the skeptical caution. But what follows? The only proper response is Wittgenstein's admonition, to "look and see." Interpretation may well be an interminable activity or happening.

To illustrate what I mean by the choreography of critique, I propose to examine two rich examples of Freudian interpretation in order to reveal the complexity and rationality of the critical evaluation of interpretations. The first example is from Freud's provocative interpretation of the personality and art of Leonardo Da Vinci. Probing this interpretation will open up the second example, the question of Freud's theory of symbolism.[1] There are both broad and narrower, more restrictive, conceptions of symbolism. My primary intention is not to make a definitive, substantive judgment about the truth or correctness of Freud's claims, but rather to focus on what philosophers call "metaquestions"—issues concerning the logic of argumentation. Freud, even in what seem to be his wildest speculations, is always arguing, always seeking to support his hypotheses with evidence and reasons. It is always relevant to ask critical questions about whether his evidence and arguments support his conclusions. Exploring those two interrelated examples will enable me to raise some general issues not only about psychoanalytic interpretation, but about the dynamics of the interpretive process.

VULTURES AND KITES

Before concentrating on what is now recognized to be a crucial mistranslation in Freud's essay on Leonardo, I want to call attention to a number of its distinctive features (all of which are important for understanding Freud's mistranslation). The study, published originally in 1910, is one of Freud's most scholarly essays.[2] In developing his interpretation, Freud cites references in German, Italian, Greek, and Latin (usually without translating them). Ernest Jones, who wrote the preface to the first English edition (translated by A. A. Brill) tells us in his biography of Freud that "perhaps the [work] for which he had the greatest affection was his book on Leonardo" (Jones, 1955, 2:401). And Jones also tells us:

> Freud was expressing conclusions which in all probability had been derived from his self-analysis and are therefore of great importance for the study of his personality. His letters of the time make it abundantly clear with what exceptional intensity he had thrown himself into this particular investigation. (Jones, 1955, 2:78)

Later, Jones adds the comment, "Much of what Freud said when he penetrated into Leonardo's personality was at the same time a self-description; there was surely an extensive identification between Leonardo and himself" (Jones, 1955, 2:432).

Jones's judicious and apparently straightforward remarks take on a rich suggestiveness when we realize that the Leonardo study is not only a classic analysis of sublimation, the conflict of artistic and scientific impulses, an exploration of the connection between infantile "sexual researches" and scientific inquiry, but also a study of Leonardo's "femininity" and latent passive homosexuality. This becomes even more intriguing when we realize the many connecting links between Freud's interest in Leonardo and his friendship with

Fleiss (Bass, 1985). I do not want to play the role of amateur psychoanalyst of Freud himself, although it is difficult to resist this temptation.

Let me note, however, that to read the Leonardo essay simply as an "application" of psychoanalytic theory would be to read it in an extremely superficial way. A close reading shows how extensively it is intertwined with many of Freud's most important themes and theses. I have already mentioned sublimation and alluded to the theory of infantile sexuality, but there are also threads leading to Freud's reflections on memory, phantasy, fetishism, narcissism, bisexuality, the phallic mother, symbolism, mythology, the writing of history, and much more. Indeed, a microanalysis of this short book reveals connecting links with almost every aspect of Freud's thinking (conscious and unconscious). The study is fascinating not only for what it reveals, but for what it conceals.

To appreciate the centrality of the crucial mistranslation (and the distortion it involves), let me turn to its precise title: *Leonardo Da Vinci and a Memory of His Childhood (Eine Kindheitserrinerung des Leonardo Da Vinci)*. The most important word here is the simple article, *Eine*. Why? Because most of what is distinctive about Freud's interpretation appears to be based on the report of a single memory/phantasy of Leonardo.

Freud himself tells us, "About Leonardo's youth we know very little," and he summarizes this information in a single paragraph. Freud claims, "The only definite piece of information about Leonardo's childhood comes in an official document of the year 1457; it is a Florentine land-register for the purpose of taxation, which mentions Leonardo among the members of the household of the Vinci family as the five-year old illegitimate child of Ser Piero" (Freud, 1910, p. 81).[3] This doesn't look very promising for an analysis of Leonardo's infantile sexual experiences, but it does highlight how much weight seems to be placed on the report of a single memory. Let me cite verbatim the English translation of Freud's statement of this memory. Freud begins the second section of his essay, "There is, so far as I know, only one place where Leonardo inserts a piece of information about his childhood. In a passage about the flight of vultures he suddenly interrupts himself to pursue a memory from early years which had sprung to his mind" (Freud, 1910, p. 82).

Now Freud quotes from Herzfeld's German translation of the Italian original, or more accurately from the German translation of the *Codex Atlanticus*, as given by Scognamiglio. Again I quote from

Alan Tyson's English translation. "It seems that I was destined to be so deeply concerned with vultures; for I recall as one of my earliest memories that while I was in my cradle a vulture came down to me, and opened my mouth with its tail, and struck me many times with its tail against my lips" (Freud, 1910, p. 82).

That's it. That is the memory the title of the work refers to as "a memory of his childhood." Let me mention one more detail. In this instance—unlike many of Freud's other scholarly references in the book—he not only cites Herzfeld's German translation (which contains two inaccuracies—Bass, 1985, pp. 117–118; Farrell, 1963, p. 15), he cites in a footnote the Italian passage that is the basis for the German translation. Almost everything that follows in Freud's study after the citation is directly or indirectly related to this brief passage, including Freud's discussion of memory, the relation of phantasy to memory, "the way in which the writing of history originated among peoples of antiquity" (Freud, 1910, p. 83) and, of course, the specific interpretation that Freud gives about Leonardo's infantile sexual experiences and how they enable us to understand and explain the enigma of his personality and important features of his art—an interpretation that concentrates on the symbolic meaning of vultures and tails. Freud succinctly tells us, "The key to all of [Leonardo's] achievements and misfortunes lay hidden in the childhood phantasy of the vulture" (Freud, 1910, p. 136).

Whether we are sympathetic or unsympathetic, Freud's imaginative ingenuity is breathtaking. For we are off on an exploration of vulture mythology among the ancient Egyptians where the vulture is a symbol of the phallic Mother Goddess and the Egyptian legend is that all vultures are females and are impregnated by opening their vaginas to the wind while in flight. This legend "had been seized on by the Fathers of the Church so that they could have at their disposal a proof drawn from natural history to confront those who doubted sacred history" (Freud, 1910, p. 90), that is, the sacred history of the conception of the child Christ by the Blessed Virgin. And, of course, Freud relates Leonardo's memory/phantasy to his experience with his own mother and even to an explanation of the famous enigmatic smile of the *Mona Lisa*. I have mentioned only a small fragment of the elaborate interpretation—an interpretation that takes the form of an explanatory narrative—that Freud spins, a fabric in which the memory/phantasy of the vulture as a phallic mother is prominently embroidered.

Although Freud both cites Herzfeld's German translation and

gives the Italian source for this translation, he fails to note that the Italian word *nibio* (the modern form *nibbio*) is mistranslated by the German word *Geier*. A nibio is not a vulture but a kite.[4]

For those who are ready to pounce upon what they take to be the willful, arbitrary, wildly speculative nature of Freudian interpretations, this error might seem to be paradigmatic of their flimsy character, which can so easily collapse under close critical scrutiny. One can easily be sympathetic with the author of a letter to the editor that was published in the January 1923 issue of the *Burlington Magazine* shortly after the appearance of the English edition of the Leonardo study. The letter was published with the title "Leonardo in the Consulting Room" and was written by Eric Maclagen.

> Sir—In view of the prominence given to Dr. Freud's little book on Leonardo in the Editorial Article of the December issue of *The Burlington Magazine*, I think it may be worthwhile to point out on what very inadequate grounds his theories are built up. ... Dr. Freud devotes pages to the Egyptian symbolism of the vulture, and any impartial reader will admit that he makes it the main basis of his argument. But Leonardo never mentions a vulture at all. He tells the story of a kite (nibio) and the Italian text is actually printed by Dr. Freud (p. 21, note 2) though none of his admirers seem to have taken the trouble to read it. (Maclagen, 1923)[5]

Now the first point I want to stress is an obvious but extremely important one, especially in light of those who are inclined to suggest that there is something arbitrary about all translation and interpretation. There is nothing arbitrary about the question of whether Freud has mistranslated the Italian word *nibio*. In many cases it is contestable whether an author has mistranslated a word. But in this instance it is clear that there is a mistranslation, and we are familiar with the procedures for determining this. This is a question of objective fact, and there are objective, that is, intersubjective, criteria for determining what are "the facts of the matter," what is true and false. To anticipate a point that will be important later in our discussion I want to affirm that in the interpretive process, one (and this is certainly true of Freud) is constantly making—implicitly or explicitly—what Habermas calls "validity claims." These claims can be challenged, and when challenged what is required is that they be supported, modified, or abandoned by the appeal to reasons—to "good reasons." What are or are not to be counted as good reasons is itself frequently rationally contestable.

My second point is also obvious and just as important. In many contexts a mistranslation may be innocuous and may not seriously affect a subsequent interpretation. But in this instance the mistranslation is crucial both for evaluating Freud's interpretation and for figuring out precisely what is going on in this essay—and even what it may be concealing.[6] This is true for the manifest reason mentioned by Maclagan that the mistranslation seems to be "the main basis of his argument." But this type of mistake is itself an exemplar of what is frequently the key to psychoanalytic interpretation, for unriddling what is repressed. One can imagine Freud or his "double" writing an entire monograph entitled, "On the Psychoanalytic Meaning of a Mistaken Translation in *Leonardo Da Vinci and a Memory of His Childhood*." Considering the internal textual evidence and the external evidence (revealed in Freud's letters) that the Leonardo study, as Jones says, "expresses conclusions which in all probability had been derived from his self-analysis and are of great importance for the study of his personality" (Jones, 1955, p. 78), the psychoanalytic significance of this singular mistake comes into sharp focus.[7]

My third point is a cautionary one. We, like Eric Maclagan, may jump to the conclusion that Freud's mistake invalidates his entire interpretation because "the Egyptian symbolism of the vulture ... [is] ... the main basis of his argument." But such an inference would be rash and a bit too facile. It suggests what Wittgenstein calls a picture that "holds us captive"—that rationally warranting an interpretation is like constructing an edifice on a firm foundation—or less metaphorically, like presenting a straightforward, deductive argument. If the foundation is weak, the entire edifice collapses; if the truth of the premises is called into question, the soundness of the argument is destroyed. Although this does occur in some instances, it is rarely the case that a complex interpretation takes on this canonical foundational or deductive form.

To put this last point more positively, once it is established—and this is important for everything that follows—that Freud has mistranslated a key term, our work in evaluating his interpretation has only just begun. For the question we must then ask is, what precisely is called into question, what precisely must be modified or rejected. For example, James Strachey, the editor of the English Standard Edition, introduces the *Leonardo* essay by acknowledging Freud's error. However, he cautions the reader: "In face of this mistake, some readers may feel an impulse to dismiss the whole study as worthless. It will, however, be a good plan to examine the situation more coolly and consider in detail the exact respects in which Freud's arguments and conclusions are invalidated" (Freud, 1910, p. 61). Strachey then proceeds to list what he thinks is and is not invalidated, and concludes as follows:

> Apart, then, from the consequent irrelevance of the Egyptian discussion—though this nevertheless retains much of its independent value—the main body of Freud's study is unaffected by his mistake: the detailed construction of Leonardo's emotional life from his earliest years, the account of the conflict between his artistic and scientific impulses, the deep analysis of his psychosexual history. And, in addition to this main topic, the study presents us with a number of not less important side themes: a more general discussion of the nature of the creative artist, an outline of the genesis of one particular type of homosexuality, and—of special interest to the history of psycho-analytic theory—the first full emergence of the concept of narcissism. (Freud, 1910, p. 62)

This judgment of Strachey is eminently reasonable. But to say that it is reasonable is not yet to endorse it or to say it is correct. Rather, it is reasonable in the sense that it can be supported and even challenged by reasons—reasons that themselves need to be carefully stated and rationally evaluated.

My primary objective is not to reach a substantive conclusion about what is valid or invalid in this singular instance of an interpretation that is based upon a mistranslation. There is a logic of argumentation, an elaborate choreography of critique involved in the moves and countermoves of analyzing and evaluating an interpretation. There is nothing arbitrary or relativistic about this activity, although there may be a great deal that is contestable, indeterminate, and even undecideable.[8]

To further illustrate and warrant my own claims, I will take up the issue that Strachey puts aside when he speaks of "the consequent irrelevance of the Egyptian discussion." I do not think it is irrelevant. On the contrary, in one respect it brings us to the heart of the matter. Suppose we put aside the question of Freud's mistranslation. Regardless of whether Leonardo's memory/phantasy was about vultures or kites, the general analysis of the significance of vulture symbolism in dreams, myths, or memory/phantasies is not affected. The substructure of Freud's theory of symbolism is implicated in this discussion. Earlier I spoke of a broader and narrower conception of symbolism. When Freud introduced the topic of symbolism—in a hesitating manner—in the original edition of *The Interpretation of Dreams*, he initially restricted its significance in two ways. First, in this context he was primarily concerned with the role of symbolism for dream interpretation. Second, he speaks of the analyst's knowledge of symbols as a complement to his or her use of the technique of free association. Freud realized that at times there are gaps in what is revealed by the patient's own associations. The analyst can only complete an interpretation of a dream by recognizing that some elements in the dream are symbols—symbols with fixed, even universal, meanings—with primarily sexual meanings. The analyst as the translator must have some knowledge of the meanings of these symbols if he or she is to interpret the dream. This is what I mean by the narrower conception or theory of symbolism. Thinking of symbolism in this manner, one could even imagine—as Freud suggests —a code book, a "dream-book," or translation manual that would list symbols and their sexual meaning. Thus it might include an entry for *tail*, "one of the most familiar symbols and substitutive expressions for the male organ" (Freud, 1910, p. 85).

But the theory of symbolism is not as self-contained as this example suggests, because it has a way of affecting the central text. For though some symbols—once it is established that they are functioning as symbols—may have fixed, permanent (sexual) meanings, Freud is always drawing upon what is involved in all symbolism as he describes it. In analyzing a dream, myth, legend, folktale, memory, phantasy, or joke, Freud searches for the sexual meaning of the elements out of which it is constructed. These elements may have many other types of meaning (Freud never denies this), but although Freud frequently says that we may never be able to reach a complete interpretation of a single dream, a psychoanalytic interpretation is always seeking hidden sexual meanings. Every symbol at once conceals and reveals. Every symbol has at least two meanings. This is why I refer to a broader and a more restrictive theory of symbolism. In any account of Freud or psychoanalysis, the theory of symbolism stands at the very center of this style of interpretation. Let us now turn to the discussion of symbolism in *The Interpretation of Dreams*.

THE LANGUAGE OF SYMBOLISM

As always with Freud, it behooves us to pay close attention to the context in which he advances his theses. In the first edition of *The Interpretation of Dreams*, the discussion of symbolism is almost incidental, at least if we judge by the space allotted to the topic. But as Strachey notes in his introduction to the Standard Edition,

> By far the greater number of additions dealing with any single subject are those concerned with symbolism in dreams. Freud explains in the "History of the Psycho-Analytic Movement" ... as well as at the beginning of Chapter VI, Section E ... of the present work, that he arrived late at a full realization of the importance of this side of the subject. (Freud, 1900, pp. xii–xiii)

A reader of the Standard Edition will find the discussion of symbolism one of the most uneven and confusing parts of the entire book. In the numerous subsequent editions that appeared during Freud's lifetime, material was added, deleted, and even transplanted. But there are more important reasons why this discussion is so confusing. Freud seems to waver in his own assessment of the significance of the use of symbolism. A telling illustration of this is a paragraph that begins by stating "how impossible it becomes to arrive at the interpretation of a dream if one excludes dream-symbolism, and how irresistibly one is driven to accept it in many cases" and ends by cautioning the reader:

> The two techniques of dream interpretation must be complementary to each other; but both in practice and in theory the first place continues to be held by the procedure which I began by describing and which attributes a decisive significance to the comments made by the dreamer, while the translation of symbols ... is also at our disposal as an auxiliary method. (Freud, 1900, p. 360)

But the reference to complementary techniques masks a difficult and unstable problem. The technique of association pulls us toward the specificity of the subject's associations, experiences, memories, and phantasies, but the appeal to symbolism pulls us toward what is general, stereotyped, and even universal. Freud is acutely aware of the problems involved in deciding when an element of a dream is to be understood as a symbol and how a symbol functions in a dream, although he is far from clear in explaining by what criteria this is to be decided.

But there are other uncertainties and peculiarities exhibited in Section E of Chapter VI of *The Interpretation of Dreams*. At times Freud seems to protest too much. He begins this section by discussing the work of Wilhelm Stekel. He says that although he does not want to belittle "the value of Stekel's services," Freud sharply criticizes the use he made "of a method which must be rejected as scientifically untrustworthy. Stekel arrived at his interpretations of symbols by way of intuition, thanks to a peculiar gift for direct understanding of them" (Freud, 1900, p. 350). Freud repeats this criticism several times with slight variations. It is almost as if Freud is anticipating and seeking to defend himself against the very charge that has been brought against his interpretation of symbols—the charge of arbitrariness in dream-interpretation. Freud emphasizes the need for "scientific trustworthiness," "critical caution," and even "strict proof."[9]

But even the most sympathetic commentators on Freud have raised serious critical questions not only about the very concept of symbolism that he employs, but about the way in which he discovers the sexual meaning of specific symbols. Let me indicate some of the central problems—problems that go to the heart of psychoanalysis and that have not been adequately resolved by Freud (or Freudians).

Every symbol for Freud has at least two meanings—its manifest and its latent meaning. Symbols represent something, and what they represent is not obvious from their manifest meanings. Freud never goes so far as to suggest that symbols have only a latent sexual meaning. This is the type of meaning with which, from a psychoanalytic perspective, he is primarily (although not exclusively) concerned. Furthermore, Freud does not see any essential difference between the way in which symbols function in dreams, phantasies, myths, folktales, and legends. Now we come to the first—and perhaps the deepest—problem: the question of how symbols become associated with what they represent. In his *Introductory Lectures*, Freud tells us

we are faced by the fact that the dreamer has a symbolic mode of expression at his disposal which he does not know in waking life and does not recognize. This is as extraordinary as if you were to discover that your housemaid understood Sanskrit, though you know that she was born in a Bohemian village and never learnt it. It is not easy to account for this fact by the help of our psychological views. We can only say that the knowledge of symbolism is unconscious to the dreamer, that it belongs to his unconscious mental life. But even with this assumption we do not meet the point. Hitherto it has only been necessary for us to assume the existence of unconscious endeavours—endeavours, that is, of which temporarily or permanently, we know nothing. Now, however, it is a question of more than this, of unconscious pieces of knowledge, of connections of thought, of comparisons between different objects which result in its being possible for one of them to be regularly put in place of the other. These comparisons are not freshly made on each occasion; they lie ready to hand and are complete, once and for all. (Freud, 1916, p. 165)

Let me put aside the sticky issues implied by speaking of "unconscious pieces of knowledge." There is still a disconcerting *aporia* here. Dreams make use of unconscious symbolic connections that "lie ready to hand." But Freud never satisfactorily explains how these connections are made and stay fixed. This is not a localized problem. It raises fundamental questions about the very nature of the unconscious and unconscious processes. We must, of course, be careful not to reify the unconscious. Even if we think of it as a model or construct, we need to understand how it works in the formation of symbolic connections. Suppose we ask bluntly: Is the unconscious linguistic or prelinguistic? We know that the answer must be for Freud: It is both. But this only forces us to probe how it can be both and more significantly precisely how the prelinguistic or nonlinguistic aspects of the unconscious are related to its linguistic and symbolic aspects. Without a satisfactory answer to this question, the entire structure of psychoanalysis is in danger of foundering (Jacques Lacan has perceived and appreciated this *aporia* more profoundly than any other Freudian. It is the *fons et origo* of his own reconstruction of Freud.).

The problems concerning symbolism spread. Freud does assume that some symbolic meanings are fixed, permanent, cross-cultural, and cross-linguistic. But it is also the case that artifacts, some of which have been invented or discovered relatively late in history or are only artifacts in a given culture, take on symbolic meaning. Thus "nailfiles," "staircases," "airplanes," can serve as symbols. But how does this happen? What mechanism is involved? One might answer that this happens because of their resemblance to other more primary and universal symbols, but this answer is a bit too facile. Resemblance is always resemblance in some respect, resemblance under some description.

What features of a symbol make it a symbol? Sometimes Freud appeals to the physical resemblances between the symbol and what it represents. Sometimes we need to observe the function of the object that serves as a symbol. Sometimes the resemblance is analogical. Thus, in the symbolic function of "playing with a child," it is not physical resemblance but rather the analogical relation that makes this a symbol for masturbation (Freud, 1900). Even when we may think we grasp the rules of this language game, there are surprises. We classify some symbols as symbols of the male organ and some as symbols of the female genitals because of their physical resemblance. But what about an "airship"? I suspect many would immediately say this is or can be a symbol for the womb or female genitals. But Freud tells us, "A quite recent symbol of the male organ in dreams deserves mention: the air-ship, whose use in this sense is justified by its connection with flying as well as sometimes by its shape" (Freud, 1900, p. 357).

The allusion I have made to Wittgenstein's notion of language games is appropriate. For one frequently has the sense that the rules of the language-game of what symbols represent is like a private language; that the rules seem to be made up as one goes along—or perhaps that there are no rules for this language-game.

I have barely scratched the surface of the questions that can be raised about the theory of symbolism, whether we focus on its general characteristics or its details.[10] My intention was not to assemble objections in order to show how mistaken, ridiculous, or unfounded are Freud's claims. Rather, it was to show that whether or not we take Freud seriously, there are gaps, *aporias*, and unresolved problems that demand careful, critical scrutiny. This examination is the process of understanding the various questions to be raised, formulating hypothetical ways of answering them, and evaluating the evidence and reasons supporting these hypotheses; it is all a part of the choreography of critique.

THE CHOREOGRAPHY OF CRITIQUE

Let us stand back and examine what I have tried to show. There is always a danger, especially in discussing Freud, of becoming mesmerized by details and neglecting a more panoramic perspective. Imagine an "Other"—a critic who may well concede much of what I have said, but wants to add a forceful *but* or *nevertheless*. This Other might object as follows: Look, Bernstein, you speak of *plumpes Denken*, but you yourself are not really radical enough. You are dodging the really tough and basic questions. What you have shown in what you call the logic of argumentation or the choreography of critique is that when we carefully analyze Freud's writings we can discern a variety of claims to truth or validity that need to be carefully assessed. But there is something too internal about your discussion. You never raise the issue of the validity of Freud's controversial style of discourse and interpretation—its very appropriateness for describing, accounting for, and explaining human behavior. Let me even be a bit more specific. Your discussion of the *Leonardo* study and the theory of symbolism shows that, on virtually any reading of the *Leonardo* study (whether the memory/phantasy is about vultures or kites), Freud appeals to a set of concepts and theoretical presuppositions in order to give an explanatory narrative of Leonardo's personality and career. But what *plumpes Denken* requires is that you confront the question of the appropriateness and validity of these basic concepts and theoretical postulates that are distinctive for psychoanalytic discourse. Consider an analogy that you suggested, although you pushed it aside earlier in your discussion. Suppose we were to investigate alchemy. Would we not also discover internally what you call a logic of argumentation—elaborate moves and countermoves within this discourse that appear to have a rationale. When we dismiss alchemy, we are not saying that it was irrational in the way in which mumbo jumbo is irrational, but rather that it rested on a series of claims that made use of concepts that were arbitrary in the sense that—regardless of what the participants in this discourse believed—can now be seen to lack any rational grounding. Have you given us any reason not to believe that someday we will look upon Freudian interpretation and psychoanalysis as the alchemy of the 20th century?

I hope it is clear that this Other is not alien to me, but is indeed my own inner critical voice. But in the spirit of moves and countermoves,

I would like to add my own significant "But. . . ." I want to respond to what my critic takes to be a *coup de grâe*. Yes, there is no *a priori* reason to think that someday we might not look back upon Freudian interpretation with a sense of its archaic quaintness, just as we today think about Aristotelian physics or even caloric or phlogiston theory. And, as in these instances, we might even be able to explain why so many rational people believed so firmly in its validity and explanatory value. But why should such a possibility be surprising or disturbing? Indeed, if I wanted to use an authority who thought of psychoanalysis in this manner, I would cite Freud himself. This is the very way in which he frequently understood what he was doing, and he even thought that we might some day displace psychoanalysis with a more biological or neurological understanding of human beings. We have become much more sensitive in our time to the variety of causes and reasons as to why one type of vocabulary—to use Richard Rorty's phrase—replaces or displaces alternatives. In the history of science perhaps the clearest instances are those that occur when a new theoretical alternative is developed that is judged by the relevant community of scientists to be superior in its descriptive and explanatory power—a judgment that can be backed up by a battery of evidence and reasons. Even if we turn to such a "soft" area as the causes and reasons for the collapse of scholastic philosophy, we can now provide an explanatory narrative to account for why this happened. Sometimes, as Foucault has shown us, the transformation of an entire mode of discourse or discursive practice can suddenly occur. But I fail to see any reason why this possibility should paralyze us now in the critical discrimination and assessment of Freud's claims. And to do this, what is required is the patient, detailed examination, the sorting out of issues, the evaluation of types of evidence and argumentation that I have sketched in my examples. This is difficult and messy work. It is messy because we frequently do not have clear procedures for determining what is true and what is false, what is better and what is worse. We know, or ought to know, that even our standards for critical evaluation are themselves rationally contestable. There rarely are any firm arguments that can substantiate validity claims, especially in advancing and warranting complex interpretations. The type of demarcation procedures that Karl Popper suggested for sorting out what is scientific and nonscientific just will not work. And Popper represents only one variation of the epistemological delusion that dreams of reconstructing all discourse so that it is commensurable—where the discourse "can be brought under a set of rules which will tell us how rational agreement can be reached or what would settle the issue on every point where statements seem to conflict" (Rorty, 1979, p. 316). A lesson we have (or should have) learned in the 20th century is that the search for rigid demarcations frequently turns out to be a screen for violent exclusionary tactics.

Although I have conceded that the complex discourse that we call psychoanalysis may someday be displaced, that we might look back upon Freudian interpretation as the alchemy of our time, I do not want to concede too much. For there are special features of Freudian interpretation that distinguish it from alchemy or such outdated scientific theories as caloric or phlogiston theory. In other contexts I have argued—along with many others—that we are beings whose social reality is, in part, constituted by the ways in which we interpret and preinterpret this reality (Bernstein, 1978, 1983). I think Anthony Giddens is right when he tells us that the social disciplines not only imply a "single level of hermeneutical problems, involved in the theoretical metalanguage, but a 'double hermeneutic' because social scientific theories concern a 'preinterpreted' world of lay meanings" (Giddens, 1977, p. 12). It is this last point that I want to stress in regard to Freud and psychoanalysis, for Freudian concepts, categories, and vocabulary have become constitutive of our preinterpreted world. We think, act, and feel differently because of the influence of Freud's doctrine. Our most intimate lives are not lived differently because phlogiston theory has been rejected, but if the vocabulary of psychoanalysis were to be abandoned (in the radical manner imagined by my critic—the Other), then we would not only tell different narratives about ourselves, we would become different beings. This is not an argument against such a possibility, but rather a commentary on what such a possibility would mean.

When Freud entitled his last major paper "Analysis Terminable and Interminable" (Die Endlichse und die Unendliche Analyse), he struck a note that had already been sounded almost forty years earlier in The Interpretation of Dreams. He did think of himself, as Rieff suggests, as the great "unriddler," but he always acknowledged that we may never come to the end of our unriddling. What he says about the endless character of analysis can be taken as a parable not only for Freudian interpretation, but for all varieties of interpretation. We are beings who desperately seek closure, totality, and finality. And when we experience how it eludes us, our deepest anxieties can be aroused. Freud, in what might seem like an old fashioned manner, spoke in his final days of the "love of Truth ... [that] precludes any kind of sham or deceit" (Freud, 1937a, p. 248). Freud did have "the mind of the moralist." And if we are to appropriate the message of this great moralist, then it means recognizing that the choreography of critique may be an endless activity—one that requires the virtues of patience, care, sympathetic understanding, sharp critical encounter, and the "love of truth."

NOTES

1. In this context I am using the term *theory* in a vague, but useful way. I do not mean to suggest that the theory of symbolism is a well-formulated hypothetical-deductive system of propositions. Rather, I want to call attention to the descriptions, analyses, and characterizations of symbolism in Freud's writings. Insofar as Freud appeals to symbolism in his interpretations and seeks to explain human behavior by appealing to the meaning of symbols, we can speak of a theory of symbolism.

2. Since the time of its publication in 1910, this study attracted a great deal of critical attention. There now exists a small library dealing with various aspects of the Leonardo study. One of the most recent essays is Bass (1985). It was Bass's stimulating essay that first put me on the track of exploring the extensive discussion of the Leonardo essay. See Bass's notes for some of the important articles and books on Freud's *Leonardo*. One should also consult Brian Farrell's superb, balanced introduction to the Penguin edition of the *Leonardo* essay (1963; see also Schapiro, 1956; Wohl and Trosman, 1955). For a polemical defense of Freud's interpretation, see Eissler, 1961. I want to thank Steven Z. Levine for sharing his extensive knowledge and bibliography of the *Leonardo* essay.

3. All references to Freud are to the Standard Edition.

4. A kite is also a bird of prey. It may be argued (and has been argued) that Freud's mistake does not seriously affect his interpretation of Leonardo's memory/phantasy because its most important feature is that a bird of prey "opened my mouth with its tail, and struck me many times with its tail against my lips." But at the very least, one can question the relevance of Freud's extensive discussion of vulture symbolism, and in particular

the identification of the vulture as a symbol for the phallic mother. One would also require an independent argument to show why a kite represents Leonardo's mother.

5. The more one pursues in detail the history of literature on the *Leonardo* essay, the more bizarre is the history of mistranslations, misunderstandings, and confusions. Maclagan's letter is a response to an editorial that appeared in the *Burlington Magazine* and is followed by the editor's reply. Even here, we detect the seeds of confusion. In the initial editorial, the editor characterizes the memory/phantasy as follows: "... when a child in his cradle, a vulture flew down to him from the sky and caressed him" (*Burlington Magazine, 41,* 256). There is no mention of the tail placed in the mouth of the child—which is the key feature of Freud's interpretation of the memory/phantasy as corresponding "to the idea of an act of fellatio, a sexual act in which the penis is put into the mouth of the person involved" (Freud, 1910, p. 86). We also know that Ernest Jones was a reader of the *Burlington Magazine*, yet there is no clear evidence that Freud ever acknowledged his mistranslation.

6. To anticipate, although the mistranslation is crucial, we need to ask "crucial for what?" Some of Freud's subsequent remarks about Leonardo and vulture symbolism are called into question. But it is a complex and subtle question whether Freud's interpretation of Leonardo's infantile sexual experiences depends on whether the memory/phantasy is about a vulture or a kite. Although I think there is some sophistry in Eissler's claims, he even says: "The fact that Leonardo actually did not write of a vulture but of a kite gives occasion to demonstrate how sensitive an instrument psychoanalysis really is" (Eissler, 1961, p. 22).

7. We should also recall what Freud himself says in another context: "In its implications the distortion of a text resembles a murder: the difficulty is not in perpetuating the deed, but in getting rid of its traces. We might well lend the word 'Entstellung [distortion]' the double meaning to which it has a claim but of which today it makes no use. It should mean not only 'to change the appearance of something' but also 'to put something in another place, to displace.' Accordingly, in many instances of textual distortion, we may nevertheless count upon finding what has been suppressed and disavowed hidden away somewhere else, though changed and torn from its context. Only it will not always be easy to recognize it" (Freud, 1937b, p. 43).

8. Farrell (1963) beautifully illustrates what I mean by the choreography of critique. He carefully reviews Freud's claims and arguments not only in light of the significance of the mistranslation, but in light of some of Freud's mistaken historical assumptions as revealed by Meyer Schapiro and others. He also displays great sensitivity in assessing what he calls Freud's "explanatory narrative." Although I do not endorse all his claims, his perceptive analysis is an invitation for further argumentation.

9. In the Standard Edition of *The Interpretation of Dreams*, Strachey

includes the following footnote taken from Freud's paper, "Additional Examples of Dream-Interpretation" (1900): "Of the many objections that have been raised against the procedure of psycho-analysis, the strangest, and, perhaps, one might add, the most ignorant, seems to me to be doubt as to the existence of symbolism in dreams and the unconscious. For no one who carries out psycho-analyses can avoid assuming the presence of such symbolism, and the resolution of dreams by symbols has been practiced from the earliest times. On the other hand, I am ready to admit that the *occurrence of these symbols should be subject to particularly strict proof in view of their great multiplicity*" (Freud, 1900, p. 360; italics added).

10. For further questions and *aporias* concerning symbolism, see Rieff (1979). See also Ricoeur (1970), especially pp. 494 ff.

REFERENCES

Bass, A. On the history of a mistranslation and the psychoanalytic movement. In J. F. Graham (Ed.), *Difference in translation*. Ithaca, N. Y.: Cornell University Press, 1985.

Bernstein, R. J. *The restructuring of social and political theory*. Philadelphia: University of Pennsylvania Press, 1978.

Bernstein, R. J. *Beyond objectivism and relativism: Science, hermeneutics, and praxis*. Philadelphia: University of Pennsylvania Press, 1983.

Bloom, H. Agon: Towards a theory of revisionism. New York: Oxford University Press, 1982.

Derrida, J. Des tours de babel. In J. F. Graham (Ed.), *Difference in Translation*. Ithaca, N. Y.: Cornell University Press, 1985.

Eissler, K. R. *Leonardo da Vinci: Psychoanalytic notes on the enigma*. New York: International Universities Press, 1961.

Farrell, B. Introduction to *Leonardo da Vinci and a memory of his childhood*. Hammondsworth, Middlesex: Penguin Books, 1963.

Freud, S. The interpretation of dreams. S.E., 1900, Vols. 4–5.

Freud, S. Leonardo Da Vinci and a memory of his childhood. S.E., 1910, Vol. 11.

Freud, S. Introductory lectures on psychoanalysis. S.E., 1916, Vol. 15.

Freud, S. Analysis terminable and interminable. S.E., 1937, Vol. 23.(a)

Freud, S. Moses and monotheism. S.E., 1937, Vol. 23.(b)

Giddens, A. *Studies in social and political theory*. New York: Basic Books, 1977.

Jones, E. *The life and work of Sigmund Freud* (2 Vols.). New York: Basic Books, 1955.

Maclagan, E. Leonardo in the consulting room. *Burlington Magazine*, 1923, 42.

Ricoeur, P. *Freud and philosophy: An essay on interpretation*. New Haven: Yale University Press, 1970.

Rieff, P. *Freud: The mind of the moralist* (3rd ed.). Chicago: University of Chicago Press, 1979.

Rorty, R. *Philosophy and the mirror of nature*. Princeton: Princeton University Press, 1979.

Schapiro, M. Leonardo and Freud: An art historical study. *Journal of the History of Ideas*, 1956, 17, 147–178.

Wohl, R., & Trosman, H. A retrospect of Freud's *Leonardo*: An assessment of a psychoanalytic classic. *Psychiatry*, 1955, 18, 27–39.

Psychoanalytic Interpretation and the Question of Validity: Commentary on Richard J. Bernstein

ROBERT L. WOOLFOLK and STANLEY B. MESSER

The theories that underlie the mental health professions are broad based and variegated. They include, at the very least, personality theory, cognitive and social psychological theory, theories of psychopathology, and the clinical theory of psychotherapy. Many who study these conceptual foundations of clinical psychology and psychiatry have come to believe that this body of theory is not, and in principle cannot be, a morally neutral structure, a corpus of objective knowledge that transcends history and culture. Systems of psychotherapy contain not only theoretical and technological features but also prescriptive, ideological components. Various commentators (e.g., Hogan, 1975; Woolfolk, 1985; Woolfolk & Richardson, 1984) have demonstrated both the culture-bound and evaluative character of personology, revealing such constructs as sublimation, social interest, and self-actualization to be prescriptive terms operating in scientific disguise and defining standards of human virtue and peccability. Psychiatric nosologies become not only vehicles for the proscription of conduct inconsistent with prevailing social norms, but also a system of labeling that facilitates those forms of social control administered by a mental health establishment.

Given these complications to a view of the mental health professions as nothing other than applied sciences parasitic upon some foundation of transhistorical, objective truth (in the manner that civil engineering derives from physics), knowledge in these areas has become problematic. The lack of a transhistorical epistemological warrant tends to prompt two kinds of responses:

1. The first, found most obviously in behavior therapy, is the positivist approach, which rules out of bounds any proposition that cannot pass some kind of verificationist or falsificationist test (cf. Ayer, 1946; Popper, 1959).
2. The second is to search for models alternative to those derived from the natural sciences with which to evaluate our practices and theories. This search, seemingly, often results in a form of relativism.

In his paper Richard Bernstein has made the hermeneutic argument that we lack any apodictic starting point, epistemologically independent of history and culture, that could serve as a foundation for our inquiries. Despite this, to use terminology Bernstein (1983) has employed elsewhere, the refutation of objectivism does not imply relativism. By describing what he refers to as a "choreography of critique," he attempts to argue for some middle ground between objectivism and relativism. Although sympathetic to his aims, we find what he says on behalf of his position to be unpersuasive.

He states that despite what appears to be a grievous flaw in Freud's analysis of Leonardo (his mistranslation resulting in a misclassification of the species of bird encountered by Leonardo in his childhood), much of Freud's speculation about vulture symbolism might nevertheless be of value and that much of the analysis does not hinge on the vulture symbol. He goes on to imply that, even if the analysis does not reveal much about Da Vinci, it nevertheless may reveal a great deal about Freud. It is difficult to argue with these contentions, but also difficult to see what they have to do with evaluating the validity claims implicit in Freud's account.

Bernstein suggests that to abandon psychoanalysis would be quite a different matter from dispensing with a physical theory or a pseudo-science such as alchemy. This is because "Freudian concepts, categories, and vocabulary have become constitutive of our pre-interpreted world" (Bernstein, 1988, p. 104). This is a plausible assertion, but again, how it really helps us evaluate the claims of psychoanalysis is difficult to see, except perhaps that it points to a possible bias in favor of psychoanalysis within our culture. Bernstein seems to feel that the burden of proof is on critics of Freud, but fails to provide an explicit basis for his inclinations.

Bernstein reminds us that interpretations and theory in psychology do make validity claims. In this he is following Habermas and is clearly correct, for what conceivable form of praxis would we be involved in if this were not the case? But how are we to evaluate such validity claims? Other than to pose the question, Bernstein offers little help. Several other writers within the hermeneutic tradition, however, have attempted to develop more explicit criteria for the evaluation of psychoanalytic interpretations.

Ricoeur (1981), who advocates viewing action as a text-analogue, suggests that we validate psychoanalytic interpretations not by the methods of verification employed in observational sciences, but rather through argumentation among practitioners who are aware of the singular meaningfulness and inexplicable uniqueness of the psychoanalytic situation. For Ricoeur, a good interpretation meets the following criteria:

It is consistent with the basic tenets of Freudian theory.

It satisfies the psychoanalytic rules for decoding the text of the unconscious.

It is therapeutically effective (when issued within a therapeutic context).

It forms an intelligible narrative.

For Habermas (1971) claims to truth and rightness admit of discursive justification and thus have to be analyzed in terms of the possibility of rational consensus. A consensus is rationally motivated to the extent it is the result of the force of the arguments advanced and not of accidental or systematic constraints on communication. This absence of constraint necessitates that the pragmatic structure of communication allows an effective equality of opportunity for participants to assume dialogic roles. In the case of psychoanalysis, Habermas assumes that the interpretations can be confirmed by the self-reflection and assent of the patient, who functions as a kind of dialogic partner. Insight must serve to facilitate the self-reflective, emancipatory powers of the patient.

One way in which the value or adequacy of interpretation has been studied empirically involves noting the patient's response to one or another kind of interpretation in psychotherapy. For example, segments of patient speech immediately before and after a transference demand (the patient's demanding affection, advice, rejection, or humiliation from the therapist) and therapist's response were rated independently by teams of judges. Ratings were made of patients' involvement and productivity, their levels of affect (fear, anxiety, love, and satisfaction), their capacity to boldly confront new material, and their degree of associative freedom (Silberschatz, Curtis, Fretter, & Kelly, in press). This procedure allowed for a tracking within the process of therapy of covariation between interpretation and categories of patient responses.

The psychoanalysts Spence (1982) and Sherwood (1969), although they do not abandon completely criteria of correspondence, discuss analytic interpretation as a form of narrative. Sherwood has placed three requirements on the adequacy of psychoanalytic interpretation:

Internal consistency (one part of the narrative does not contradict another part)

Coherence (ability to accommodate an individual's behavior within a narrative and make it intelligible therein)

Comprehensiveness (the degree to which the explanation is complete and incorporates the totality of the individual's life, case history, or psychodynamics)

Spence, in his discussion of the "narrative truth" of analytic interpretation, focuses on the criteria of subjective satisfaction and therapeutic efficacy.

Exposure of the inadequacies of a natural science-technological model of psychotherapy and psychological theory has been an important aspect of contemporary critical endeavors. Moving away from verificationist, correspondence-based standards of evaluation has resulted in psychoanalytic interpretation being judged on pragmatic, aesthetic, coherence, and consensual criteria. But the abandonment of the search for a method of verification grounded on apodictic epistemological bedrock, in our view, does not make empirical test irrelevant to psychoanalysis. If psychotherapy is a language game other than that played by applied science, it is at the very least a game in which it is important to keep score. Pragmatic criteria for interpretation must refer to efficacy requirements with some empirical content. Furthermore, consistency and coherence do not occur within an explanatory vacuum. Interpretations of human action inevitably contain points of contact with that realm of human capabilities that has been partially mapped by the cognitive and biological branches of psychology. We must square our interpretations with what we know about the natural world. We are with Bernstein in believing that the working out of some alternative to the Scylla of positivism and the Charybdis of Nietzsche's "weightlessness of all things" is important both to psychology and to the culture at large.

REFERENCES

Ayer, A. J. *Language, truth and logic.* New York: Dover, 1946.

Bernstein, R. J. *Beyond objectivism and relativism.* Philadelphia: University of Pennsylvania Press, 1983.

Bernstein, R. J. Interpretation and its discontents: The choreography of critique. In S. B. Messer, L. A. Sass, & R. L. Woolfolk (Eds.), *Hermeneutics and psychological theory: Interpretive perspectives on personality, psychotherapy and psychopathology.* New Brunswick, N. J.: Rutgers University Press, 1988.

Habermas, J. *Knowledge and human interests,* trans. J. J. Shapiro. Boston: Beacon Press, 1971.

Hogan, R. Theoretical egocentrism and the problem of compliance. *American Psychologist,* 1975, 30, 533–540.

Popper, K. R. *The logic of scientific discovery.* London, England: Hutchinson, 1959.

Ricoeur, P. *Hermeneutics and the human sciences,* trans. J. B. Thompson. New York: Cambridge University Press, 1981.

Sherwood, M. *The logic of interpretation in psychoanalysis.* New York: Academic Press, 1969.

Silberschatz, G., Curtis, J. T., Fretter, P. B., & Kelly, T. J. Testing hypotheses of psychotherapeutic change processes. In H. Dahl & H. Thoma (Eds.), *Psychoanalytic process research strategies.* New York: Springer, in press.

Spence, D. *Narrative truth and historical truth.* New York: Norton, 1982.

Woolfolk, R. L. What's at stake in the mental illness controversy. *American Psychologist,* 1985, 40, 468.

Woolfolk, R. L., & Richardson, F. C. Behavior therapy and the ideology of modernity. *American Psychologist,* 1984, 39, 777–786.

Rejoinder to Robert L. Woolfolk and Stanley B. Messer

RICHARD J. BERNSTEIN

I fully endorse the statement, "The abandonment of the search for a method of verification grounded on apodictic epistemological bedrock ... does not make empirical test irrelevant to psychoanalysis." This is in part what it means to say that psychoanalytic hypotheses make a claim to validity—a claim that is open to the critical scrutiny of the community of inquirers. Furthermore, I think that neither Habermas nor Ricoeur deny the need for empirical testing. On the contrary, they insist upon it insofar as they recognize that psychoanalytic explanations are a species of causal explanations. But the really tough problems arise at the very point where Robert Woolfolk and Stanley Messer conclude their comment. Precisely what is meant by an "empirical test" of psychoanalysis? This is not a merely rhetorical question, but a substantive one. Despite many claims and counter claims there is (as of now) no widespread rational agreement about what parts of psychoanalytic theory have been confirmed or disconfirmed by empirical tests. Even more important and more fundamental, there is still a great deal of disagreement (and confusion) about the very meaning and criteria for the empirical testing of psychoanalysis. Metaphors such as claiming that "our interpretations must *square with* what we know about the natural world," and that "it is important *to keep score*" are not very illuminating unless they are unpacked and specified with precision. So the challenge I would present to Woolfolk and Messer is to spell out in detail what empirical testing, squaring interpretations with our knowledge of nature, and keeping score really mean. I would also ask them to reflect on why the record to date of attempts to confirm or disconfirm empirically psychoanalytic theories, hypotheses, and interpretations is so poor.

The tendency to think that hermeneutical or interpretive approaches to psychoanalysis are an alternative to an empirical concern with testing and confirmation is to reify a false (and disastrous) dichotomy. A primary contribution of the hermeneutical emphasis in understanding psychoanalysis has been to explode simplistic (and even some sophisticated) myths about what counts as a proper empirical test of psychoanalytic validity claims and to open new questions about empirical testing. It behooves us to admit our ignorance and—whatever our epistemological allegiance—to seek new creative approaches to the issue of an empirical validation of psychoanalytic hypotheses, explanations, and interpretations. Unless this is done, and done with sensitivity to the complexities of interpretive causal explanations, tough-minded appeals for empirical tests can too easily degenerate into mere rhetorical flourishes.

Chapter 5

What Happens When the "Brute Data" of Psychological Inquiry Are Meanings: Nurturing a Dialogue between Hermeneutics and Empiricism

DONALD MEICHENBAUM

The purpose of this paper is to indicate that there is fundamentally nothing incompatible between a hermeneutic approach and an empirical approach to psychological investigation. In fact, a productive dialogue between the two approaches that would benefit each could be established. Following a brief description of hermeneutics and an examination of the implications of this approach for psychological inquiry, I will consider the nature and impact of the so-called "cognitive revolution" on empirical psychological inquiry. One thrust of this cognitive movement has been an increasing recognition of the important role of meaning, appraisal processes, and subjectivity in the study of human behavior. One outcome of the shift to a more cognitive perspective is that it opens new avenues of potential dialogue between hermeneutic and empirical lines of inquiry.

WHAT IS HERMENEUTICS?

Hermeneutics has been described as the art and science of interpretation. As Packer (1985) and Steele (1979) have noted, hermeneutics emerged in the 17th century as an interpretive discipline that was devoted to establishing the proper interpretation of biblical scripture.

It was designed to uncover and reconstruct the message from God that the text supposedly contained. As Packer (1985) notes, the term *hermeneutics* refers to Hermes, messenger of Greek gods, and "himself god of eloquence and cunning as well as of roads and thefts" (p. 1082). It was later expanded to apply to any literary text as well as to the understanding of historical periods (Dilthey, 1976). Wilhelm Dilthey (1831–1911), who contributed much to the hermeneutic tradition, admonished historians to interpret events in context and cautioned them against judging past events in terms of present standards. "According to Dilthey understanding is subject to time and change; no past is fixed and no present is to be thought of as somehow outside time. We survey the past from within our own horizon and that horizon is always changing" (Kermode, 1985, p. 7).

As Kermode (1985) indicates, hermeneutics holds that meaning changes and that the past is inextricably tied to the present of the interpreter. "*There* and *then* cannot be detached from *here* and *now*, and objectively inspected" (p. 7).

In time hermeneutic inquiry was extended to the interpretation of human action. As an approach to understanding, hermeneutics highlights the need to reconstruct the "world of meaning" surrounding an event. In the same way that a biblical or literary scholar attempts to understand a particular passage by referring to the corpus of the work, the student of human behavior must refer to the historical and cultural context that is constantly changing. The same ostensible behavior may have quite different meanings, and there is a need to assess and determine these meanings if we are to understand the nature of human behavior. Moreover, the hermeneutic tradition sensitizes investigators to the complications involved in this task by reminding us that the context of the interpreter (the investigator) contributes to the nature of the interpretation. In short, hermeneutics has evolved into a general line of inquiry that is concerned with the processes by which investigators interpret the meaning of human action.

IMPLICATIONS OF A HERMENEUTIC VIEWPOINT FOR PSYCHOLOGICAL INVESTIGATION

As Stanley Messer noted in an announcement to this conference, "Hermeneutics insists upon the inseparability of fact and value, detail and context, observation and theory." Context is critical in understanding human behavior. As we shall consider below, the "decontextualism of measurement" or the need to appreciate the context-bound nature of measurement has become a rallying cry for those who have embraced a hermeneutic approach.

Closely aligned with a concern with social context is an appreciation of the changing nature of behavior. Perhaps this viewpoint has been most clearly articulated by Klaus Riegel (1973) who argued that the study of all human behavior is essentially developmental in nature. Individuals change as well as do their environments. As Faulconer and Williams (1985) note, the study of human action is the study of temporal events. The fact that we are temporal beings in a temporal world has important implications for an empirical approach to psychological inquiry.

Hermeneutics reminds us that not only does human behavior and its contexts change, but so do investigators and their contexts. Investigators are not detached, dispassionate observers and reporters of facts who track "reality." Like the historian, the psychological investigator is constantly making choices and interpretations. The selection of concepts, instruments, or units of analysis reflects a basic process of interpretation. As Bowers (1977) noted:

> Our conceptualization of a phenomenon, however implicit or unarticulated, has a profound and tenacious impact on what we decide to measure and record. In other words, what man brings to nature in the form of intuition, ideas and (pre)conceptions is as important to an objective understanding of the world as what nature presents to man. (p. 68)

A similar sentiment was expressed by Gadamer (1975) who observed that to have a method is to already have an interpretation. Faulconer and Williams (1985) comment that investigators choose and trust their methods on the basis of some already existing interpretation that Gergen (1982, 1985) reminds us is likely to change over time.

Moreover, those whom we study are neither insensitive nor indifferent to the fact that they are being studied. Investigators in the physical sciences, on the other hand, do not have to be concerned that the objects of their study (e.g., planets, rocks, molecules) are aware of being investigated. The objects of psychological inquiry (people) often do change and are influenced by their reactions to being under scrutiny. Although this fact has long been observed, little recognition of it is reflected in the manner in which psychological inquiry is conducted. Rarely does one see subjects queried or treated as collaborators in the study of psychological phenomena. Rarely does one see behavior studied in a social and interactional context. As Wachtel (1980) has admonished, experimenters still treat subjects with an implacable stance that often detracts from the transactional nature of psychological inquiry. Hermeneutics forces psychological investigators to confront their false sense of objectivity and epistemological privilege.

AN EXAMPLE OF A HERMENEUTIC VIEW OF PSYCHOLOGICAL INQUIRY

A recent set of studies by Gergen, Hepburn, and Comer (in press) nicely illustrates some of the concerns that arise from a hermeneutic approach. Their research was due to the decontextualism of personality research as reflected in personality inventories. A mainstay of psychological inquiry has been the use of paper-and-pencil personality questionnaires. Although there is nothing inevitably antithetical between such an assessment approach and the dictates of hermeneutic inquiry, the problem arises when the investigator is called upon to interpret the meaning of subjects' responses. Such interpretation is further complicated by the observation that the meaning of items may change over time. As an example, Gergen et al. offers an item from the Authoritarian F scale that today may be obsolete: "Homosexuals are hardly better than criminals and ought to be severely punished." Gergen et al. (in press) observe that as our sensibilities change so does the meaning of the test items and so does the nature of our constructs. Although the relation between this test item and changing social norms is quite obvious, Gergen and his colleagues challenge the field to consider where similar concerns may arise even in the case of less blatant examples. They also question the flexibility of the nature of psychologists' explanatory conventions.

In order to demonstrate their case, Gergen et al. (in press) examined the very popular personality scale, Locus of Control (LOC, Rotter, 1975), which assesses an individual's penchant for internal and external views of the personal control of reinforcement. They presented subjects with "a puzzle of sorts," namely, items from the LOC scale and asked them to offer descriptive adjectives, personality statements, and predictions of how individuals who endorse different items might behave in real life situations. They found that items on the personality test permit a wide range of interpretation. More specifically, they demonstrated that

1. any item on the LOC scale could be plausibly interpreted as an expression of virtually any common trait term,
2. judges could offer a plausible rationale for interpreting randomly selected items from the LOC scale as indicators of multiplicity of traits, and
3. judges could offer multiple explanatory means by which people can demonstrate how a given item is an expression of various common traits.

For example, in examining whether any response can express any trait, consider the item, "There is a direct connection between how hard I study and the grades I get" (scored Internal). Subjects were able to offer plausible explanations of why someone who is shy, logical, or impulsive might endorse such an item. Subjects were also able to view such item endorsement as fitting a variety of personality dispositions such as being narrow-minded vs. broad-minded, optimistic vs. pessimistic, fearful vs. brave. Given the multifaceted nature of human behavior and our interpretative flexibility, there was little that could not be explained. Gergen et al. (in press) demonstrated that personality items can reflect various constructs and behavioral relationships.

Such findings, however, should come as little surprise to either researchers or clinicians. First, consider researchers. How many investigators have pored over correlational matrices with their graduate students and interpreted significant relationships in a particular way? The investigator may develop convincing explanations of why two variables go together in a certain manner. He or she might even get carried away and consider the possible moderator and mediating variables. This flight of fancy by the researcher may be interrupted by the student who might sheepishly note that the investigator had the variables labeled in the "wrong" direction—what was high on one variable went with what was low on the other variable—not as the investigator had suggested. Never to be dismayed, the verbally fluent, ingenious professor readily reverses the hypothesis, offering as plausible and as convincing an explanation as before, reflecting the flexibility of interpretation.

Consistent with the findings of Gergen et al. (in press) on the flexibility of interpretation, this example should come as little surprise to those studying to obtain a Ph.D. in psychology. Clearly, one of the things graduate school teaches is exactly such interpretative flexibility.

Not to be outdone, clinicians are equally facile. Just consider the classic enterprise of the clinical case conference. Could one think of a better examplar to demonstrate the hermeneut's case? Given the multifaceted and multicausal nature of human behavior, one cannot help but relish the varied explanations of a client's behavior by various professionals (psychiatrist, social worker, psychologist), let alone those within the same profession who hold diverse theoretical perspectives (e.g., psychoanalytic, behavioral, family systems).

The clinic case conference gives a new definition to the concept of interpretative flexibility. No wonder Paul Meehl (1973), in a telling piece, explained why he does not attend clinical case conferences.

Finally, the onus of interpretative flexibility should not be laid only at the feet of professionals. Clients also show remarkable skill in being able to interpret their behavior from a variety of theoretical and therapeutic perspectives. In fact, at one point I have suggested that such interpretative flexibility ensured the financial support of all the various schools of psychotherapy in North America—a considerable feat (Meichenbaum, 1977).

Clients show remarkable ability to make sense out of almost any psychotherapeutic approach. You can ask patients to relax, to engage in primal scream, to act out their dreams, to talk to themselves, to perform embarrassing behavioral acts, to disregard and to disengage from their spouses' maladaptive behavior, and so forth. For this, not only will patients pay good money, but they will convince themselves and others that it is helpful.

Are all of our clients walking "closet hermeneuts"? In answering this rhetorical question, we must recognize that knowledge, including self-knowledge, results from a constructive process that is subjective, relative, and provisional. In fact, the ways in which scientists, clinicians, and hermeneuts find and impose meaning may be quite similar and thus the proper domain of psychological inquiry.

WHAT HAPPENS WHEN THE "BRUTE DATA" OF PSYCHOLOGICAL INVESTIGATION ARE MEANING?

The term *brute data* was used by Taylor (1971) to refer to the acts of people (behaviors), as identified and recorded by scientists, which supposedly are "beyond interpretation." These are the observational building blocks for the empiricist. The empiricist whom Taylor has in mind, however, is someone who holds a rather outdated view of behaviorism. Following the model of the natural sciences and embracing positivistic notions of objectivity, behaviorism eschewed mental events as elements of proper explanations of behavior. From this perspective the task for the empiricist is to grind out the facts or record the brute data. Taylor takes the behaviorist to task, and appropriately so, for failing to recognize that inherent in the collection of so-called brute data are interpretation, meaning, and human values.

The cognitive revolution caused a major shift in psychological inquiry (Dember, 1974). The focus has shifted to the nature of mental events and their interrelationships with both the emotions and social behavior. If one does not equate empiricism with behaviorism, then an interesting dialogue may be established between the empirical and hermeneutic approaches.

The cognitive view highlights the fact that human beings are not the passive recipients of environmental inputs, but, rather, active, aware appraisers and interpreters, whose perceptions and interpretations are framed in the context of their existing knowledge structures. Individuals are not merely passively shaped by environmental input, but are active, often unwitting creators of and contributors to their circumstances. As Walter Mischel (1973) commented:

> The image is one of the human being as an active, aware problem-solver, capable of profiting from an enormous range of experiences and cognitive capacities, possessing great potential for good or ill, *actively constructing* his or her psychological world, and influencing the environment, but also being influenced by it in lawful ways—even if the laws are difficult to discover and hard to generalize. (p. 253, emphasis added)

The cognitive view highlights the fact that individuals come to know the world through their actions and their consequences. Human beings are active constructive agents. They seek to make sense out of their experience. In some very essential features they operate like hermeneuts. Much of cognitive psychology and social psychology has been directed at learning how human beings go about the very process of creating data and making interpretations and decisions, a task that strongly resembles hermeneutic inquiry.

As Taylor (1971) notes, hermeneutics represents an attempt to elucidate, to make sense of an object of study; to generate a clarifying interpretation when something is confused, incomplete, cloudy, seemingly contradictory; to make decisions under conditions of uncertainty.

A great deal of empirical effort has gone into studying exactly how individuals conduct such interpretative activities. Although a full description of these efforts is beyond the scope of this chapter, a few examples will illustrate the natural confluence of the empirical and hermeneutic perspective. (See Meichenbaum and Gilmore, 1984, for a more detailed account.)

In order to appreciate the ways in which the interpretative process currently is being studied, there is a need to draw a distinction between cognitive events, cognitive processes, and cognitive structures. As we consider each concept, we can raise questions about the implications they have for understanding the nature of hermeneutic inquiry. Quite briefly, cognitive events refer to the conscious, identifiable, or readily retrievable thoughts, images, and accompanying feelings that individuals experience when the automaticity of their acts is interrupted. When the scripted nature of one's behavior is broken, as in the case of an individual who has to make a decision under conditions of uncertainty, individuals engage in what Plato called an "internal dialogue." The appraisals, expectations, attributions, self-statements, images, or what Beck (1976) called "automatic thoughts," influence our interpretative processes.

In the same way that individuals talk to themselves when having to interpret ambiguous events, so do hermeneuts talk to themselves when having to make decisions under conditions of uncertainty. The nature and impact of such thoughts and feelings on the decision-making process has become a major research focus (e.g., Janis & Mann, 1977; Kahneman, Slovic, & Tversky, 1982). Is the decision-making process of hermeneutic inquiry in any basic ways distinct from the decision-making process of how one negotiates one's daily lives? I think not! The concern with finding, imposing, and creating meaning, and even with the nature of self-deception, is a primary concern of current empirical efforts. The results of such research will have important implications for understanding how hermeneuts conduct their inquiries.

Closely related to the issue of hermeneutic inquiry is the basic concept of cognitive processes. Cognitive processes refer to the mental habits or heuristics, rules, and procedures that guide thinking and information processing (see Kahneman et al., 1982). A number of cognitive processes have been identified that influence the way we process information. Among these are search and storage mechanisms, inferential and retrieval processes. Two processes worth noting are confirmatory bias and mental heuristics.

Confirmatory bias refers to the process by which we selectively perceive, remember, and interpret experience so as to filter out disconfirmations of strongly held beliefs. As Snyder (1981) so aptly observed, "Seek and ye shall find." In other words we are in some sense all like the television character Archie Bunker as we search for information that is consistent with our views of ourselves and the world. Moreover, we actively create the very data, especially in social situations, that confirm our initial hunches. As the adage goes, "If we possess a hammer, then the world is viewed as being filled with nails." Moreover, we are likely to actively seek, and sometimes create, a world full of nails.

Our hermeneutic efforts are also influenced by a variety of mental habits, or what Tversky and Kahneman (1977) call "mental heuristics." When making a decision under conditions of uncertainty, we often call forth the most available (salient, ready at hand) instance and use it as the basis to make a decision. Our interpretative processes are influenced by such factors as saliency, recency, and stereotyped preconceptions rather than being influenced by other, perhaps more relevant, features, such as the base-rate frequency or occurrence of the event. Nisbett and Ross (1980) and Turk and Salovey (1985a) have enumerated a variety of processes such as illusory correlation, differential recall due to moods, primacy effects, and the like, that influence interpretation. The conclusion to be drawn from the present discussion is that each of us engages in hermeneutic inquiry every day and that many factors affect such inquiry, often exerting their influence without our awareness. With the cognitive revolution in psychology, the empirical tradition has turned its attention to how these factors exert their influence.

Finally, the concept of cognitive structure captures the major preoccupation with the nature of meaning. Once again this concept could bear its own close scrutiny. At this point one need only appreciate that individuals' assumptions, beliefs, commitments, or what is known as self-schemas, influence how events are appraised and how individuals habitually construe themselves and the world. Cognitive structures, or what Meichenbaum and Gilmore (1984) called "core organizing principles" (COPS), should be viewed as hypothetical constructs that are useful for purposes of understanding the coherence and thematic unity in an individual's thoughts, feelings, and behavior.

For example, consider a clever study by the sociologist Kieser (1969) who interviewed and observed members of a Chicago street gang. Interestingly, the gang members divided their daily activities into two rather colorfully labeled events: (1) high-risk activities (for example, "humbugging," "gang-banging," "wolf-packing," and "hustling"), and (2) low-risk activities ("gigs," "games," "sets," and "pulling jive"). It was in the former set of risk activities that one earned peer acceptance (earned one's "rep," displayed "heart," or showed one was no "punk"). Thus, acceptance by one's peers in the gang represented a primary current concern (Klinger, 1977) that influenced how situations were perceived in terms of risk levels, with the associated potential for raising or lowering esteem within the group. Peer acceptance influenced individuals' emotions, thoughts, and actions (e.g., approach or avoidance). The need for status in the gang and for the social approval of peers produced a "readiness set" or appraisal system that operated automatically in influencing thoughts, feelings, and behaviors of the gang members. Moreover, how gang members behaved and the reactions their behavior elicited from others were taken as evidence confirming their appraisal system and current concerns.

As Taylor and Crocker (1981) note, such cognitive structures serve a number of adaptive functions in the interpretative process. They help individuals to identify stimuli quickly, fill in missing information, categorize events, set goals, attach importance, select strategies, solve problems, evaluate outcomes, and resist counterschematic inputs. These are the same tasks that Dilthey advised historians to address when interpreting historical and literary works and that Heidegger implied when he discussed the hermeneutic study of human action. In short, the parallels between our daily search for meaning and the nature of hermeneutic inquiry are striking.

This is further underscored when we appreciate that the nature of one's cognitive structures is not "set in stone." Cognitive structures change over time as reflected in such concepts as black pride, women's lib, gay rights, and the like. Changing such cognitive structures and the accompanying feelings, thoughts, and behaviors is a primary concern of cognitive behavior modification and cognitive therapy procedures (Beck, Rush, Hollon, & Shaw, 1979; Meichenbaum, 1985). One primary concern of such efforts is how individuals appraise events, as well as their ability to cope with such events. A major clinical tool is to establish a collaborative, empirically-based relationship between the client and the therapist so the client can perform "personal experiments." In this way the client can begin to collect anomalous and disconfirmatory data. The therapist helps the client treat such data as evidence in order to begin to change the nature of his or her cognitive structures.

At this point the intent is not to convey the mechanics of such a treatment approach, but instead, to suggest that one could conceptualize cognitive behavior modification as a form of teaching clients the nature of hermeneutic inquiry. Clients are taught the transactional nature of their behavior (namely, the interdependence between thoughts, emotions, social interactions, and their resultant consequences). As collaborators, they are guided, cajoled, challenged, and taught ways to notice, interrupt, and reverse maladaptive cycles. This teaching is experimental, inductive, affective, and self-discovery based as contrasted with approaches that are didactic, expository, and deductive. In fact, a comparison of the writings of Heidegger (as reviewed by Packer, 1985) and the writings of cognitive behavior therapists provides a strikingly fascinating parallel. Although neither the hermeneuts nor the cognitive theorists tend to cite each other, the similarities between them are indeed instructive.

In summary, when the brute data of psychological inquiry are meaning and interpretation, appraisal processes, and the social process and multiple factors that influence them, then the incompatibility of a hermeneutic and an empirical approach no longer is the case. In fact, there seem to be some lessons that each approach could learn from the other.

WHAT CAN EACH APPROACH (EMPIRICAL AND HERMENEUTIC) LEARN FROM THE OTHER?

The empiricist needs to more readily appreciate the dialectical nature of knowledge. The empiricist needs to become more sensitive to the often implicit role that the investigator's interpretations play in the scientific process.

As the hermeneuts have highlighted, the empiricist needs to appreciate the important role of social context and the relative and provisional nature of what one is studying. Since the nature of one's scientific concepts is likely to change, there is a need for the empiricists to think in developmental and temporal terms. Not only do individuals change over time but so do contexts. This implies the need for a more process-oriented ipsative-longitudinal research approach as suggested by Lazarus and Folkman (1984) who advocate that individuals, as well as social contexts, be studied over time. There is a need to study human behavior in its social context rather than in a "sterile" laboratory setting where investigators behave in an implacable manner. Such standardized settings often miss the social nature and reciprocal aspects of behavior. It is the very "stuff of social contexts" that helps investigators better understand the meaning of behavior. Moreover, the hermeneutic tradition reminds us that the so-called laws and principles of behavior, as well as the nature of our constructs and the validity of our instruments, are likely to change over time.

Finally, if interpretation plays such an important role in both lay and scientific endeavors, there is a need to study interpretative processes. How do the lay person, the scientist, the hermeneut, make decisions under conditions of uncertainty? A shift to the study of interpretation will mean that the brute data of psychological inquiry will be meanings.

The hermeneut needs to learn not to equate empiricism with behaviorism. Since the coming of the so-called cognitive revolution, many interesting parallels can be noted between hermeneutic thought and cognitive inquiry.

There is also a need for hermeneuts to appreciate that the processes of interpretation in which they engage may not be too different from the ways in which people in general go about the act of interpretation. Moreover, the types of errors, biases, and distortions that influence such judgmental processes likely affect the hermeneut's own professional efforts at interpretation. The chapters in this volume by Bernstein, Spence, and others underscore the variety of ways in which investigators have drawn premature, inaccurate, and often misleading interpretations based on limited and often ambiguous data sources. Those who engage in hermeneutic inquiry, as well as those who engage in clinical diagnosis, could benefit from training and inoculation against such errors and biases.

Arkes (1981) and Turk and Salovey (1985b) have nicely enumerated the variety of errors one may make in forming interpretations.

The interpretation of responses to an inkblot test, the meaning of an individual's behavior, or the meaning of a literary work or a historical period are each likely to be influenced by factors of which the interpreter is not fully aware. The empirical work on decision making has a number of important lessons (guidelines) to contribute to the art and science of hermeneutics. In fact, hermeneuts may represent a unique population for empirical investigation.

In summary, both the empirical and hermeneutic approaches to inquiry not only have a good deal in common, but most importantly, they have even more to learn from each other. Both approaches are likely to benefit from interacting.

REFERENCES

Arkes, H. R. Impediments to accurate clinical judgment and possible ways to minimize their impact. *Journal of Clinical and Consulting Psychology*, 1981, 49, 323–330.

Beck, A. *Cognitive therapy and emotional disorders*. New York: International Universities Press, 1976.

Beck, A., Rush, J., Hollon, S., & Shaw, B. *Cognitive therapy of depression*. New York: Guilford Press, 1979.

Bowers, K. W. There's more to Iago than meets the eye: A clinical account of personal consistency. In D. Magnusson & N. Endler (Eds.), *Personality at the crossroads*. Hillsdale, N. J.: Erlbaum, 1977.

Dember, W. Motivation and the cognitive revolution. *American Psychologist*, 1974, 29, 161–168.

Dilthey, W. The types of world view and their development in metaphysical systems. In H. P. Rickman (Ed.), *Dilthey: Selected Writings*. Cambridge: Cambridge University Press, 1976.

Faulconer, J. E., & Williams, R. N. Temporality in human action: An alternative to positivism and historicism. *American Psychologist*, 1985, 11, 1179–1188.

Gadamer, H. G. *Truth and method*. New York: Seabury Press, 1975.

Gergen, K. J. The social constructionist movement in modern psychology. *American Psychologist*, 1985, 40, 266–275.

Gergen, K. J. *Toward a transformation in social knowledge*. New York: Springer-Verlag, 1982.

Gergen, K. J., Hepburn, A., & Comer, D. The hermeneutics of personality description. *Journal of Personality and Social Psychology*, in press.

Janis, I., & Mann, L. *Decision making*. New York: Free Press, 1977.

Kahneman, D., Slovic, P., & Tversky, A. *Judgment under uncertainty: Heuristics and biases*. New York: Cambridge University Press, 1982.

Keiser, L. *The vice lords: Workers of the streets*. New York: Holt, Rinehart, & Winston, 1969.

Kermode, F. Freud and interpretation. *International Review of Psycho-Analysis*, 1985, *12*, 3–12.

Klinger, E. *Meaning and void: Inner experiences and the incentives in people's lives*. Minneapolis: University of Minnesota Press, 1977.

Lazarus, R. S., & Folkman, S. *Stress, appraisal and coping*. New York: Springer-Verlag, 1984.

Meehl, P. Why I do not attend case conferences. In P. Meehl (Ed.), *Psychodiagnosis: Selected papers*. Minneapolis: University of Minnesota Press, 1973.

Meichenbaum, D. *Cognitive behavior modification: An integrative approach*. New York: Plenum Press, 1977.

Meichenbaum, D. *Stress inoculation training*. New York: Pergamon Press, 1985.

Meichenbaum, D., & Gilmore, J. B. The nature of unconscious processes: A cognitive-behavioral perspective. In K. S. Bowers & D. Meichenbaum (Eds.), *The unconscious reconsidered*. New York: John Wiley, 1984.

Mischel, W. Toward a cognitive social learning reconceptualization of personality. *Psychological Review*, 1973, *80*, 252–283.

Nisbett, R. E., & Ross, L. *Human inference: Strategies and shortcomings of social judgment*. Englewood Cliffs, N. J.: Prentice Hall, 1980.

Packer, M. J. Hermeneutic inquiry in the study of human conduct. *American Psychologist*, 1985, *40*, 1081–1093.

Riegel, K. F. Developmental psychology and society: Some historical and ethical considerations. In J. R. Nesselroade & H. W. Reese (Eds.), *Life-span developmental psychology: Methodological issues*. New York: Academic Press, 1973.

Rotter, J. B. Some problems and misconceptions related to the construct of internal vs. external control of reinforcement. *Journal of Consulting and Clinical Psychology*, 1975, *43*, 56–67.

Snyder, M. Seek and ye shall find: Testing hypotheses about other people. In E. Higgins, C. Herman, & M. Zanna (Eds.), *Social cognition: The Ontario symposium*. Hillsdale, N. J.: Erlbaum, 1981.

Steele, R. S. Psychoanalysis and hermeneutics. *International Review of Psycho-Analysis*, 1979, *6*, 389–411.

Taylor, C. Interpretations and the sciences of man. *Review of Metaphysics*, 1971, *25*, 3–34.

Taylor, S., & Crocker, J. Schematic basics of social information processing. In E. Higgins, C. Herman, & M. Zanna (Eds.), *Social cognition: The Ontario symposium*. Hillsdale, N. J.: Erlbaum, 1981.

Turk, D., & Salovey, P. Cognitive structures, cognitive processes and cognitive behavior modification: Judgments and inferences of the clinician. *Cognitive Therapy and Research*, 1985, *9*, 19–35.(a)

Turk, D., & Salovey, P. Clinical reasoning, inference and judgment: Bias inoculation. In R. Ingram (Ed.), *Information processing approaches to psychopathology and clinical psychology.* New York: Academic Press, 1985.(b)

Tversky, A., & Kahneman, D. Causal schemata in judgments under uncertainty. In M. Fishbein (Ed.), *Progress in social psychology.* Hillsdale, N. J.: Erlbaum, 1977.

Wachtel, P. L. Investigation and its discontents: On some constraints on progress in psychological research. *American Psychologist,* 1980, 35, 399–408.

Hermeneutics and Empiricism: Commentary on Donald Meichenbaum

JEROME WAKEFIELD

Can the meanings of human behavior be studied empirically, like any other object of scientific inquiry? Hermeneutics is the discipline that deals with the methodology of interpreting meanings, and the standard view among hermeneuticists is that the study of meaning possesses some essentially nonempirical features. In his chapter, "What Happens When the 'Brute Data' of Psychological Inquiry Are Meanings: Nurturing a Dialogue between Hermeneutics and Empiricism," Donald Meichenbaum argues that in fact, "There is fundamentally nothing incompatible between a hermeneutic approach and an empirical approach to psychological investigation." Meichenbaum's attempt to integrate these two seemingly opposed traditions parallels his valuable past contributions to integrating behavioral, cognitive, and psychodynamic ideas, but I do not think that he succeeds as well in this case. Although I am very sympathetic to Meichenbaum's ultimate goal of an empirical science of meaning, I think he misdiagnoses the source of the rejection of empiricism by hermeneuticists and consequently fails to confront the true obstacles to integration. I will focus on clarifying exactly what the dispute between hermeneutics and empiricism is about.

HERMENEUTICS AND THE COMPATIBILITY THESIS

Before turning to Meichenbaum's argument, I need to say something about the concepts of hermeneutics and empiricism as I will understand them. Hermeneutics, as Meichenbaum explains, is the art and science of interpretation, which in turn is the attempt to "make sense" of a text by elaborating, uncovering, and reconstructing its meaning. For example, literary criticism and biblical interpretation are typical hermeneutic endeavors. Hermeneutics is potentially relevant to psychology because *text* can be taken in a broad enough sense to apply to the behavior, verbalizations, and conscious mental states of a person who is being treated or studied. In therapy and in the cognition laboratory, the psychologist routinely attempts to uncover and reconstruct aspects of the person's meaning system lying behind these manifest states, and this activity can be considered a possible instance of hermeneutics.

Meichenbaum's claim that hermeneutics and empiricism are compatible raises a messy terminological issue. The question is how to interpret the compatibility claim in order to make it neither trivially true nor trivially false. On the one hand, if hermeneutics is defined as the study of meaning, it becomes so broad that the compatibility claim becomes trivially true. Empiricists are unquestionably studying meanings, so some empirical studies would certainly fit this definition of hermeneutics. On the other hand, hermeneutics traditionally rejects empiricism as a possible methodology for studying meanings. If this central thesis is incorporated into the definition, empiricism is by definition not hermeneutics, and the compatibility thesis becomes trivially false. Obviously, neither of these trivial arguments is of interest.

Now, hermeneuticists do not deny that empiricists can attempt to study meanings, they just deny that such a project can succeed in providing the desired understanding. So the fact that some empiricists have tried to study meaning is not in conflict with hermeneuticists' rejection of empiricism. Moreover, hermeneuticists do not reject empiricism out of sheer dogma. They advance specific claims about the nature of meaning that they think disqualify meaning as a subject of empirical study. The question is whether the reasons given by hermeneuticists for rejecting empiricism are cogent. Therefore, when Meichenbaum claims that hermeneutics and empiricism are compatible, I will interpret him as claiming that hermeneuticists have no good reason for denying that the empirical study of meaning is a viable possibility. To prove his point, Meichenbaum must show that the doctrines of the hermeneutic tradition about the nature of meaning that underlie the denial of empiricism are either false or actually compatible with empiricism.

COGNITIVISM, EMPIRICISM, AND MEANING

Empiricism is an even vaguer and broader term than *hermeneutics*, covering all procedures that consider the evidence of the senses. On such a broad construal, the claim that hermeneutics is empirical becomes too weak to be of interest. Instead, I will limit myself to a consideration of the currently dominant empirical framework for the study of meaning, which I will call "cognitivism."[1] This is the approach that recently inherited the mantle of power from behaviorism as a result of the cognitive revolution (Baars, 1986). Cognitivists approach the study of meaning by combining traditional scientific methods of causal-explanatory scientific inquiry with a certain thesis about the nature of meaning. To explain what this cognitivist thesis is, I must first say something about what I mean by *meaning*.

As I use the term in relation to psychology, *meaning* refers to the "aboutness" or "directedness" of certain states and activities of persons, in which their patterns of behavior and states of mind are highly organized and responsive to objects (taken in the broadest sense, including human "objects") and situations outside themselves. It is due to these highly discriminating and organized responses that we say that these outside objects have meaning for a person. Classical examples of such directed and meaningful states include intentional action, such as walking to the store in order to pick up some beer; skillful activity, such as banging a nail with a hammer or playing chess; perception, including the way the world looks from one's unique vantage point; and mental states, such as beliefs, desires, and emotions.

There are various theories of the nature of meaning that attempt to explain how people can be directed at the world in the way that they are. One of these theories is the cognitivist thesis about meaning I mentioned earlier, and it has become virtually synonymous with the notion of meaning within recent empirical psychology. This view holds that a person can be directed at an object because that person's mind contains a representation of the object. Mental representations are typically thought of as analogous either to pictures of the object (visual images) or to sentences describing the object (thoughts) or some other kind of explicit representation that enables one to relate to the object. Since we obviously do not have enough images and thoughts in our conscious awareness to explain all of our directed behavior, cognitivists generally hold that these representations are capable of being unconscious.

In the case of certain mental states, such as desires and beliefs, it is generally agreed that representations must be involved. A person's desire, for instance, consists partly of a representation of the thing the person wants, and that representation is crucial to organizing the person's goal-oriented behavior in pursuit of the desired object. Similarly, to believe that a particular assertion is true is for the content of that assertion to be represented in one's mind and for that representation to play a certain role in guiding one's behavior. A philosophical term for these kinds of mental states that are directed at objects via representations is *intentionality*. The representation is called the *content* of the intentional state, and the thing in the world that is represented and at which the intentional state is directed is called the *object* of the intentional state. This philosophical terminology corresponds to a colloquial use of *object*, as in "the object of my affections." It is also the source of Freud's term *object* as it has come down to us in the phrase "object relations theory." The cognitivist theory of meaning might therefore be said to be the thesis that all meaning works the same way that beliefs and desires do, that is, representationally. The new empirical science of meaning on which Meichenbaum bases his argument is essentially the investigation of such mental representations, the rules governing their interactions, and their role in causing behavior.

Granted that beliefs and desires are representational states, it is a tremendous theoretical leap to suggest that all meaningful behavior must be mediated by mental representations. Yet, perhaps because we are so intimately acquainted with our own beliefs and desires and have an intuitive grasp of intentionality, the intentionality model for meaning has proven extremely attractive, and this theoretical leap has been regularly attempted. Freud, for example, asserted that all purposeful activity on the part of the organism, including instinctually driven activity, must be mediated by ideas, which was his term for what are now known as mental representations. In fact, the cognitivist approach is currently so all-pervasive that it might seem to be the only possible view, so it must be emphasized that the representational view is just one approach to how meaning works. I will discuss an alternative account of meaning later on, the (existential) phenomenological view,[2] which suggests that activity can be directed without the need for representations.

Cognitivism leads to a very elegant and appealing—though not necessarily correct—view of what one is doing when one interprets the meaning of behavior or of any "text." Ultimately, meaning consists of mental representations in the mind of the person who generated the behavior, and the meaning of the behavior consists in those intentional states that were causally responsible for the occurrence of the behavior. So, if the desire for bread caused you to walk to the store, then that desire is part of the meaning of your behavior. Applied to literary criticism, this theory yields the approach of E. D. Hirsch (1967, 1976), in which the interpretation of a text always consists of the discovery of the intentions that were in the author's mind when creating the text.[3]

On the cognitivist view, there is in principle a single correct answer to the question of what the meaning of a behavior is, no matter how difficult it may be to establish the correct answer in practice and no matter how complex the answer might be. This is because there is in principle a single correct description of the content of the representational state(s) in the person's mind that caused the behavior. For example, the image in one's head might be of sitting and happily eating bread, or the mental content might consist of the thought, "It would be great to have some fresh bread." The cognitivist holds that representational states are determinate in meaning because the content of a mental sentence or a mental picture, like the contents of sentences and pictures generally, can be discerned and described from their structure alone. If meanings are inherently determinate, then an interpretation is an attempt to use language to match as closely as possible the actual content of the intentional state, and the interpretation either gets it exactly right or suffers from some degree of inexactitude. Thus, for example, there is within the psychoanalytic tradition a concern about how an inexact interpretation—one that does not exactly match the true literal content of the intentional state being interpreted—can still have a therapeutic effect (Glover, 1931; Spence, 1982).

If the content of a representation is manifest in its structure in the way that the meaning of a sentence is manifest from its grammar, does that mean that the content of a representation can be determined completely independently of its context? Not quite, because even the cognitivist allows that other representations in a person's mental system can affect the meaning of a given representation. For the sophisticated cognitivist, the mind is a *system* of representations, and the meaning of one cognition will in part be determined by the network of cognitions of which it is a member and with which it interacts. The meaning of a certain image of a parent's face, for example, will be determined in part by the context of other images and thoughts about the parent, memories of when the parent displayed that facial expression, and so on. Similarly, the meaning of a thought like "I am a nogoodnik" depends on beliefs about the meaning of the word *nogoodnik*. Or, the meaning of a dream that is at first mysterious becomes clearer as one learns the thoughts and desires and images that preceded it and formed its context.

Most cognitivists, then, adhere to a form of "meaning holism" which asserts that the content of an intentional state is partly a function of its position within the person's entire network of intentional states. But for cognitivists the system of representations as a whole is unambiguous and exhaustive of a person's meaning system; there is nothing more one would need to know to determine the meanings of behavior. For convenience of expression, I will speak as if cognitivists believe that each idea has a determinate meaning in isolation, but the reader should keep in mind that it is really the whole system of ideas that have a determinate meaning.

Cognitivists believe that meanings are determinate entities hidden "in the head" of the individual, and this view of meaning leads them to employ traditional empirical strategies in the attempt to uncover those entities, which means they pursue an observationally-based causal inquiry. The cognitivist typically justifies attributions of meaning by appeal to observations that confirm or disconfirm relevant causal hypotheses about representations in the mind of the subject. In the simplest case, the subject reports a thought, but in more complex cases the existence of certain affects, or speeded up or slowed down reaction times to tachistoscopically presented stimuli, or symptoms, and many other responses, can all be taken to indicate the presence of nonreported representations that are causing the observed behavior. Alternative hypotheses about meanings are ruled out by reference to predicted observable phenomena, and hidden ("nonobservable") meanings can be studied through their causal interaction with more accessible ("observable") meanings. Note that the cognitivist approach to the study of meaning has the interesting feature that there is absolutely nothing methodologically special about it that would differentiate the study of meaning from the study of any other empirically studyable entity, such as electrons or DNA. The methods are essentially the same because the goals—a causal-explanatory account of behavior in terms of hidden entities—are the same as in all theoretical empirical inquiry.

I have spelled out a few features of the cognitivist version of empiricism that I believe are currently dominant in psychology. I now turn to Meichenbaum's argument that hermeneutics and empiricism are compatible, which I am interpreting as an argument that hermeneutics and cognitivism are compatible. I will argue that central to traditional hermeneutic approaches are doctrines that imply that the cognitivist enterprise is conceptually flawed and must fail and that Meichenbaum fails to confront these arguments.

HERMENEUTICS AND THE DISTINCTIVENESS THESIS

The overall structure of Meichenbaum's argument is essentially as follows: Hermeneutics is the study of meanings; hermeneutics and empiricism have been thought to be incompatible only because empiricism has been confused with behaviorism; but now that the cognitive revolution has occurred, cognitive psychologists are engaged in the empirical study of the subject's and patient's meaning system, so empiricism and hermeneutics are no longer incompatible. Meichenbaum implies that the cognitive psychologist utilizes hermeneutics at two levels. First, hermeneutics enters into the content of psychological theory, because psychological theory portrays each person as interpreting the meanings of other people's behavior, so that the subject is practicing a hermeneutics of everyday life. Second, hermeneutics enters into the methodology of psychology because the psychologist must use hermeneutic modes of inquiry to understand the subject's meaning system. So, both the model of human functioning and the methodology used to test that model are hermeneutic in nature.

Meichenbaum's argument begins with a diagnosis of why so many people irrationally (according to him) hold that hermeneutics and empiricism are incompatible. The answer he gives is that there is a widespread tendency to mistakenly equate empiricism with behaviorism. Behaviorism in its pure form denies that meanings have a legitimate role in understanding human behavior, so behaviorism and hermeneutics are indeed incompatible approaches to psychology. But behaviorism is not synonymous with empiricism; it just happens to be the form of empiricism that dominated academic psychology in the United States for several decades. The cognitive revolution has changed all that, and the empirical study of behavior is now focused on the cognitions through which the individual interprets his or her environment. If Meichenbaum's diagnosis of the problem were correct, the shift to the empirical study of cognition should constitute an easy rapprochement between hermeneutics and empiricism.

Meichenbaum's diagnosis is partially correct in that there is a tremendous amount of confusion in the hermeneutic camp about the nature of empirical inquiry. Grünbaum's (1984) recent book documents the hermeneuticist's misconceptions in some detail. Such confusions do often lead hermeneuitcists to ignore the possibility of a sophisticated empirical inquiry into meaning, and to reject the straw man of behaviorism in favor of the hermeneutic approach on the grounds that hermeneutics at least confronts the problem of meaning. The argument for hermeneutics becomes considerably more difficult when the alternative is a cognitivist empiricism that is equally willing to grapple with meaning, albeit in a different way.

But Meichenbaum's diagnosis is also wrong in a critical way. Many hermeneuticists are quite aware of cognitivist attempts to study meaning and yet continue to believe that hermeneutics is incompatible with empiricism. The source of their rejection of empiricism lies not in a mistaken equation of empiricism and behaviorism, but in their account of meaning. Indeed, if there is one doctrine that unites the varied set of thinkers who are traditionally categorized as hermeneuticists, it is that the study of meaning involves basically different processes and constraints than are used in the scientific scrutiny of other objects, irrespective of whether those objects are behaviors or representations.[4] I will call this traditional core doctrine of hermeneutics the *distinctiveness thesis*. The distinctiveness thesis implies that interpretation cannot be carried out as a traditional causal-explanatory inquiry into items in the mind and thus implies the impossibility of succeeding with a cognitivist approach. In order to understand why hermeneuticists reject cognitivism it is necessary to understand the sources of the distinctiveness thesis in hermeneutic theory, which I will consider shortly.

It is the distinctiveness thesis that makes hermeneutics so provocative and controversial. It also poses a challenge to the herme-

neutically-minded empiricist to explain in some detail how a hermeneutic empiricism can be coherently constructed. Meichenbaum
ignores this challenge due to his incorrect diagnosis of the
hermeneuticist's objection to empiricism, and thus fails to consider
the real reasons for the hermeneuticist's belief that hermeneutics and
empiricism are incompatible.

EPISTEMOLOGICAL VERSIONS OF HERMENEUTICS

The grounds hermeneuticists have for maintaining the distinctiveness thesis, that is, for maintaining that the study of meaning must be
methodologically distinct from empiricism, are of two sorts. The first
is that there is something about the interpretative situation that
makes it impossible for interpreters to discover the meanings they are
after if they are limited to empirical methods. This is an epistemological thesis about how we come to know about meanings, and it asserts
that empirical inquiry is not capable of providing the desired knowledge. The second reason is that the nature of meaning is such that a
purely empirical approach of the sort exemplified by cognitivism is
not appropriate. This is an ontological thesis about what meanings
are, in particular, that they are not determinate items in the mind
that can be discovered by empirical methods. I will consider examples of each of these forms of hermeneutics in some detail before
returning to evaluate the remainder of Meichenbaum's argument.

Epistemologically-based hermeneutics may agree with cognitivism
that meanings are determinate mental entities, but it holds that there
is something methodologically special about the process of finding
out these meanings. For example, Dilthey (read one way) and, most
recently, Kohut have held that there is a special procedure, which
Dilthey christened *Verstehen* and Kohut calls "empathy," which is a
kind of immediate understanding of another person's subjective
internal state, and that this method of obtaining knowledge is unique
to the sciences of man and sets them off from the natural sciences.
Empathy is not empirical by traditional standards because it is not
open to public verification. Also, since the ability to empathize with a
given person varies greatly with personality and life experience, it
will obviously matter to the results of the investigation who the
investigator is, in a way that it shouldn't in principle matter in
physics, where almost anyone can read the appropriate meters. The

observer's capacities and range of empathy consequently constrain the data and make the data observer-relative in a way that does not hold true in physics. Nonetheless, this view does not involve any profound form of relativism about meaning because the meanings are really in there and the observer will be either correct or incorrect, the empathy will be accurate or inaccurate. The empathy view is in sharp contrast to the view common among cognitive psychologists that no special method like *Verstehen* or empathy is necessary for working out the correct account of a person's meaning states. Most cognitivists accept that cleverly designed empirical measuring techniques, such as reaction time experiments, should be able to tell you what the hidden meanings are without the necessary intercession of an empathizing observer. However, cognitivists engaged in therapy tend to avoid this epistemological issue by considering empathy itself to be an empirical technique useful for discovering the contents of the patient's mind. I will come back to this last point.

Interpretive methodology—an examination of the internal structure of a given text for evidence of hypothesized further meanings using such criteria as coherence, comprehensiveness, understanding —is another special method that is sometimes thought to be essential to getting at the hidden meanings of a text. Some versions of interpretive methodology accept representationalism about meanings and are purely epistemological in source. The monks who founded hermeneutics in the course of interpreting the Bible might have been in this situation. Suppose that they were interpreting the Bible on the assumptions that (1) the Bible as it has come down to us is literally the word of God; (2) in asserting what he does in the Bible, God intended to say things that go beyond the literal meaning of the text, so that these additional or alternative intended meanings consist of representational states in God's mind; (3) God is not now and never will be available to tell us what these additional meanings are. Clearly, no empirical or even empathic investigation is going to help here to judge God's true intentions. The situation demands an interpretive approach not because the meanings involved are different sorts of entities than the cognitivist believes in, but because the situation is one in which there is no access to the text we really want to read (in this case, the one that exists in God's mind), and we have to reconstruct it as best we can by examining and "filling out" another related text, the Bible, to which we do have access. Interpretation is forced upon us by our epistemological position, which-precludes a direct causal-explanatory inquiry into the hidden representational meanings.

To the degree that Freud's position is hermeneutic, it is also strictly of the epistemological variety. In many ways it is similar to the monk's position. Freud is clearly looking for causal explanations of symptoms, and he believes that the causes of symptoms reside in meanings that are representational states, which he calls "ideas" (Vorstellung), that are in the mind of the patient. However, the crucial meanings are unconscious and not available for empirical scrutiny, so the therapist is forced to use hermeneutic-style reasoning to figure out what the hidden text might be, based on the evidence of the patient's conscious text. However, unlike the monk, who will never get a "yea" or "nay" from God in response to his interpretations, the therapist does eventually get some independent verification. Correct interpretations eventually cause the patient's unconscious meaning to become conscious and to become part of the available text.

I have presented several cases where the belief in an epistemological constraint on the study of meaning leads to the distinctiveness thesis. However, epistemologically-based versions of the distinctiveness thesis are inherently unstable. For one thing, there is always the possibility that new empirical methods will, or already have, overcome the pragmatic difficulties that were claimed to force a nonempirical methodology on the interpreter in the first place. If, for instance, measurements of anxiety during subliminal presentations of conflictual material could indicate which sentences expressed unconscious ideas (Silverman, 1983), then interpretation would no longer be necessary. Secondly, there is a tendency to reconsider some of these methods and to conclude that they are really empirical after all, as when it is argued that empathy can be interpersonally calibrated and used as an empirical method, like a sixth sense.

ONTOLOGICAL VERSIONS OF HERMENEUTICS

This brings me to the second possible ground for the distinctiveness thesis, which is the view that meaning itself has a distinctive nature as an object of study that puts special constraints on methodology. This is an ontological thesis, that meanings cannot be studied in the way the cognitivist does because they are not the kinds of things the cognitivist thinks they are. This is a stronger ground for the distinctiveness thesis and one that is not subject to the sorts of problems noted above in the case of epistemological hermeneutics. For in this case the need for nonempirical interpretative methods is tied to the nature of the meaning and is not merely a pragmatic happenstance due to our inability to empirically acquire knowledge that is potentially there. The most important example of this sort of claim is the phenomenological thesis that most meanings do not consist of representational states or other "items in the head." Phenomenology's rejection of cognitivism is prompted by an ontological consideration, namely, that there is no determinate representational text anywhere, hidden or otherwise, that entirely determines the proper interpretation.

The existential phenomenologists Heidegger (1962) and Merleau-Ponty (1962) argue that most human functioning involves a direct relation of the human being to the world without the mediation of mental representations. Merleau-Ponty claims that there is a meaningfulness and purposefulness in the way the body directs itself in the world, a feature he calls "body-intentionality." At first glance this position seems paradoxical. How can the body even know where it is or what it is doing without mental representations to tell it? It is hard to give a positive account of this idea, although Hubert Dreyfus and I try to say much more in this volume. The difficulty is partly that there is no vocabulary for this new level of explanation, the body-intentional level. It cannot be described in behavioral/mechanical terms, because it does involve meaning and is holistic and highly directed. Nor can it be described in cognitive/ideational terms, because these meanings are not representational. Merleau-Ponty conceives of the relation of body and world to be analogous to the formation of a perceptual Gestalt, where the parts (i.e., the body and the world) organize themselves into a meaningful whole. Not only does nonrepresentational meaning have its locus in the body, but even representational states cannot be understood without setting them in the bodily nonrepresentational context. For example, an image of a hammer is only understood due to a bodily sense of how to use a hammer, which is not part of the network of representations. So, representations are not the source of all directed action (the skill of hammering a nail is not exhausted by any set of representations), and meaning goes beyond the entire representational network. Merleau-Ponty suggests that representational states do often occur and are helpful when there is a breakdown in smooth functioning, leading to a startle reaction or other type of disorganization of the bodily relation to the world and a need to attend explicitly to the situation and thus regain a smooth pattern of functioning. He also notes that when we attend to our past behavior and try to represent to ourselves now how we were functioning then, our current representation of what we were doing tends to get projected into our picture of our past self as a mental representation that existed then, so that we experience a retrospective illusion that we experienced more representations than we actually did.

Whereas Merleau-Ponty emphasizes the bodily background of action and cognition, Heidegger's account of nonrepresentational meanings and directedness emphasizes how the individual's action fits into a background of cultural practices and how its sense derives from that context. The meaning of action can be read from the directedness of the action seen within the pattern of practices that constitute the individual's social milieu. It is these practices, and not any representations in the individual's head, that determine the meanings attributable to the individual. The background of social practices and cultural institutions give specific objects and actions —and even mental representations when they do occur—their meanings, and these influences, although somehow stored in the nervous system, need not be represented in each individual's mind. For example, the very same representational state, such as a certain idea about suffering, might mean saintliness in one culture and masochistic pathology in another, due not to other cognitions but just to the social context in which they occur.

For Merleau-Ponty and Heidegger, directed behavior must be understood in terms of the way it fits in with the background organization of the body and of the culture, and those bodily and cultural meanings are not representations in anyone's mind that are like pictures or sentences with determinate content that can mechanically be read off or gotten exactly and objectively "right." Consequently, their meaning is inherently ambiguous (Merleau-Ponty is known as the philosopher of ambiguity because the relation of body and world, like all gestalts, can be legitimately interpreted in many different ways) and essentially requires interpretation in a way that representations do not. Thus, an interpretation is a creation of a useful way of seeing one's behavior and not an attempt literally to match the structure of an internal representation.

I said earlier that there is no good language as of now for

describing the nonrepresentational background. Thus, phenomenologists often end up describing the background using the
cognitivist language of representational states. The phenomenologist, like the cognitivist, may tell the patient that he or she
has certain assumptions or beliefs or schemas, like the belief that
everyone is superior to him or her, and it might seem that the
phenomenologist is identifying a picture self-statement in the mind
of the patient, as a cognitivist would. But, on the phenomenologist's
account, some of these interpretations do not correspond to any
representational states in the person's mind. Rather, it is at best a way
of talking or theorizing about patterns in a person's behavior, the way
a person's body is organized to relate to the world, the way they fit
into broader social categories, and their patterns of experiences as
molded and constrained by social categories. The phenomenologist is
not just filling in hidden or unnoticed mental representations, he or
she is going beyond the entire representational system and ascribing
to the patient meanings that are not written anywhere in the mind,
but are the background from which the contents of the mind emerge.
The language of representational states is used here to convey
something that is not really representational in nature. This situation
is extremely confusing, but may be the best that the phenomenologist
can do for now.

WHAT CAN COGNITIVISM LEARN FROM HERMENEUTICS?

Having clarified the reasons for the hermeneuticist's rejection of
cognitivism, I now want to consider Meichenbaum's two claims
about the relation of hermeneutics to empirical psychology, focusing
on the phenomenological form of hermeneutics.

First, Meichenbaum suggests that hermeneutics can be incorporated into the psychologist's theory of cognitive activity, because
ordinary people are in fact closet hermeneuticists. There is clearly
some truth in Meichenbaum's claim. To take an extremely simple
example, when I see my neighbor returning from the store with
bread, I might interpret the manifest behavior and infer that the
neighbor desired bread. This interpretation of the meaning behind
the observed action seems to presuppose certain hermeneutic tenets
of coherence, rationality, and so on, in the formulation of the

meaning of behavior. The question then is whether human behavior generally involves such interpretations.

Not just any response to meaning qualifies as an interpretation. An interpretation is an attempt explicitly to represent the meaning of a text.[5] To a cognitivist it is obvious that there must be an explicit interpretation when people respond to meanings in their environment, because the cognitivist holds that all responses to external meanings involve beliefs (i.e., conscious or unconscious mental representations) about the meanings being responded to. However, from the phenomenological perspective behavior is not generally interpretive in this way. The phenomenologist suggests that most everyday behavior is just skillful negotiation of the human and physical environment which is not accomplished via explicit representations, but by a direct response in which the body-world relationship is self-organizing. Representations may be involved, but by no means do they exhaust the means by which persons maintain their directedness. When we live out meaningful situations like hammering a nail, or making love, or even talking, relatively few representations are involved, but direct bodily adjustment to the world is going on continually. It is tempting to call these everyday responses "interpretations" to emphasize that they are one way of many possible ways of responding to the situation, but that is just a metaphor, and theories of interpretation do not capture the nature of such processes. Hermeneutic interpretation is precisely an attempt to give an explicit interpretation of these noninterpretive everyday responses. In sum, the phenomenologist holds that everyday responses do not generally constitute interpretations in the sense the cognitivist requires if human behavior is to be modeled upon interpretive processes.

Meichenbaum's second point is that the empiricist is reconstructing the meanings of the subject, so the empiricist is also doing hermeneutics. The cognitive scientist can then learn from the hermeneuticist methodological lessons about the difficulties in discerning the meanings in a text, such as the role of the investigator's conceptual scheme, the theory-ladenness of the data, the influence of context on meaning, the reactivity of meanings to the setting and to the actions and demeanor of the researcher/therapist, the provisional nature of one's theories and data, and so on.

Again, I think that there is something true, but also something very confusing, in this second point of Meichenbaum's. Certainly the findings of hermeneutic theory can illuminate the interpretive activity of the scientist "reading" the meaning system of the subject or patient. But how can it illuminate it? According to the phenomenologist, the cognitivist is basically wrong about the nature of the meanings he or she is attempting to interpret, and there is an inherent ambiguity to interpretation that no amount of empiricism can resolve. Furthermore, interpretation has to go beyond the representational contents of the mind to encompass the bodily tendencies and stances of the person, as well as the cultural context, in ways that are not represented in the mind of the person being interpreted. If the cognitivist learns these lessons, he or she will no longer be a cognitivist.

But what of Meichenbaum's list of more specific methodological lessons that hermeneutics can teach cognitivists? None of the features on Meichenbaum's list is special to the study of meanings; they apply to any sophisticated scientific investigation. For example, physics has nothing to do with meaning, yet physics can be holistic, the data can be theory-laden, the data can be sensitive to context and reactive to experimenter effects, and so on. The central feature of hermeneutics is, I believe, the distinctiveness thesis and not these other principles. A confusion over this point led to a suggestion at the conference on which this book is based that Adolf Grünbaum, an eminent empirical philosopher who has recently published an extended attack on hermeneutic interpretations of Freud's theory (Grünbaum, 1984), is himself a hermeneuticist. I believe that this idea originated in the fact that Grünbaum is a sophisticated enough empiricist to accept holism, the theory-ladenness of data, and other such contemporary empiricist doctrines. Because all of those doctrines are compatible with a rejection of the distinctiveness thesis, Grünbaum's adherence to those doctrines is not sufficient to show he is a hermeneuticist. I am not saying that scientists cannot learn the lessons mentioned by Meichenbaum from hermeneutics, only that there is nothing unique about hermeneutics in teaching these lessons, and the need for the lessons has nothing uniquely to do with the cognitive revolution or the study of meanings.

I have not attempted to solve the difficult problem of the relationship of hermeneutics and empiricism, and I have not attempted to evaluate whether the cognitivist or phenomenological approach to meaning is preferable. Rather, I have tried to display the complexity and depth of the issue, and to explain why Dr. Meichenbaum's paper, valuable as it is, fails to come to grips with some of the most interesting and difficult aspects of the problem he himself posed.

NOTES

1. There are many related doctrines that might be called cognitivism. I will be focusing on one aspect of cognitivism, *representationalism* (explained in the text), and presenting what I consider to be an ideal or pure version that is held by some of those called cognitivists, but not by all.

2. What I will refer to in this paper as "the phenomenological view" is really one particular version of phenomenology, an integration of the views of Heidegger (1962) and Merleau-Ponty (1962). This branch of phenomenology is sometimes known as "existential phenomenology," and should especially be distinguished from Husserl's transcendental phenomenology, which in some respects comes close to being a cognitivist approach.

3. As I have conceptualized his position, Hirsch is a cognitivist. Yet he is often called a hermeneuticist since he is concerned with the interpretation of literary texts. However, Hirsch's position is actually opposed to the heart of traditional hermeneutic theory, as will become clear below. This is why, for example, Ken Gergen described Hirsch at a recent conference as "an empiricist in hermeneuticist's clothing."

4. See especialy Ricoeur (1974) and Taylor (1985).

5. I follow Heidegger here in distinguishing the sheer living out of meaningful activity (he calls this *Auslegung*) from the specific activity usually called *interpretation* (Heidegger uses the term *Interpretierung*). On Heidegger's account everyday meaningful activity need not involve an explicit formulation of the nature of the meanings being responded to. Such everyday activity is often said to be the individual's interpretation of his cultural background in the metaphorical sense that the individual is fitting into the set of cultural meanings in one way and not others. The theory of interpretation as I understand it, and as it is relevant to the tasks facing the psychologist, is concerned primarily with the process by which meanings are explicitly formulated. This is the activity in which critics, therapists, social scientists, and others engage when they attempt to explicitly formulate the meaning of a text or activity. Although everyday meaning may by nature often be nonrepresentational and nonexplicit, an interpretation of meaning must always be an explicit formulation.

REFERENCES

Baars, B. J. *The cognitive revolution in psychology.* New York: The Guilford Press, 1986.

Glover, E. The therapeutic effect of inexact interpretation. *International Journal of Psycho-Analysis*, 1931, *12*, 397–411.

Grünbaum, A. *The foundations of psychoanalysis: A philosophical critique.* Berkeley: University of California Press, 1984.

Heidegger, M. *Being and time,* trans. J. Macquarrie & E. Robinson, London: SCM Press, 1962.

Hirsch, E. D., Jr. *Validity in interpretation.* New Haven: Yale University Press, 1967.

Hirsch, E. D., Jr. *The aims of interpretation.* Chicago: University of Chicago Press, 1976.

Merleau-Ponty, M. Phenomenology of perception, trans. C. Smith. London: Routledge & Kegan Paul, 1962.

Ricoeur, P. *The conflict of interpretations.* Evanston, Ill.: Northwestern University Press, 1974.

Silverman, L. H. The subliminal psychodynamic activation method: Overview and comprehensive listing of studies. In J. Masling (Ed.), *Empirical studies of psychoanalytic theories* (Vol. 1). Hillsdale, N. J.: Erlbaum, 1983.

Spence, D. P. *Narrative truth and historical truth: Meaning and interpretation in psychoanalysis.* New York: W. W. Norton & Company, 1982.

Taylor, C. Interpretation and the sciences of man. *In Philosophical papers 2,* Cambridge: Cambridge University Press, 1985.

Chapter 6

Are Hidden Motives in Psychoanalysis Reasons but Not Causes of Human Conduct?

ADOLF GRÜNBAUM

Freud, I claim, treated the explanations offered by his theory of repression as a species of causal explanations. Thus, he uses psychic conflict to give a causal explanation of the genesis of neuroses, repressed wishes to explain dream-instigation causally, and repressions of unpleasant thoughts to give a causal account of slip-formation. Moreover, Freud's depiction of the dynamics of his therapy offered the resolution of psychic conflict, coupled with affect-release, to provide a causal explanation of therapeutic gain. In my recent book I question these various causal explanations by arguing that their purported clinical validations were basically flawed (1984). I do not question whether these accounts are, in fact, causal. Rather I contend that, qua causal accounts, their clinical credentials were poor.

But, precisely the causal construal of the motivational explanation of human actions that had been at the foundation of psychoanalysis for over 70 years has been vigorously denied in some versions of the so-called "hermeneutic" reconstruction of psychoanalytic theory. As these anticausal versions would have it, human intentionality, both conscious and unconscious, calls for explanations by means of the agent's reasons. And these elucidations of human behavior, we are told, defy incorporation in the genus of causal explanations. It will be one of my concerns to clarify the notion of a causal antecedent relevant to Freud's causal claims. Suffice it to say for now that in Freud's theory of psychic determinism, a causal antecedent clearly need not be a physical event; instead, a causal antecedent for Freud can be—and indeed often is—a mental event. This elementary point needs to be mentioned only because it has sometimes been over-looked.

The British psychologists A. Gauld and J. Shotter (1977, pp. 12–13) claim that explanation of action by reasons is even logically incompatible with explanation by causes. This thesis of incompatibility is likewise championed by the American psychoanalyst G.S. Klein (1976, p. 13). On Klein's account clinical explanations in psychoanalytic theory and therapy "read [or decipher] intentionality" (pp. 23, 26, 71), and they "state reasons rather than causes" (p. 56) when they unlock so-called meanings (p. 48). Hence we are told that, contrary to Freud, the psychoanalytic enterprise cannot—and should not—emulate either the explanatory or the epistemic standards of the natural sciences. Psychoanalysis, we are now being told, is concerned with meaning and language, thus being a science *sui generis*, a science in a class by itself. And, according to this view, it was misguided on my part to demand that the theory of repression meet the standards of validation to which we hold causal hypotheses in the empirical sciences.

But I must emphasize that, as an alleged reconstruction of psycho-analytic explanations, the generic disallowance of causal explanations of human conduct poses the following key question: Can Freudian theory be reconstructed at all, short of mutilating it beyond recognition, unless one does countenance motivational explanations that are causal? What if the answer is that Freudian explanations are inherently causal? Then the insistence on noncausal explanations of human behavior would boomerang, leaving no scope for a reconstruction of psychoanalysis, only for its repudiation. Yet those who advocate the noncausal construal do not wish to repudiate psychoanalysis. Instead, they see themselves as putting Freud's theory on a suitably humanistic foundation.

I claim that their proposed conception of unconscious motives as noncausal or acausal reasons cannot be accommodated in Freud's explanatory edifice short of dismembering it. Indeed, I shall contend that when we explain human conduct by means of either conscious or unconscious motives, we thereby generate a species of causal explanation. For brevity, let me use an acronym for the opposing thesis that explanatory reasons cannot belong to the genus cause: I shall call the latter doctrine the "reasons versus causes" thesis, or simply "R vs. C." Let me now develop my contention that explanatory reasons for human conduct are a particular species of cause.

EXPLANATORY REASONS AS A SPECIES OF CAUSE

As my Pittsburgh colleague Kurt Baier has pointed out (1958), when we speak of reasons for our behavior, we must be careful to distinguish the role of reasons in the explanation of action from their function in either deliberation before acting, or in justification afterward. As Baier has put it:

> In *explanation*, the word "reasons" ... is ... used to claim that some fact (which is declared to be *the* reason) has actually *moved* the agent to act as he did. ... In explanation, it is indeed true that no factor can be *the* reason why the agent did something or can be *the agent's reason for* doing something, unless the agent actually was moved to act in this way by that factor. ... in deliberation and in justification, however, a fact may be said to be a reason for doing something, although the agent was *not* moved by it to do that thing, or although he knows that he will not be moved by it. (p. 149)

In short, explanatory reasons are motivating reasons, though other sorts of reasons may well not be motivating. These distinctions are important for psychoanalysis, if only because of their role in Ernest Jones's notion of the defense mechanism of rationalization. Rationalization in this sense pertains to an agent's construction of a false rationale for what he or she did. Such situations have the following two features: (1) the desire and belief avowed by the agent as his motives (or "reasons") for what he did are quite different from the actually operative, true motives, and (2) the agent offers the false explanation to justify his conduct to others, and even to himself, being more or less aware that his actual, causally operative motives could not legitimate his behavior. Thus, when one of us rationalizes his or her behavior in Ernest Jones's sense, the avowed reasons are only purportedly rather than actually explanatory. And though masquerading as both explanatory and justificatory, the reasons given by the agent are, at best, only justificatory. Let us be mindful, therefore, that the reasons of concern to us here are of the explanatory sort.

R vs. C develops its case by reference to the so-called "practical syllogism," which has the following form: An action is held to be carried out for a reason, and the reason is that the agent aims to achieve a goal, G, and believes that the action will issue in the attainment of G. For example, assume I wish to quench my thirst. Suppose also I believe that if I walk down the hall, I'll find a water fountain. Hence I walk down the hall to the fountain. Pointing to the stated reason for the action, the thesis R vs. C denies that an agent's state of having a reason for action, in the explanatory sense, can belong to a species of the genus "cause."

As mentioned initially the purported hermeneutic reconstruction of psychoanalytic explanations is offered within the framework of the R vs. C thesis. But I claim that this supposed noncausal version of psychoanalysis is predicated on a grievous mistake. To state the error, let us consider the relation of causal relevance between an antecedent X and an outcome Y. Those who regard a noncausal reconstruction of Freudian explanations to be feasible, and indeed illuminating or even vital, have insisted that only a physical antecedent X can be causally relevant to an outcome Y. But, I submit, they have unfortunately overlooked that the causal relevance of an antecedent state X to an occurrence Y does not at all require the physicality of X. Instead, I maintain, causal relevance is a matter of whether X makes a difference to the occurrence of Y in the sense of affecting the incidence of Y.

But let me mention at once a possible misunderstanding of the relation of causal relevance. In order to do so, consider a universe of discourse to whose members the properties X and Y are meaningfully applicable. For example, being paranoid, and being homosexual are attributable to living persons, but not to chairs or to radios. Since breathing, for example, is a necessary condition for being a living person, it is also necessary for being a paranoid living human. But, for the same reason, breathing is a necessary condition for being a nonparanoid living person. Hence, within the class of living persons, breathing does not make a difference to being paranoid or affect the incidence of paranoia, although it is a necessary condition for being paranoid. For brevity we can say that breathing is not causally relevant to being paranoid as such. Using the formulation given by Wesley Salmon (1984, p. 128), we can say that breathing does not even partition the reference class of human beings, let alone such that the probability of being paranoid is affected by being someone who breathes.

By contrast, within the framework of Freud's theory of paranoia, having strong repressed homosexual desires is indeed causally relevant to being paranoid as follows: The presence of strong homosexual repressions increases the probability of being paranoid, and indeed only those who harbor such repressions become paranoiacs. In short, being a repressed homosexual makes a difference to becoming paranoid or affects the incidence of paranoia.

Clearly, this brief caveat against deeming any and every necessary condition for Y to be causally relevant to it does not pretend to offer general criteria for causal relevance. It does claim, however, to have said enough to make it evident that a mental or psychophysical antecedent X can make a difference or affect the incidence of some event or other, no less than a physical antecedent can do so. For example, gastroenterologists sometimes say to patients who suffer from stomach ulcers: It does not matter what you eat; it is what eats you that matters. This sobering declaration asserts the causal relevance of psychic aggravation to the persistence or even the genesis of stomach ulcers. Why, I ask, is it not obvious to students of psychoanalysis that the ontological status of an event (i.e., whether it be physical or mental) is irrelevant to its functioning as a cause?

This irrelevance should be a banality, I claim, for the following reasons: If, for example, a repression R is indeed the psychic pathogen of a neurosis N, then the presence of R is causally relevant to the incidence of N, precisely because R does make a difference to becoming afflicted by N. And R is held to affect the incidence of N no less than a chemical carcinogen affects the somatic incidence of cancer, or as certain psychic dispositions are held to affect psychosomatically the incidence of ulcerative colitis.

Hence, those who operate under the myth that a cause must be a physical agency of one sort or another run afoul of a simple fact: When the motives of agents qualify as causes of their actions and when, say, solar magnetic storms produce poor radio reception, the causal relevance derives, in both cases, from the same key fact. In either case the antecedent makes a difference to the corresponding outcome or affects the incidence of the pertinent outcome.

Plainly, if an agent is actually moved to do A by having a certain reason or motive M—so that his having the motive M explains his action A—then this very presence of M made a difference to his having done A. But, if so, then the agent's having M qualifies as having been causally relevant to what he did.

To illustrate the relation of causal relevance, first take a deliberately pedestrian example of conscious action. Consider a person who desires to read a book that she believes to be normally available at some library. If that combination of desire and belief actually prompts her to go there to borrow the book, then her reason (motive) M for doing so qualifies as explanatory just because M makes a difference to going. When the agent neither needs a book, nor has any other business at the library, i.e., when she has no motive (reason) for going there then she indeed refrains from going. Plainly, by affecting the incidence of visits to a library, having a reason that prompts one to go there qualifies as causally relevant to making such visits. *Mutatis mutandis*, the same conclusions apply to more sophisticated instances of acting from reasons, e.g., in the case of an agent who, motivated by family bonds, deliberately gives nepotistic preference to a relative in authorizing a promotion.

Hence, it emerges that the analysis I have offered does vindicate the view expressed by the psychologist Robert Holt (1981), who wrote: "For years, I have operated on the assumption that a [motivating] reason is one kind of cause, a *psychological* cause, and that various types of causes can be handled in the same study without confusion" (p. 135). And in a comprehensive chapter, "Recent Work on the Free-Will Problem," the Norwegian philosopher Harald Ofstad (1983) points out that even when the term *reason* is not used to label a causal factor, "the statement that an action was done for a reason does not imply that it was not caused" (p. 49).

No wonder, therefore, that in the context of the psychoanalytic clinical theory of psychopathology, the ontological identity of unconscious motives as mental rather than physical phenomena hardly robs them of their hypothesized causal role. Indeed, as early as 1897, this Freudian theory of repression emphatically abjured an exclusively physicalistic construal of the attribute of causal relevance. Thus, within the psychic world depicted by Freud, it is simply wrongheaded to maintain that, in virtue of being mental, repressed desires cannot function as a motivational cause. As well aver the inanity that because an explosion involves natural gas, this eruption cannot qualify as a cause of the collapse of a building and of the deaths of its occupants.

Quite properly, therefore, Freud deemed explanatory reasons to be a species of motive, and motives—whether conscious or unconscious—in turn, a species of the genus of cause. Moreover, he allowed that some motives might not even be mental. Thus, he characterizes the psychoanalyst's quest for "sufficient motives" as a refined implementation of our "innate craving for causality" (Freud, 1910, p. 38). Indeed, sometimes he speaks interchangeably of motives and causes. For example, he hypothesized an obsessive patient's "flight into [psychological] illness," such that the patient's mental anticipation of being incapacitated by the illness was actually "the *cause* or *motive* of falling ill [psychologically]" (Freud, 1909, p. 199) italics in original; in the German original *Gesammelte Werke* [Freud, 1941, 7, p. 420], the wording is "die Ursache, das Motiv des Krankenwerdens"). More generally, as Robert Shope (1973) has carefully documented exegetically, "Freud does not maintain that dreams, errors, or symptoms are motivated or express motives in an everyday sense" (p. 291). Instead, Shope (1973, pp. 290–292; in press, sec. 2) points out that Freud employs "motive" in a technical sense akin to the etymological one. In his parlance a motive is an exciting, instigating cause that moves us to action. Nevertheless, Freud does not overlook the fact that mental causes of human behavior—conscious or repressed —have properties over and above those of purely generic causes! But particular sorts of physical causes also have properties over and above belonging to the genus "cause."

In sum Shope (1973) gives several citations to support the following conclusions:

> The sense which Freud gives to the expression "motive for" is indicated by his willingness to speak of the "motive force" behind the dream as the "dream-instigator." ... He is concerned ... with the sense in which the motor supplies the motive power and force behind the motion. Freud thus finds it natural to speak of wishes as the only things which can "set the apparatus in motion" or "at work" (Freud, 1900, p. 567). This reference to forces as exciting causes is built into the very meaning of the term "motive" as Freud uses it. (p. 292)

It is therefore unavailing for Stephen Toulmin (1954) to invoke none other than the psychoanalytic dream theory as support for the following ill-founded pseudo-antithesis: "The kernel of Freud's discovery is the introduction of a technique in which the psychotherapist begins by studying the *motives for*, rather than the *cause* of neurotic behaviour" (p. 138; italics in original). To prepare the ground for this dubious exegesis, Toulmin had offered the following purportedly paradigmatic case of causal explanation of human conduct: A person acts in a certain way "because he was given an injection of cocaine twenty minutes ago" by someone else (p. 134). Toulmin contrasts this supposed model of explaining action causally with instances in which wanting to go home is offered as the reason for some behavior. The issue posed was whether motivational explanations in psychoanalysis qualify as a species of causal explanations. And the intended moral of Toulmin's comparison is that no motivational explanation of an action can qualify as being causal.

But, qua paradigm of a causal explanation of conduct, Toulmin's example of the cocaine injection totally begs the question at issue in the present context by assuming that all causes must be physical. For in this illustration, the explanatory physical injection of cocaine automatically excludes, at the outset, the agent's desires and beliefs, be they conscious or unconscious. Evidently, Toulmin has illicitly traded on some of the common nontechnical uses of the terms "reason," "motive," and "cause" in ordinary discourse about human behavior.

By means of such question-begging reliance on the parlance of daily life, he believes to have established that "the [therapeutic] success of psychoanalysis ... should reemphasize the importance of 'reasons for action' as opposed to causes of action" (p. 139). And in this way he believes to have vindicated his initial contention that "troubles arise from thinking of psycho-analysis too much on the analogy of the natural sciences" (p. 134). Alas, Toulmin's argument provides yet another illustration of the obfuscating effects of the ordinary language approach to philosophical understanding, an approach whose demise from sheer sterility and boredom occurred none too soon on both sides of the Atlantic. In addition, Toulmin avowedly rested his case not only on his cocaine injection example, but also on the alleged success of psychoanalytic treatment outcome. But at the time he wrote, there was no evidence at all that psychoanalytic treatment outcome exceeds the gains from spontaneous remission, or the gains from telling one's troubles to one's favorite bartender or clergyman. And even today there is hardly any cogent evidence that professional psychoanalytic therapy does better than placebo treatments or than nonprofessional therapies. There is essentially no such evidence, if only because the requisite comparative studies have yet to be carried out.

The proponents of the R vs. C doctrine include not only the aforementioned writers, but also the American psychoanalyst Roy Schafer, who was the Sigmund Freud Professor at the University of London some years ago. These writers have secured spurious plausibility for their thesis of acausality by ignoring that—in psychology, no less than in physics and somatic medicine—causal relevance is a less demanding, logically weaker relation than either being causally sufficient or being causally necessary.

In medicine, for example, there is evidence that heavy tobacco smoking is indeed causally relevant to cardiovascular disease and to lung cancer. But it is a commonplace that such smoking is neither causally necessary nor causally sufficient for acquiring these illnesses. For example, radon gas may contribute to the development of lung cancer by nonsmokers. And I know of smokers who console themselves with the fact that the comedian George Burns still chain-smokes at age 90 or so. When asked what his doctor has to say about that, he replied: "Oh, my doctor, he is dead." Familiar as such examples of mere causal relevance are, the aforementioned authors try to make philosophical capital out of taking no cognizance of the properties of causal relevance as such.

In this vein Schafer claims falsely that every cause is even both necessary and sufficient for the occurrence of the outcome to which it is causally relevant. In an unavailing attempt to impugn the causal role of motives in psychoanalysis, he gives examples of psychoanalytic explanations in which the adduced motives—which he calls "reasons"—neither assure the occurrence of the syndrome they serve to explain, nor are required for its occurrence. Having used a false premise of causal universality, he is then able to conclude that so-called unconscious reasons cannot belong to the genus of cause. Hence as Schafer (1976) would have it, "We rely on reasons—reasons that ... make actions comprehensible. We do not rely on causes—causes that are the conditions regularly antecedent to the actions in question. Causes are the conditions in the absence of which the specific action would not be performed, and in the presence of which it must be performed" (pp. 204–205).

But as Freud explained (1896), the tubercle bacillus is not disqualified from being the specific cause of tuberculosis merely because many carriers of this bacillus do not develop this disease. And Freud made just this point in order to disabuse people of the notion that infantile seduction episodes cannot be the specific causes of adult hysteria, merely because many people have had such childhood experiences without becoming hysterics.

Moreover, psychoanalytic theory features the so-called "principle of causal over-determination" that Breuer and Freud introduced in their *Studies on Hysteria* (Freud, 1895a, b; 1896; 1905). Freud also

called this principle much more accurately, and much less misleadingly, *"the principle of the complication of causes"* (Freud, 1901, pp.
60–61; italics in original). According to this causal precept, clinical
phenomena are normally attributable to a conjunction and/or temporal succession of causes, each of which is only a partial cause,
precisely because—at best—these causally relevant factors are only
jointly, rather than singly, causally sufficient for the production of
the given clinical phenomenon. I submit that Schafer's account, as
well as Gauld's and Shotter's, are simply oblivious of this fundamental principle of causal explanation in the psychoanalytic clinical
theory. One of their key grounds for claiming that a motive cannot
qualify as a cause of behavior, but only as a "reason," is that a motive
is typically not sufficient for the occurrence of the ensuing action.
But a motive can be causally relevant without being causally sufficient, as we saw.

More generally, one must wonder—within their scheme of
causality—in what current branches of the natural sciences their
notion of cause, as both necessary and sufficient for the effect, does
have a bona fide use. No such concept of causality is found in
statistical physics, e.g., in the theory of radioactive decay, or in
somatic medicine. In the former branch of the natural sciences, the
causally relevant antecedents featured in its explanations are hardly
both sufficient and necessary for the occurrences they explain, as
demanded by the stated hermeneutic depiction of causality. Indeed,
the antecedents are not even sufficient, as is stressed in elementary
textbooks of physics. In medicine syphilis is causally necessary for
paresis but hardly sufficient, since only a minority of syphilitics
become victims of paresis. Seemingly unaware that his largely quixot-
ic requirements for causality go mostly unfulfilled in the theories and
applications of the contemporary natural sciences, Schafer invokes
these requirements to draw the ill-founded conclusion that Freudian
theory is barred from using the concept of causality "in any rigorous
and untrivial sense" (1976, p. 205).

Apparently, like so many others, Schafer has relied on a mythologi-
cal conception of the natural sciences to erect a pseudo-contrast
between them and psychoanalysis. This sort of myth-making is not
confined to hermeneutic psychologists. Thus, there are philosophers
who make similarly sweeping, global claims about the differences
between the natural and the human sciences. For example, as Ricoeur
(1970, p. 365) would have it, whereas there are observational facts to
be explained in the natural sciences, there are, strictly speaking, no

such facts in psychoanalysis. And his reason for this initial dichotomy is that "the analyst does not observe, he interprets." But, to the serious detriment of his hermeneutic case, he overlooks that insofar as the interpretative activity of an observer militates against the existence of "data"—i.e., of facts to be explained—the received natural sciences are on the same epistemic footing as the interpretative clinical inferences drawn by analysts.

Let us return to the practical syllogism with a view to determining its relevance, if any, to psychoanalytic explanations. I shall argue that—at least more often than not, if not typically—the practical syllogism fails to apply in classical, paradigmatic psychoanalytic explanations. As we recall this sort of syllogism takes the following form: An action A is held to be carried out, because the agent aims to achieve a goal G, and believes that A will issue in the attainment of G. In short, a specified desire-cum-belief set is the "reason" for doing A. But, as I have argued, insofar as reasons for conduct are, in fact, thus explanatory (rather than, say, only justificatory), they are causally relevant to that conduct by making a difference to its occurrence. And this conclusion itself is already enough to gainsay the R vs. C thesis. As a corollary we see that the practical syllogism as such can be coherently applied, at least to consciously motivated action or behavior, by those who deem motives to be a species of cause (e.g., Moore, 1983), no less than by proponents of the R vs. C thesis.

But, to the additional serious detriment of applying the R vs. C thesis in psychoanalysis, I maintain that, in the context of psychoanalytic explanation, this thesis of acausality comes to grief even further. It founders also, because, as will now be seen, very important classes of Freudian explanations simply defy assimilation to the practical syllogism. And yet just that syllogism is the explanatory paradigm crucial to the claim that repressed motives qualify as reasons for behavior and that psychoanalytic understanding of human conduct lends support to the R vs. C doctrine.

Some examples will now tellingly illustrate just how Freud's explanatory reliance on unconscious motives violated the practical syllogism by not conforming to it from the outset.

According to the psychoanalytic etiology of paranoia, repressed homosexual love is—in both males and females—causally necessary for having paranoid delusions (Freud, 1915). This very postulate itself is, of course, incompatible with the R vs. C claim that neither unconscious nor conscious motives can be a species of cause. But I am now concerned to show that the explanatory role of desires in Freud's etiology of paranoia is refractory to the practical syllogism, a paradigm that is typically presupposed by the R vs. C thesis.

Freud postulates a kind of causal microstructure as mediating between the hypothesized repressed homosexuality and the engendered paranoid delusions (Freud, 1911). The account he gives is claimed to apply to both male homosexuality and lesbianism, although male pronouns are used to state it. Freud assumes that the mediating causal dynamic operates essentially as follows: Given the social taboo on homosexuality, the failure to repress homosexual impulses may well issue in feelings of severe anxiety and guilt. This anxiety could then be eliminated by converting the love emotion "I love him" into its opposite "I hate him," a type of transformation that Freud labeled "reaction formation." Thus, the pattern of reaction-formation here is that once a dangerous impulse has been largely repressed, it surfaces in the guise of a far more acceptable contrary feeling, a conversion that therefore serves as a defense against the anxiety associated with the underlying dangerous impulse.

When the defense of reaction-formation proves insufficient to alleviate the anxiety, however, the afflicted party may resort to the further defensive maneuver of "projection," in which "I hate him" is converted into "He hates me." This final stage of the employment of defenses is then the full-blown paranoia. Thus, this rather epigrammatic formulation depicts reaction-formation and projection as the unconscious defense mechanisms that are actuated by homosexual desires, which are the postulated specific pathogen of paranoia. Now, the question is whether Freud's explanation of paranoid behavior conforms to the practical syllogism's desire-cum-belief set. In particular, we must ask: In the psychoanalytic explanation of a paranoiac's delusional conduct, can the afflicted agent be warrantedly held to have "reasons" for his behavior such that he unconsciously believes that behavior to be a means of attaining the fulfillment of his homosexual longings? Can the paranoiac be warrantedly said to have unconsciously intended his delusional persecutory thoughts and comportment to accomplish his repressed erotic objectives?

As Robert Shope has documented extensively, Freud does not regard psychopathological symptoms, slips (parapraxes), and manifest dream contents as forms of intentional actions. Yet, quite compatibly, he did hypothesize the causes of these phenomena to be repressed intentions in the rudimentary sense of being unconscious strivings. Moreover, as Shope shows further, "It is extremely difficult, in fact, to find an analyst who reports that a patient recalls not just the presence of an unconscious wish or intention but an [unconscious] intentional or voluntary connection it had with a symptom or error [slip]!" (1973, pp. 292–293, n. 11).

Thus, to my knowledge psychoanalytic practice has furnished no empirical evidence that paranoiacs unconsciously believe their delusional conduct to be a means toward the realization of their repressed erotic objectives. Finally, Shope (1973, p. 290, n. 9) calls attention to the fact that, whereas Freud's German original speaks of the intention in whose service ("in deren Dienst") an obsessive woman behaved compulsively, the Standard Edition renders this in English as "the intention with which she was performing the obsessional action" (Freud, 1917, p. 277). In this way the English rendition obscures the fact that Freud "usually refuses to say that the person intended the act to accomplish the suppressed or repressed intention or desire," though he claims, of course, that the intention produces the action.

Thus, consider Freud's report of the memory-slip of forgetting the Latin word *aliquis*, which he attributed to the subject's repressed pregnancy fear (Freud, 1901). This well-known case, I submit, fails to conform to the practical syllogism. Notably, there is not a shred of evidence that the male subject underwent his memory lapse in the unconscious belief—however foolish—of thereby realizing his desire that his paramour not be pregnant. Therefore, the proponent of the R vs. C thesis has no basis for claiming that the subject unconsciously intended his own mnemonic failure as a means of achieving the much desired freedom from pregnancy, even if his desire itself is deemed to qualify as an "intention."

As Morris Eagle (1980, p. 368–369) has stressed, there is a major gap between a mere wish and a plan to realize it. But without a plan the agent's conduct cannot be held to have been envisaged by him as a means to the fulfillment of his wishes. Nor, as Eagle points out further (p. 371), can the stated gap be bridged by Roy Schafer's purely verbal device of calling such conduct "disclaimed actions." Such semantic baptism does nothing toward assimilating Freud's motivational explanations to those in which the motives qualify as "reasons for action" in the sense of the practical syllogism. In short, there was no unconsciously planned action, based on a belief in a means-ends connection. And without it Freud's example cannot be held to instantiate the practical syllogism.

Robert Shope (1973, p. 301) helpfully calls attention to other illustrations of the poignant absence of evidence for the operation of an unconscious belief in a means-ends connection. Significantly, Freud (1895a) disavows any role of intended, voluntary action in the operation of typical defense mechanisms, such as the process of hysterical conversion of psychic distress into straightforward physical pain. The agent in Freud's world is unconsciously intent upon a certain instinctual goal. But as for the behavior that is causally engendered by this yearning, the agent is hardly intent on this ensuing behavior qua action toward his goal.

There are even actions with conscious motives whose explanation fails to conform to the practical syllogism. Michael Moore (1980, 1983) has given an illuminating example to make this point: "Suppose X is a prisoner who wants very much to get out of prison. He rattles the bars of his cell 'because he wants out.' His rattling the cage is an action he performs, and his desire causes it; yet he doesn't rattle the bar *in order* to get out because he does not believe for an instant that he can shake loose the bars" (1980, p. 497; 1983, p. 35). Thus, X expresses his desire for freedom by rattling the cell bars. But—given X's lack of the pertinent belief—this desire does not qualify as his reason for his action in the sense of the practical syllogism, although a secondary desire-to-express the desire for freedom may so qualify.

Let me state the upshot of my account of psychoanalytic explanations *vis-à-vis* the practical syllogism. Consciously motivated, premeditated action A is, of course, the centerpiece of the practical syllogism. The premises of that syllogism feature not only the agent's goal G, but also his or her belief that A is conducive to the realization of G. As we saw, however, in at least some of the paradigm cases of psychoanalytically-explained conduct C, the explanatory motives do not include an unconscious belief that C is a means toward the realization of the repressed aim. Hence, at least in these cardinal cases, behavior that is held to be engendered by repressed desires does not conform to the practical syllogism. And therefore such behavior fails to be a species of intended actions, although the impulse that instigates it may be said to be a repressed intention.

In short, when one says that intentionality is explanatory in psychoanalysis, the legitimacy of this location is often only Pickwickian, or metaphorical. By the same token, the hermeneutic advocate of the reasons vs. causes thesis can derive little support, if any, from using the ambiguous, much-abused term "meaning" here as a synonym for "intentionality." And, incidentally, this lesson illustrates once again the abject poverty of ordinary language philosophy as an avenue to the conceptual elucidation of theories, whose hallmark is their transcendence of common sense! We need such theories because common sense, at best, does not go far enough and, at worst, is just primitive.

In a last ditch effort, the champion of R vs. C might try to fall back on the thesis that the connection between motivating reasons and actions is logically necessary rather than logically contingent, regardless of whether the motives are conscious or repressed. To say that a connection is logically necessary in this context is to say that its negation is self-contradictory or logically incoherent. A logically necessary connection between motives and action would not be causal, as David Hume taught the world. But this desperate fallback will not do at all. Surely, it is logically contingent, I submit, rather than logically necessary that a psychological motive does make a difference to the actual overt behavioral occurrence of an action. And it is not only conceivable, but may actually happen that a paralytic wills an action but cannot perform it. Thus, even when an action is consciously intended, the willing of its performance hardly renders it logically necessary that its successful execution will actually materialize. Paraplegics, victims of strokes or of Parkinson's disease, and various sorts of other paralytics appreciate this state of affairs all too well. No matter how strong their desire or motive to perform a certain action or movement to achieve a goal, they often or even always fail. Yet this commonplace seems to have been lost on those exponents of the R vs. C thesis who claim that reasons for actions make their execution logically necessary.

In sum, various sorts of paralysis clearly belie the purported logically necessary connection between conscious motives and their implementation by actions. And the aborting of someone's consciously intended actions by other agents attests that that person's volition to perform them hardly assures their successful execution in point of fact. *A fortiori* such execution is clearly not logically necessary.

By the same token, if the connection between repressed motives and the ensuing behavior were logically necessary, it would indeed gainsay the causal role of repressed motives to the credit of the R vs. C thesis. But, as I shall now show, the claim that psychoanalytically explained conduct is logically necessitated by its unconscious motives is demonstrably wrong.

Consider our earlier example of the micro- and macrostructure of Freud's etiology of paranoia. Is it not clear that the hypothesized transformation of reaction formation—in which "I love him" is supplanted by "I hate him"—is no less logically contingent than, say, Newton's inverse square law of gravitation? Since Freud did not even claim universality for such reaction formation on the part of the homosexually repressed, how could that transformation of affect be deemed logically necessary? The universality he did claim was the converse one that every paranoiac had undergone reaction formation to his or her repressed motives. Equally plainly, the further transformation of projection, in which "I hate him" is superseded by "He hates me," is logically contingent. *A fortiori*, it would be absurd to claim that the contingently mediated connection between the repressed homosexuality and the paranoiac's delusional behavior is logically necessary: Evidently, that linkage is fully as logically contingent as the fact that there is conservation of linear momentum, a connection exemplified by the motions of two colliding billiard balls. The same conclusion is reached upon considering further cases, such as other examples of Freudian reaction formation like the following: "An exaggerated sympathy can be a defense against an impulse to cruelty" (Wallerstein, 1976, p. 220). Hence, the hermeneutic advocate of the R vs. C thesis cannot salvage his doctrine by claiming a logically necessary connection between Freudian motives and the conduct they are supposed to explain.

Let me now recapitulate the substance of my argument thus far. I posed the question whether the latent motives postulated in psychoanalysis are reasons but not causes of human conduct. It has emerged that psychoanalysts and philosophers who claimed that Freudian explanations feature reasons rather than causes drew a pseudo-contrast. In cardinal cases the explanatory repressions turned out not to qualify as motivating reasons in the sense of the practical syllogism. There can therefore be no question of these repressions being such reasons as opposed to causes. And in any case these latent contents hardly forfeit their causal relevance in virtue of being unconscious desires. Indeed, their explanatory role in psychoanalysis derives from their causal relevance. Thus, there was nothing illicitly physicalistic or otherwise alien in Freud's thesis that unconscious desires are a species of the genus "cause." Nor did such speciation impoverish these desires, because he fully allowed them to possess endlessly fascinating properties of their own, over and above those of mere generic causes.

The now demonstrated failure of the R vs. C thesis makes it unavailable as a prop for the hermeneutic conception of psychoanalysis, which is offered as an emphatic alternative to Freud's own scientific aspirations for his enterprise.

CODA ON INTENTIONALITY

Do the phenomena of full-blown intentionality spell a dichotomous explanatory moral that casts doubt on the very feasibility of causal explanations of human desires or beliefs?

Let us take a simple belief such as the belief that "All men are mortal." Clearly, the statement A "All men are mortal" is logically equivalent to its contrapositive C "All non-mortal entities are non-men." Yet, notoriously, a person who does believe A may fail to believe C, may not know whether he or she believes C, or may even disbelieve C.

Hence, despite the logical equivalence of A and C, it does not follow from "Person X believes 'All men are mortal'" that "Person X believes 'All non-mortal entities are non-men.'" This nondeducibility illustrates the so-called logical "intensionality" characteristic of statements pertaining to the phenomena of human intentionality.

Alas, I once had a beginning student in introductory logic who failed to appreciate the logical equivalence of the above statements A and C even after its demonstration. Thus, when assenting to A he did not know whether to believe C. Indeed, negation and the complements of sets posed such inferential hurdles for him that he asked me despairingly to "keep everything positive."

Does the stated logical intensionality lend support to the acausal generation of, say, beliefs (e.g., rationalizations in Ernest Jones's sense) that—according to classical psychoanalytic theory—are presumed to have been engendered by unconscious motives? I submit that no cogent reasons have been given by hermeneuts or others to doubt the operation of a perhaps neurological cause that would explain (1) the cognitive inability of our hapless student to appreciate the logical equivalence of a statement to its contrapositive, a deficiency that makes for a corresponding gap in his beliefs, and (2) the ability of some of the rest of us to apprehend the pertinent logical equivalence and to give the ensuing creedal assent. A like assessment seems to be applicable to those beliefs that may be the object of psychoanalytic explanation.

Do the restrictions on deducibility governing intensional contexts spell a methodologically dichotomous moral for the human sciences vis-à-vis the physical ones? Those who believe that the quantum theory is best represented in a nonstandard logic rightly do not conclude that quantum physics requires an epistemology differing *toto genere* from that of the received natural sciences. Why then should the need for the elaboration of intensional logics have such dichotomous import?

True enough, human beings—unlike some purely physical entities—are themselves interpretative agents, whose conduct is the object of theoretical interpretation by psychologists, anthropologists, and others. But the crucial question is what investigative and validational lesson is to be learned from this important difference in the constitution of the object of interpretative study and from intensionality. I have argued that, at least in the context of psychoanalysis, the moral drawn by the hermeneuts is ill-founded.

NOTE

This chapter draws on material in section 4 of the lengthy Introduction of my *The Foundations of Psychoanalysis: A Philosophical Critique*, University of California Press, 1984.

REFERENCES

Baier, K. *The moral point of view.* Ithaca, N. Y.: Cornell University Press, 1958.

Eagle, M. A critical examination of motivational explanation in psychoanalysis. *Psychoanalysis and Contemporary Thought*, 1980, 3, 329–380. This article was reprinted from *Mind and medicine: Explanation and evaluation in psychiatry and the biomedical sciences*, edited by L. Laudan, Pittsburgh Series in the Philosophy and History of Science, Vol. 8. Berkeley, Los Angeles, London: University of California Press, 1983.

Freud, S. Studies on Hysteria. S.E., 1895, Vol. 2.(a)

Freud, S. A reply to criticisms of my paper on anxiety neurosis. S.E., 1895, Vol. 3.(b)

Freud, S. The aetiology of hysteria. S.E., 1896, Vol. 3.

Freud, S. The interpretation of dreams. S.E., 1900, Vol. 4–5.

Freud, S. The psychopathology of everyday life. S.E., 1901, Vol. 6.

Freud, S. Fragment of an analysis of a case of hysteria. S.E., 1905, Vol. 7.

Freud, S. Notes upon a case of obsessional neurosis. S.E., 1909, Vol. 10.

Freud, S. Five lectures on psycho-analysis. S.E., 1910, Vol. 11.

Freud, S. Psycho-analytic notes on an autobiographical account of a case of paranoia. S.E., 1911, Vol. 12.

Freud, S. A case of paranoia running counter to the psycho-analytic theory of the disease. S.E., 1915, Vol. 14.

Freud, S. Introductory lectures on psycho-analysis. S.E., 1917, Vol. 16.

Freud, S. *Gesammelte Werke*. London: Imago, 1941.

Gauld, A., & Shotter, J. *Human action and psychological investigation*. London: Routledge & Kegan Paul, 1977.

Grünbaum, A. *The foundations of psychoanalysis: A philosophical critique*. Berkeley, Los Angeles, London: University of California Press, 1984.

Holt, R. C. The death and transfiguration of metapsychology. *International Review of Psycho-Analysis*, 1981, 8, 129–143.

Klein, G. S. *Psychoanalytic theory*. New York: International Universities Press, 1976.

Moore, M. M. The nature of psychoanalytic explanation. *Psychoanalysis and Contemporary Thought*, 1980, 3, 459–543.

Moore, M. M. *The nature of psychoanalytic explanation*. In L. Lauden (Ed.), *Mind and medicine: Explanation and evaluation in psychiatry and the biomedical sciences* (Vol. 8). Pittsburgh Series in the Philosophy and History of Science. Berkeley, Los Angeles, London: University of California Press, 1983.

Ofstad, H. Recent work on the free-will problem. In K. G. Luccy & T. R. Machan (Eds.), *Recent work in philosophy*. Totowa, N. J.: Rowman & Allanheld, 1983.

Ricoeur, P. *Freud and philosophy*. New Haven: Yale University Press, 1970.

Salmon, W. *Scientific explanation and the causal structure of the world*. Princeton: Princeton University Press, 1984.

Schafer, R. *A new language for psychoanalysis*. New Haven: Yale University Press, 1976.

Shope, R. K. Freud's concepts of meaning. *Psychoanalysis and Contemporary Science*, 1973, 2, 276–303.

Shope, R. K. The significance of Freud for modern philosophy of mind. In *Contemporary philosophy*, Vol. 4, of G. Floistad (Ed.), *Philosophy of mind*. Boston: Nijhoff, in press.

Toulmin, S. The logical status of psycho-analysis. In M. MacDonald (Ed.), *Philosophy and analysis*. New York: Philosophical Library, 1954.

Wallerstein, R.S. Psychoanalysis as a science: Its present status and its future tasks. In M. M. Gill & P. S. Holzman (Eds.), *Psychology versus metapsychology: Psychoanalytic essays in memory of George S. Klein*. New York: International Universities Press, 1976. (This volume is Monograph 36 of *Psychological Issues*, vol. 9, no. 4.)

A Plea for Differences:
Commentary on Adolf Grünbaum

RICHARD J. BERNSTEIN

Adolf Grünbaum is a master of what might be called the "adversarial" or "confrontational" mode of argumentation. This is a style of argumentation that has been dominant in contemporary Anglo-American philosophy, and Grünbaum is one of its most skillful practitioners. According to this style, when one is confronted with a position or thesis that one takes to be mistaken or confused, one relentlessly "goes after it." The "Other" is viewed as an opponent. And the aim is to locate specifically what is wrong in the opponent's position, to expose its weaknesses. The practice of this style of argumentation requires attention to details, to working through specific claims and arguments in order to show up their falsity, and sometimes to expose their triviality. There are great advantages to this style of argumentation: It is never satisfied with vague claims, it helps to pinpoint issues in dispute, and it exposes difficulties that require serious answers. But there are also dangers. For in being primarily concerned with exposing weaknesses, with showing the absurdities in what is taken to be mistaken, we can be blind to what the Other is saying, and to the "truth" that may be implicit in what he or she is contributing to the discussion.

The adversarial confrontational style can be contrasted with a model of dialogical encounter. Here one begins with the assumption that the Other has something to say to us and to contribute to our understanding. The initial task is to see the Other's position in its strongest possible light. Conflict is just as important in dialogical encounters. But we risk our own prejudgments. We are committed to the ideal that we may genuinely learn from each other, that there may be, as Gadamer phrases it, a "fusion of horizons." This is a play, a to-and-fro movement in a genuine dialogue, a seeking for a common ground in which we can understand our differences. This style of argumentation also has its distinctive virtues and dangers. In our attempt to listen to the Other and to seek common ground, we may inadvertently obscure serious differences and conflicts. We need both styles of argumentation; each can serve as a corrective to the exclusive use of one of these styles of argumentation. In seeking to understand and appreciate the contributions of hermeneutics to our understanding of psychoanalytic discourse, we need to counterbalance adversarial argumentation with dialogical encounter.

From this perspective let me turn directly to Grünbaum's paper. I agree with almost everything he says in this paper. It is what Grünbaum does not say—and only barely suggests—that troubles me. Grünbaum's primary concern here is with a limited but important thesis announced in his opening sentence: "Freud, I claim, treated the explanations offered by his theory of repression as a species of causal explanations." He is not concerned in this paper with assessing the adequacy or clinical validation of Freud's causal explanations, but with the task of challenging those who claim that Freudian explanations are not causal explanations.

I want to enumerate the points of agreement between Grünbaum and myself. Like Grünbaum, I believe the textual evidence that Freud himself claimed to be offering causal explanations is overwhelming. Even more important, the attempt to reconstruct psychoanalysis in a manner that eliminates its causal claims would be to emasculate it. In this context we can say that it would castrate psychoanalytic explanation. The sharp dichotomy between reasons and causes is untenable. The "practical syllogism" is inadequate to capture what is involved in psychoanalytic explanations.

I am sure that Grünbaum would recognize that he is not the first to make many of these points in challenging the reasons versus causes thesis. He cites others who support his views. Let me cite another distinguished philosopher who makes virtually the same claims about psychoanalysis.

One of the implications of this dichotomy between the two 'language-games' of action and movement bears directly on the point at issue in our discussion: according to these analysts, our motives for acting can in no way be assimilated to the causes by which we explain natural events. Motives are reasons for our action, while causes are the constant antecedents of other events from which they are logically distinct.

v   Can psychoanalytic theory be reformulated on the basis of this distinction? Some authors have thought so and have interpreted psychoanalysis as an extension of the vocabulary of action (intention, motives, etc.) beyond the sphere where we are aware of what we do. Psychoanalysis, according to this interpretation, adds nothing to ordinary conceptuality except the use of the same concepts of ordinary language in a new domain characterized as 'unconscious'. . . . But what is completely omitted in this reformulation is the very paradox of psychoanalytic theory, namely, that it is the becoming unconscious as such that requires a specific explanation so that the kinship of meaning between conscious and unconscious contents may be recognized. Now, the explanatory schema capable of accounting for the mechanisms of exclusion, banishment, reification, etc. completely challenges the separation of the domains of action and movement, along with the dichotomy between motive and cause. . . . What is remarkable about psychoanalytic explanation is that it brings into view motives which are causes and which require an explanation of their autonomous functioning.

Now Grünbaum might well consider this to be a strong endorsement of his own position. There is one catch to this: I have just cited Paul Ricoeur.[1] And according to Grünbaum, Ricoeur is supposed to be one of the "bad guys"—one of those hermeneuts whose claims are ill-founded, who obscure and banalize the issues. Indeed, if I wanted to play the game of scoring negative points, I could also show that many of the claims and arguments that Grünbaum offers against the reasons versus causes thesis are paralleled in the work of Jürgen Habermas—another supposedly confused hermeneut that Grünbaum attacks in *The Foundations of Psychoanalysis* (1984). Now something has gone wrong here when we find the same or similar claims and arguments being made by those whom Grünbaum is presumably attacking. Perhaps Grünbaum has missed the point about what some of those persons he classifies as "hermeneuts" have been saying.

My central claim is that Ricoeur and Habermas are primarily concerned with explicating the type of causal explanations that are essential for psychoanalytic explanations. Causal explanations in psychoanalysis differ from causal explanations in physics because we must take account of the interpretive strategies of human beings. Indeed, if we take Grünbaum's claims seriously we are led to confront the very issues that have been central to the rich and diverse tradition of hermeneutics.

Although Grünbaum cautiously begins his paper by specifying that his target is "some versions of the so-called 'hermeneutic' reconstruction of psychoanalytic theory" that vigorously deny that motivational explanations of human actions are causal explanations, he abandons this caution and toward the end of his paper speaks without qualification of hermeneuts. But to lump together such thinkers as Gadamer, Ricoeur, and Habermas with those whom he explicitly attacks is on a par with the loose and obscuring way of speaking that would label Grünbaum, Popper, and Carnap as positivists.

If I were to adopt the adversarial mode of argumentation, I might note a remarkable fact about Grünbaum's paper—namely, that he tells us very little about what he means by "causes" and "reasons," or how these treacherous concepts are to be constructively and rigorously analyzed. And much of what he does tell us is either inadequate or begs important issues. Throughout, he reiterates that causal explanations are a "genus," and that explanations offered by Freud's theory of repression are a species of this genus. But he does not tell us precisely how this genus is to be characterized, nor what are the differentia that set off the species of psychoanalytic causal explanations. The closest he comes to telling us what *cause* means is when he speaks of "causal relevance" and says, "The antecedent makes a difference to the corresponding outcome, or affects the incidence of the pertinent outcome." But there are many antecedents that "make a difference"—whether in common sense or scientific discourse —where we do not say they are causes. Indeed, what Grünbaum does when he uses such phrases as "makes a difference" or says an "agent actually was moved to act" or claims that "having a reason prompts one" is to play on our preanalytic sense of what *cause* means. He does not make much headway in conceptually analyzing what is a causal explanation and what is distinctive about causal explanations in psychoanalysis.

Indeed, what I find troubling about Grünbaum's presentation is the way in which he inadvertently falls into a trap that he so trenchantly notes. At one point he tells us, "This lesson illustrates once again the abject poverty of ordinary language philosophy as an avenue to the conceptual elucidation of theories, whose hallmark is their transcendence of common sense! We need such theories because common sense, at best, does not go far enough and, at worst, is just primitive." I heartily agree. But Grünbaum's paper is filled with "common sense" distinctions that, at best, do not go far enough and, at worst, are just primitive. He speaks of reasons and causes without attempting to characterize what these concepts mean, or how we are to identify reasons. He relies on the distinction of the mental and the physical, as if this common sense distinction were transparent. He even speaks of conscious and unconscious motives as if we knew how to draw this distinction. He refers to desires and beliefs as if these were labels for well-defined concepts. Grünbaum relies on what some of our philosophic colleagues have dubbed "folk psychology." I think we need to be extremely careful in explicating these concepts —especially if we want to understand the character of causal explanation in psychoanalysis.

Now I do not want to suggest that it is incumbent upon Grünbaum to resolve problems that have perplexed philosophers for centuries before he can begin to argue against the mistaken thesis that Freudian explanations are not causal explanations. But I do want to maintain that Grünbaum has not taken us very far in understanding the distinctive characteristics of causal explanations in the discipline of psychoanalysis that relies so heavily on interpretive strategies. And I also want to claim that some of those whom Grünbaum classifies as hermeneuts—such as Habermas and Ricoeur—have been struggling with these very issues. I can make my main point by quoting Grünbaum from his final paragraph: "True enough, human beings —unlike some purely physical entities—are themselves interpretative agents, whose conduct is the object of theoretical interpretation by psychologists, anthropologists, and others. But the crucial question is what investigative and validational lesson is to be learned from this important difference in the constitution of the object of interpretative study and from intensionality." This is the crucial question that Grünbaum does not answer.

If we are to make some progress in answering it, then our (and his) first task is to probe what we mean when we speak of human beings as interpretative agents. This opens up a complex array of questions as we try to understand what is meant by human agency and what is meant by interpretation. I think we cannot make much progress in understanding what is distinctive about causal explanations in psychoanalysis until we probe these questions. This is demanded by Grünbaum's *own way* of positing the "crucial question." But I fail to see that he has carried us very far in understanding the change that takes place when we try to understand causal explanations as they pertain to interpretative agents. In the spirit of dialogic encounter, I would plea that we should at least recognize that some of those whom Grünbaum damns as hermeneuts have been attempting to probe and clarify the very issues that Grünbaum himself takes to be central, but which he has not—at least in this paper—seriously confronted.

NOTES

1. Paul Ricoeur, "The Question of Proof in Freud's Psychoanalytic Writings," (1977). Reprinted in *Paul Ricoeur: Hermeneutics and the Human Sciences*, ed. and trans. John B. Thompson, (Cambridge: Cambridge University Press, 1981). In *The Foundations of Psychoanalysis*, Grünbaum discusses the article of Ricoeur from which I have quoted. In a section entitled "Are Repressed Motives *Reasons But Not Causes*," he writes: "Some of the appeal of a hermeneutic construal of psychoanalysis does not derive from the specific arguments given by Ricoeur and Habermas. Instead, this purported reconstruction gains plausibility from assorted cognate theses that pertain to the role of intentionality in human action. As we are told in some quarters, explanation of action by *reasons* is incompatible with explanation by causes." Nevertheless, Grünbaum in his oral comments on my response suggested that Ricoeur changed his position on this issue between the publication of *Freud and Philosophy* (1970) and his paper "The Question of Proof in Freud's Psychoanalytic Writings" (1977). But I would argue that this is mistaken. On the contrary, a central feature of *Freud and Philosophy* was to grapple with the paradox that psychoanalysis is at once a causal and a hermeneutical discipline. In Grünbaum's terms Ricoeur seeks to elucidate the "species" of causal explanation that characterizes psychoanalytic explanation. So, too, when Habermas considers psychoanalysis in *Knowledge and Human Interests* (1971) and argues that it is an exemplar of a critical social science, he emphasizes that it is a discipline that seeks to produce nomological knowledge, and consequently seeks causal explanations. Habermas has consistently criticized hermeneutics for its failure to do justice to the role of causal explanation in the social disciplines.

There is another confusing aspect of Grünbaum's presentation. I do not want to suggest that he is attacking a "straw man"; he cites a number of thinkers who have advocated the reasons versus causes thesis and who think they are defending a hermeneutic orientation. But as Grünbaum knows, the discussion of the reasons-versus-causes thesis occurred in the context of Anglo-American ordinary language philosophy without any explicit reference to, or knowledge of, the continental tradition of hermeneutics. In the 20th century, hermeneutics has become central primarily because of the work of such thinkers as Heidegger, Gadamer, and Ricoeur. None of these thinkers has advocated or endorsed the reasons-versus-causes thesis.

REFERENCES

Grünbaum, A. *The Foundations of Psychoanalysis*. Berkeley: University of California Press, 1984.

Habermas, J. *Knowledge and human interests*. Boston: Beacon Press, 1971.

Ricoeur, P. *Freud and philosophy*. New Haven: Yale University Press, 1970.

Ricoeur, P. The Question of proof in Freud's psychoanalytic writings, 1977. (Reprinted in J. B. Thompson (Ed.), *Paul Ricoeur: Hermeneutics and social science*. Cambridge: Cambridge University Press, 1981.)

Rejoinder to Richard J. Bernstein

ADOLF GRÜNBAUM

Richard Bernstein begins with matters of style rather than of substance, contrasting the adversarial with the dialogical style of argumentation. The former mode, he tells us, is featured by contemporary Anglo-American philosophy; the latter is found in the continental European philosophy of such writers as Ricoeur and Habermas. And he depicts me as a practitioner of the confrontational style of argumentation.

I submit that any reader of my *Foundations of Psychoanalysis* (1984) would find that the examination of Freud's clinical theory presented there is altogether dialogical. Indeed, several exponents of Karl Popper's wholesale indictment of psychoanalytic theory as pseudo-scientific have taken me to task for just that. But it is also true that much of my lengthy Introduction is adversarial in its treatment of Habermas and Ricoeur. There, I have documented why I find their writings on psychoanalysis obfuscating and distressingly undisciplined, besides being scientifically untutored.

The most recent case is furnished by Habermas's evasive and dismissive comment on a section of my paper (Grünbaum, 1983) entitled "Critique of Habermas's Charge of 'Scientistic Self-Misunderstanding'." In a footnote Habermas (1984) writes:

I do not find any basis in Freud for the strict separation between a clinically justified theory of neurosis and a metapsychological superstructure that Adolf Grünbaum proposes in "Freud's Theory: The Perspective of a Philosopher of Science," *Proceedings and Addresses of the American Philosophical Association* (1983), vol. 57, no. 6 [the issue is no. 1, not no. 6]. This separation makes the specific roots of Freudian theory in the experiences of the analytic dialogue unrecognizable. Such an operation may be useful for the argumentative purpose of assimilating Freudian theory to the standard model of unified science, only to then reject it for failing to measure up to its standards. At the same time, it expresses the simple decision not to consider the hermeneutic character of this science. (p. 249, fn. 25).

Habermas's claim that I have proposed a "strict separation between a clinically justified theory of neurosis and a metapsychological superstructure" is just a red herring. As I had pointed out in the paper he cites, "The separation of the clinical theory of repression from that metapsychology within the [Freudian] edifice is not always sharp" (p. 6). Moreover, none of my numerous detailed objections to Habermas's views require such a clear-cut borderline. Ironically, as indicated by the very title of his chapter, "The Scientistic Self-Misunderstanding of Metapsychology" (Habermas, 1971, chap. 11), his own charge of "scientistic self-misunderstanding" against Freud is predicated on the existence of a significant, if not strict, distinction between the two systems of hypotheses.

By the same token, as I showed (1984, Introduction, sec. 5), the psychoanalyst George S. Klein (1976, p. 12) rests his hermeneutic construal of psychoanalysis on the supposition that he has exorcized the "heavy and hopeless burden of the expendable metapsychology" while having articulated the clinical theory. In fact, starting with an influential paper by David Rapaport (1960), the distinction between the clinical theory and the metapsychology has been and is invoked by students of psychoanalysis to this day (Holt, 1985, p. 290).

In any case, nowhere did I use that distinction for the purpose of "assimilating Freudian theory to the standard model of unified science" as Habermas would have it. It is a commonplace that throughout his life, Freud considered psychoanalysis to be "a natural science like any other" (1940, p. 158). Yet Habermas pretends disingenuously that it was I who foisted this scientific conception on Freud's theory, "only to then reject it for failing to measure up to its standards." Indeed, as was reported in a German newspaper in

Habermas's own city (Kerz, 1986), Freud—along with Albert Einstein, Ernst Mach, and others—signed a manifesto calling for a unity-of-science approach to all the special sciences. Furthermore, Habermas makes a mockery of my painstaking arguments, declaring without ado that my purported misassimilation "expresses the simple decision not to consider the hermeneutic character of this science." Evidently, this charge also begs the question. Is this a mode of disputation that Bernstein considers "dialogical"?

Nor is there the slightest attempt to deal with my challenge in Habermas's more recent statement on psychoanalysis (1985). In response to the question, "What is your attitude to psychoanalysis today?," the closest he comes to the issue at hand is to say: "I have not done any work myself on Freud's metapsychology since the end of the sixties" (p. 87).

Bernstein does not come to grips at all with the 36 pages I devoted to Habermas (1984, pp. 7–43). Instead, he opines, just in passing, that much of my case against R vs. C is "paralleled in the work of Jürgen Habermas." And these alleged parallels are presumably to impung my censorious assessment of Habermas. But Bernstein's purported parallels are, at best, just verbal, if only because Habermas makes the untenable claim that successful psychoanalytic therapy dissolves and overcomes or subdues the causal linkage between the unconscious motive for neurotic conduct and the neurosis. According to Habermas this alleged therapeutic subduing of a causal connection as such shows that the law-like causal nexus present in the causality of nature does not inhere in the therapeutic dynamics of the psychoanalytic treatment process of self-reflection. As I wrote in the paper (1983) cited by Habermas:

> What the patient has indeed overcome is his pathogenic repression as well as his neurosis, but hardly the causal connection between them. To terminate an *effect* by undercutting the cause required for its production is patently *not* tantamount to overcoming the causal connection that links them. On the contrary, it is to illustrate it. Hence in Freud's clinical theory, just as in physics, there can be no question at all of "dissolving" a causal linkage between an antecedent C and its effect E on the strength of terminating the recurrence of E by preventing the further realization of C. Far from having elucidated the role of causality in psychoanalysis, Habermas's importation of the causality of fate has only obfuscated it. (pp. 8–9)

In fact, Habermas's dissolution thesis boomerangs, since it could be applied equally misleadingly to the severance of an electric circuit by the throwing of a switch or to the therapeutic dissolution of gallstones by taking suitable medication (Grünbaum, 1984, pp. 12–13).

In the discussion of Bernstein's comments at the conference, I pointed out that his depiction of my treatment of hermeneutics had simply not heeded the following passage in my book (1984):

> In his full-length book on Freud, Paul Ricoeur (1970, pp. 359–360) endorses Toulmin's claim that psychoanalytic explanations are *not* causal, just *in virtue* of being motivational. As Ricoeur saw it then, in psychoanalysis "an explanation through motives is irreducible to an explanation through causes ... a motive and a cause are completely different," instead of the former being a species of the latter. Hence, one must welcome that, under the influence of Michael Sherwood (1969), Ricoeur did have second thoughts in his later work (1981, pp. 262–263) and, commendably enough, repudiated the ordinary language approach to Freudian explanations along with the "dichotomy between motive and cause." (p. 73)

Yet Bernstein still ignores this documentation of Ricoeur's change of view, and adduces against me precisely the pages in Ricoeur's (1981) book that I had commended in the passage just cited. Thus, in the long endnote of Bernstein's commentary, he quotes selectively from my 1984 book, so as to turn a blind eye to Ricoeur's 1970 endorsement (p. 360) of Toulmin's R vs. C.

Bernstein likewise overlooks that, in opposition to Freud, Ricoeur (1970, p. 360) had also written: "Since it deals with a psychical reality, psychoanalysis speaks not of causes but of motives." But, as I was glad to observe, thereafter Ricoeur had become convinced that "what is remarkable about psychoanalytic explanation is that it brings into view motives which are causes" (1981, pp. 262–263). How then can Bernstein see himself entitled to reject, as he does (n. 1), my contention that Ricoeur espoused R vs. C in 1970, though he repudiated it afterward?

Indeed, by Bernstein's own account (n. 1), Ricoeur's 1970 book grappled with the paradox that psychoanalytic explanation is at once causal and hermeneutical. But if in 1970 Ricoeur already saw psychoanalytic motivational explanations as a species of causal explanation, as claimed by Bernstein, how then could such speciation have been a paradox for Ricoeur? For my part I credit Ricoeur with appreciating that a species of a given genus has properties over and above those of the genus, and that these further attributes hardly conflict with the generic ones. Thus, I contend that, in his book (1970), Ricoeur saw a paradox because he then did espouse, as I documented, Toulmin's R vs. C for Freud's motivational explanations, which then drove him to relegate causal explanation in psychoanalysis to the metapsychological domain of Freud's hypothesized psychic energy model (1940, pp:163–164). In short, Bernstein flies in the face of Ricoeur's book (1970), when he concludes (n. 1), "None of these thinkers [Heidegger, Gadamer, and Ricoeur] has advocated or endorsed the reason-versus-causes thesis."

Do I qualify my theses at the start of my paper as pertaining to some—rather than all—hermeneutic reconstructions of psychoanalysis, only to abandon this qualification toward the end by speaking *simpliciter* of hermeneuts *tout court*? As Bernstein would have it, I do. But the last paragraph of my paper immediately preceding its coda does nothing of the kind. And in the coda itself I am concerned with a "methodologically dichotomous moral for the human sciences *vis-à-vis* the physical ones." As is patent from my context there, it is this precept that I address when I conclude that "the moral drawn by the hermeneuts is ill-founded."

Bernstein is oblivious to the wider context of my book (1984) in which the R vs. C occupies only 15 pages (pp. 69–83). Thus he complains that I do not say precisely how the genus of causal explanations is to be characterized, "nor what are the differentia that set off the species of psychoanalytic causal explanations." And he adds that insofar as I do explicate the relation of causal relevance in my paper, there are "plenty of" counter examples to it. As he puts it in general terms: "there are plenty of antecedents that 'make a difference' ... where we do not say they are causes." But, alas, Bernstein has now chosen to ignore my demonstration, during my oral reply to him at the meeting, that his purported counterexamples are based on a misunderstanding. To obviate just that misconstrual, the above published text of my paper now contains a new paragraph. Therein, I used the example of breathing to explain why, in the context of psychoanalytic theory, breathing is not causally relevant to becoming paranoid, whereas being homosexually repressed is thus relevant. In brief, within the class of living humans, breathing does not make a difference to becoming paranoid, if only because paranoiacs and nonparanoiacs each breathe.

More generally, it is not necessary to write a whole treatise on causation to show that R vs. C has no legitimate place within psychoanalytic theory. As Bernstein knows, it was the avowed objective of my paper to provide that demonstration. And for that purpose, I claim, the causal relevance of an attribute X possessed by a living person P to P's also having the property Y can be defined as follows: X is causally relevant to Y in the class C of P's just in case X partitions C into two subclasses in which the probabilities of Y are different (cf. Salmon, 1984, esp. p. 128). For brevity, I said that the causal relevance of X to Y is a matter of X's making a difference to the incidence of Y.

Finally, Bernstein employs a double standard when claiming that, at least in the conference paper, "Grünbaum has not taken us very far" in understanding issues of causal explanation in psychoanalysis. These are issues, he says, that "those whom Grünbaum damns as 'hermeneuts' have been attempting to probe and clarify." Here he presumably refers to the corpus of Ricoeur's and Habermas's writings on psychoanalysis. By contrast, in addressing my views he turns a blind eye to almost all of what I did say in my book (1984), focusing instead on what I did not accomplish in a mere paper of 22 typescript pages. But even if one does take the corpus of the prohermeneutic literature on psychoanalysis, Bernstein gives no evidence whatever that it fulfills the demand he made upon me: To say precisely how the genus of causal explanations is to be characterized and "what are the differentia that set off the species of psychoanalytic causal explanations."

In sum, I find nothing in Bernstein's comments to blunt my case for concluding that the hermeneutic reconstructions of psychoanalysis have, at least for the most part, merely darkened counsel.

REFERENCES

Freud, S. Physical qualities. S. E., 1940, vol. 23.
Grünbaum, A. Freud's theory: The perspective of a philosopher of science. 1982 Presidential Address to the American Philosophical Association (Eastern Division). *Proceedings and Addresses of the American Philosophical Association*, 1983, 57, 5–31.
Grünbaum, A. *The foundations of psychoanalysis: A philosophical critique*. Berkeley, Los Angeles, London: University of California Press, 1984.

Habermas, J. *Knowledge and human interests*, trans. J. J. Shapiro. Boston: Beacon Press, 1971.

Habermas, J. Habermas: Questions and counterquestions. *Praxis International*, 1984, 4, 229–249.

Habermas, J. A philosophico-political profile. *New Left Review* (May-June 1985), No. 15, pp. 75–105.

Holt, R. The current status of psychoanalytic theory. *Psychoanalytic Psychology*, 1985, 2, 289–315.

Kerz, J. PH. Ideologiekritik oder Naturwissenschaft von der Seele. *Frankfurter Allgemeine Zeitung* (April 9, 1986), No. 82, p. 33.

Klein, G. S. *Psychoanalytic theory*. New York: International Universities Press, 1976.

Rapaport, D. The structure of psychoanalytic theory. *Psychological issues*, 1960, Monograph No. 6 (Vol. 2, No. 2). New York: International Universities Press.

Ricoeur, P. *Freud and philosophy*. New Haven: Yale University Press, 1970.

Ricoeur, P. *Hermeneutics and the human sciences*, trans. J. B. Thompson. New York: Cambridge University Press, 1981.

Salmon, W. *Scientific explanation and the causal structure of the world*. Princeton: Princeton University Press, 1984.

Sherwood, M. *The logic of explanation in psychoanalysis*. New York: Academic Press, 1969.

Chapter 7

On the Problem of Accepting Facticity and Pursuing Possibility

SALVATORE R. MADDI

An apt starting point for my paper is the well-known prayer whose origins are traced differently by different persons:

> God grant me the serenity to accept
> things I cannot change,
> The courage to change the things I can,
> And the wisdom to know the difference.

It is this wisdom that I would like to understand better. Perhaps it is some God-given state of grace, and that is all there is to it. Before concluding that, however, it may be worth struggling a bit to discover more. Accordingly, the question that pervades this paper is, "What help can existentialism provide that minimizes the companion risks of wasting time and energy trying to change the unchangeable, and of foolishly conserving time and energy through readily accepting as unchangeable that which can be changed?" Because psychologists are especially concerned with prescriptive considerations of individual development, they are perhaps more suited to struggling with this question than are philosophers.

Developed over a number of years, my position on personality has been detailed elsewhere (e.g., Maddi, 1967, 1970, 1980, 1985; Kobasa & Maddi, 1977). I will only summarize it here, highlighting points of special relevance to present aims. Although I have been

influenced by existentialism, that body of thought is certainly heterogeneous and I have not been scrupulous in subscribing to all its parts.
I have been most influenced by Søren Kierkegaard, Jean Paul Sartre,
Victor Frankl, and Rollo May, though my course has been to pick
what seemed useful in their work and elaborate it in my own way.
Carl R. Rogers's humanistic efforts have also affected me, though I
now find the person-centered approach limited. My steadfast aim has
been to render formulations that are clearly delineated, empirically
testable, and practically useful, being wary of the risk of oversimplifi-
cation that comes with such a direction. In all this I have benefitted
from the wise influence of my colleague, Suzanne C. Kobasa. What
has emerged over the years seems to me a recognizable form of
existential psychology, though there might well be disagreement
about this.

OVERALL THRUST TOWARD POSSIBILITY

In defining personality, theorists are attempting to characterize the
pervasive, integrative tasks and directions of human functioning. I
find Sartre's (1956) depiction of personality as "a blend of facticity
and possibility" essentially useful. At any moment, our personalities
combine the givens that we cannot change and should accept with the
possibilities for change that can still be imagined and are worth
pursuing.

It is clear that, according to existentialism, the best thrust of
human functioning is toward possibility. Minimizing facticity leaves
one's options open for personal growth through new experiences.
This way lies freedom, renewal, richness, sensitivity, deepening
understanding, sophistication in the best sense. But facticity cannot
be avoided completely. It is inherent in our experience, not only in
our own limitations, but also in what we have become, even if in that
becoming we have pursued possibility vigorously. Hence, our sense
of what is possible is intertwined with what we perceive as given, and
the dynamic balance between the two gives our lives its particular
flavor.

THE DECISION-MAKING PROCESS

However satisfying or terrible is our present, it does not remain static. Fully lived, the present is impelled toward the future. This is because a person who is vigorously thinking, feeling, and acting, all the while in interaction with others who are doing likewise, will inevitably encounter changing, new experiences. It is important to recognize that the changes in experience involved need not be large and obvious (e.g., taking a new job). They may be small and subtle (e.g., shifting one's perception of a problem, or working through one's anger until a sense of hurt emerges). In contrast, when a person inhibits thinking, feeling, and acting, and is either socially isolated or interacts with similarly inhibited others, then the present will slip into the past through the increasing repetitiveness of unchanging experiences.

Given the inevitably changing nature of the present, persons are faced with the choice of the future or the past in that unending series of decisions that characterizes our lives as human beings. To become aware of this choice sets the stage for making decisions more effectively (Kierkegaard, 1954). Awareness is especially important because the future is the way of possibility, and embracing the past builds facticity.

Consider a female professor who has taught at a particular college for many years and then is offered a job as an administrator at another college. Given that she can continue to teach at the new college, taking the offered job is probably choosing the future (the unfamiliar), whereas remaining where she is probably involves choosing the past (the familiar). To do something new is developmentally more valuable than persisting in the old. However, she can remain in the original job without choosing the past by adding an administrative dimension to her functioning or changing the direction of her teaching, because such redirections will also bring new experience.

Given the thrust of existentialism toward personal growth through new experience, rejecting the future and embracing the past (e.g., remaining at the original job without changing a thing) treats that which is familiar as facticity, as somehow unchangeable. Sometimes the familiar is justifiably regarded as facticity, and sometimes this is merely an expedient, the easiest way out.

What would motivate choosing the past as an expedient? The usual existential answer emphasizes the painful concomitants of choosing the future. When contemplating or doing something new, one experiences anxiety that can be called ontological in recognition of its being a natural concomitant of facing something unknown and unpredictable. For existentialists experiences are no less developmental because they are painful. Indeed, there is probably no development without some emotional pain. Friedrich Nietzsche (1964) put this dramatically as "whatever does not kill me makes me stronger." In *The Once and Future King*, E. B. White (1983) put it more charmingly when the young King Arthur sinks into depression after a personal reversal and seeks the counsel of Merlin who, as a wizard, should know everything. Merlin insists that to overcome depression, Arthur must learn from the reversal, as learning is all that lasts. The message in this is that one thing making it easy to slip into regarding unnecessarily past-oriented decisions as imperatives is the natural anxiety of facing an uncertain future.

It is true that existentialists regard choosing the past as courting ontological guilt and that this should motivate choosing the future instead. But the ontological guilt is not, in any usual decision-making situation, as vivid as the ontological anxiety. The guilt is experienced as a sense of having missed out on something, but something the value of which was dubious and mingled with anxiety anyhow. It is only after a considerable history of choosing the past that ontological guilt accumulates to the point where one begins to wonder whether one's life has been a waste and whether anything is meaningful. This "sickness unto death" (Kierkegaard, 1954) is awful, but is a much more gradual accretion than fear of the unknown, or future.

So, unless one is careful, the past will be chosen as the easiest way out. The familiar will be misconstrued as necessity, and day-to-day life will appear secure and easy. In our extended example, the professor may conclude that her colleagues and students at the original college need her to stay there and function exactly as before, and she may comfort herself with being around all those people and circumstances that she has come to know so well. But development and vitality will be jeopardized with this conformist choice (Maddi, 1970) and despair will loom on the horizon. There is good reason in this to inquire further how one can identify the circumstance when a decisional alternative is truly unchangeable and needs, therefore, to be accepted as facticity.

This is not to say that the conformist choice, shrinking from the anxiety of the future by embracing as facticity a past that is misperceived as unchangeable, is the only decisional mistake persons make. Although this kind of error may indeed be the most common, there is another mistake in which something actually unchangeable is reacted to as if it were in the realm of possibility. This is aptly called extravagant, a flight into a false future (Maddi, 1980). In the case of our professor, suppose that her present home, social, and intellectual life define her so completely that fundamental change was no longer a real option. However, suppose that she felt somehow compelled to accept the offer and moved to the new college, only to find that her husband and children would not accompany her, she missed them and her friends intensely, her new colleagues were not stimulating enough for her, and she detested administrative work, longing instead for the day-to-day freedom to come and go that she had relinquished. As a result of her move, she might have made an error from which there was no recovery. Had she accurately perceived the facticity inherent in the old life, she might have declined the new position and instead added features to the old life. She could have incorporated what seemed attractive to her in the new position without the loss of what was crucial in the old.

Thus, in our attempt to understand the bases on which mistakes are made in the determination of whether some experience is or is not unchangeable, we would do well to consider not only the conformist but also the extravagant choice. Is the usual existential emphasis on shrinking from ontological anxiety a sufficient basis for understanding both mistakes? What motivates the intriguing unwillingness to accept real facticity and insist that it is possibility instead? In answering this last question, do we want to reconsider the motivational bases of the conformist mistake as well?

FACTICITY DUE TO INSURMOUNTABLE LIMITATIONS

In existentialism there is no experience without perception and thought. This is not to say, however, that input—the world and our bodies impinging upon our minds—is irrelevant. In the continual, complex interaction between person and world, experience is constructed. We must understand this transaction more precisely if there is any hope of considering how persons can construe facticity and possibility accurately and act accordingly. Specifically, we must consider when the input from data sources for experience contributes such insurmountable limitations that it forces a sense of facticity on us.

The input, or raw material, for experience is from four sources that are approximately characterizeable as biological, ecological, socio-economic, and individual. Each of these sources makes a contribution to facticity and possibility. Important for facticity are the limitations defined by the structural features of these sources.

Of the four, the biological source provides the most vivid examples of givens. These express the limitations inherent in having a particular anatomy and physiology. As a species, we humans have limitations by comparison with other species. Relatively speaking, our night vision and sense of smell is not as highly developed as in some other animals. Furthermore, particular persons have limitations with regard to others. If you have the reproductive organs of a male, you are not capable of giving birth. If you are born deaf, it will be very hard to become a debater. Future medical technology may erase these limitations, but at present they are givens.

Reasonably vivid examples are next easiest to find regarding ecology and involve such matters as weather patterns, natural resource distribution, and human alteration of the physical environment. If you live in Alaska, you would be foolhardy to wear shorts and sandals when going for a walk in winter. Any Italian government would have to consider the implications for industrialization of a land with sparse supplies of coal and oil. If we pollute the Great Lakes, we will be at considerable risk on eating the fish from those waters. Ecological limitations can certainly be overcome, but represent a source of facticity unless and until that happens.

Being based to some degree on conventions, socioeconomic sources for facticity are even less compelling as examples. They are the stuff of laws, norms, roles, credentials, and income. You cannot become president of the United States without having been born here. You would be well advised to be licensed if you wish to practice medicine, and to have a large income if you want to buy a Rolls Royce car. If you value your freedom and voting rights, it is best in many societies not to murder your enemy. Certainly laws, norms, and the like can change, and so too will social facticity. But it is also possible to be deviant, to flout conventions, more easily than one can transcend biological and ecological limitations.

There are certain extreme and relatively rare conditions, however, when socioeconomic sources for facticity can be quite compelling. There are conditions of poverty so desperate that malnutrition or starvation affects the ability to engage in the very cognitive functions that are required for construing experience and contemplating decisions. A splendid neurologist I spoke with in Brazil who had responsibility for conducting electroencephalographic examinations on patients at a free city hospital bemoaned conditions that would bring poor people into the hospital in such a starved state that accurate readings could not be obtained until after they had been fed. Starving people may have lost any vigorous ability to contemplate possibility. Political oppression may also introduce facticity even if there is no special socioeconomic limitation. Financially advantaged Jews were still burned by Nazis. It might, of course, be argued that in the case of oppression, financial or political, there remains always some possibility, if not through contemplation of a better life at least through accurate recognition of one's plight. Alan Wheelis (1974) insists that though some Jews went to the gas chambers and ovens steadfastly denying what was happening, others better able to exercise the little freedom left to them by thinking at least knew that they were going to their deaths. Nonetheless, these Jews who achieved awareness in doing so accepted the facticity that they would be put to death.

Individual sources of facticity are perhaps the least universal of all, representing as they do the history of decisions each person has made up to that time. Specifically, settled beliefs about one's own characteristics, worth, requirements, strengths, and weaknesses contribute to facticity. Thus, if you think of yourself as shy and unattractive, it may be hard to approach others you would want to know. Having accepted yourself as stolid and unimaginative, it would be difficult to approach a career in art. If you have spent years of time and energy being a psychologist, it may seem less possible as the years go by to pursue another demanding profession, say architecture, no matter how attractive it may seem in the abstract. As with other sources of facticity, one's sense of self may change, but it will have to if individual givens are to be altered.

FACTICITY DUE TO EXPERIENTIAL AGREEMENT

Human endeavors are generally complex enough to involve more than one source of experience. Hence, it is natural for these experience sources to interact. Although many forms of interaction are possible, two in particular are important here. Experience sources may operate in a complimentary, cumulative manner, or they may be in conflict.

When Sartre (1956) asserted that the waiter at a Paris cafe cannot become a cabinet minister, he was presumably pointing to socioeconomic and individual sources of experience acting complimentarily. As to norms, France of that time did not foster much upward mobility. A waiter's parents would likely have been in that same sort of occupation. The waiter would not have received the right kind of education to serve as a credential for public office. Because of this, it is unlikely that there would be access to funds to support any public bid for a ministry. These are socioeconomic givens. In terms of individual givens, the waiter would not think of him or herself as anything remotely approaching a cabinet minister. Whether such a ministry were disdained or coveted, it would seem too remote to take seriously for oneself. Whether content or discontent with this, the waiter would consider his or her more mundane daily work fitting. Thus, an individual sense of self and social forces would combine to deepen the sense of facticity. In general, the more the complimentarity between sources of experience, the more the clarity hat something is a given.

Also, sources of experience can agree in indicating that something is in the realm of possibility. If a French person, for example, had been born into the upper middle class and a family of public servants, had passed the requisite school tests and received the right degrees, had cultivated the appropriate friends and backers, and had nurtured thoughts of public office for years, then a bid at a ministry would appear in the realm of possibility.

Sources of experience can also interact in a conflicting manner. For example, a male adolescent, who had a strong, supple body with quick reflexes (biological experience source), might find a career as a baseball player attractive (personal experience source) but be hampered by living in a mountainous, cold region that discouraged outdoor sports (ecological experience source) and by having parents who disrespected athletic careers (social experience source). Because of the conflict between experience sources as they bear on the decision of whether to pursue a baseball career, there is ambiguity as to what is possible and what is not. In the case of ambiguity, there is no unequivocal case for facticity, and it is well to treat the decisional alternatives as possibilities. Thus, the adolescent could as well explore a career in baseball as turn away from it to something else. Whichever direction he tries, there will be obstacles. If he attempts a career in baseball, he will have to contend with his parents' unsupportive attitude and unfavorable ecology. If he turns away from that career, he will have to find something that will fulfill his desires and use his physical prowess. But in the struggle to pinpoint possibility in ambiguous circumstances, to follow directions despite some obstacles, there is much to be learned that is of developmental value.

Very likely in our complex world, the most frequent situation occurs when interacting experience sources are in conflict. Thus, it should be commonplace to find persons struggling to resolve ambiguities through the decision-making process. What advice can be given concerning this difficult process?

The easiest procedures for resolving conflict between experience sources is to follow the preponderance. If three out of four experience sources agree, then one might develop a direction consistent with them regardless of where the fourth would lead. This, however, is not necessarily the most effective conflict-resolution tactic. Suppose three of four experience sources constitute obstacles to a particular direction. Is it developmentally most valuable to give up the direction? Accepting the existential emphasis on pursuing possibility as most important, a person might well want to explore a certain direction even if it were supported by only one of several experience sources. What is there about this attraction to a baseball career that is so compelling? How much would the person be willing to give up in pursuit of that career? Is there anything else that would give the same sense of satisfaction? There are answers to such questions that would justify trying to become a baseball player no matter what obstacles loomed, as long as one could hope to find a way around them.

In focusing on this extended example, I do not wish to give the impression that what is important is invariably pursuing your attractions. Imagine a change in the example such that to ecological and social obstacles is added an individual one—the person is not particularly attracted to a baseball career. All that is left to suggest the baseball career as a possibility is the strong, supple body with quick reflexes. If, over time, the person observes again and again how this body responds well to and in baseball, he might at some point decide to follow this talent wherever it would lead. Now, of course, the person might find some other use of the talent that attracted him more than baseball, and this other use might seem on balance even more fulfilling. But the point is that compelling evidence from even a solitary experience source might make all the difference in deciding on a possible direction. Once a direction is pursued, it is, of course, useful if (and even likely that) additional information gained in the process will support the perhaps initially fragile decision. The fewer the experience sources that support a direction pursued, the initially more anxiety-provoking will the direction be. But this anxiety is not a contraindication for existentialists, once again because of their strong emphasis on development through new experience.

It is also true that facticity can be defined by only one experience source, even when all others suggest possibility. The insurmountable limitations discussed previously are cases in point. For example, if someone has a serious heart condition or a crippled leg, this contraindicates a baseball career no matter how much the personal desire and socioecological support for it. Having gracefully accepted this facticity, one might even be able to steer a course that is maximally relevant to playing baseball. One might, for example, become a manager, or join the front office of a baseball team. In this fashion one could stay satisfyingly close to what was desired and socioecologically supported.

The preceding several paragraphs have suggested that the direction decided on is arrived at through some rational sorting of evidence and resolving existing conflicts through a process not unlike weighting the relevant components differentially and summing algebraically. Perhaps an algorithm of this sort can do the job. From a subjective point of view, however, the decision may appear to emerge intuitively. Focusing on the whole process surely alerts us to an initial phase in decision-making in which the various relevant sorts of information are juxtaposed, examined, digested, and reexamined, rejuxtaposed, and redigested. But there is also a period of just "living with" or "sleeping with" all the evidence. When a decision finally emerges, it appears rather intuitive and is sometimes a bit of a surprise to the person. This intriguing combination of rational and intuitive functioning is not unlike what has often been described as the creative process.

MINIMIZING FACTICITY THROUGH SYMBOLIZATION, IMAGINATION, AND JUDGMENT

The thrust of the immediately-preceding discussion is that as long as there is some small basis for considering a decision-making alternative in the realm of possibility, it is developmentally worthwhile to pursue it. In this attempt the person must rely on the cognitive processes of symbolization, imagination, and judgment. Vigorous use of these cognitive functions is one way of decreasing the likelihood of mistaking possibility as facticity and facticity as possibility.

The more the person symbolizes, imagines, and judges, the greater will be the richness and meaningfulness of experience (Maddi, 1967). In symbolizing one abstracts from concrete experiences categories that represent or classify the experiences. For example, the larger a person's vocabulary, the finer the distinctions and the more overarching the similarities that can be recognized regarding experience. In imagining one combines and recombines symbols mentally in a manner that represents the complexities of external experience. The more a person imagines, the greater the fund of new ideas there will be regarding experience. In judging one evaluates imaginative and external experience along preferential and ethical lines. The more a person judges, the more definite the stance taken toward living.

One function of the vigorous use of the cognitive processes of symbolization, imagination, and judgment is to render one's life more meaningful. This is because the end result of symbolizing is more categories with which to recognize experience; of imagining, more new ideas about what might be done; and of judging, more preferences and values (Maddi, 1970; Kobasa & Maddi, 1977). A more important implication for present purposes is that through vigorous symbolization, imagination, and judgment, one can increase the sense of possibility. Less will appear to be unchangeable because you will be able to draw fine distinctions, imagine alternatives, and have a definite stance that is likely to be idiosyncratic because it is elaborate and complex. In this context the chances of all relevant experience sources agreeing that a decision-making alternative is unchangeable are definitely lower. Also, in the case of conflict between experience sources, even if most point toward facticity, the chances of finding a way to construe possibility nonetheless are greater with the kind of vigorous cognitive functioning already mentioned.

In being socialized most people are directly taught certain symbols, ideas about change, values, and preferences. This is a large part of the shared patterns of meaning that define the culture of which each of us is a part. This does not mean, of course, that no individual change is possible. One source of change is the interpersonal conflict we can experience when interacting with others who, though members of our society, had different socializing agents. In being confronted with differences between our understandings and those of another, we have the option of changing. Another source of change, perhaps more important, is inherent in our having been socialized to symbolize, imagine, and judge vigorously. Through vigorous cognition we can transcend the particular symbols, ideas about change, values and preferences that are conventional in our culture and develop others in a creative process as we attempt to construe our experiences.

To return to our baseball example, a person who desires such a career and who symbolizes, imagines, and judges vigorously might be quite able to deal with the opposition of parents and an inhospitable climate in various ways. The person might transcend the ecological limitation by moving to a warmer, flatter terrain or by arranging to practice indoors. The precise nature of the parental opposition would be discerned, and the person would have ideas about how to circumvent it or would accept the disagreement without jeopardy to everything in the relationship. When the experience that defines our existence is that which we construe, rather than something more objective, it behooves us to symbolize, imagine, and judge vigorously. It is important, therefore, for us to understand what factors increase the likelihood of this vigorous cognition.

WHEN SYMBOLIZATION, IMAGINATION, AND JUDGMENT FAIL

One way of discerning the factors that control the vigorousness of symbolization, imagination, and judgment is to observe some culturally accepted examples of significant failure to exercise these cognitive functions. Perhaps in this way we can gain insight into what goes wrong when persons do not explore their own experience sources sufficiently to make the best decision for them, instead short-circuiting the process and ending by mistaking possibility for facticity and facticity for possibility.

The protagonist of Alexander Solzhenitsyn's *Cancer Ward* (1969) is in a hospital being treated for stomach cancer. A fragile but marvelous affection begins to develop between him and a female physician who ministers to him. Near the end of the novel he is released, the hospital having treated him as well as it could. As he leaves, the physician invites him to her home. It is clear that they are now in love with each other. As she waits and waits for him, her sadness deepens as it becomes clear that he will not arrive. Apparently, he did not see an intimacy with her as in the realm of possibility. But, of course, it was. She clearly loved and respected him, and wanted to take care of him. He loved and needed her very much, and she made the overture. They could have shared something beautiful together. One supposes that he could not bear the thought that he would die and that she would be party to that. This seems so odd, though, for no one knew his condition better than she, and if he were to die, that would make their time together all the more intense. As they are depicted by the author, both characters have the capacity to love despite adversity and are quite used to physical infirmity.

Presumably, his pride got in the way. With his stomach cancer, he fancied himself no longer a fit candidate for her love. He felt it was too late for him. He chose to overlook, thereby, other ways in which he could well have construed the experience. It was within his phenomenal purview to think that love is not lessened by brevity, or intimacy by infirmity. He could easily have concluded that it is never too late as long as there is emotional intensity. That he gave up on the relationship, treating it as outside the realm of possibility and in that fashion overlooking the obvious signs of her love, is a kind of conformity. Conventionally, one should be able to offer to a potential lover a sound, healthy body.

It is when symbolization, imagination, and judgment are not vigorously expressed that one ends in conformity (Maddi, 1967). The otherwise sensitive hero of Cancer Ward should have been able to transcend conventionalities through cognitive effort. Presumably, his vivid sense of inferiority and the associated depressive affect clouded the decision-making process such that only some but not all the relevant experience was taken into account.

Certainly, Cancer Ward is only a novel. But it grips us because we know there are many circumstances in which we wonder whether we mistook possibility for facticity. At a conference I recently attended, a speaker won acclaim by suggesting that depression may have evolutionary value. The example used was of the ape community. When a male ape successfully challenges a previously dominant male for the relevant females, the deposed ape goes into a kind of depression, withdrawing, sulking, not eating. After a period of time, the depression will lift, and the demoted status of the ape will have been accepted by all. The evolutionary point is that the withdrawal avoided further confrontation and at least kept the ape alive. The obvious parallel was drawn to human depression. I could not help wondering whether there is such a thing as an evolutionarily useful depression being prolonged enough to become disfunctional. This seems especially possible at the human level because of our huge cognitive capacity. When is it functional for a human to sink sufficiently into depression that a desired intimacy is lost, whether this involve a competitor or not? When does self-protection (with the implication of a legitimate facticity) shade over into conformity (with the implication of mistaking possibility for facticity) driven by a sense of inferiority?

Something similar to what has been suggested is also true in the case where facticity is mistaken for possibility. This is a more extravagant circumstance than the opposite mistake, and it is therefore not surprising to find good examples of it in mythology, which is by definition about extraordinary happenings. In myths there are many instances where strong emotions and compensatory sentiments block otherwise remarkable characters from perceiving facticity accurately (Maddi, 1981).

The Theban myths are relevant here. As the king of Thebes, Creon proclaimed that Polyneices, killed attacking the city, should not receive the burial rites by which souls pass successfully into the next life. Although Polyneices, a son of the former king, was to be king himself and was attempting to claim this right when killed, Creon decided that he had committed treason by the attack and was therefore not entitled to burial. Polyneices' sister, Antigone, defied the proclamation and buried her brother, whereupon Creon brought about her death. But Haemon, Creon's son, committed suicide because of his great love for Antigone, his fiance. Creon was overwhelmed by his loss, and his downfall ensued.

Clearly, Creon did not exercise imagination and judgment fully in posing and evaluating consequences before his decision to condemn Antigone. Had he done so, he would have realized that Haemon desperately loved Antigone (indeed, he had told his father this), and Antigone had no choice but to bury her brother on pain of losing her own soul along with his. Creon would also have realized that he could not withstand the loss of his son. Recognizing all this facticity, he would have had to act differently. Actually, it would not have been difficult, given Greek culture, for him to conclude that familial obligations are as important as considerations of state in the matter of death. An ingenious solution would have been to permit a family member to bury Polyneices, while still denying him state sanction.

Creon's failing in imagination and judgment, his extravagance in insisting on his way, can be traced to the compensatory sentiment of pride. Actually, Creon only became king when Polyneices and his brother, the sons of the former king, were both killed in battle. Creon previously had been passed over for the kingship, and having now gained it unexpectedly was puffed up with his own power. Operating from what must have been a sense of inferiority, he probably felt that Polyneices' receiving a hero's burial would somehow diminish his own new status by reminding the populace of their loss. It is an excess of pride, compensating for inferiority feelings, that clouded his vision of facticity.

In the myth of the Trojan wars, there is a good example of the same clouding function that concerns Hector, a normally sensible and capable person. Achilles had retired from the fight following a dispute with Agamemnon, the Greek field commander. With Achilles out of the fight, the Trojans swept the Greek forces to the sea, destroying their ships, and cutting off their escape route. As leader of the Trojan forces, Hector knew that it had been prophesied that only when Achilles was fighting could the Trojans lose. He also knew that Achilles would fight only if his own ships were attacked. The question arose in the Trojan council from a clear perception of facticity, a strategy that might have led eventually to a complete Trojan victory. But in his extravagance Hector insisted that the attack be pressed. Achilles, of course, reentered battle and killed Hector, an event not only unfortunate personally, but disastrous for the Trojan cause.

Why was Hector suddenly so blind and injudicious? He seemed to be experiencing a compensatory kind of emotional pride. He knew that Achilles was a much better warrior than he. He must also have sensed that the Trojan position had been deteriorating slowly with the passage of each month. The gnawing frustration of the situation, coupled with a creeping sense of inferiority, probably led him to overvalue the victory achieved in Achilles' absence. He became drunk with victory in compensation for his sense of inferiority. This euphoria rendered him fatally incapable of the imagination and judgment so clear in the counsel of Polydamus.

It is worth hypothesizing that a sense of personal inadequacy leading to blinding emotions can sufficiently interfere with cognitive functioning in the decision-making process allowing inaccuracies in perceiving facticity and possibility to be more likely. The necessary process of exploring and sorting experience, searching for leads in making decisions, and then trying to live with the decisions made, is a complex and arduous matter under the best of circumstances. Add to this the ingredient of a sense of personal inferiority with its propensity to fuel either passive depressiveness or compensatorily blind pride, and the likelihood of mistaking facticity and possibility for each other is greatly increased. The person, feeling inferior, may latch on to any sign of defeat or victory, short-circuiting all that goes into a comprehensively sound decision.

PERSONALITY HARDINESS AS THE OPPOSITE OF INFERIORITY FEELINGS

If inferiority feelings can decrease the likelihood of accurate identification of facticity and possibility, is there some positive human outlook that can reverse this trend? Something along the lines of an answer to this question is implied in several existential formulations. For Kierkegaard (1954), the concept was faith. Through a rational process of thought, the person arrives at the point of making a decision for the future or the past. Kierkegaard likened this to standing at the edge of an abyss, contemplating whether to jump in. At that point more cognitive activity will not really help. What is needed additionally for Kierkegaard is faith, an otherwordly conviction that in choosing possibility one is creating experience and, in that sense, doing the kind of thing that God does. In exercising the part of us that is most godly, we have faith that we are drawing ourselves closer to Him and in that fashion gaining paradise. In later, more secular times, Paul Tillich (1952) used the concept of courage to accomplish the explanation of choosing possibility no matter what the cost in anxiety. The notion of courage begins to highlight the person's trust in his or her own special or unique abilities despite the awesome complexities of the world.

The concept of hardiness, introduced by Kobasa (1979) and elaborated on in various reports (e.g., Maddi & Kobasa, 1984), is in the more secular tradition of Tillich. Hardiness has the advantage of being conceptually detailed and has stimulated much recent research (e.g., Kobasa, 1979, 1982, 1985; Kobasa, Maddi & Kahn, 1982; Kobasa, Maddi, Puccetti, & Zola, 1985; Kobasa & Puccetti, 1983). The connotations of hardiness concern strength. But it is not the ego strength of the psychoanalyst, which emphasizes the control of antisocial impulses. Rather, hardiness is the strength of resiliency. There are three components to hardiness: commitment, control, and challenge. These components refer to the content of assumptions that persons make concerning themselves, their world, and the interaction between the two.

Persons high in the commitment component assume that they and their worlds are both interesting and worthwhile, so that involvement in the interaction of the two is easy. Such persons find something to provoke curiosity or suggest importance in whatever they are doing or contemplating doing. Persons high in the control component believe that they can influence what is going on around them, and are willing to act on that belief. They are commonly organizing, coordinating, planning. Persons high in the challenge component believe that life is by nature a developmental phenomenon, and that changes are a stimulus to personal growth through learning. They can learn from a change even when it signifies a failure in their ability to control events.

Commitment, control, and challenge are not the same, though they compliment each other. One can imagine differing patterns of the three characteristics. Antonovsky's (1979) sense of coherence, for example, might be translated into hardiness terms as involving high levels of commitment and challenge and a relatively low level of control. Persons with this personality pattern would be quite content with involving themselves in the world around them and understanding their place in it without trying much to change it. As it is emerging in theory and research, the Type A behavior pattern (e.g., Rosenman, Friedman, Straus, Jenkins, Zyzanski, & Wurm, 1970) might well be translated into hardiness terms as being just the opposite of coherence, namely, high control and relatively low commitment and challenge. The impatience of the Type A pattern suggests the lack of curiosity about the sense of importance of ongoing activities that expresses low commitment. Type A persons also have great time urgency, suggesting inability to accept the inevitability of imperfect control over complex phenomena that expresses low challenge. Indeed, the brittle, vulnerable quality of Type A persons may be this very absence of the mellowing qualities of commitment and challenge.

Persons uniformly high on all three aspects of hardiness have something close to a prerequisite for the pursuit of authenticity so valued by existentialists (Maddi, 1985). Approving of themselves and their worlds (commitment), hardy persons will have a basis for the continual exploration of experience that is consistent with trying to identify what is possibility and what is facticity. Believing in and acting as influencers (control), they will have a basis for choosing the future, as its uncertainty will not seem too terrible to confront. Seeing their lives as an unfolding development (challenge), they will have a basis for learning through not only successes but, more importantly, through failures. Overall, they will be in the best position to engage in vigorous symbolization, imagination, and judgment and to use these cognitive processes in future-oriented decision making. Ontological anxiety will still be there for them, but it will not seem so overwhelming because they are grounded in their sense of capability for living.

Not so for persons uniformly low in commitment, control, and challenge. The absence of commitment is alienation, a state in which neither oneself nor one's world seems particularly interesting or worthwhile. Such persons are frequently bored and do as little as possible. The absence of control is powerlessness, whereby one imagines oneself the passive victim of circumstances. Such persons are fearful and take no initiative. The absence of challenge is threat, which involves thinking that life is best when there is easy stability, comfort, and security. Such persons react to changes as disruptions from which there is little to be learned.

From an existential viewpoint, the disadvantage of being low in hardiness involves a high risk of mistaking possibility for facticity and facticity for possibility. The sense of inferiority inherent in not finding oneself interesting or worthwhile and in feeling unable to make a difference is not a sound basis for shouldering ontological anxiety and getting on with formulating one's unpredictable future. In this regard defining life as being about easy stability, comfort, and security saps any enthusiasm for learning through new experiences. Alienation, powerlessness, and threat combine to render it too dangerous to explore the limits to one's experience in order to determine what can and cannot be done. Such exploration just does not seem worthwhile (alienation), feasible (powerlessness), or satisfying (threat). Instead, the pervasive sense of inferiority and futility, surrounded as it would be with strong negative emotions, leads to short-circuiting the admittedly complex and taxing process of exploring experience through symbolization, imagination, and judgment. This shows up in either excessively conformist or wildly extravagant choices. Another way of saying this is that persons low in hardiness are likely to mistake possibility for facticity, and facticity for possibility.

It is intriguing to consider the conditions making for one as opposed to the other of these mistakes in identifying facticity and possibility. Perhaps when the absence of personality hardiness is a long-standing developmental fact, one's typical mistake is that of conformism, namely, to think of as facticity that which is actually possible. But when the low level of hardiness is an acute reaction to a period of intense stress on the part of someone ordinarily adequate in this personality style, then maybe the mistake is more likely to be that of extravagance, namely, to think of as possibility that which is actually unchangeable. Perhaps, under such conditions, the person strives compensatorily for an older level of competence still remembered, but fails due to the blindness of the effort.

CAN OTHERS HELP?

The strong subjectivistic emphasis of existential positions would seem to preclude persons helping each other in the complex process of accepting facticity and pursuing possibility. If one person cannot ever really know another person, then how can they provide any legitimate assistance to each other? Certainly not by imposing on the person one's own direction and approach to life. At most, one can justify helping the person become able to construct and reflect on experience in a manner conducive to finding his or her own direction and approach. In the frame of reference being developed here, this means helping the person grow in personality hardiness so that vigorous use of symbolization, imagination, and judgment will be brought to bear on the sorting of experience and the making of decisions in a manner consistent with personal growth. There are implications in this stance for both child-rearing and counseling.

Child-rearing practices

In discussing how hardiness comes about, Kobasa and Maddi (1977) differentiate between early and later development. Early development, coinciding roughly with the childhood years, involves the parents and significant others in facilitating the growth of hardiness assumptions in the young, unformed person (Maddi & Kobasa, 1984).

How do some persons come to experience themselves and their worlds as interesting, worthwhile, and satisfying, whereas others find them dull, meaningless, and frustrating? This difference in sense of commitment may well result from the overall degree to which the interactions they had with their parents were supportive, in the sense

of facilitating satisfaction, and providing encouragement and acceptance. Children will attempt to satisfy their needs and potentialities
in many ways. When parents meet these efforts with approval,
interest, and encouragement, the child feels supported and satisfied
and, on this basis, comes to view self and world as interesting and
worthwhile. But if parents are generally hostile, disapproving, or
neglectful, the child comes to view self and world as empty and
worthless. What is important in the development of commitment is
that parental support be preponderant. It matters little if a few
interactions are traumatic or wonderful.

There are many reasons why parents might be chronically unsupportive of their children. They might, for example, be too wrapped up
in their work lives away from the family or be continually resentful
because they never wanted children in the first place. Another
problem is that parents may be so overwhelmed that they become
neglectful and ungiving to their children. Nor can it help if parents
do not love each other. In contrast, parents who find family interaction fulfilling, who are managing to cope with their own problems,
and who appreciate rather than resent their children, are much more
likely to be supportive of them.

There is a particularly damaging (though subtle) way in which
parents can be unsupportive and thereby undermine the child's sense
of commitment to self and world. This occurs when parents impose
on the child preconceived notions of what is acceptable and admira-
ble despite signs that this is at variance with the natural expressions
of the child's capabilities. A female child who is naturally very
physically active may be regarded by her parents as unladylike. They
may support her only for signs of emotional sensitivity and passivity.
A naturally sensitive and emotional male child may be considered
unmanly and be supported only when he shows signs of physical
prowess and aggression. In this way children may conform to parental
expectations rather than express their capabilities openly. The result
is a developing person who appears outwardly adjusted but carries
around a nagging, restless sense that something important is missing,
that life as currently lived is not enough. To avoid this sense of
alienation in their offspring, parents must support them not from
rigid preconceptions of what will be best but from respect for the
individuality that will result if they are less insistent.

Why do some persons believe that, and act as if, they can influence
ongoing events, whereas others passively succumb to being victims?
This difference in control may reflect the overall proportion of

mastery, as opposed to failure experiences, in early life. As they grow older, childrens' developing physical and mental capabilities lead them to try to accomplish things. Their own needs and abilities define many goals for them to strive toward. When children succeed they have a sense of mastery—and when they fail, a sense of powerlessness. Arenas for mastery or failure include cleaning and dressing oneself, finding one's way outside the home, interacting with others, getting school work done accurately, riding a bicycle, and so forth.

As they develop it is best for children when the tasks they encounter are just a bit more difficult than those they can easily perform. If the tasks are too easy, then succeeding at them will not bring a sense of mastery. Conversely, if the tasks are too hard, the child is likely to fail and feel powerless. What builds control is for the child's interaction with the environment to involve a predominance of tasks that can be mastered because they are just a bit more difficult than he or she can easily manage (McClelland, 1958). If that is so, children will sense that they are able to influence things if they struggle and will learn a willingness to act on that sense. But if the large proportion of the child's tasks are so hard as to provoke failure, powerlessness will be learned instead.

When children encounter too many difficult tasks, often it is because parents are either neglectful or are subtly competing with their offspring. If children encounter, instead, too many easy tasks, it usually means that parents are being overprotective. Both problems express resentment toward and domination of the child. But parents genuinely interested in their children feeling and acting in an initiating, competent fashion make the effort to ensure that the tasks encountered are generally of moderate difficulty.

Why do some persons expect life changes to be frequent and instructive, whereas others expect stability and regard change as disruptive of security? This difference in a sense of challenge reflects the degree to which a person's early environment changed and whether that change was regarded as richness or chaos. An environment may have many large, obvious changes (e.g., trips to foreign countries, changes in residence, and frequent visitors to the home). But more subtle changes (e.g., varying tasks to perform around the home, interacting with parents and siblings who talk and act in differing ways, having many hobbies) are perhaps even more important.

Neither obvious nor subtle changes are by themselves sufficient to build a sense of challenge in the unformed child. Indeed, children may be overwhelmed by continual change unless they are helped to see it as richness rather than chaos. Parents must themselves see changes as interesting and developmentally valuable so that they can communicate this to their children. In the communication parents must encourage children to use their mental capabilities to conceive of the challenges as signs of richness and possibility. In contrast, parents who are themselves disrupted by changes, and communicate this, are understandably unable to help their children learn to feel challenged rather than threatened.

Putting together the three developmental themes outlined above gives a general sense of what kinds of family atmosphere breed hardiness in children. The social and physical environment changes frequently and includes many moderately difficult tasks. Parents encourage their children to construe the changes as richness and support their efforts to perform the tasks successfully. More generally, the parents are warm and enthusiastic toward the children so that their interactions are usually pleasant, rewarding, and supportive of individual expression.

In this atmosphere children are very likely to develop personality hardiness, taking it with them as they become older and eventually leave their families of origin. It should not be thought that these conditions of early development are restricted to socioeconomically advantaged families. Being largely established by the parents, atmosphere is only loosely connected to socioeconomic conditions. Indeed, some wealthy and powerful parents neglect their children beyond all hope of their developing personality hardiness. In contrast, some parents who are poor and socially marginal manage nonetheless to construct environments for their children that are developmentally beneficial.

Once the rudiments of hardiness have been learned, the youngster enters into what we call later development (Kobasa & Maddi, 1977) to signify that there is enough personality structure present to permit self-initiated learning. In particular, the youngster with rudimentary hardiness can learn through failure experiences. In contrast, the youngster not having developed hardiness is too self-protective to risk failure, too insecure to face it squarely when it happens, and too rigid to let it spur reconsideration of decisions and directions.

These days, there is increasing concern about the plight of adolescents, in whose age group there is a frightening increase in alcohol and drug abuse, serious accidents, and suicide. Experts frequently contend (e.g., Moore, 1982) that the adolescent period is too tumultuous and should, therefore, be rendered more simple, less demanding, and more predictable. Even if any of us had the power to bring such a thing about, I am not at all sure it would be desirable. There is, after all, much to be learned about oneself and the world in the adolescent experience that sets the stage for the rest of life. In later development adolescence is only the first phase. It seems to me (1982) that youngsters may be able to handle the stresses and strains of the adolescent period if they have emerged from childhood with the rudiments of personality hardiness.

Elaborately adapting Kierkegaard, we (Kobasa & Maddi, 1977) have contended that persons must pass through stages of aestheticism (roughly hedonism) and idealism (roughly inflexible ideals) before reaching a full-bodied authenticity. In order for aestheticism and idealism to be given up so that one can move on, they must be disconfirmed by failure experiences properly understood. It is only the youngster who emerges from childhood with the rudiments of hardiness who will be sufficiently resilient to learn by failure and hence be able to enter into aestheticism and idealism vigorously and give them up through their disconfirmation just as vigorously. Insofar as a normative task of adolescence is to try to reject aestheticism, we should not consider tampering with the adolescent's environment in some vain hope of making it easier, so much as concentrating on facilitating the development of hardiness in the preceeding period of childhood.

Counseling for Hardiness

Can persons who have not developed personality hardiness in childhood be helped later in life? If hardiness can be learned in childhood, there is little reason to believe that it cannot be learned later. But learning it later may be rendered especially difficult because the unproductive habits of a nonhardy past must be broken in order that commitment, control, and challenge be instilled. This suggests the utility of counseling or a psychotherapeutic approach. But whatever sort of counseling procedure is involved needs to be consistent with the existential emphasis on helping the person find his or her own particular directions in the general effort after authenticity.

There are several counseling approaches in common use that appear relevant because they are cognitively based, explicitly concerning assumptions made about self and world. On careful scrutiny, however, they emerge as too directive to be very existential. These include rational-emotive therapy (Ellis, 1977), assertiveness training (Rimm & Cunningham, 1985), affirmations, EST and its new incarnation, FORUM, and stress-inoculation training (Meichenbaum, 1977). Ostensibly, all these approaches aim to increase the person's sense of worth and confidence so that the stresses of everyday life can be better coped with. Also, all employ cognitive methods in attempting to produce these aims. On these grounds they would appear to be relevant. The main problem, however, is that they interpret to the person what is realistic and what is not, forcing him or her to adopt this imposed frame of reference on experience. In general, these approaches start from some version of the assumption that persons are unrealistic in having a low sense of worth or confidence and can feel and act more assertively through thinking about themselves more positively (realistically). It is common for the counselor to identify how persons are being unrealistic and to supply bases for thinking better. In all this there is a remarkable absence of sensitivity to the specifics of a person's particular life and subjective experience. Ironically, such approaches may alienate persons from deep self-understanding, substituting instead a surprisingly conventional formulation of their troubles. From an existential viewpoint, these approaches should tend to produce indiscriminate rigidity in thought and action rather than the freeing of the decision-making process, coupled with the resiliency to accept feedback from this process, that would seem more consistent with finding one's own directionality.

By a laborious process of observing and interacting with clients, searching all the while for how to help them without merely imposing external views, we have developed counseling procedures for encouraging personality hardiness in adolescents and adults (Maddi, 1985; Maddi & Kobasa, 1984). This procedure employs three interrelated techniques through which the client is led to cope with stressful circumstances by transforming them and thereby resolving the problem. The feedback from this coping process is then used by the client to reflect on the underlying assumptions he or she has made concerning self, world, and the interaction between them. Throughout, clients work with their own assumptions, understandings, and goals, trying always to stretch them through imagination and evaluate them through personal judgment. If they become better able to cope with their problems transformationally, they have ample experience to grow in the sense of commitment, control, and challenge marking personality hardiness.

Using the three interrelated techniques to help persons develop hardiness is a skilled clinical activity. It would not be appropriate or possible to detail it sufficiently here so that others could even begin to learn how to be hardiness trainers. My aim in what follows is merely to give some idea of why the techniques fit the kinds of assumptions made by existential psychologists.

The starting point is a problem-solving technique we call *situational reconstruction*. Starting with a description of the problem or stressful circumstance, the person is led by the steps of the exercise to imagine versions of the circumstance that are even worse, and somehow better. The person is encouraged to consider what would have to shift in the circumstance in order to increase the likelihood of the better and worse versions. Then the person explores what he or she could personally do to help bring about the better versions and stave off the worse versions. This leads to a reaction plan that is then carried out. If the exercise goes well, the feedback obtained throughout provides a basis for deepening one's sense of commitment, control, and challenge.

But the person may find it difficult to carry out the imaginative or action features of situational reconstruction. When this happens it is sometimes because some strong emotion surrounding the stressful circumstance has been pushed out of attention and is therefore not available as information as to the person's relevant underlying assumptions. This is a time when we use the second technique, called *focusing* (Gendlin 1978). For our purposes this is a good technique with which to push aside conventional levels of meaning, and through focusing on bodily messages search for some more emotional, personal, individualistic meaning. If the person indeed finds some meaning of this sort, then he or she tries situational reconstruction again, utilizing the new information. If the blockage to successful completion of this technique has been removed, then the process goes forward as described in the previous paragraph.

If, however, no amount of situational reconstruction and focusing resolves the problem, then we conclude that the person has confronted an aspect of facticity, a given of experience. The emphasis then shifts to accepting this facticity serenely, i.e., without further losing one's sense of commitment, control, and challenge despite being unable to solve or change a problem. In this, our technique of *compensatory self-improvement* is helpful. It requires the person to identify a second problem or stressful circumstance, preferably related to the first one which is being accepted as a given, and to work on the second instead. This working is accomplished, once again, with situational reconstruction and focusing.

As the experiences in counseling accumulate, the person copes with more and more problems with these three interrelated techniques and obtains extensive feedback with which to grow in a sense of commitment, control, and challenge. The techniques encourage the person to deal more directly with problems, to take the initiative in decision making and action and to identify facticity and possibility. Throughout, it is the person who defines problems, whose imaginative and action processes are directed toward solving them, who concludes after appropriate struggle that facticity is present, and who reflects on underlying assumptions that have been made concerning self, world, and the interaction between them. The techniques stimulate and partially guide these processes but do not impose the counselor's categories, ideas about change, values, and preferences on the client.

THE WISDOM TO KNOW THE DIFFERENCE

I have covered a lot of ground in highlighting the decision-making process as the basis for identifying what is unchangeable and what is possible. We reflected on experience of insurmountable limitations and exploration of complimentarity and conflict among experience sources. Also considered was the transcendent role of symbolization, imagination, and judgment. Determining what is facticity and what is possibility emerged from all this as a truly complex matter engaged in under the aura of the inevitable anxiety of facing the new and unknown.

My proposal is that it is personality hardiness that gives persons the best chance to decide consistently for the future, discerning carefully but forthrightly what is likely to be possible and unchangeable for them. Conversely, it is a sense of inferiority marking the absence of hardiness that courts mistakes of conformity and extravagance by confusing facticity and possibility. I have also taken on the psychologist's task of considering how hardiness comes about both through the normal developmental process and by counseling efforts.

There is much in personality hardiness that lends the courage to change the changeable and the serenity to accept the unchangeable called for in the prayer I mentioned at the beginning of this chapter.

Similarly, hardiness emerges as a prerequisite for the "wisdom to know the difference," in that it facilitates complete and honest exploration of one's relevant experiences, whether remembered, currently perceived, or anticipated. The rest of wisdom is the accumulation of understanding, or personal growth, that results from the hard work of forging a fulfilling life.

NOTE

Preparation of this paper was supported in part by National Institute of Mental Health grant MH 39672.

REFERENCES

Antonovsky, A. *Health, stress and coping*. San Francisco: Jossey-Bass, 1979.

Ellis, A. The basic clinical theory of rational-emotive therapy. In A. Ellis & R. Grieger (Eds.), *Handbook of Rational-Emotive Therapy*. New York: Springer, 1977.

Gendlin, E. *Focusing*. New York: Everest House, 1978.

Kierkegaard, S. *Fear and trembling and the sickness unto death*, trans. W. Lorie. Garden City, New York: Doubleday, Anchor Books, 1954.

Kobasa, S. C. Stressful life events, personality and health: An inquiry into hardiness. *Journal of Personality and Social Psychology*, 1979, 42, 707–717.

Kobasa, S. C. The hardy personality: Toward a social psychology of stress and health. In G. S. Sanders & J. Suls (Eds.), *The social psychology of health and illness*. Hillsdale, N. J.: Lawrence Erlbaum, 1982.

Kobasa, S. C. Personality and health: Specifying and strengthening the conceptual links. In P. Shaver (Ed.), *Self, situations and social behavior*. Beverly Hills, Calif.: Sage Publications, 1985.

Kobasa, S. C., & Maddi, S. R. Existential personality theory. In R. Corsini (Ed.), *Current personality theory*. Itasca, Ill.: Peacock, 1977.

Kobasa, S. C., Maddi, S. R., & Kahn, S. Hardiness and health. *Journal of Personality and Social Psychology*, 1982, 42, 168–177.

Kobasa, S. C., Maddi, S. R., Puccetti, M., & Zola, M. A. Effectiveness of hardiness, exercise, and social support as resources against illness. *Journal of Psychosomatic Research*, 1985, 29, 525–33.

Kobasa, S. C., & Puccetti, M. Personality and social resources in stress-resistance. *Journal of Personality and Social Psychology*, 1983, 45, 839–850.

McClelland, D. C. Risk-taking in children with high and low need for achievement. In J. W. Atkinson (Ed.), *Motives in fantasy, action, and society*. Princeton, N.J.: Van Nostrand, 1958.

Maddi, S. R. The existential neurosis. *Journal of Abnormal Psychology*, 1967, 72, 311–325.

Maddi, S. R. The search for meaning. In M. Page (Ed.), *Nebraska symposium on motivation*. Lincoln, Nebr.: University of Nebraska Press, 1970.

Maddi, S. R. *Personality theories: A comparative analysis* (4th ed.). Homewood, Ill.: Dorsey, 1980.

Maddi, S. R. Myth and personality. *Journal of Mind and Behavior*, 1981, 2, 145–153.

Maddi, S. R. Personality development. In C. D. Moore (Ed.), *Adolescence and stress*. Washington, D.C.: NIMH Science Reports Series, 1982.

Maddi, S. R. Existential psychotherapy. In S. J. Lynn & J. P. Garske (Eds.), *Contemporary psychotherapies*. Columbus, Ohio: Charles Merrill, 1985.

Maddi, S. R., & Kobasa, S. C. *The hardy executive: Health under stress*. Homewood, Ill.: Dow Jones-Irwin, 1984.

Meichenbaum, D. *Cognitive-behavior modification: An integrative approach*. New York: Plenum, 1977.

Moore, C. D. (Ed.). *Adolescence and stress*. Washington, D.C.: NIMH Science Reports Series, 1982.

Nietzsche, F. *Complete works*, ed. O. Levy. New York: Russell & Russell, 1964.

Rimm, D. C., & Cunningham, H. M. Behavior therapies. In S. J. Lynn & J. P. Garske (Eds.), *Contemporary psychotherapies*. Columbus, Ohio: Charles Merrill, 1985.

Rosenman, R. H., Friedman, M., Strauss, R., Jenkins, C. D., Zyzanski, S. W., & Wurm, H. Coronary heart disease in the Western Collaboration Study: A follow-up experience of 4-½ years. *Journal of Chronic Diseases*, 1970, 28, 173–190.

Sartre, J.P. *Being and nothingness*, trans. H. Earnes. New York: Philosophical Library, 1956.

Solzhenitsyn, A. *Cancer ward*, trans. N. Bethell & D. Burg. New York: Ferrar, Straus and Giroux, 1969.

Tillich, P. *The courage to be*. New Haven, Conn.: Yale University Press, 1952.

Wheelis, A. *How people change*. New York: Harper & Row, 1974.

White, E. B. *The once and future king*. New York: Berkeley, 1983.

Existentialism and Human Development: Commentary on Salvatore R. Maddi

JANE FLAX

At the beginning of his essay, Salvatore Maddi mentions the special concern psychologists have for "prescriptive considerations of individual development." He goes on to give an account of the contributions an existentialist approach can make to the question of what constitutes the desirable direction for human development as well as some of the impediments to such development.

My concern in these remarks will also be with the existentialist concept of individual development and the ethics derived from it. I will identify some of the presuppositions necessary to and underlying this concept and some of my questions about these presuppositions. Finally, I will briefly explore some of the social, ethical, and clinical implications of the existentialist norm, especially in contrast to a possible feminist alternative.

As is well known, existentialism includes a definite set of ethical and metaphysical commitments. Confronted with qualities conceptualized as antinomies at least since the 17th century, the existentialist "resolves" their problematic nature by simply annihilating one of the pair. Thus transcendence, mind, reason, the future, the heroic or agonistic, and doing are retained at the expense of immanence, the body, feeling, the quotidian, and being. In existentialism, also, the person is conceptualized as a self-constituting monad, and everything outside this monad is experienced as an (at least) potential impediment to the freedom of the monad to pursue its own projects and thereby to continually reconstitute itself.

These commitments are present in Maddi's paper as well. "Facticity" is seen only as imposing limitations on the growth of the individual. The new represents the way to "freedom, renewal, richness, sensitivity," and so on. Our lives are seen as being constituted in and through a series of (cognitive) decisions. The substance of these decisions is a choice between "shrinking from the future" or "embracing the past." According to Maddi, "to do something new is developmentally more valuable than persisting in the old." Choosing the past entails some sort of failure or constriction; either one is paralyzed by or seeks to avoid the ontological anxiety invariably evoked by confronting the new or external data from the world or our bodies impinging unavoidably upon the mind. Despite Maddi's acknowledgment that sometimes facticity cannot be overcome, a serene acceptance of limits feels like a second-rate compromise within the context of this essay.

Since people are constituted in and through their decisions, they should be able to make these decisions with maximal rationality. In this context rationality means the capacity to correctly distinguish between facticity and possibility in any given situation. However, our decision-making processes may be inhibited by certain feelings (such as a sense of inferiority). The opposite of a sense of inferiority is *hardiness*, Maddi's developmental norm.

It is worth reiterating the three components of hardiness. Hardy persons believe the self and world are worthwhile; they believe they can influence what is going on and that change is basically positive (e.g., it is a "stimulus to personal growth").

My uneasiness with this set of presuppositions can be best expressed by first noting what is excluded from this developmental norm. First, the hardy person never lives in the present. The past is prologue to the future, but there is nothing in between. The familiar, the day to day, has no value in itself. In fact, the day to day, what exists and the work required merely to maintain it, are devalued in existentialism. Sartre, for example, calls the "in itself" (which grounds the quotidian) "slime." This slime fills him with disgust, loathing, and terror. Consider this extraordinary, but not atypical passage from *Being and Nothingness*:

> The slimy seems to lend itself to me, it invites me. . . . But it is a
> trap . . . The slime is like a liquid seen in a nightmare, where all

its properties are animated by a sort of life and turn back against me. Slime is the revenge of the In-itself. A sickly-sweet feminine revenge which will be symbolized on another level by the quality "sugary". ... A sugary sliminess is the ideal of the slimy; it symbolizes the sugary death of the For-itself. ... A consciousness which became slimy would be transformed by the thick stickiness of its ideas. From the time of our upsurge into the world, we are haunted by the image of a consciousness which would like to launch forth into the future, toward a projection of self, and which at the very moment when it was conscious of arriving there would be slyly held back by the invisible suction of the past and which would have to assist in its own slow dissolution in this past which it was fleeing, would have to aid in the invasion of its project by a thousand parasites until it completely lost itself. (1966, pp. 747–748)

In reading such passages, we begin to suspect that this self's endless movement toward the new is also a sort of flight, that the source of existentialist anxiety is not just fear of the unknown—or rather that this formulation of its problem is partially a screen for a different sort of fear—fear of commitment, of intimacy, of the complex negotiations that are required to sustain relationships between self and other—whether that other be a lover or a community.

By privileging change and action, we obscure the possibility that a constant need for the new can also be a symptom of illness. As Dorothy Dinnerstein (1976) points out in her extraordinary reworking of existentialism, psychoanalysis, and feminism: "There is no hint in this account that what appears to be a 'freely chosen project' can in fact be chosen out of neurotic inner compulsion; that the person's 'undefined need to transcend himself' can in fact be a need to escape something essential in himself" (p. 212).

The potentially compulsive quality of this endless projection of the self into the future can be seen in the experience of a borderline or schizoid person. Such persons do not have a defect in cognitive decision making. They can correctly assess what they are capable of doing, and they consistently push themselves to the limits of possibility. However, they cannot feel themselves, experience themselves, as doing anything. Their self is not filled by choosing the future; in fact, they feel more and more depleted. They suffer, not from fear of the new, not from an inability to act, but from fear of *being* itself.

The norm of hardiness also seems to exclude the capacity to enter into relationships with others or to give oneself over to the needs of a community, a child, or a friend. In existentialism the individual is profoundly isolated; "One person can never really know another person." One always risks the death of the self in a relationship with an other.

Despite the existentialist separation of self and society or the claims of existentialist therapists not to impose values on clients, it is clear that the privileging of the new over the old, or of doing over being are only possible or intelligible in certain sorts of societies. First, such norms reflect a society in which constant accumulation (whether of goods or experience) is considered highly desirable. Second, such norms reflect a society in which the work of creating bonds between self and other, whether personal or political, is devalued or rendered publicly invisible. Such devalued work in our society includes childrearing and the nourishing of civic virtue. Third, such norms presuppose a division of labor in which some are able to project themselves into the future because others are firmly rooted in the present, cleaning, preserving, cooking, taking care of the children, providing food and shelter, and what Sara Ruddick (1984) calls "attentive love"—"intense, pure, disinterested, gratuitous, generous attention" (p. 223)[1]. In our gender-divided society, many of these household and care-giving virtues and activities are primarily practiced by women—which is not to say that we should all merely abandon the projection of self into the future (what Dinnerstein calls "history making") for the cultivation of domestic virtues.

In fact, the activities and ethics of attentive love and of history making are distorted when they are not balanced by and integrated with the other. The projection of the self toward "freecome," unbounded by attentive love for others, our ecology and present and past experience is all too easily transformed into domination and objectification of self and other. Attentive love without concern for the self and its transcendental powers is all too easily transformed into a bitter, self-sacrificing resentment that victimizes self and others.

The concept of subjectivity in existentialism is thus partial and incomplete. That which it excludes is in fact essential to the possibility of such subjectivity existing at all, but given the nature of existentialist subjectivity, it is not clear how these necessary but excluded qualities could be included in or reconciled with its distinctive commitments. (Thus Maddi remains puzzled over how, given the distinctively existentialist premises, one person could ever help another.)

What do these philosophical reflections have to do with the practice of psychotherapy? First, they should encourage us as clinicians to be more self-reflective about the dangers inherent in our commitment to our own projects as therapists. We too tend to favor doing over being, curing the sick "Other" over being in a relationship with a person who in many ways is not unlike our self.

As Harold Searles (1979) points out in his essay, "The 'Dedicated Physician' in the Field of Psychotherapy and Psychoanalysis," our commitment to doing, to "curing" someone defined as sick, as an Other unlike our self, can blind us to the ways such a stance drives our patients (more) crazy. First, this stance can encourage us to disavow our own feelings and the powerful effects these have on the other and the therapy process as a whole. This denial of our own feeling states can make the patient feel disconnected from and abandoned by the therapist. It can also repeat the experience in a family in which aspects of the emotional reality of the situation were dismissed as projection or fantasy produced by the (now) patient. Third, the therapist's need for progress or growth may be experienced by the patient as only the latest in a long series of demands for performance and decisions on the part of others in the patient's life. Sometimes our patients most need time and space to just be —despairing, confused, or pleasuring. They need us to be with them, perhaps absorbing or containing their feeling states, perhaps just there as a passive but facilitating environment.

In order to recognize and meet such needs within the therapy process, the therapist has to move beyond the monadic and agentic views of the self that constitute core aspects of existentialism. The therapy process is a kind of relational work in which both therapist and patient struggle to acknowledge, develop, and reciprocally exchange their capacities for both attentive love and history making within the context of a unique and delimited relationship. Only under such conditions can one person really help another.

NOTE

1. Hubert Dreyfus pointed out to me at the Rutgers conference that an analysis of Kierkegaard's comments on marriage would provide further support for my critique of existentialism (Kierkegaard, *Either/Or* [Vol. 2].

New York: Anchor, 1959, especially pp. 312–332). On p. 316 Kierkegaard says, "Woman explains finiteness, man is in chase of infinitude."

REFERENCES

Dinnerstein, D. *The mermaid and the minotaur: Sexual arrangements and human malaise*. New York: Harper & Row, 1976.

Ruddick, S. Maternal thinking. In J. Treblicot (Ed.), *Mothering: Essays in feminist theory*. Totowa, N. J.: Rowman & Allanheld, 1984.

Sarte, J. P. *Being and nothingness*. New York: Washington Square Press, 1966.

Searles, H. F. *Countertransference and related subjects; selected papers*. New York: International Universities Press, 1979.

Rejoinder to Jane Flax

SALVATORE R. MADDI

Jane Flax's comments indicate that she has not heard what I had to say. My position should not be confused either with Sartre or the stereotypical male, who pursues his career agentically while leaving his wife at home to do the drudgery.

Flax's critique contends that my position (1) does not appreciate the present, (2) considers facticity nothing but limitation, (3) amounts to isolation and a compulsive need for change from fear of commitment and intimacy, and (4) may manipulate clients into trying to change when what they need is to rest and share relationship with their therapists. She does not understand my position and ends by advocating something that must be regarded as odd.

However engrossing, exciting, frustrating, painful, boring, or satisfying the present may be, it does not remain static. As long as there are thinking, feeling, and acting persons involved with each other and the broader society, the present rushes to become either the future (something new) or the past (something old). This continual transformation of our present does not necessarily involve dramatic changes (e.g., moving residences, starting relationships); cognitive (e.g., a new perspective on a friend's problem) and emotional (e.g., anger gives way on reflection to an underlying sense of hurt) shifts are quite enough. Perhaps Professor Flax does not appreciate this point because she is dealing exclusively with dramatic changes rather than the more subtle internal changes. Be that as it may, an essential part of appreciating one's present is understanding its changing nature.

My expressed position on facticity is that it is an important part of one's personality, an inevitable outcome of living fully, and something to be truly and sincerely accepted rather than disdained. I could not have started my paper with that prayer calling for serenity in accepting the unchangeable, or ended it by communicating that essential feature of our psychotherapy that helps clients accept facticity serenely, were my position accurately depicted by Flax. Facticity is a living, real part of ourselves that should not be abhorred. I recall the thought from one of Shakespeare's sonnets that recognizes that whoever loves me loves everyone I've ever loved. Intimate relationships (and lots of other experiences) from our past influence what we are and may become. So the person who loves you should have no trouble appreciating and accepting those who entered significantly into your developmental process.

What is a problem, and I was quite clear about this, is when something is misconstrued as unchangeable. Such false facticity has little developmental value (the Freudians would call it *defensive*). Let me also remind Professor Flax that I rendered misconstrual of something as in the realm of possibility an equal developmental hazard. How can I, therefore, be guilty of advocating a compulsive need for change, or be unable to understand the importance of what is truly unchangeable? Elsewhere (Kobasa & Maddi, 1977; Maddi & Kobasa, 1984) I have taken pains to distinguish a genuine developmental thrust from mere adventurousness or novelty-seeking. Indeed, adventurousness defines a category of psychopathology for me (Maddi, 1970).

In all this Flax has also misunderstood the role of personality hardiness. It is not itself the developmental norm. Rather, it functions as prerequisite for accurately perceiving facticity and possibility. The developmental norm is more accurately carried in the prayer I quoted, and at the end of my paper, I make clear that reaching this combination of courage, serenity, and wisdom involves a mix of hardiness and the experiences of living fully that it encourages. It should be clear in all this that mine is certainly not a bloodless, merely cognitive agentic position.

Flax also contends that I advocate isolation, perhaps out of fear of commitment or intimacy. In this, she seems to be focusing on some connotations of the control aspects of hardiness, but neglecting the commitment and challenge aspects. By definition, persons high in hardiness have little difficulty making commitments and are not threatened by obstacles, seeing them as challenges instead. Hardiness should aid commitment and intimacy, not preclude it. The developmental norm I have postulated (Maddi, 1967; Kobasa & Maddi, 1977) takes intimate (rather than contractual or minimal) relationships as an essential ingredient. There is no implicit contradiction to this posed by the emphasis on growth through choosing the future, unless one has an excessively gross view of change (dramatic and external shifts, rather than internal, subtle ones).

It is at this point that Flax begins to fall into an odd advocacy. Let me point out that it is she who apparently finds child-rearing and homemaking mere drudgery requiring an abject, uncritical commitment (which she calls *reflexive love*). The hardy parent, female or male, would find interest in, be able to influence, and learn through the activities of child-rearing and homemaking, so they would not appear as drudgery. Important in this would be such a parent's recognition of the importance of helping the child develop through choosing the future rather than the past.

The oddity of her position deepens when she combines views on borderline and schizoid persons into a nonexistent composite. Schizoids do tend to be isolates, but neither to suffer over that nor consider their lives empty. They certainly do not push themselves toward change. Some borderline persons feel unfulfilled, but bounce back and forth in action and thought in a manner that reveals an underlying cognitive deficit—they can hardly be characterized as making decisions soundly. Once Flax's mistaken combination of these two psychopathological states is unraveled, her criticism, of course, falls apart.

The ultimate oddity emerges when she worries that my position may manipulate clients into trying to change even though they may want to rest, share, and be nurtured. She aligns herself with that deepening pessimism in the psychoanalytic movement that contends that therapy is about understanding more than change. Doesn't therapy have to be about both to make sense? It is, after all, not just friendship or intimacy, but a contrived relationship to help the client.

If therapy is seen as being about both understanding and change, then my position qualifies as relevant to both. The techniques involved encourage and guide clients who are struggling to change problems they have defined as needing change, and the struggle is conducted respecting their own subjective understanding of things. If after struggle they must accept facticity, they are helped to do so gracefully, without giving up on themselves. From the point of view

of conceptualization and technique, Flax appears to have misconstrued my approach.

There are, of course, incapable therapists who misuse whatever
approach they try. Let me assure Professor Flax that my clients feel
respected and nurtured in their pain and vulnerability, but also
encouraged and supported in their goal of a better life, even when
they have begun to lose hope of attaining it. I refer Flax once again to
the prayer with which my paper begins; as a therapist it is not enough
to just make the client comfortable, you must also do what you can to
foster that combination of courage, serenity, and wisdom.

REFERENCES

Kobasa, S. C., & Maddi, S. R. Existential personality theory. In R. Corsini
    (Ed.), *Current personality theory.* Itasca, Ill.: Peacock, 1977.
Maddi, S. R. The existential neurosis. *Journal of Abnormal Psychology,*
    1967, 72, 311–325.
Maddi, S. R. The search for meaning. In M. Page (Ed.), *Nebraska symposium
    on motivation.* Lincoln, Nebr.: University of Nebraska Press, 1970.
Maddi, S. R., & Kobassa, S. C. *The hardy executive: Health under stress.*
    Homewood, Ill.: Dow Jones-Irwin, 1984.

ONTOLOGICAL HERMENEUTICS

Chapter 8

Humanism, Hermeneutics, and the Concept of the Human Subject

LOUIS A. SASS

It is easy to ignore the differences between intellectual movements that share a common enemy—especially when that enemy looms like a colossus over the field in question. This, it seems to me, is the case in psychology, where humanistic and hermeneutic approaches tend to be equated because of their shared opposition to the objectivism and scientism of the mainstream. It is true, after all, that philosophers like Heidegger (1962), Gadamer (1976, 1984), and Ricoeur (1981), and their followers in the social sciences (e.g., Geertz, 1973, 1983; Taylor, 1985; Rabinow & Sullivan, 1979; Haan & Bellah, 1983), are committed to developing an alternative to the methods and models of the natural sciences—as is also the case with humanistic and "third force" psychologists generally. Further, both humanists and hermeneuticists are heirs to the intellectual tradition of Romanticism, itself largely a reaction against the Enlightenment tradition of objectivism, the intellectual source of mainstream empirical psychology (Shalin, 1986). Indeed, both these groups can be called *humanistic* in a broad sense—if by this we mean committed to developing an approach respectful of the special characteristics of human experience and action, and free of the positivism, mechanism, and reductionism of 19th-century physical sciences and the social sciences modeled on them. However, along with these affinities are significant differences that should not be forgotten.

There is another, more restrictive sense of the term *humanism* that would apply to much of third force psychology, at least in America, but not at all to the hermeneutic tradition I will discuss—an approach that could almost be called a kind of *anti*humanism. This chapter is devoted to working out the distinction between humanism and this most influential school of hermeneutics—the tradition of Heidegger and his followers, known as *ontological hermeneutics* or *hermeneutic phenomenology*.[1] Humanistic psychology is a particularly appropriate foil to use in an exposition of the hermeneutic perspective, for it is perhaps the purest manifestation in the social sciences of the sort of humanism against which ontological hermeneutics has pitted itself; also, the humanistic movement in psychology has had a profound impact on contemporary culture through its influence on people's aspirations and self-images. Thus it exemplifies, at both a theoretical and a practical level, many of the aspects of modern humanistic thought and culture to which Heidegger and other hermeneuticists are so strongly opposed.

By considering both affinities and differences between these schools, I hope to provide a clarification and critique of key tenets and central assumptions of both perspectives. Unlike previous studies that have concentrated on methodological and epistemological aspects of hermeneutics (Bernstein, 1983; Packer, 1985; Gergen, 1982; Polkinghorne, 1983; Kuhn, 1977), my focus is primarily on *philosophical anthropology*—the image of man or fundamental conception of human subjectivity that guides theory and practice. Although I will engage in some mild polemics in favor of hermeneutics, the main purpose of this comparative study is expository: to introduce the hermeneutic perspective to social scientists unfamiliar with, or mystified by, this important but difficult approach.

Perhaps the most characteristic feature of humanistic psychology is the emphasis it places on the conscious human subject. This centrality of the subject has a number of overlapping aspects that can, somewhat arbitrarily, be described as emphases on four purported qualities of the subject: freedom, privacy, uniqueness, and self-transparency (the latter refers to a certain faith in the certitude and clarity of subjective experience). Each of these emphases has both a descriptive and a prescriptive import in humanistic psychology. On the one hand, the human condition is supposedly defined by the presence in all human beings of these characteristics; on the other hand, the healthy or optimally functioning person is seen as someone who both recognizes this human universal and manifests it in especially clear fashion. Those in the tradition of ontological hermeneutics (the tradition of Heidegger, Gadamer, and Ricoeur) take a different position on each of these aspects of human subjectivity.

In the first section of this chapter, I describe the views of humanistic psychology on each of these issues, concluding with a consideration of philosophical sources. Then I turn to the contrasting approach of hermeneutics, whose sources are rather different. In this section, the linchpin of the essay, I discuss differences between the hermeneutic phenomenology of Heidegger and the, in a sense, more humanistic "transcendental phenomenology" of his teacher Husserl; special attention is paid to Heidegger's notion of the "horizonal" nature of human existence. Next, I consider the implications of accepting the hermeneutic philosophical anthropology for two issues of broad relevance to psychology and psychotherapy: first, the conceptualization of interpersonal communication and understanding, both in everyday life and the human sciences; second, prescriptive notions about "authenticity" and the nature of human fulfillment. Whereas the first of these issues bears upon epistemological matters, the nature and limits of psychological interpretation, the second concerns ethics and values, conceptions of what is the "healthy" or "genuine" way to live. I conclude the essay by considering some of the implications of hermeneutics for psychotherapeutic practice and, finally, for our general approach to psychological knowledge.

As we shall see, many of the conceptual polarities by means of which humanistic psychology has traditionally defined itself, whether explicitly or implicitly, are dissolved or transcended by what is, in my view, the more complex and sophisticated position of hermeneutics. Third force psychology would, therefore, avoid certain characteristic exaggerations and oversimplifications—not to mention certain forms of naïveté—if it were to embrace the philosophical anthropology (and associated methodology) of hermeneutics.

A few cautionary words should be said about my approach. First, I am not primarily concerned with the exegesis of philosophical positions as such—with the accurate and detailed portrayal of the meaning of philosophical texts in all their subtlety and complexity. I am concerned, rather, with the place of these ideas in the stream of intellectual history, where a simplified version of the ideas in question is often what matters. Second, I will be taking a distanced, bird's eye view of a vast terrain, concerning myself with major formations and fault lines and necessarily ignoring subtle differences. Thus, I will focus on the overall spirit of humanism and hermeneutics, positions that are, admittedly, quite heterogeneous in nature. Third, I will be interested in maximizing differences, since hermeneutics and humanism have not been adequately distinguished in the psychological literature.[2]

HUMANISTIC PSYCHOLOGY

Freedom

At its inception third force psychology in America defined itself largely in opposition to the first two forces, behaviorism and psychoanalysis, each of which was seen by the humanists as propounding an overwhelmingly deterministic vision of human nature. In the introduction to his influential anthology of 1967, *Challenges of Humanistic Psychology*, James Bugental spoke of this controversy as "a battle for man's soul" (p. 9). Against both the reactive approach of stimulus-response (S-R) psychology and the mechanistic instinctualism of classical psychoanalysis, influential humanists (or protohumanists) like Allport (1961), Rogers (1961), and Bugental (1965, 1967) argued that the human being's most distinctive and important feature was the capacity for volitional choice. Lip service may have been paid to such constraining factors as culture, nurture, or biological inheritance, but far greater emphasis was placed on the capacity for free will, which was generally seen as capable of outweighing these deterministic factors.

This vision of man was not only descriptive but also prescriptive: thus, to be "proactive" rather than "reactive" was treated as both an essential defining feature of human nature in general and also as the goal or ideal toward which psychotherapy should strive. Nowhere is this central theme of humanism more clearly stated than in Hubert Bonner's article on "The Proactive Personality" in Bugental's anthology. Bonner (1967) writes, "We are all proactive," then describes the kind of person whose mode of being seems to raise this essential feature of the human to its highest pitch: "The proactive person, then, like every healthy and creative individual, resists engulfment by customs and rigid habits, the impairing force of narrow enculturation, and all barriers to a free and active forward movement of his personality. He has both the will and the capacity ... to transform himself in the light of his personal goals and values" (p. 65). As an example of a person who knows that "the future of man is largely of his own making," Bonner chooses Jean Genet, as described in Jean-Paul Sartre's famous existentialist study. Genet, writes Bonner, "has become deeply aware that in his acts of choice about his own life he had freed himself from the destructive forces of his past. He has 'cured' himself in the sense that he has transcended his prior reactive life and directed himself proactively toward a future" (p. 65).

Uniqueness

The second major facet of the humanist anthropology is the emphasis on individuality or the essential uniqueness of the person, and this too has both a descriptive and a prescriptive force. The descriptive emphasis on uniqueness as being a crucial if not definitive feature of human nature was, perhaps, given its clearest and most influential statement by Gordon Allport, an important influence on humanistic psychology who stressed the essentially idiographic nature of personality. Although, as Maddi (1980, p. 129) has pointed out, Allport's position on this issue was rather extreme, the tendency to emphasize and valorize individuality is in fact characteristic of all "fulfillment theorists" (Maddi's term for a group that includes the humanists).

We have already encountered the prescriptive emphasis in Bonner's valorization of "*personal* goals and values" as against those of culture, tradition, or personal history—referred to by him, rather disparagingly, as "rigid habits, the impairing force of narrow enculturation." Similar values are implicit in Carl Rogers's (1961) prizing of the uniqueness of each person's experience and in Maslow's (1955, 1962) central notion of self-actualization. In emphasizing the human being's "need for individuation, for being himself as a person" (Bonner, 1967, p. 65), and in identifying freedom and authenticity with the fulfillment of this individuality, the humanistic psychologists are taking up ideas that have a long history in Western culture, dating back at least to the Renaissance (Greenblatt, 1980) and reaching a kind of climax during the period of romanticism (Trilling, 1971; Taylor, 1975; Berman, 1980).

Privacy

Closely related to both the uniqueness and the freedom of the human person is the notion of the essential privacy or, as one might also put it, the subjectivity or inwardness of human reality. According to Bugental (1967, pp. 6–9), the "basic subjectivism of all experience" and the "privacy of the subjective" is actually "the cornerstone of humanistic psychology." Further, what he calls "the ultimate subjectivity of all that we call objective" applies both to experience and to action. Thus, all knowledge for him is intrinsically a statement about ourselves: "I mean, very literally, that any statement we make about the world (the 'out there') is inevitably, inescapably, a statement about our theory of ourselves (the 'in here')." Further, our behavior in the world is, supposedly, best understood by grasping the inner, and often unique, point of view taken by the actor: "While man's reactiveness is certainly recognized, the humanistic psychologist regards this as less distinctive of the human experience." Consequently, such a psychologist gives "primary concern to man's subjective experience and secondary concern to his actions."

For most of the major humanists, this essential quality of innerness—in one sense a universal characteristic of the human—is also the appropriate goal for human improvement. Thus, according to Rogers (1961, p. 189), the "fully-functioning person" is one for whom the locus of evaluation, especially self-evaluation, comes from within.

Such a vision of human nature seems to foster a belief in the essential privacy or even hiddenness of human reality: thus, it stresses not only that there is no objective reality "out there" (or, at least, not one of primary importance for psychology), but also that what we might call "subjective" reality exists not as a shared "we-world" but as a dispersion of separate and unique perspectives. The peculiar pathos of this romanticist/modernist vision of isolated consciousnesses was perhaps best expressed by Virginia Woolf in a famous passage that suggests that reality has to be understood not as a kind of illuminated stage at which we are all looking, but as more akin to a vast and dark forest in which, scattered about, wander lone individuals carrying lamps, each restricted to his own separate pool of light.[3]

Given their emphasis on privacy and uniqueness, significant communication or understanding between subjectivities might, for the humanists, necessarily seem to be deeply problematic, perhaps even impossible. The strange but perhaps not surprising fact is, however, that humanists who take such a view have generally believed in the possibility of a sort of perfect empathic communication, the achievement of which, given their premises, seems almost mystical or magical in nature.[4] Thus, in a recent article on psychotherapy, Moustakas (1986) writes of the state he calls "Being-In." Although admitting that this state may never be perfectly achieved, Moustakas obviously believes it can be closely approached: "When I am Being

In, I am totally immersed in the other; I enter every expression, nuance, thought, feeling; every scene or portrait, seeing it exactly as it is depicted. Being In puts me totally in the world of the other. My attitude and interest are focused on being aware and understanding from the vantage point of the other ... I do not select, interpret, advise, or direct" (pp. 100–101).

This conception of empathy seems deeply and intrinsically paradoxical: the humanistic emphasis on the privacy and uniqueness of each person's experience would seem to place the object of empathic knowing (i.e., the others subjectivity) quite out of reach; the humanistic emphasis on the inevitable subjectivity of all knowledge would seem to declare the knower's inevitable inadequacy to the task of understanding. (Also, note that the world of the other, though foreign to the interpreter, is presumed to be immediately intelligible to the Other who lives it; thus, from this point of view, the difficulty of understanding seems to reside only in the crossing of the gap separating knower from known, not in the understanding of *what* one knows once one enters the world of the other.)

Self-transparency

Moustakas's apparent belief in the fundamental importance of grasping the immediate, unintegrated data of conscious experience brings us to the last of the four aspects. In addition to being the essential wellspring of freedom and locus of uniqueness and privacy, human subjectivity is also the main source of certitude and clarity about human existence. Here we encounter a well-known aspect of humanistic psychology, its reliance on the spirit if not the letter of phenomenology—a philosophy, founded by Edmund Husserl (1962, 1969), that, according to a recent overview of humanism, "begins and ends with the phenomena or experiences immediately presented to consciousness" and values such data on the grounds that they are "all we can know with certainty" (Tageson, 1982, p. 57).

As Husserl himself well knew, his philosophical project had much in common with Descartes' search for a source of certainty in the presumably indubitable facts of human experience itself (the title of one of Husserl's books is *Cartesian Meditations*). Husserl's fundamental method involves the setting aside or "bracketing" of all belief in the reality of the external world in order to clear the way for a (presumably) unbiased description of experience as it presents itself immanently or phenomenally—i.e., stripped of all scientific and naturalistic assumptions re causality and objective existence. This method, which Husserl called the *phenomenological reduction* or *epoché*, directs attention toward acts of consciousness and their intentional objects, thereby opening up for analysis "an infinite realm of being of a new kind" (quoted in Dreyfus, 1982a, p. 7). Like Descartes' method of doubt, Husserl's approach can be called a kind of foundationalism: an attempt to discover a realm of indubitable and transparent meanings or experiential entities that can provide a firm basis on which to build valid knowledge about human existence. Several third force psychologists describe this Husserlian objectivity as involving "fidelity to phenomena"—*phenomena* being understood by them as experiences that are "direct," "immediate," and "prelinguistic," not involving the "interpretations" or "constructions" of natural science or common sense (Colaizzi, 1978, p. 52; Valle & King, 1978, pp. 9–12).

Taken together, the belief in the essential certitude and innerness of experience (i.e., self-transparency and privacy) constitute a position that can be termed *subjectivist*: i.e., both assumptions imply that human reality is actually constituted by the individual subject, whose inner experiences are considered to provide a bedrock foundation for the world.

This faith in such a foundational realm of private, immanent experiences has obviously had important methodological implications for third force psychology. As Bonner (1967, p. 62) says, the reliance on "descriptive phenomenology," "immediate cognition," and "self-anchored perception" implies and assumes that "a person carefully observing his own subjective experience can add substantial and dependable insight into the nature of human behavior." This view has been taken to justify concentrating on conscious subjectivity to the relative exclusion of other realms. Thus, in the words of its practitioners, humanistic psychology tends, both as science and therapy, to "accept immediate experience with only a passing glance at congruence with external events" (Temerlin, 1965, p. 71) and, as mentioned above, to give "primary concern to man's subjective experience and secondary concern to his actions" (Bugental, 1967, p. 9). The following statement by William Tageson (1982, p. 55) illustrates the tendency to accept the testimony of conscious experience almost as indubitable, especially when it concerns the nature of the self or of subjectivity itself: " 'Common sense' that is derived from my lived experience tells me I am somehow a stable center of existence, a 'self', persisting through all the changes and stages of my life."[5]

This fourth aspect of the humanist notion of the human subject concerns what might be called the fundamental self-transparency of consciousness: the availability or nonhiddenness of the most fundamental facts of human existence. This belief also must be understood as having both a descriptive and a prescriptive force—descriptive because, as we have seen, it implies a vision of human nature as involving a form of fundamental and unquestionable self-knowledge; prescriptive because it assumes that the actualization of this potentiality is a kind of ultimate good. Thus, as Tageson (1982, p. 39) states, humanistic psychologies in general tend to assume that "to the extent that *all* my personal data are available to my awareness, can be openly owned by me," I'll be "a genuinely caring person."

Humanistic Psychology—A Summing Up

As with their stressing of freedom, the humanists' emphasis on the other facets of human subjectivity developed, at least to some extent, in reaction against the then-reigning paradigms of traditional behaviorism and psychoanalysis. The concern with uniqueness meant a rejection of the behaviorist pursuit of general laws of learning applicable across people or even across species, and also a rejection of the psychoanalytic preference for typologies of neurotic types. The insistence on privacy and self-transparency implied a rejection of the positivistic kind of foundationalism, which is rooted in the supposedly unquestionable nature of public or behavioral data. It also meant rejecting the sometimes Procrustean reductionism of psychoanalysis, where dogmatic speculations about the unconscious seemed to be valued over the more nuanced, unique, and empirical facts of an individual's conscious experience. In 1967 Bugental (p. 7) recognized the extent to which humanism in psychology was defined by what it was not but looked forward to a future when negation would play a less important role. One might ask whether such a change has come about during the quarter century of humanistic psychology's existence—and, if so, whether this has significantly modified the philosophical anthropology described above.

To answer this question is necessarily hazardous, given the heterogeneity of what might better be described as the humanistic psychol-*ogies*. Certainly, there are some third force psychologists who would not be comfortable with the four premises as I have stated them, especially among those with strong ties to more recent developments in European thought (Giorgi, 1970; Polkinghorne, 1983) and those interested in transpersonal psychology (Valle & Harari, 1985). (Some of these might identify more closely with the hermeneutic position.)

Nevertheless, it seems to me that these four premises, with the vision of Man they constitute, remain the core of what might be called "mainstream American humanistic psychology." Thus, in the most recent book-length survey of humanistic psychology, Tageson (1982) asserts that, despite their variety, humanistic psychologists share an emphasis on the proactive rather than reactive nature of man and on "self-reflective awareness"—qualities that clearly imply freedom, privacy, and self-transparency. Among the seven major themes of humanistic psychology Tageson lists are: the phenomenological approach, self-determination, person-centeredness, the ideal of authenticity, and the actualizing tendency—all of which correspond to the aspects of humanism discussed above. (The other two, holism and self-transcendence, concern features of humanism that do not differentiate it from the hermeneutic position.)

That the values of humanistic psychology have remained essentially the same—namely, a valorizing of innerness and uniqueness and a faith in the validity of the person's self-awareness combined with a distrust of external sources of value—is apparent in Tageson's rousing summary of the humanistic "principle of self-actualization":

> There is considerable danger that [the person's] potential for a *uniquely creative, particularized* integration or solution will be lost in the shuffle. ... [Humanistic psychology holds] the belief that there exists *within the individual an actualizing tendency unique* to his or her *specific* organism. ... That somehow, in the deepest sense and perhaps unconsciously for most of us, *I know best what is 'good for me'*, how best to integrate *the unique potential* that *differentiates me* from all other individuals, and that therefore represents *my unique contribution* to the mosaic of society or humanity as a whole. (p. 216, emphasis added)

Philosophical Sources

Whereas the major negative influences on humanistic psychology came from psychoanalytic and behavioral psychology, the major positive influences derived from the discipline of philosophy. It is not that American humanistic psychologists necessarily had a deep or scholarly knowledge of relevant trends in continental philosophy (though some surely did); their conception of psychology seems, however, clearly indebted to the ideas propounded and approaches legitimated by certain German and French thinkers. As a way of summarizing and simplifying what could otherwise be an infinite task of tracing influences and affinities, we might locate these positive philosophical sources in the work of Wilhelm Dilthey, Edmund Husserl, and Jean-Paul Sartre. At least two of these thinkers were also important influences on the development of the ontological hermeneutic approach. (Dilthey is often considered to be the father of modern hermeneutics, and Husserl was Heidegger's mentor.) But, whereas humanistic psychology seems essentially to have adopted the views of these thinkers (albeit in diluted form), the ontological hermeneutic tradition developed largely in reaction against the influence of these important philosophers.[6]

It was Dilthey who, in the late 19th century, crystallized for the modern era the idea of a specifically human kind of science—the *Geisteswissenschaften*—distinct from the sciences of the physical world. As conceived by Dilthey (1976), such sciences would be directed toward the study of cultural and psychological "worlds," the possibility of whose radical differentness from one's own was accepted and even emphasized. Such sciences would accept the experiential or spiritual nature of their objects, and therefore would be based not on external observation or causal explanation, but on "some sort of understanding gained through sympathetic experience" (Hughes, 1958, p. 197). Like his predecessor Schleiermacher, Dilthey accepted the project of traditional philological study—to discover the intention of the author of a text. Dilthey's famous method of *Verstehen* (derived from a distinction made by the historian-philosopher Droysen), emphasized the grasping of the subjectivity of other people and cultures, the re-living or co-living of the inner lives that are expressed in texts or other objective expressions of human experience (Guignon, 1983, p. 51; Howard, 1982, p. 111). This is certainly similar to the empathic approach of Moustakas, Rogers, and other humanists, who want to "enter the subject's private world of conscious experience" or "to grasp his or her internal frame of reference" (Tageson, 1982, p. 309). Like the humanists with their interest in the experiential and the idiographic, Dilthey was concerned not to explain but to understand the inner and individual life; he rejected as inappropriate the explanatory modes of the natural sciences, with their use of causal determinism or explanation by subsumption under general statistical laws (Palmer, 1969).

The importance of Husserl has already been mentioned; it derives from his laying-out, in the early years of the 20th century, of a particularly rigorous, radical, and ambitiously self-confident program for the study of consciousness, which he declared to be the foundation of all knowledge (Kockelmans, 1967). Husserl is the most technically difficult of the philosophers under discussion, and his influence on humanistic psychology was probably the most indirect of the three. The majority of humanistic psychologists have not employed Husserl's method of phenomenological bracketing or reduction in a rigorous fashion. Yet their above-mentioned faith in immediate cognition or self-anchored perception (i.e., self-transparency) seems to involve the Husserlian assumption that it is possible to separate out a pure and certain realm of subjective or immanent experience by bracketing or suspending any positing of the existence of a world beyond consciousness itself. Husserl's philosophy, like that of some humanistic psychologists, can seem at times to approach a form of solipsism (or, at least, an extreme subjectivism) in which the universe's very meaning and claim to existence is seen as depending on human consciousness.

The last of the philosophical influences is the most famous of the existentialists, Jean-Paul Sartre. In his early work, Sartre (1956a) presented the most radical and influential doctrine of the essential freedom of human consciousness, an aspect that he saw as intimately related to the supposed self-transparency of consciousness. The metaphysical vision of *Being and Nothingness* offers an almost Manichean contrast: on the one hand, the dark, contingent, and deterministic realm of the objects of consciousness, exemplified by viscous physical matter; on the other, the realm of consciousness itself, whose essential features are supposed to be utter freedom and absolute self-awareness. In Sartre's conception of human existence, "there is no determinism—man is free, man *is* freedom" (1956b, pp. 291–292).[7]

ONTOLOGICAL HERMENEUTICS

As I have said, the rejection of objectivism—of positivistic methodologies and mechanistic models—is as basic to contemporary hermeneutics as it is to humanistic psychology. Recent hermeneutic thought, which is largely derivative of Heidegger, has, however, been equally concerned to avoid an error of the opposite kind: that of according too much centrality to the human subject in action and experience. It was Heidegger who, largely in reaction against the phenomenology of Husserl, his mentor, first called for a "second Copernican revolution" to disabuse man of his illusion of being the center or foundation of the experiential universe. The philosophers

Gadamer and Ricoeur, and social theorists like the philosopher/ political theorist Charles Taylor and the anthropologist Clifford Geertz, have followed Heidegger in criticizing the tendency, so common in modern thought, to overestimate the role of the isolated, conscious subject. They agree in rejecting the humanistic penchant for conceiving of consciousness as a private, an inner, a self-transparent, or a constitutive realm.

Husserl's Transcendental Phenomenology

In order to understand the nature of this rejection, so central to hermeneutics, there is no more pivotal place to begin than with Heidegger's disagreements with Husserl. Difficult, at times technical, as this discussion may be, it is worth pursuing in some detail. Heidegger's rejection of Husserl is absolutely critical to any understanding of ontological hermeneutics. And, since Husserl provides the most explicit and rigorous rationale for one of the central tenets of humanism (the assumption of self-transparency), Heidegger's arguments against Husserl can be understood as applying to humanism also. Further, if one can grasp the basis of Heidegger's rejection of what has been called *Husserlian subjectivism*, it will be much easier to understand the other central themes of the hermeneutic tradition and to see how they differ from those of humanism.

We will begin, then, with the issue of self-transparency, first in Husserl, then in Heidegger. Later we will turn to the other three closely related humanistic themes, as well as to the thought of Dilthey and Sartre—whose humanistic views are in fairly sharp contrast with those of the ontological hermeneutic tradition.

Husserl attempted to found a "First Philosophy," a philosophical position that would dispense with all metaphysical, ontological, and epistemological presuppositions and return "to the things themselves": i.e., to the things of the world as directly given in experience. The phenomenological reductions mentioned above (known as *bracketing* or the *epoché*) played a crucial role in this founding movement since these techniques were designed to suspend the prejudices and interpretations characteristic of both the philosophical and scientific traditions and of what Husserl called the "natural attitude" of everyday life, including belief in the transcendently real object (the object existing "in itself," beyond human consciousness). Left behind after this process of distillation would, supposedly, be only the barest and most indubitable data of immediate or immanent experience—

data that, in Husserl's view, would then stand forth clearly before the steady gaze of phenomenological observation, where they could be given a direct and certain description via the method he called *phenomenological intuition*.[8] Husserl believed that this method could provide "an absolute grounding of science" based on the certain evidence found in what he called *"transcendental solitude,* the solitude of the ego" (quoted in Guignon, 1983, p. 43). Now let us consider just what, in Husserl's view, is supposed to be revealed once all scientific assumptions and the naive natural attitude are bracketed.

Because of the considerable confusion concerning the phenomenological reduction, it is worth first pointing out that it does not imply a reduction of experience to something like sense data, nor an actual doubting of objective existence, nor even an ignoring of the very issue of objective existence. To perform the reduction is to suspend one's taken-for-granted assumptions of the actuality of objects and the objective world. In this special act of reflection, we "turn our attention *away from* the object being referred to (and *away from* our psychological experience of being directed toward that object), and turn our attention *to* the act, more specifically to its intentional content" (Dreyfus, 1982a, p. 6). Our attention is not thereby directed to the "raw feels" or brute sensations postulated by sense-data empiricism, but to the meanings and objects-as-meant of normal experience; these may include the experience of actual existence, which, instead of being either assumed or ignored, is itself thematized as an object of contemplation (for phenomenology *is* concerned with the question of "what it *means* for something to count in our experience as an actually existing reality") (Hall, 1982, p. 184; also see Dreyfus & Haugeland, 1978, pp. 228–229).

According to Husserl, two kinds of phenomena are isolated and revealed (i.e., rendered perspicuous or transparent) by this method of phenomenological reduction and intuition. First, the method is supposed to reveal the necessary and intrinsic characteristics of the (immanent) object of experience: e.g., the essential nature of what is experienced as a table, a triangle, or a being in the category "human." Second, the phenomenological reductions supposedly reveal the existence of the "transcendental ego," a consciousness persisting through time that is discovered to be the existing foundation, the *sine qua non*, of all actual and possible experiences (cf., Husserl, 1969, pp. 69–72). Notice that these objects (or are they products?) of phenomenological description—the meanings or objects-as-meant, and the ego or transcendental activity by which they are meant—have at least a rough correspondence with the traditional (Cartesian) philosophical distinction between object and subject (cf., Dreyfus & Haugeland, 1978, p. 229).[9]

It is also significant that Husserl's method, known as that of *transcendental phenomenology*, seems to reveal the primacy of one side of this polarity: the subject is discovered to have ontological priority over the world. That is, consciousness is found to be the "supporting ground of reality," the "primordial region" that makes possible or constitutes "*all* the forms of being that comprise reality (including natural being, logical being, ... conscious being, and so on)" (Jennings, 1986, p. 1236; DeBoer, 1978). (The ego is called *transcendental* because it is a constant that runs through —transcends—all possible acts or moments of experience.) A kind of solipsism is implied in Husserl's description of phenomenological epoche as the reduction of psychic life to what he calls "the realm of transcendental-phenomenological self-experience": "The Objective world, the world that exists for me, that always has and always will exist for me, the only world that ever can exist for me—this world, with all its Objects, I said, derives its whole sense and its existential status, which it has for me, from me myself, *from me as the transcendental Ego*, the Ego who comes to the fore only with transcendental-phenomenological epoché." (Husserl, 1969, p. 26). Further, even other people are "first of all, others for me who receive from me, whatever meaning of validity they have for me. They can be of assistance to me as fellow subjects only after they have received their meaning and validity from me. As transcendental ego I am thus *the absolutely responsible subject* of whatever has existential validity for me" (quoted in Guignon, 1983, p. 44).[10]

In addition to that between subject and object, there is another traditional philosophical distinction whose ghost pervades Husserl's thought: the Platonic distinction between quality and substance or essence and existence. In the following passage, for example, Husserl takes it as self-evident that the meaning-imbued everyday lifeworld consists of cultural interpretations (i.e., qualities, meanings, or essences) imposed by the human subject in some active way on top of a more fundamental, and passively experienced, world of independent "mere things": "Anything built by activity necessarily presupposes, as the lowest level, a passivity that gives something beforehand ... The 'ready-made' object that confronts us in life as an existent mere physical thing (when we disregard all the 'spiritual' or 'cultural' characteristics that make it knowable as, for example, a hammer, a table, an aesthetic creation) is given, with the originality of the 'it itself,' in the synthesis of a passive experience" (quoted in Dreyfus & Haugeland, 1978, p. 235).

In Husserl's view one could obtain certain knowledge of these essences (the "characteristics that make [the mere physical thing] knowable as, for example, a hammer ...") by a method of "eidetic reduction," a sort of thought-experiment in which one imaginatively transforms phenomena in order to separate essential from accidental characteristics. The essence-existence distinction and also the subject-object distinction were important tenets of Husserlian phenomenology since they implied that it was possible to capture the truth about human experience by giving clear and distinct descriptions of its separable components or elements. The primacy of transcendental subjectivity was important because it implied that, in a sense, nothing was really lost as a result of the bracketing: if everything meaningful derives from "me, as the transcendental ego," then everything important about human existence can still be described from within the position of "the transcendental-phenomenological *epoché*."

Even in his early work, Husserl obviously recognized that the natural attitude of "everydayness" (*Alltaglichkeit*, the pervasive attitude of our everyday experience, in which the world is taken as real and independent of the mind) was an element of human experience. At first, however, he did not treat this attitude as an especially central topic to be investigated phenomenologically. This relative neglect of the natural attitude is, perhaps, not altogether surprising if one reflects on the potentially paradoxical relationship between such an attitude and the phenomenological method that was the foundation of Husserl's enterprise. After all, the natural attitude is precisely that which is suspended by the *epoché*; one might well wonder, therefore, whether one could then take this very attitude as the object of phenomenological study, of study within the *epoché*. This amounts to asking whether it is possible simultaneously to suspend the natural attitude and to invoke it as an object of contemplation. In other words, is everydayness, the very atmosphere of our normal engagement in the world, something that can be contemplated at a remove? And, if the answer is no, what implications might this have for Husserlian transcendental phenomenology? Does it undermine his project in some fundamental way, or merely demonstrate the recalcitrant nature of one potential domain of phenomenological inquiry (i.e., everydayness)?

Since Husserl, in his earlier work, did not attempt a phenomenology of everydayness, he did not have to confront these questions directly—at least not until they were broached by the seminal work of his student Martin Heidegger. But *Being and Time*, Heidegger's first major work, which was published in Husserl's journal, took as its central topic this very everydayness and implied profoundly negative conclusions regarding the ultimate viability of Husserlian phenomenology. Heidegger came to believe that Husserl's phenomenology was neither pure nor presuppositionless; that it was actually deeply complicit with the philosophical tradition Husserl wanted to go beyond. For, in Heidegger's view, Husserl's attempt to escape the natural attitude of everydayness was a futile task; far from providing a radically new route to clear and certain knowledge (the self-transparency that Husserl had claimed), it was in fact a philosophically conventional move, and also one that was ultimately self-deceiving. As we shall see, Heidegger's understanding of everydayness made him question not only the above-mentioned tenets of Husserlian phenomenology (i.e., the essence-existence and subject-object distinctions, and the priority of the subject), but also something even more fundamental: the assumption, which seems implicit in Husserl's method, that the essence of human consciousness is primarily manifest in acts of contemplative knowing rather than in acting (cf. Guignon, 1983, pp. 60–61).

Heidegger—Dasein's Horizonal Nature

It is clear that, in Husserl's thought, the contemplative attitude of phenomenological observation is accorded the privileged role: it is seen as capable of revealing the indubitable elements or foundations of all experience. (In his later work, Husserl, responding to the challenge represented by Heidegger's work, argued that even the "natural attitude" could be made the object of this kind of detached reflection.) Heidegger argues, by contrast, that the fundamental mode of human existence—that on the basis of which all other modes must be understood—is not detached knowing but engaged activity. In his view other modes of experience, like the disinterested contemplation of the scientist or philosopher, are preceded, both temporally and logically, by everyday situations of involvement with the world. Thus, for Heidegger, everydayness is not just a possible mode of existence; everyday engagement, as it is lived prereflectively, is both the primordial foundation from which derive all other modes and the key for understanding all other modes (Heidegger, 1962, 1979). And, according to Heidegger, a careful, unprejudiced investigation of a typical everyday situation of engaged activity shows the untenability of certain philosophical assumptions that have pervaded Western philosophy at least since the time of Descartes and that persist, albeit in disguised from, in the philosophy of Husserl.[11]

On Heidegger's account there is in the lived-world no real split between subject and object, between an inner and an outer realm, or between essence and existence. Man and world, like quality and substance, are knitted together inextricably by the purposes and activities by which their very reality is constituted. Thus, *Dasein* ("Being-there," Heidegger's term for human existence) is not a confrontation of separate entities or forms of being, since subject and object simply cannot be defined or even conceived in isolation: "Self and world are not two entities [but] the basic determination of Dasein itself in the unity of the situation of Being in the World." Consequently, it makes no sense to argue that the knowing subject is more fundamental than the world that is known. Nor is it possible to isolate a realm of pure subjectivity in which absolute certitude is possible. As a way of illustrating these points, let us begin with Heidegger's favorite example of engaged everydayness, the situation of a carpenter hammering a nail.

For Heidegger, the paradigmatic object in the human world is something like the carpenter's hammer: not a mere physical thing or an idea or sensation contemplated from a position of scientific or philosophic detachment, but a tool that is used. Such a tool seems to occupy what, from a traditional Cartesian point of view, is a middle realm: it cannot be equated with either the subject or the object of Cartesian philosophy (nor with the quality or substance of Platonic philosophy). Rather, it seems to be the locus of both subject and object, self and world, quality and substance (or better, it undermines these distinctions themselves).[12] Thus, a hammer is not a "hammer" by virtue of some objective characteristics that it has in itself, apart from its place in the human world. Nor is its "hammerness" something that comes from a subjective inner space (the realm of individual and private consciousness) to be projected onto a material or sensory substrate. And so, on Heidegger's account, not only the subject-object distinction, but also that between quality (or meaning) and substance (whether conceived as material or sensory) turns out to be misleading. If one takes an unprejudiced look at the lifeworld, Heidegger argues, one finds not only that the hammer's "hammerness" is out there in the world, but that the external world is "always already" imbued with human purpose and meaning.[13]

The most primordial way in which objects present themselves is in the mode of what Heidegger calls the "ready-to-hand": as tools, goals, obstacles, and so on, i.e., as those objects encountered in concern that he calls "equipment." For Heidegger, it is therefore artificial and distorting to separate, as did Husserl, the "object that confronts us ... as an existent mere physical thing" from the "'cultural' characteristics that make it knowable" (Husserl, quoted in Dreyfus & Haugeland, 1978, p. 235). For, says Heidegger: "The less we just stare at the hammer-Thing, and the more we seize hold of it and use it, the more primordial does our relationship to it become, and the more unveiledly is it encountered as that which it is—as equipment" (Heidegger, 1962, p. 98).[14] And, in this primordial situation of engagement, the hammer's reality—its Being—is taken for granted: the carpenter does not feel himself to experience chimeras dependent on his own consciousness; he encounters solid entities that guide or resist his actions and that are visible to other subjects.[15] (Subjectivity, one might say, is subordinate to Being, rather than vice versa.)

As crucial to the nature of equipment as the quality of engagement (what, in a traditional, non-Heideggerian vocabulary, might be called a unity of subject with object) is the quality of complete interrelatedness (a unity of object with object). Heidegger emphasizes that a particular item of equipment can never be understood in isolation since it only exists as such in a purpose-imbued context of other equipment, in an "equipmental totality" unified by a referential context and an in-order-to structure. Thus, in the following characteristic passage, Heidegger emphasizes that the objects in one's world are not separate entities but constituents of a unified field (a field that itself is constituted by the purpose-imbued unity of subject and object):

Taken strictly, there 'is' no such thing as *an* equipment. To the Being of any equipment there always belongs a totality of equipment, in which it can be this equipment that it is. Equipment is essentially 'something in-order-to ... ' ... Equipment—in accordance with its equipmentality—always is *in terms of* its belonging to other equipment: ink-stand, pen, ink, paper, blotting pad, table, lamp, furniture, windows, doors, room. These 'Things' never show themselves proximally as they are for themselves, so as to add up to a sum of *realia* and fill up a room. What we encounter as closest to us (though not as something taken as a theme) is the room; and we encounter it not as something 'between four walls' in a geometrical spatial sense, but as equipment for residing. (Heidegger, 1962, pp. 97–98)

Elsewhere, Heidegger writes, "Being as a whole is what we have continually before us and around us. . . . Being as a whole always has completeness in some degree; everything about us is interlocked with everything else. All things have a character of belonging together" (quoted in Grene, 1976, p. 41).

Given this view, one cannot build up an adequate understanding of human reality by describing separate objects or meanings that might seem to be its components. The very nature of both things and essences is determined by their place in a web of human meaning that cannot itself be treated as a mere object of knowledge. It is therefore impossible, for example, to carry out the Husserlian project of analyzing the common-sense background of everyday involvement by treating it as a complex abstract structure composed of constituent beliefs understood as context-free elements (cf., Dreyfus, 1982a, pp. 8, 23). In Heidegger's view, then, experience always involves what might be called an implicitly sensed "ground," "horizon," or "clearing," which is the context or totality within which experience occurs. This horizonal character, which undercuts both the opposition of subject and object and the seeming independence of object from object, as well as the primacy of the subject, is also the most important aspect of human existence, for it is the very condition or possibility of anything at all appearing or having meaning. It—and not consciousness or the transcendental ego—is the "primordial region," since it is the only place where man or any aspect of his world can find their being.[16] However, for our present concerns, the most crucial fact about this all-important horizonal character of human existence—neglected by those who assume the essential self-transparency of human experience—is that it is necessarily imbued with a deep and, in a sense, paradoxical quality of obscurity or concealedness.

The Non-transparency of Horizons

The concealedness of horizons is quite unlike that of the Freudian unconscious, for it is not the product of a motivated act of repression—something that, on principle at least, might not have taken place. Rather, it is a kind of structural or inevitable fact of human consciousness. Also, its concealment is intimately or intrinsically connected with the condition of being visible. Instead of hiding, like a shameful object, far away in some dark recess of the mind, its presence is almost too obvious, too self-evident. This paradoxical obscurity is captured in Heidegger's description of the object of (hermeneutic) phenomenology as: "something that lies *hidden*, in contrast to that which proximally and for the most part does show itself; but at the same time it is something that belongs to what thus shows itself; and it belongs to it so essentially as to constitute its meaning and its ground" (1962, p. 59). Merleau-Ponty compares the horizon to the light in a room: something that cannot be seen precisely because it is the medium by which everything is seen (Dreyfus & Wakefield, 1988).

Perhaps the best way of understanding the paradoxical obscurity of Dasein's horizons is to move from the particular horizons of, say, a carpenter's workshop to a consideration of the broadest horizons of all, those of everydayness itself. Everydayness is, on Heidegger's account, characterized by a pervasive and lived sense of the sheer existence or reality of the world—what he calls the "Being of entities." (This sense is, in Heidegger's view, more fundamental and encompassing than the feeling of the reality of a constituting ego; yet the foundational importance of this very feeling of the Being of entities is ignored by transcendental phenomenological method, which brackets the feeling and then treats it as just another thematizable mental content.) As Heidegger understands it, this aspect of everydayness is both too all-encompassing and too close to the human subject to be readily known or recognized. It is, after all, the implicit context within which or against which objects may emerge, like figures against a ground. ("Being is essentially broader than all the beings, because it is the clearing itself," writes Heidegger [1973].) It cannot become a figure itself because, in Heidegger's view, there just is no more all-encompassing context that could serve as a ground against which Being could be revealed as figure. And so, the horizon of Dasein is in a sense everywhere and nowhere, not a possible object of experience precisely because it is the very medium of experience itself—the very "light of one's eye or atmosphere of one's thoughts."[17]

Heidegger makes a similar point in discussing the supposed existence of the "I," by which he seems to mean something equivalent to Husserl's transcendental ego or what the humanist Hubert

Bonner calls the stable self (see above). So long as one adopts a contemplative attitude, the nature and existence of this "I" may seem indubitable, thus a haven of foundational certitude in contrast to the dubiousness of the world. (This is how Husserl discovered the transcendental ego from which, supposedly, "the objective world . . . derives . . . its entire meaning and its claim to existence.") In fact, says Heidegger, this "I" may be an artifact of the "mere reflective awareness" which, rather than revealing something real, does not "disclose Dasein in its everydayness, if it discloses Dasein at all" (1962, p. 151).[18] Heidegger believes that there is a more fundamental, less artificial mode of self-experience—he calls it *Dasein*, being-there— in which the "I" in some sense pervades its world, is its horizons: "Dasein *is* its world existingly"; "Even one's *own* Dasein becomes something that it can itself proximally 'come across' only when it *looks away* from 'Experiences' and the 'centre of its actions,' or does not as yet 'see' them at all" (1962, pp. 416, 155). Yet, since this more fundamental mode of being cannot be isolated and objectified, it must of necessity remain somewhat obscure: "If that which is accessible by mere 'giving' [i.e., the 'I' 'discovered' by Husserlian transcendental phenomenology] can be determined, there is presumably an ontological horizon for determining it; but what if this horizon should remain in principle undetermined?" (Heidegger, 1962, p. 151).

According to Heidegger, then, the essential stance or method of Cartesian philosophy and its central philosophical tenets form a mutually supportive web of illusion. As we have seen in the case of Husserl, the very adoption of an attitude of detached and passive observation seems to lead to doctrines that institute a new variant of the traditional subject-object and quality-substance distinctions. Husserl's rather Cartesian vision of a primordial experiential world of immanent objects stripped of their worldhood (i.e., their externality and their irreducibly holistic nature) and felt to be constituted by an essentially private contemplative ego seems, in fact, to be an artifact of his method of detached and passive observation. At the same time, belief in such doctrines seems to encourage adopting such a contemplative stance or method, since the very idea of a primordial object devoid of subjective interpretation, existing somehow "in-itself," seems to justify, even to demand, the taking-up of a detached and objective attitude toward one's object of study. Heidegger considered transcendental phenomenology to be an instance of the "objectivistic subjectivism" of the modern age (Gadamer, 1976, p. 49). In treating its subject matter, lived-experience, as something that can be contemplated at a distance and subjected to the experiment-like manipulations inherent in the various reductions, it seems to have misleadingly imported into the domain of subjectivity a certain almost atomistic conception of the physical universe; experiences are treated as if they were inner "things."

Clearly, then, the thrust of Heidegger's hermeneutic view of human existence is opposite to that of Husserlian phenomenology, as well as to the positions of Sartre and the humanistic psychologists, who take for granted the essential self-transparency or intelligibility of consciousness. If the horizonal nature of Dasein is central to its very nature (as is revealed by an examination of engaged everydayness), then it is no longer possible to retain faith in the transparency and certitude of phenomenological description. For, as we have seen, not only does the horizon not offer itself to the direct intuitive grasp of observation within the *epoché*; observation can even be misleading and distorting. Consequently, on the hermeneutic view, the realm of subjectivity—the relationship of consciousness with itself—no longer appears as an epistemologically privileged realm, a haven of certainty in a world of unjustified assumptions and claims. Hermeneutic phenomenology recognizes that what Ricoeur has termed "the narrow and narcissistic 'I' of immediate consciousness" is fraught with its own special sources of deception; and that "the fascination with subjective certainty can be as deceptive as the fascination with the world of the object found in prephenomenological philosophies" (Ihde, 1971, p. 7).

This is not, however, to say that Man is doomed to complete ignorance of his own horizonal nature; after all, *Being and Time* is itself an attempt to elucidate human existence. But it does mean that Dasein can know its own being only in an approximate, tentative, and indirect way, not through some quasi-scientific method of direct intuition, with access to certain and foundational data. Human subjectivity cannot be understood as an analyzable combination of isolable and fully specifiable mental entities or aspects that either do or do not exist in a determinate fashion (or that exist to a specifiable degree). It is, rather, an interweaving texture of only partially specifiable themes and backgrounds that exist at various levels of implicit and explicit awareness, often merging imperceptibly with one another. A recognition of the horizonal nature of experience means that understanding is never at the foundational beginning of some impeccable and surefire methodology, but always, as Ricoeur says, *in media res.*[19] Nor can Dasein take its own ordinary self-understanding at face value (as does the humanist Bonner, for example, in asserting the existence of a stable, transcendent self). For, on the hermeneutic view, experience is not transparent to itself; it is a kind of text-analogue, an intrinsically obscure object that needs to be interpreted to bring to light its hidden meaning, and that can be evoked only by an approximate and metaphoric, perhaps even quasi-poetic mode of description.[20] Essential to any adequate characterization or evocation of human existence will be a recognition of precisely what transcendental phenomenology's detachment keeps it from grasping: the primacy of Being and the utter inseparability (or rather, the unity) of subject and world.

The all-important role that man's horizonal nature plays in Heidegger's thought should now be clear, as should the way this realization undermines belief in one aspect of the humanist philosophical anthropology, self-transparency. The self-presence of the Husserlian or Cartesian ego (the ego of Descartes' *cogito ergo sum*) has, in Ricoeur's vivid words, been found to be a "wounded *cogito,* which posits but does not possess itself, which understands its ordinary truth only in and by the confession of the inadequation, the illusion, and the lie of existing consciousness" (Freeman, 1985, p. 297). If we investigate in more detail the nature of these horizons, we will understand why the Heideggerian tradition of ontological hermeneutics also rejects the other facets of the humanist image of the human subject: privacy, uniqueness, and freedom. And, we shall begin to see what implications this rejection has for knowledge and practice in the human sciences. Next, I will discuss the public nature of Dasein's horizons, and then, in the following sections, will consider the implications of this philosophical anthropology for understanding the nature of communication and interpretation, and for notions of authenticity and human fulfillment.

The Public Nature of Horizons; Man's Linguisticality

In *Being and Time,* Heidegger places great emphasis on the shared and public nature of the contexts of significance (the horizons) that mediate human awareness. To a great extent, it is the customs and institutions of a given culture, not the idiosyncratic perspectives of isolated individuals, that channel and constitute human experience. "The 'subject' of everydayness," writes Heidegger, is "*not* the egotistical particular, not the ontically isolated individual" but rather "the

Anyone" or "the They"; the "They" "articulates the referential context of significance" (quoted in Guignon, 1983, p. 108).

Thus, even the nature of our self-interpretations or self-understandings are largely determined by the possibilities laid open by a shared "we-world" (Guignon, 1983, p. 104). For, it is only in accordance with the culture's images and roles that we can behave in a coherent manner, only in accordance with its modes or templates of knowledge that we can know ourselves. Heidegger therefore rejects the common assumption—accepted by Husserl and many of the humanists—that a certain awareness of self is prior, temporally or logically, to the discrimination of others or the constitution of cultural forms and practices. "It is not 'I,' in the sense of my own self that 'am,' but rather the others, whose way is that of the Anyone," writes Heidegger. "In terms of the Anyone and as the Anyone, I am 'given' proximally to 'myself'" (quoted in Guignon, p. 108). Accordingly, Ricoeur calls on the thinker to "break out of the enchanted enclosure of oneself, to end the prerogative of self-reflection" (Ricoeur, 1967, p. 356). For, as Gadamer puts it, "the focus of subjectivity" is "only a distorting mirror," and the route to true self-understanding must go by way of an understanding of culture and history: "In fact, history does not belong to us, but we belong to it. Long before we understand ourselves through the process of self-examination, we understand ourselves in a self-evident way in the family, society and state in which we live. ... The self-awareness of the individual is only a flickering in the closed circuits of historical life" (1984, p. 245).

We see, then, that Heidegger, Gadamer, and Ricoeur all reject Husserl's idea of the possibility of a direct, unmediated encounter with the things of experience, insisting instead on the all-important role played by a shared context or background of historical and cultural interpretations. But so far, we have not considered what, for all these thinkers, is the most important source of these interpretations that form the implicit clearing of all experience: namely, language. Gadamer and Ricoeur follow Heidegger in taking a constitutive rather than merely instrumentalist view of the relationship between language and experience, and in this they differ from both Husserl and Dilthey (cf. McIntyre & Smith, 1982, pp. 87–88; Guignon, 1983, p. 117). Such a view is inconsistent with Husserl and other forms of Cartesianism since it swallows up both the Cartesian poles of experience, undercutting the purity and independence of the object even as it compromises the freedom of the subject. The resulting view of language also offers the most serious challenge to the humanist conception of the privacy and transparency of experience and of the freedom and uniqueness of the individual.

With regard to the experiential world, the hermeneutic thinkers take a position akin in certain respects to the Whorf-Sapir hypothesis (a hypothesis which, in one of its strong forms, argues that even such basic conceptual/experiential distinctions as those between quality and substance, subject and object, or action and object are constituted by language and are not translinguistic universals).[21] On the hermeneutic view, there is no "prior grasp of the *nonsemantic significance* of the contexts in which we find ourselves" (Guignon, 1983, p. 117), for these contexts are actually constituted by language. Though this view is espoused somewhat ambivalently in *Being and Time*, it emerges as one of the most prominent themes in Heidegger's later work, and is also central to the thought of Gadamer and Ricoeur (Guignon, 1983). "Words and language are not wrappings in which things are packed for the commerce of those who write and speak," writes Heidegger in *An Introduction to Metaphysics* (1961, p. 11). "It is in words and language that things first come into being and are." Similarly, Gadamer's *Truth and Method*, which accepts Heidegger's later position, insists on the "linguisticality" of man: for "language is not just part of the equipment with which men who are in a world are outfitted; rather, it depends on language and is brought forth in language that humans have a world at all" (quoted in Guignon, pp. 124–125). It is obvious that the objects of experience cannot be encountered in the way attempted by many phenomenological psychologists—i.e., without mediation by any interpretation—if language, which is itself a kind of interpretation, is "always already" everywhere.

If language could thus be said to dominate or determine its object, this is no less true of its relationship to the speaking (or listening) subject. Here the hermeneutic view is reminiscent of that of Saussure and the later structuralists, who declare the priority of the linguistic system over any particular individual act of speaking or understanding (Sturrock, 1979).[22] Thus, Gadamer (1984) emphasizes a certain passivity, the fact of being caught up in something so vast and internally determined as to be largely beyond the grasp of one's knowledge or control: "When you take a word in your mouth you must realize that you have not taken a tool that can be thrown aside if it won't do the job, but you are fixed in a direction of thought which comes from afar and stretches beyond you" (p. 496).

In the penultimate paragraph of his major work, *Truth and Method*, Gadamer refers approvingly to the famous essay by the

German romantic, Heinrich von Kleist, "On the Gradual Elaboration of Thoughts while Speaking." In that essay, written in 1805, Kleist argues that it is an illusion to think that speaking at its most articulate involves the precise communication of ideas that have already been clearly thought out in the mind and are then deliberately expressed. Rather, writes Kleist, "As they say in France, 'l'appétit vient en mangeant' and from our own experience we might in parody assert, 'l'idée vient en parlant' " (Kleist, 1982, p. 218). Kleist is saying that language has a kind of creative genius of its own: it does not simply express but actually generates thought. As Gadamer glosses Kleist's point: "We speak and the word goes beyond us to consequences and ends which we had not, perhaps, conceived of" (1984, p. 497). Kleist seems to have been sensitive to an error equally characteristic of both the rationalist and much romanticist thought of his time: the tendency to locate meaning in the mind of the individual subject. "For it is not we who 'know'," he wrote in his essay, "it is rather a certain condition, in which we happen to be, that 'knows'." A similar view of how individual thought and experience is subordinate to and embedded in the larger transpersonal system of language is expressed in Heidegger's famous statement that "language speaks me" and in the portentous last lines of his "Letter on Humanism": "Thought by its speaking traces insignificant furrows in language. They seem even more insignificant than the furrows the peasant with deliberate steps traces in the field" (1973, p. 181).

Gadamer makes an argument about the essentially enigmatic nature of language that is obviously indebted to Heidegger's more general argument about the essential obscurity of the horizons of Dasein. Since "we are always already encompassed by the language that is our own," it is impossible to get far enough away from language to illuminate fully the nature of this phenomenon that can be described neither as objective nor as subjective. Thus, he says, it is part of the nature of language to have "a completely unfathomable unconsciousness of itself" (Gadamer, 1976, p. 62).

For the ontological hermeneuticists, then, human beings are constituted by their self-interpretations; but, for the most part, these interpretations are not unique, freely chosen, or consciously recognized, since they are deeply embedded in the public and determining facts of language, culture, and history, and are so pervasive as to be nearly invisible. Clearly, such a vision calls into question not only the notion of self-transparency, but also the other facets of the humanist philosophical anthropology: freedom, uniqueness, and privacy.

But, though it may be impossible on the hermeneutic account for a human being to have a self-reflective grasp of the linguistic and cultural context that imbues his own experience, the very pervasiveness of this context does assure that communication between human beings may be less problematic than it might otherwise seem—a point that has certain implications for the nature and goal of interpretation in the human sciences. This is the topic of the next section.

THE NATURE OF COMMUNICATION; THE GOAL OF INTERPRETATION

Humanism Versus Hermeneutics

On the hermeneutic account, communication does not seem as difficult, mysterious, or mystical as is the case for the humanists; it is viewed as a necessary, natural, and constitutive aspect of human existence rather than as a problematic and ultimately distorting transformation of a more primary private human essence.[23] These different views of communication derive directly from the differing philosophical anthropologies assumed by humanism and by ontological hermeneutics.

According to the humanist view, the shared medium of language necessarily homogenizes and thereby distorts the referent of communication, since the latter is understood to involve a unique, inner, and preverbal level of experience. But, if one makes the hermeneuticist assumption that experience is intrinsically language-imbued, and that the horizons of experience involve shared or public contexts of significance, then neither the experience of the speaker nor that of the listener will any longer seem so irredeemably separate, nor so exquisitely unique. If even prereflective experience is already language-imbued, already molded by public ways of knowing, then the description of such experiences in a verbal and shared language need not imply an essential contamination or dilution of some original, unique, and ineffable essence.

A methodological implication of the hermeneutic philosophical anthropology is that the process of understanding human beings, or even a single human being, does not essentially depend on capturing or identifying with an ephemeral realm of inner experiences (as in the hermeneutics of Schleiermacher and Dilthey); it requires only the careful elucidation and interpretation of shared and objectified forms. As we have seen, for Heidegger the true locus of selfhood is not seen as existing behind the public persona, nor as a point of consciousness set back at a remove from the objects of experience (as in Sartre and Husserl). Dasein is "in the world"; it just is the horizons of its world since there is no inner self or pure consciousness existing apart from these horizons. And not only are these horizons shared, they are also, to a large extent, public and observable, since the customs and institutions of relevance are always objectified in the symbolic forms of the culture in question.

What this means for social science methodology is suggested by the hermeneutic anthropologist Clifford Geertz (1983) in the following discussion of his own researches into what might seem the most inner of topics, the nature of selfhood in several non-Western cultures: "In each case, I have tried to get at this most intimate of notions [the experience of self] not by imagining myself someone else, a rice peasant or a tribal shiek, and then seeing what I thought, but by searching out and analyzing the symbolic forms—words, images, institutions, behaviors—in terms of which, in each place, people actually represented themselves to themselves and to one another" (p. 58).

According to Geertz we should understand understanding not as a matter of somehow getting inside someone else's head, but as looking over the shoulder of the other at the text he himself is reading. And this, presumably, is what Gadamer means when, in disagreement with Schleiermacher and Dilthey, he defines hermeneutical understanding as "not a mysterious communion of souls, but a sharing of a common meaning" (1984, p. 260). As conceived by the modern hermeneuticists, then, understanding is not a subjectivist process since its object is neither private nor unique. Gadamer: "When we try to understand a text, we do not try to recapture the author's attitude of mind but, if this is the terminology we are to use, we try to recapture the perspective within which he has formed his views" (1984, p. 259).[24]

The Prejudice against Prejudices

It is clear that, in emphasizing the constitutive role of culture and language, Gadamer does not mean to imply that the horizons of human understanding are closed or static. This would be to succumb to what Karl Popper has called "the Myth of the Framework"—the view that says, "We are prisoners caught in the framework of our theories; our expectations; our past experiences; our language" (quoted in Bernstein, 1983, p. 84). On such a view, it would be impossible on principle to "recapture the perspective within which [someone else] has formed his views" since one would be irredeemably caught within one's own rigid perspective.

In fact, one of Gadamer's main concerns has been the criticism of what he calls the "prejudice against prejudice"—the conviction, stemming from the scientism of the Enlightenment, that the ideals of truth and liberation demand a bringing-to-light and a sloughing-off of all one's unexamined assumptions and traditional beliefs (Gadamer, 1984, pp. 239–240). As we have seen, the Heideggerian conception of the horizons of consciousness suggests that any such attempt would be a fool's errand—not only futile but even self-deluding. If what has been called (by Schleiermacher) the *hermeneutic circle* is a valid characterization of the conditions of all knowing, then prejudices or kinds of foreknowledge are always present and always required as the organizing and orienting devices without which perception would be blind: "Prejudices, in the literal sense of the word, constitute the initial directedness of our whole ability to experience" (Gadamer, 1976, p. 9). Any attempt to dispense completely with prejudices would, in all likelihood, lead not to their eradication but only to their deeper concealment and perhaps to a certain impoverishment of knowing vision (as is the case with radical behaviorism and other forms of positivism that only seem to be theory-free). In Gadamer's view, in fact, prejudices should be understood not only as potentially blinding but also as potentially liberating and illuminating: they are "biases of our openness to the world" (Gadamer, 1976, p. 9). We can best grasp this point if we consider Gadamer's discussion of linguistic communication.

The traditional (Diltheyan or humanist) view makes the mistake of treating meaning as if it were determinate—an object-like entity of a special inner sort residing in the mind of the speaker. In the modern hermeneutic tradition, by contrast, meaning is conceived of both as shared and as having an essential ambiguity. The true or essential meaning of an utterance is not imagined as residing in the consciousness of the speaker and only as being somehow reflected in the mind of the listener. Gadamer emphasizes, rather, that the listener actually contributes to the meaning since "understanding is not merely a reproductive but always a productive attitude as well" (1984, p. 264).

In calling understanding *productive*, Gadamer is not simply point-ing out the empirical fact that a listener may understand an utterance differently than does its speaker. More importantly, he is arguing against the common temptation to think of this productive nature of understanding as involving some kind of contamination of the original essence of what was "really" meant (which, presumably, would be the speaker's intended meaning). Gadamer would see this way of understanding understanding as erroneous—even though it is almost irresistible to most people because it assumes so much of the traditional Cartesian metaphysics that pervades modern thought, affecting even thinkers like Dilthey (i.e., the assuming of the exis-tence of an inner mental realm, and the conceiving of this realm in an objectivist manner: as containing entities analogous to material objects in their quality of determinateness or definiteness).[25] Actual-ly, in Gadamer's view the listener's or reader's understanding may well involve the foregrounding or rendering explicit of what may appropriately be thought of as already existing, albeit implicitly, in the original utterance.

If, as Heidegger and Gadamer suggest, meaning is, to an important extent, actually generated by language, then it resides not in the mind of the individual speaker or writer but, in a sense, in the dialogue itself. Uttering words must not, on the Heideggerian account, be thought of as merely an instrumental manipulation to achieve previ-ously decided-upon ends. It is better conceived as an act of immer-sion, of participation in something whose vast and systemic nature sets up reverberations of which one may not even be aware, even when one is oneself their instigator. On this account it is a mistake to equate the "true meaning" of the discourse with the thoughts, conscious or unconscious, that pass through the speaker's mind— whether before, during, or even after the speaking of his discourse; such thoughts represent but an impoverished shadow of the full richness of the communicative event.[26]

Therefore, to see the foregrounding brought about by the listener's prejudices as a distortion while treating the speaker's conscious intention (if there was one) as the "truth" would run counter to the general Heideggerian emphasis on the importance of the horizonal nature of experience. Also, it would involve an unacceptably subjec-tivist valorizing of a private and inner realm. For, if meaning is social, if it exists in the dialogue, then it legitimately depends, to a significant extent, on the person who listens. All this implies that the meaning of a text is essentially indeterminate, since it depends on and varies with the contexts of understanding within which it is received. "The text's career," says Ricoeur, "escapes the finite horizon lived by its author" (Freeman, 1985, p. 305).[27]

This "productive" view of understanding casts the role of the listener's biases and prejudices in an entirely different light. If the primary goal of interpretation is not the passive reflection of what was in the speaker's mind, but the full explicitation of the meanings lying implicitly in the discourse or text-analogue, then the listener's or interpreter's prejudices can be understood to play a positive rather than negative role in that "fusion of horizons" characteristic of all true understanding. Once the illusion of capturing the single determinant meaning is given up, the horizons brought to bear in understanding can be seen as having at least the potential to be enriching rather than contaminating. For, only with the aid of the "biases of one's openness to the world" (Gadamer) is it possible to bring forth the many meanings that, so to speak, lie enfolded within the text.[28]

But it is not only the object that is, in a sense, transformed in the act of interpreting. Gadamer also emphasizes the fluidity of the interpreter's horizon, its capacity to change over time, largely as a result of the fusion with and accomodation to the horizon of what is interpreted. For this reason Gadamer is at odds with Diltheyan hermeneutics and other forms of cultural or linguistic relativism because of their tendency to hypostatize cultures or communities of understanding, treating these as if they were radically distinct, almost mutually incomprehensible worlds. Such a view would, in fact, be the equivalent on the collective plane of the humanist tendency to conceive of individual subjectivities as defined by *innerness* and *uniqueness*. And, asks Gadamer, isn't this really a romantic myth, the image—half-glorified, half-lamented—of a tragic but quite illusory condition of isolation?:

> Or is this a romantic reflection, a kind of Robinson Crusoe dream of the historical enlightenment, the fiction of an unattainable island, as artificial as Crusoe himself, for the alleged primary phenomenon of the solus ipse? But in reality just as the individual is never simply an individual, because he is always involved with others, so too the closed horizon that is supposed to enclose a culture is an abstraction. The historical movement of human life consists in the fact that it is never utterly bound to any one standpoint, and hence can never have a truly closed horizon. (1984, p. 271)

Despite its multifacetedness, however, the meaning of a text, utterance, or other act cannot be thought of as completely indeterminate (as is argued by some deconstructionists and other relativistic poststructuralists [White, 1978]). For, though it may be impossible to discover a single meaning, this does not mean that anything goes, that listeners can legitimately ascribe any meaning to any discourse. The hermeneutic approach is a sort of "middle way" between objectivism and relativism.[29] It is obvious that the hermeneutic view of interpretation as a fusion of horizons does not offer the sort of surefire technique promised by foundationalist approaches, be they empiricist or (transcendental) phenomenological. Interpretation always begins *in media res* since one always encounters objects in the context of familiar horizons, never as stripped-down indubitables. But, although it does not proffer the Cartesian dream of absolute certainty, hermeneutics does hold out the prospect of a valid and public kind of knowledge—one based not on some kind of timeless certainty but on the relative persuasiveness, within a particular interpretive community, of the various interpretations offered. It seems, in many ways, to be more modest and pragmatic than either the positivistic hope for absolute certitude or humanism's mystical dream of an empathic communion of souls.[30]

In the view of Gadamer and Ricoeur, the Diltheyan (and humanistic) attempt to divest oneself of one's own biases and capture the supposed subjective intentions and experiences of the other can actually have a somewhat paradoxical effect: by, in a sense, trying too hard to get at the author's original experience, the humanist may, ironically enough, end up actually trivializing the author's perspective. For if one concentrates on the chimera of the author's experience, just as it was presumably lived by him, one tends to encounter a subjectivized reality; one seems, so to speak, to experience the other's experience rather than his world. Instead of encountering the other's vision as something that could seriously challenge one's own biases about reality or the proper conduct of life, one might treat the other's experience as an interesting and self-enclosed exotic artifact; and this, of course, is not how he himself experienced it (unless, perhaps, he was somehow encouraged to take a rather narcissistic stance toward his own experience). Therefore, against this (typically humanist) attempt "to recover behind the text, the lost intention," Ricoeur, echoing Heidegger, argues that interpretation should "unfold, in front of the text, the 'world' which the text opens up and discloses." For: "What is to be interpreted in the text is a proposed world which I could inhabit and in which I could project my ownmost possibilities" (Ricoeur, 1981, pp. 111, 112). Here the post-Heideggerians are criticizing something widespread in modern and especially modernist culture: the tendency, discussed in Heidegger's famous essay, "The Age of the World View," to experience reality as constituted by and subordinate to the subjective states of an individual or a consciousness.

As we have seen, this latter, subjectivist view seems to be implicit in the philosophical underpinnings of much of humanistic psychology, especially in the thought of Husserl and Dilthey, with their focus on immanent experience or subjective worlds. Such approaches can have the practical effect of treating human beings as an array of isolated and incommensurable subjectivities. Since each person's (or culture's) experience just is what it is, there is little point in criticizing its validity, but also little possibility for serious communication. Thus, for example, from a hermeneutic point of view, there might seem to be something trivializing, perhaps ultimately condescending and even countertherapeutic, in, say, the subjectivist approach to psychotherapy of Carl Rogers or the humanistic psychoanalyst Heinz Kohut—with their all-too-benign and selfless acceptance and valorizing of the patient's experience-as-such (Rogers's "unconditional positive regard," Kohut's "vicarious introspection"; cf. Kahn, 1985). A hermeneutic approach would not, of course, mean the authoritarian imposition of a single reality—that of the therapist. It would, however, leave open the possibility of a more probing and ultimately challenging dialogue that more directly confronts traditional issues of values and of (objective) truth.

AUTHENTICITY AND SELF-FULFILLMENT

Two Strains of Romanticism

It may be illuminating to locate the ideas under consideration in the larger context of intellectual history, especially in relation to the Romantic movement to which both humanistic psychology and ontological hermeneutics are heir. Later, this will help to clarify how the hermeneutic and humanistic schools differ in certain of their prescriptive emphases—i.e., in their conception of what it is to live an "authentic" or fulfilled human existence.

As we have seen, the humanistic psychologists oppose objectivism, mechanism, and rationalism, the ideals that have informed not only behaviorism but most of mainstream American psychology. In their view mainstream psychology has alienated man from his own being by treating subjectivity as an unimportant or merely derivative phenomenon. Against this prevailing scientism, the humanists have championed the essential inwardness of human consciousness and the freedom of the human individual. These positions, both positive and negative, are, to a great extent, the same as those taken by many of the romantics who reacted against the scientistic legacy of the 17th-century Enlightenment; in this sense humanistic psychology, like certain of its philosophical influences (Dilthey and Sartre, e.g.) has strong affinities with romanticism.

There is, however, another strain of romanticism which, though on the surface less extreme, may ultimately be more radical in its rejection of the scientism and Cartesianism of the Enlightenment; it is to this that hermeneutics is heir. This strain is not the solitary romantic egoism of Lord Byron, Goethe's Young Werther, or the Sartrian existential hero—with their extreme commitment to freedom and self-determination—but, rather, the romanticism of those who longed for a sense of community (*Gemeinschaft*) and placed as great an emphasis on the need for tradition and social order as on that for self-expression. (This second group includes writers like Schlegel, Herder, Schiller; cf., Taylor, 1975, pp. 3–51; Shalin, 1986.)

From a hermeneutic point of view, the approaches both of humanistic psychology and of the first strain of romanticism actually seem to perpetuate certain central values and assumptions of the Enlightenment; namely, the values of individualism, of freedom, and of enlightenment itself. Thus, the humanist emphasis on individual subjectivity is reminiscent of the atomism of the 17th century, when atomism permeated the understanding of the psychological as well as the physical universe (McPherson, 1962). Also, the humanists' rather absolute concept of the freedom of the human subject, often understood in stark contrast to the mechanistic determinism of the material world, seems to depend on the kind of mind-body dualism espoused by Descartes; though obviously rejecting the application of scientistic methodology and materialism to human nature, humanism does then, at a deep level, accept the metaphysical dichotomies that made materialism possible in the first place. Finally, humanistic psychology (like other perspectives in psychology, including classical psychoanalysis) seems to treat knowledge, and especially self-knowledge, as an almost unquestionable ideal; in this way it accepts perhaps the most central assumption of the Enlightenment: the notion that awareness is an unmitigated good, that knowledge will make you free.

Since the middle of the nineteenth century, many of these individualistic and subjectivist themes have increasingly been criticized both for their theoretical and their practical implications and consequences (Heller, Sosna, & Wellbery, 1986, p. 1; Dallmayr, 1981, pp. 1–37). Emphasis on the individual has been seen as leading to a rampant possessive individualism that encourages and justifies destructive attempts to dominate both nature and one's fellow man (McPherson, 1962; Horkheimer & Adorno, 1972; Wallach & Wallach, 1983); and also to the condition of the disinherited mind detached from any sense of community and bereft of the sacred canopy of transcendent religious meanings and values (Heller, 1975; Berger, 1977; Bellah, Madsden, Sullivan, Swidler, & Tipton, 1985). Other critics have pointed out certain ironies that haunt the humanist aspirations for freedom, self-knowledge, and authentic self-expression. The very desire to find one's "true self" may lead to a continual adopting and shedding of roles, and thus to an ultimate estrangement from all roles or ways of being (Trilling, 1971, pp. 26–52). The desire to manifest one's radical freedom may lead to a kind of inner division and self-enslavement, for it may require that one part of the self, the ego, dominate other parts that are less conscious and controlled (Taylor, 1975, pp. 22, 33). In a startling and provocative analysis, Foucault (1977) has even suggested that the humanist aspiration for self-knowledge and integrity of personality are creations of a modern disciplinary society in which power need not be imposed from without since it already permeates the individual's self-monitoring soul.

As I have said, the ontological hermeneuticists are in the tradition of the second strain of romanticism—a tradition that emphasizes community as prior to individuality and that seeks to transcend the dualisms of mind versus matter and of freedom versus determinism.[31] This is also the tradition of those romantics who accepted that human existence required an element of opaqueness or incomprehensibility. One can, in fact, detect the roots of Heidegger's notion of the obscurity of horizons and of Gadamer's defense of prejudice in the statement from the German romantic Friedrich Schlegel: "But is incomprehensibility really something so unmitigatedly contemptible and evil? Methink the salvation of families and nations rests upon it. . . . Every system depends in the last analysis . . . on some such point of strength that must be left in the dark, but that nonetheless shores up and supports the whole burden and would crumble the moment one subjected it to rational analysis" (quoted in Shalin, 1986, pp. 94–95).

The first strain of romanticism is largely animated by its objection to the tendency to understand and treat human beings on the analogy of inanimate things and thereby to deny the distinctive nature of subjectivity, the inner perspective. One could thus say that this first strain reacted primarily against a certain alienation from without—an alienation rooted in Enlightenment scientism and highly characteristic of the technological society of modernity. The latter sort of romanticism, in contrast, is more concerned about an alienation from within: i.e., an overaccentuation of the inwardness and separateness of the human being. Such a form of alienation is fostered not only by Enlightenment atomism but also by the first strain of counter-Enlightenment romanticism, and it has come to be especially prominent in the literary and artistic culture of modernism, where the privacy and individuality of consciousness is valorized as against the inauthenticity of the public persona and the outer world (Sennett, 1974; Trilling, 1971; Heller, 1975).

Roughly speaking, therefore, one could say that, whereas humanism and the first strain of romanticism are predominantly reactions against the technologistic society of modernity, the Heideggerian version of hermeneutics, which is related to the second strain, is in at least equally strong reaction against the subjectivistic culture of modernism. The significance of these differences will become more evident if one compares the humanistic with the (ontological) hermeneuticist notion of authenticity.

Authenticity

It is true that Heidegger, like the humanists, stresses man's teleological and temporal essence, sets himself against all materialist or deterministic views of human nature, and criticizes modes of existence based on unthinking conformism. An authentic existence must, in his view, include some sense of (and acceptance of responsibility for) how one "projects" oneself into "possibilities" (1962, p. 185). But Heidegger is equally concerned to avoid the voluntaristic picture characteristic of writers like Sartre, who overemphasize the freedom and self-transparency inherent in human existence.

The image of man that is explicit in Sartre and at least implicit in much of humanism is of an agent who is able to choose freely because he stands apart from the social world and consciously recognizes ("thematizes") a set of alternatives for action or understanding. Against this image, which is consistent with both the Husserlian and Cartesian notions of an ego standing over against its objects, Heidegger opposes his own horizonal picture of human existence: "Projecting [oneself into possibilities] has nothing to do with comporting oneself towards a plan that has been thought out, and in accordance with which Dasein arranges its being," writes Heidegger (1962, p. 185). Such a (mistaken) view would have some measure of truth if the choices in question existed always within a horizon or clearing, as if these choices were akin to objects contemplated from a position of detachment (but then, of course, the horizon would just be static and taken-for-granted). Heidegger writes, "The character of understanding as projection is such that the understanding does not grasp thematically that upon which it projects—that is to say, possibilities. Grasping it in such a manner would take away from what is projected its very character as a possibility, and would reduce it to the given contents which we have in mind" (1962, p. 185).

In fact, however, according to Heidegger, the most important instances of human "projecting" involve transformations of horizons themselves—movements in and out of modes of being that must necessarily remain largely obscure to the human subject who lives them precisely because they are, as it were, the light, the frame, or the lens by means of which any particular thing can be known. Because human consciousness is lived rather than known, it cannot have a self-transparent knowledge of its own projecting.

The lack of self-transparency does not, of course, imply that any sense of freedom is mere illusion, for to maintain this would be to lapse back into the deterministic side of Cartesianism, or into the too-extreme antisubjectivism of French structuralist and post-structuralist writers like Althusser, Lacan, and Derrida (Sturrock, 1979). But it does rule out the usual image of an absolute freedom, that of a pure consciousness holding the world, others, and its own moods and beliefs at arm's length. For Heidegger, therefore, to live authentically does not depend so much on the contents of one's self-awareness (as is emphasized in Sartre's notion of bad faith, e.g.) as it does on the style of one's existing and acting. This "art of existing is not self-reflection," writes Heidegger, "but is rather solely the clarity of action itself" (quoted in Guignon, 1983, p. 75; also cf. Guignon, 1984).

Clearly, this conception of authenticity and human fulfillment differs, at least in emphasis, from the typical humanist conception of being true to one's inner self: for Heidegger, self-expression (if one can even use the term) is not conceived as an escape from the constraining roles and expectations of society in favor of expressing an essence imagined to be inner and unique (as with the "proactive personality"). In fact, in his famous "Letter on Humanism" of 1947, an essay directed against Sartre's humanistic existentialism, Heidegger (1973) attacks the humanist/existentialist ideal of individual freedom and expression as an inauthentic obscuring of the truth: "So-called private existence does not mean yet, however, essentially and freely being human. It merely adheres obstinately to a negation of the public. It remains an offshoot dependent on the public and nourishes itself on its mere retreat from the public. So it is witness, against its own will, of its subjection to the public" (p. 150).

Heidegger, Gadamer, and Ricoeur are not, of course, saying that individuality, freedom, or critical self-reflection have no role to play in human existence. But they are arguing that these traditional humanist ideals cannot exist in a pure form, and further, that they should not be imagined as existing in contrast with or opposition to the communal, the social, or the traditional. I have already mentioned hermeneutics' middle position regarding knowledge and interpretation. With regard to the self, the Heideggerians also take a kind of "middle way" between the humanist glorification of subjectivity and individuality and the antihumanist denial of it that has been so prominent in French poststructuralism. As might be expected, Heidegger's concept of authentic existence cannot be captured in any simple slogan (a point that seems to have escaped many of his exegetes, as Guignon [1984] points out). What he prescribes is neither a straightforward merging with community, tradition, or nature nor a romantic-heroic expression of separateness and individuality. (Heidegger [1973, p. 151] warns against both "the seduction of the public" and "the impotence of the private.") Authenticity for Heidegger is a mode of being the Anyone, in which one simultaneously accepts one's social nature and rootedness in the past, while also taking on responsibility for the options that these factors do allow. For Heidegger, then, neither language nor act, neither the larger cultural systems nor the individual consciousness, can be said to have priority over the other; rather, they are in a circular and inseparable relation with each other. And although, as Charles Taylor (1985) has said, this may be a "crashing truism," "the fog emanating from Paris in recent decades makes it necessary to clutch it as a beacon in darkness."

The hermeneutic alternative to objectivism and relativism and to humanism and antihumanism does feel at times like something less than a revelation, as if it were but the incontrovertible yet unexciting product of common sense itself. If we understand the term in its literal sense, however, we would have to say that the ontological hermeneutic position is far more radical than the polarized positions it attempts to overcome. In rejecting these extremes, the hermeneutic position is attempting to do without certain dimensions or binary oppositions in which philosophy and psychology have for centuries been rooted, and which have largely informed our questions, our techniques, and our abiding arguments: e.g., inner versus outer, self versus world, subjective versus objective, act versus system, individual versus society, and freedom versus determinism. What, we may ask, would a psychology based on hermeneutic principles look like? What, if any, implications would this epistemology and philosophical anthropology have for the practice of our field? Though it would take too many pages to elaborate and defend these implications, I would like, in concluding, at least to indicate a few of them, first for psychotherapy and finally for more general methodological issues.

CONCLUSION

By moving the conscious human subject out of his central place, such a "second Copernican revolution" would foster greater awareness of the role of cultural and historical factors in the constitution of experience and behavior, as well as greater concern with action in the world as opposed to the inner life. In psychotherapy such a shift in perspective would seem to mandate less emphasis on the supposedly unique and private aspects of the patient's subjectivity. Preoccupation with such quintessentially modernist concerns as getting in touch with one's "true" or "inner" self, or discovering the autobiographical sources of one's idiosyncratic traits, would not, of course, become taboo. Yet these themes—so central to both humanistic/ existential and psychoanalytic therapies—would be downplayed somewhat in comparison with more traditional concerns of the moral or practical life—such as exploration of one's relationship to shared ethical norms, of the truth or adequacy of one's understanding of external social reality, and of the meaning, interpersonal impact and appropriateness of one's concrete actions in the world.

Emphasis on human freedom—whether as a source of optimism, as in humanistic psychology, or of "anguish," as in pop existentialism—would be tempered by a greater concern with and respect for the inertial aspects of a human life: i.e., its embeddedness in biological, cultural, and historical contexts that must be conceived not as obstacles to self-fulfillment but as their very being and ground. In this respect (as in others) a hermeneutic approach would also differ from behavior therapy, which is surprisingly humanistic in its belief in, and advocacy of, self-determination and self-control, and in its tendency to ignore cultural frames of reference (Woolfolk & Richardson, 1984). A hermeneutic appreciation of the horizonal non-transparency of human experience would also undermine the (phenomenological/humanistic) tendency to take the patient's experience at face value, as well as the notion, characteristic of psychoanalysis, that the truth of experience is something preexisting and determinate, residing in the inner space of the patient's unconscious and passively waiting to be discovered. The hermeneutic view of insight would see it as an exploratory, dialogic interpretive process in which patient and therapist play closely analogous roles—each in a nondogmatic way bringing to bear habitual preconceptions in order to illuminate meanings that lie, in a sense, not in the patient's mind but in the text-analogue they have before them, i.e., the patient's actions and reported experiences. A hermeneutic appreciation of the role of horizons also suggests that conscious insight is both more complex and potentially dangerous than it might otherwise seem. For, if insight thematizes what was previously horizonal, then it involves not just a discovery but also a radical transformation (and, possibly, an alienation) of what had previously been a taken-for-granted foundation for existence.

In closing, let us turn to more general implications for modes of knowing in psychology. Clearly, hermeneuticists would oppose the tendency, common enough in most fields of psychology, to develop theories that ignore their own embeddedness in specific cultural, historical, and linguistic contexts—e.g., theories of motivation, of person perception, or of the self-concept that naively purport to express universally valid principles (cf. Gergen, 1973). They would encourage more use in psychology of techniques and perspectives from fields in the humanities, like literary studies and cultural anthropology, which are particularly applicable to the understanding of linguistic texts and cultural institutions. Further, they would make a place for a mode of writing very different from what is standard in our field: for a literary, essayistic discourse that seeks not objectivism and neutrality but the kind of illumination that can come from image, metaphor, and other figures of speech. In this way, a hermeneutic turn would mean not only a crossing of disciplines but also that blurring of the genres of science and literature that Geertz (1983) has called for in the social sciences in general.

Hermeneuticists would be equally as suspicious of mainstream psychology's reliance on quantitative methodologies as of the phenomenological-humanistic aspiration to be "not less but more empirical," to "see the patient as he really is" rather than as "merely a projection of our own theories *about* him" (May, 1958, p. 3). Presumably, they would encourage the kind of objectivity without objectification implicit in the hermeneutic circle—where one attempts to use all kinds of analogies and theories to understand the engaged perspective of one's subjects, but to do so without imposing, in Procrustean fashion, an already assumed theory of mind or personality. Finally, hermeneutics would encourage in the psychologist an ironic and self-critical, but by no means despairing, awareness of both the value and danger of presuppositions—and with this, a realization that though knowledge can never be value-free, it is not naive to seek truth.

NOTES

1. Certain other traditions that have been called "hermeneutic" are not treated in the present essay: e.g., the Marxist-influenced critical hermeneutics of Habermas, the methodological hermeneutics of Betti and Hirsch, and the social hermeneutics of the Wittgensteinians (see Howard, 1982; Hoy, 1978). In the view of many, it is the thought of Heidegger, Gadamer, and Ricoeur that is the central line of the contemporary hermeneutic tradition (cf. Palmer, 1969); and it is in their writing that philosophical anthropology plays an especially important role.

Also, for the purposes of the present essay, the differences among Heidegger, Gadamer, and Ricoeur are not of central importance and will not be discussed. Nor will I be able to discuss how their theories changed over time. I should say, however, that I will be primarily concerned with the early

Heidegger, the period of *Being and Time*. Re. these issues, see Palmer, 1969; Ihde, 1971; Dreyfus, 1984.

2. The fairly diverse movement of third force psychology may increasingly include work that is less in line with the humanism that originally inspired it (e.g., transpersonal psychology, Valle and Harari, 1985).

3. I have recast the lines from Woolf's essay on modern fiction that describe life as "a luminous halo, a semi-transparent envelope."

4. Virginia Woolf also yearned for this kind of total communion. For a discussion of this aspect of her work, see Naremore (1973), pp. 225, 242.

5. Similarly, in his essay "Existentialism is a Humanism," Sartre (1956b) writes that "outside the Cartesian *cogito*, all objects are no more than probable" and that "There is [an absolute] truth which is simple, easily obtained and within the reach of everybody: it consists in one's immediate sense of oneself" (p. 302).

6. Actually, both Dilthey and Husserl are tricky cases because their philosophies can be read in a number of different ways. Dilthey's views went through a number of different stages, the last of which has significant affinities to ontological hermeneutics. Heidegger (1962, pp. 429, 449) emphasized his affinities to Dilthey. I will, however, concentrate on Gadamer's (1984) and Ricoeur's (1981) more critical readings of Dilthey—readings that have the merit of capturing the major influence of Dilthey's thought (even though they might not do full justice to his later writings). Re. Dilthey, see Guignon (1983); Howard (1982); Hoy (1978). Husserl's philosophy is also characterized by considerable ambiguities and can be interpreted in a more "idealist" or a more "existentialist" fashion. On the more "idealist" reading, Husserlian phenomenology requires and assumes a consciousness able to achieve complete awareness of its own acts and objects. On the existentialist reading, phenomenology is a progressive and unending analysis of phenomena that never lose a certain obscurity. Husserl called his phenomenology a form of "transcendental idealism," but there is evidence for both readings in his writings. In the present essay, I have adopted the idealist reading. I concentrate on Husserl's *Ideas* and *Cartesian Meditations*, works emphasizing the Cartesian project of finding a certain basis for a philosophy that is rigorous and scientific. Re. these ambiguities in Husserl, see the essays by Kockelmans, Edie, and Kwant in Kockelmans' anthology (1967), pp. 221–251, 393–408.

7. According to Follesdal (1981) Sartre's concept of freedom derived largely from a misreading of Husserl's notion of intentionality.

8. Incidentally, there is a fundamental uncertainty about whether the objects of this intuition should be understood as perceptual or conceptual in nature—i.e., as revealing something like a "concrete sensuous appearance" or "perceptual Gestalt" or "perceptual Gestalt" or as concerning abstract concepts or meanings (Dreyfus, 1982b).

9. Their conceptions are not, of course, identical. Descartes conceives of the subject as having the same ontological status as its objects, as being a

fact in the world, whereas Husserl conceives of the subject as being a transcendental ground *of* the world.

10. Incidentally, Husserl's is not a *metaphysical* solipsism, since he brackets rather than denies the objective existence of the external world. What he calls his *transcendental idealism* must be understood within the phenomenological context produced by the reduction. Thus, to assert that consciousness has a (logical) priority over the real world does not mean that it literally produces things, but that it is "a necessary (though not sufficient) condition for the reference of experience to the real world" and for "the existence of a set of meanings without which objective reference of any sort would be impossible" (Hall, 1982, pp. 181, 176–179).

11. For my reading of Heidegger, I am relying primarily on Heidegger (1962, 1979). Also, I am very indebted to the interpretations offered by Hubert Dreyfus and by Charles Guignon.

12. One inevitably encounters a dilemma in describing Heidegger's views. In opting to use a traditional philosophical vocabulary (as I have often done), one runs the risk of distorting Heidegger's thought; however, not to use such a vocabulary would render the description incomprehensible to those not already steeped in the position.

13. In Heidegger's view Husserl's attempt to dispense with all the prejudices of philosophy and natural science had not been radical enough. If one really wanted to return "to the things themselves," one needed to liberate oneself from traditional techniques and methods, not just from traditional philosophical claims and assumptions. According to Heidegger Husserl's method of detached phenomenological observation accepted the objectivist methodology of Cartesian science, and in this sense was scientistic (despite Husserl's claims to the contrary). The more appropriate and radical move would be not to bracket but to accept the world of everydayness.

14. One of Husserl's criticisms of Heidegger was that the latter's privileging of a particular type of human experience—tool use—was itself unjustified. How, after all, could Heidegger know that this mode of experience was more basic or central than other modes? Didn't this very choice show that Heidegger was not really, as he claimed, approaching existence without any presuppositions? (cf. Dreyfus and Haugeland, 1978). It was just, one might say, that the presuppositions accepted by Heidegger were more pragmatist than intellectualist in nature.

15. For Heidegger, the carpenter cannot be said to "believe" in the reality of the hammer, for this would imply too thematized an awareness.

16. Heidegger claimed of *Being and Time* that "all subjectivity of man as subject is left behind in that work" (quoted in Guignon, 1984, p. 322).

17. I have borrowed this phrase from Sartre (1950), who uses it in a rather different context.

It seems to be this horizon of everydayness, with its implicit faith in the actuality of the world, to which Heidegger is referring in the following passage: "That which remains *hidden* in an egregious sense, or which relapses and yet gets *covered up* again, or which shows itself 'in disguise,' is not just this entity or that, but rather the *Being* of entities" (1962, p. 59).

18. Thus, one of the pitfalls into which reflective awareness is likely to fall is the tendency to conceive of the subject as a quasi-reified entity, existing somehow in itself, apart from its objects: "What if this kind of 'giving-itself' on the part of Dasein should lead our existential analytic astray and do so, indeed, in a manner grounded in the Being of Dasein itself? Perhaps when Dasein addresses itself in the way which is closest to itself, it always says, 'I am this entity,' and in the long run says this loudest when it is not this entity" (Heidegger, 1962, p. 151).

19. Everydayness could be said to be "foundational" for Heidegger. However, his very understanding of everydayness precludes him from being "foundationalist" as that term is usually used. Thus, for Heidegger there is no certain method or source of data by which one can build up an indubitable knowledge of human existence.

20. *Being and Time* is itself a deeply paradoxical book, since it is an attempt to describe precisely those aspects of human existence whose very nature is to remain unseen, unnoticed. For a discussion of the inherent paradoxes in Heidegger's position, see Dreyfus and Haugeland (1978). Later in his career, Heidegger rejected the route of describing in favor of a more "poetic" attempt to evoke Being (Halliburton, 1981).

21. In another respect, however, the ontological hermeneutic position is not equivalent to a strong version of the Whorf-Sapir hypothesis, for (as will be explained below) it does not believe in the mutual incommensurability of different linguistic worlds. (A useful summary of the Whorf-Sapir hypothesis can be found in Slobin, 1971, pp. 120–133.)

22. The ontological hermeneutic position is, however, more moderate than that of many structuralists and poststructuralists, who deny almost completely the role of the subject in discourse.

23. For an account of modernism's propensity to take the nonhermeneutic view that language is inevitably contaminating, see Susan Sontag's (1966) essay, "The Aesthetics of Silence."

24. When Ricoeur turned from transcendental phenomenology to hermeneutics, he wrote a book (1967) on the cultural symbolism of evil in Western society.

25. Gadamer (1984, p. 210) refers to Dilthey's "Cartesianism." Also see Howard (1982), p. 140.

26. Thus, whereas traditional empiricists criticize the empathy-view as impractical and unscientific—"inner experience" being difficult to obtain and virtually impossible to verify—the hermeneuticists add to this the criticism that the goal of such a search is not all that important anyway.

27. Similarly, Gadamer writes that "not occasionally only, but always, the meaning of a text goes beyond its author" (1984, p. 264).

Incidentally, the hermeneutic turn is not just a matter of reversing the causal priority, now placing it on words rather than on meanings. On such a view, one could still see meaning as essentially subjective or psychological; it would just be that meaning is now a precipitate of language rather than its inspiration. But the Gadamerian account (like that of the later Wittgenstein) is more radical than this, for it denies that meaning can be equated with a private psychological state at all.

28. One might contrast the hermeneutic view of the essential ambiguity or multiplicity of meaning with the traditional Freudian view. Thus, e.g., Freud describes the interpretation of dreams as a matter of discovering the original dream-thought that underlies the manifest content. Here meaning is not essentially ambiguous, for there is a single determinate meaning (or several determinate meanings) that happen to be hidden, but that, once unearthed, turn out to be determinate and self-transparent.

29. Here is one of several ways in which the hermeneutic view resembles the position of the later Wittgenstein, who argued that linguistic meaning must necessarily have certain public criteria, even though these criteria are impossible to specify completely. Neither Gadamer nor Wittgenstein argues that speaker and listeners don't have inner states, only that these states cannot be taken as the decisive criteria of the meaning of their utterances, for these meanings are necessarily subject to the indeterminate yet in some ways constraining rules of the shared language.

30. The methodological question of precisely how one adjudicates between different interpretations is a particularly problematic and controversial issue in hermeneutics (c.f. Hoy, 1978)—one that cannot be treated at sufficient length here, where my focus is on philosophical anthropology.

31. In romanticism mind-matter dualism was overcome by means of an organicist metaphysics whose root metaphor is the biological organism. The concept of the biological organism is purposive without necessarily being conscious and is rooted in the material world without being subject to simple causal determinism of a mechanical sort (Abrams, 1958).

REFERENCES

Abrams, M. H. *The mirror and the lamp: Romantic theory and the critical tradition.* New York: Norton, 1958.

Allport, G. *Pattern and growth in personality.* New York: Holt, Rinehart, & Winston, 1961.

Bellah, R., Madsden, R., Sullivan, W., Swidler, A., & Tipton, S. *Habits of the heart: Individualism and commitment in American life.* Berkeley: University of California Press, 1985.

Berger, P. *Facing up to modernity.* New York: Basic Books, 1977.

Berman, M. *The politics of authenticity: Radical individualism and the emergence of modern society.* New York: Atheneum, 1980.

Bernstein, R. J. *Beyond objectivism and relativism.* Philadelphia: University of Pennsylvania Press, 1983.

Bonner, H. The proactive personality. In J. Bugental (Ed.), *Challenges of humanistic psychology.* New York: McGraw-Hill, 1967.

Bugental, J. (Ed.). *Challenges of humanistic psychology.* New York: McGraw-Hill, 1967.

Bugental, J. (Ed.). *The search for authenticity: An existential-analytic approach to psychotherapy.* New York: Holt, Rinehart, & Winston, 1965.

Colaizzi, P. F. Psychological research as the pheneomenologist views it. In R. S. Valle and M. King (Eds.), *Existential-phenomenological alternatives for psychology.* New York: Oxford University Press, 1978.

Dallmayr, R. F. *Twilight of subjectivity: Contributions to a post-individualist theory of politics.* Amherst, Mass.: University of Massachusetts Press, 1981.

DeBoer, T. *The development of Husserl's thought.* The Hague: Nijhoft, 1978.

Dilthey, W. *Selected writings.* Cambridge: Cambridge University Press, 1976.

Dreyfus, H. *What computers can't do.* New York: Harper & Row, 1979.

Dreyfus, H. Introduction. In H. Dreyfus (Ed.), *Husserl, intentionality and cognitive science.* Cambridge: MIT Press, 1982.(a)

Dreyfus, H. Husserl's perceptual *noema.* In H. Dreyfus (Ed.), *Husserl, intentionality and cognitive science.* Cambridge: MIT Press, 1982.(b)

Dreyfus, H. Beyond hermeneutics: Interpretation in late Heidegger and recent Foucault. In G. Shapiro & A. Sica (Eds.), *Hermeneutics: Questions and prospects.* Amherst: University of Massachusetts Press, 1984.

Dreyfus, H. *Being-in-the-world: A commentary on Heidegger's Being and Time, Division I.* Cambridge: MIT Press, in press.

Dreyfus, H., & Haugeland, J. Husserl and Heidegger: Philosophy's last stand. In M. Murray (Ed.), *Heidegger and modern philosophy.* New Haven: Yale University Press, 1978.

Dreyfus, H., & Wakefield, J. From depth psychology to breadth psychology: A phenomenotogical approach to psychopathology. In S. Messer, L. Sass, & R. Woolfolk (Eds.), *Hermeneutics and psychological theory.* New Brunswick, New Jersey: Rutgers University Press, 1988.

Føllesdal, D. Sartre on freedom. In P. Schilpp (Ed.), *The philosophy of Jean-Paul Sartre.* La Salle, Ill.: Open Court, 1981.

Føllesdal, D. Husserl's notion of *noema.* In H. Dreyfus (Ed.), *Husserl, intentionality, and cognitive science.* Cambridge: MIT Press, 1982.

Foucault, M. *Discipline and punish.* New York: Vintage/Random House, 1977.

Freeman, M. Paul Ricoeur on interpretation: The model of the text and the idea of development. *Human Development*, 1985, *28*, 295–312.

Gadamer, H. G. *Philosophical hermeneutics*. Berkeley: University of California Press, 1976.

Gadamer, H. G. *Truth and method*. New York: Crossroad, 1984.

Geertz, C. *The interpretation of cultures*. New York: Basic Books, 1973.

Geertz, C. *Local knowledge*. New York: Basic Books, 1983.

Gergen, K. Social psychology as history. *Journal of Personality and Social Psychology*, 1973, *26*, 309–320.

Gergen, K. *Toward transformation in social knowledge*. New York: Springer-Verlag, 1982.

Giorgi, A. *Psychology as a human science*. New York: Harper & Row, 1970.

Greenblatt, S. *Renaissance self-fashioning*. Chicago: University of Chicago Press, 1980.

Grene, M. *Philosophy in and out of Europe*. Berkeley: University of California Press, 1976.

Guignon, C. *Heidegger and the problem of knowledge*. Indianapolis, Indiana: Hackett, 1983.

Guignon, C. Heidegger's "authenticity" revisited. *Review of Metaphysics*, 1984, *38*, 321–339.

Haan, N., & Bellah, R. *Social science as moral inquiry*. New York: Columbia University Press, 1983.

Hall, H. Was Husserl a realist or an idealist? In H. Dreyfus (Ed.), *Husserl, intentionality, and cognitive science*. Cambridge: MIT Press, 1982.

Halliburton, D. *Poetic thinking: An approach to Heidegger*. Chicago: University of Chicago Press, 1981.

Heidegger, M. *An introduction to metaphysics*. Garden City, New York: Anchor/Doubleday, 1961.

Heidegger, M. *Being and time*. New York: Harper & Row, 1962.

Heidegger, M. Letter on humanism. In R. Zaner & D. Ihde (Eds.), *Phenomenology and existentialism*. New York: Putnam's, 1973.

Heidegger, M. *History of the concept of time: Prolegomena*. Bloomington: Indiana University Press, 1979.

Heller, E. *The disinherited mind*. New York: Harcourt, Brace, Jovanovich, 1975.

Heller, T. C., Sosna, M., & Wellbery, D. E. (Eds.). *Reconstructing individualism: Autonomy, individuality, and the self in western thought*. Stanford, California: Stanford University Press, 1986.

Horkheimer, M., & Adorno, T. W. *The dialectic of enlightenment*. New York: Seabury Press, 1972.

Howard, R. *Three faces of hermeneutics*. Berkeley: University of California Press, 1982.

Hoy, D. *The critical circle: Literature, history and philosophical hermeneutics*. Berkeley: University of California Press, 1978.

Hughes, H. S. *Consciousness and society*. New York: Vintage/Random House, 1958.

Husserl, E. *Ideas: General introduction to pure phenomenology*. New York: Colliers Books, 1962.

Husserl, E. *Cartesian meditations: An introduction to phenomenology*. The Hague: Martinus Nijhoft, 1969.

Ihde, D. *Hermeneutic phenomenology: The philosophy of Paul Ricoeur*. Evanston, Ill.: Northwestern University Press, 1971.

Jennings, J. Husserl revisited. *American Psychologist*, 1986, *41*, 1231–1240.

Kahn, E. Heinz Kohut and Carl Rogers: A timely comparison. *American Psychologist*, 1985, *40*, 893–904.

Kleist, H. von. On the gradual fabrication of thoughts while speaking. In P. B. Miller (Ed.), *An abyss deep enough: Letters of Kliest with a selection of essays and anecdotes*. New York: Dutton, 1982.

Kockelmans, J. J. (Ed.). *Phenomenology: The philosophy of Edmund Husserl and its interpretation*. Garden City, New York: Doubleday, 1967.

Kuhn, T. *The essential tension*. Chicago: University of Chicago Press, 1977.

Maddi, S. *Personality theories: A comparative analysis*. Homewood, Ill.: Dorsey Press, 1980.

Maslow, A. Deficiency motivation and growth motivation. In M. R. Jones (Ed.), *Nebraska Symposium on Motivation*. Lincoln, Neb.: University of Nebraska Press, 1955.

Maslow, A. *Toward a psychology of being*. New York: Van Nostrand Reinhold, 1962.

May, R. The origins and significance of the existential movement in psychology. In R. May, E. Angel, & H. F. Ellenberger (Eds.), *Existence*. New York: Basic Books, 1958.

McIntyre, R., & Smith, D. W. Husserl's identification of meaning and noema. In H. Dreyfus (Ed.), *Husserl, intentionality and cognitive science*. Cambridge: MIT Press, 1982.

McPherson, C. B. *The political thought of possessive individualism: Hobbes to Locke*. Oxford: Clarendon Press, 1962.

Moustakas, C. Being in, being for, and being with. *The Humanistic Psychologist*, 1986, *14*, 100–104.

Naremore, J. *The world without a self: Virginia Woolf and the novel*. New Haven: Yale University Press, 1973.

Packer, M. J. Hermeneutic inquiry in the study of human conduct. *American Psychologist*, 1985, *40*, 1081–1093.

Palmer, R.E. *Hermeneutics: Interpretation theory in Schleiermacher, Dilthey, Heidegger, and Gadamer*. Evanston, Ill.: Northwestern University Press, 1969.

Polkinghorne, D. *Methodology for the human sciences: Systems of inquiry*. Albany: State University of New York Press, 1983.

Rabinow, P., & Sullivan, W. M. *Interpretive social science*. Berkeley: University of California Press, 1979.

Ricoeur, P. *The symbolism of evil*. New York: Harper & Row, 1967.

Ricoeur, P. *Hermeneutics and the human sciences*. Cambridge, England: Cambridge University Press, 1981.

Rogers, C. R. *On becoming a person*. Boston: Houghton Mifflin, 1961.

Sartre, J.-P. *Baudelaire*. New York: New Directions, 1950.

Sartre, J.-P. *Being and Nothingness*. New York: Philosophical Library, 1956.(a)

Sartre, J.-P. Existentialism is a humanism. In W. Kaufman (Ed.), *Existentialism from Dostoevski to Sartre*. Cleveland: Meridian Books, 1956.(b)

Sennett, R. *The fall of public man*. New York: Vintage Books, 1974.

Shalin, D. N. Romanticism and the rise of sociological hermeneutics. *Social Research*, 1986, 53, 77–124.

Slobin, D. *Psycholinguistics*. Glenview, Ill.: Scott, Foresman, 1971.

Sontag, S. The aesthetics of silence. In *Styles of radical will*. New York: Delta/Dell, 1966.

Sturrock, J. (Ed.). *Structuralism and since: From Levi-Strauss to Derrida*. Oxford: Oxford University Press, 1979.

Tageson, W. C. *Humanistic psychology: A synthesis*. Homewood, Ill.: Dorsey Press, 1982.

Taylor, C. *Hegel*. Cambridge: Cambridge University Press, 1975.

Taylor, C. *Philosophical papers* (vol. 1, 2). Cambridge: Cambridge University Press, 1985.

Temerlin, M. K. On choice and responsibility in a humanistic psychotherapy. In F. T. Severin (Ed.), *Humanistic viewpoints in psychology*. New York: McGraw-Hill, 1965.

Trilling, L. *Sincerity and authenticity*. Cambridge, Mass: Harvard University Press, 1971.

Valle, R. S., & Harari, C. Current developments in transpersonal psychology. *The Humanistic Psychologist*, 1985, 13, 11–15.

Valle, R. S., & King, M. An introduction to existential-phenomenological thought in psychology. In Valle & King (Eds.), *Existential-phenomenological alternatives for psychology*. New York: Oxford University Press, 1978.

Wallach, M. A., & Wallach, L. *Psychology's sanction for selfishness: The error of egoism in theory and therapy*. New York: W. H. Freeman, 1983.

White, H. The absurdist moment in contemporary criticism. In *Tropics of discourse*. Baltimore: Johns Hopkins University Press, 1978.

Woolf, V. Modern fiction. In M. A. Leaska (Ed.), *The Virginia Woolf Reader*. San Diego: Harcourt, Brace, Jovanovich, 1984 (orig. publ. 1919).

Woolfolk, R., & Richardson, F. Behavior therapy and the ideology of modernity. *American Psychologist*, 1984, 39, 777–785.

Chapter 9

From Depth Psychology to Breadth Psychology: A Phenomenological Approach to Psychopathology

HUBERT L. DREYFUS and
JEROME WAKEFIELD

Philosophical accounts of the nature of the mind are useful to psychologists because they suggest the form that explanations of mental phenomena should take. By the same token, underlying philosophical conceptions can limit the flexibility of a field in its search for explanations of new or previously ignored phenomena and may have to be adjusted as the concerns of the field evolve. We believe that a change of focus in the field of psychoanalysis since Freud's day, from neurotic symptoms to character styles and personality disorders, has led to a situation where the original philosophy of mind underlying Freud's thinking is currently not very useful in moving the field forward. In fact, some features of that philosophy have simply been jettisoned without explicit discussion in much subsequent theorizing about ego development, object relations theory, and characterology. In this paper we will first make explicit some strands of the philosophy of mind that influenced Freud, considering some of its strengths and weaknesses as a guide to clinical theorizing. Then we will set out some features of an alternative approach to mental phenomena suggested by recent hermeneutic philosophers, similarly examining the implications of this view for theories of psychopathology and therapy, and contrast this view with Freud's. We believe this alternative view is worth exploring because it may provide a more useful way of understanding global character styles and disorders than has so far been provided within the traditional view.

In his psychological theorizing, Freud generally presupposed a traditional conception of the mind that we shall call the *epistemological* view of mind. Epistemology is the theory of knowledge, and we call Freud's view epistemological because it was originally developed by Descartes to explain how a subject can have knowledge of objects outside itself.

The epistemological conception of mind is roughly that the mind consists of a set of ideas, analogous to images or descriptions, that represent the outside world and may correspond or fail to correspond to what is actually out there in the world. The mind is a set of representations, and through these representations the person knows and relates to the world.

This view of the mind reached its culmination in Franz Brentano's notion of intentionality. According to Brentano, what is unique about mental states such as perception, memory, desire, belief, and fear is that they are all "of" something or "about" something. That is, you can't simply remember or desire or believe, you must remember or desire or believe something; your mental state must contain a specific idea or content that directs it at some feature of the world. Brentano claimed that it is this directedness or aboutness, called by him *intentionality*, which is characteristic of the mind and nothing else.

One student who followed Brentano's courses in Vienna was Sigmund Freud. He accepted the intentionalist conception of mind as a set of mental states directed toward objects by means of representations. However, the entire tradition from Descartes to Brentano had maintained that all intentional states must be conscious, whereas Freud learned from his work with hypnosis that not every mental representation was immediately accessible to reflection. Thus Freud was led to introduce the notion of an unconscious that, just like the conscious mind, was directed toward objects by means of representations, but whose representations were not directly accessible to the conscious subject. Even unconscious instinctual impulses, according to Freud, must be directed via unconscious ideas. For example, libidinal energy has its effect on our behavior by cathecting a specific representation or idea of some object, which we then desire for sexual gratification.

The epistemological conception of mind, joined with the idea that some mental contents can be unconscious, led to Freud's epistemological conceptions of pathology and therapy. Freud accounts for pathology by hypothesizing that representations that are deprived of consciousness remain causally active but are not integrated into the web of conscious mental states, and so manifest themselves to consciousness as symptoms. Thus the epistemological account of mind when used to account for pathology becomes a depth psychology concerned with representations buried in the unconscious. Corresponding to these epistemological views of mind and pathology, there is an epistemological conception of the therapeutic process. In depth psychology the basic problem is that some mental contents are unconscious, and not properly integrated into the ego's overall set of representations. Therapy thus consists of helping the patient to uncover the hidden contents and to reintegrate them into his overall mental system. Since the patient has strong motivations for keeping these contents hidden, the therapist must contend with the patient's resistance to allowing the contents to emerge.

As is well known, Freud's clinical focus was on neurotic symptomatology. His central insight was that such symptoms, as well as many other seemingly meaningless behaviors, could be understood as meaningful actions. Given this approach, the epistemological framework was well suited to Freud's theoretical endeavors. Once Freud came to see symptoms as meaningful actions, his epistemological view gave him a simple implicit framework for constructing explanations by hypothesizing underlying representational states analogous to the beliefs and desires that on the epistemological model explain ordinary action.

But not all versions of psychoanalysis are committed to understanding all psychological phenomena in terms of specific mental contents. From Wilhelm Reich's classic work on character analysis down to the current focus within ego psychology and object relations theory on neurotic styles and character pathology, there is a long and currently active psychoanalytic tradition that focuses on overall styles of behavior and experience. Theoreticians of character styles usually end up implicitly deviating from the representational approach to explanation because the epistemological view—for reasons to be explained later—does not provide an illuminating framework for explaining such styles in the way it does for symptoms. In short, reducing character and style to the effects of specific beliefs, desires, schemata, and other representational states just doesn't seem to be a useful strategy. Despite this, the idea that representations must mediate between subject and action has seldom been explicitly questioned in the psychoanalytic literature, and alternatives to the epistemological explanatory framework have not been systematically explored. The remainder of this chapter will be an attempt to distill a nonrepresentational approach to the explanation of pathology from the works of recent hermeneutic philosophers as a step toward developing an alternative possible framework for current practice.

Recently, philosophers such as Martin Heidegger and Maurice Merleau-Ponty, reacting against the Cartesian tradition, have developed an alternative model of the mind's relation to reality. This account is so radical that, strictly speaking, these philosophers do not refer to the mind at all. Rather they prefer to speak of the way that the whole human being is related to the world. Indeed, even "relation" is misleading, since it suggests the coming together of two separate entities—human being and world—whereas these philosophers see mind and world as inseparable. So they are finally driven to replace the epistemological relation of subject and object with a way of being they call "being-in-the-world," in which human being is a kind of space in which coping with certain kinds of beings becomes possible. Since ontology is the study of that which determines entities as entities, this approach to the mind is called *ontological*.

The ontological view does not deny that human beings sometimes have mental states by which their minds are directed towards objects. Rather, the ontologists assert that mental states presuppose a context in which objects can show up and make sense, so that the context both opens up and limits the kinds of objects that can be represented or can be dealt with directly. According to Heidegger, this context is provided by social practices. The shared practices into which we are socialized provide a background understanding of what counts as objects, what counts as human beings, and ultimately what counts as real, on the basis of which we can direct our actions towards particular things and people. Heidegger calls this background understanding of what it means to be, which is embodied in the tools, language, and institutions of a society and in each person growing up in that society, but not represented in that person's mind, and understanding of Being. This understanding of Being creates what Heidegger calls a *clearing* (*Lichtung*) in which entities can then show up for us.

The clearing is neither on the side of the subject nor the object—it is not a set of implicit and explicit beliefs nor a set of facts—rather it contains both and makes their relation possible. It is a context that both opens up and limits the kinds of objects we can deal with—or, as Heidegger puts it, what things can show up for us *as*, for example, *as* a hammer, or *as* a person.

Merleau-Ponty, following Heidegger, compares this clearing to the illumination in a room. The illumination allows us to perceive objects, but is not itself an object toward which the eye can be directed. He argues that this clearing is correlated with our bodily skills and thus with the bodily stance we take toward people and things. Each person not only incorporates his culture, but also his subculture and the understanding of human beings and of objects that is his family's variation of the current social practices. Finally, each person has his or her own embodied understanding of what counts as real, which is, of course, not private but is a variation on the shared public world.

The ontological view leads to an alternative account of the unconscious, of psychopathology, and therapy. Merleau-Ponty claims that pathology occurs when some aspect of a person's relationship to particular objects in the world merges into the context on the basis of which objects are encountered. When this happens the person's world or clearing becomes restricted and rigid. The person suffers from a lack of possibilities that he cannot understand and over which he has no control. To highlight the contrast between Freud and Merleau-Ponty, this ontological account of psychopathology as the expanding of content into context, might be called *breadth* psychology.

On this ontological view, pathology occurs when a particular way a person relates to some people or some objects becomes a way of relating to all people and all objects, so that it becomes the form or style of all relationships. That is, some aspect of the epistemological relation of a subject to other persons and objects, which should take place *in* the clearing, becomes a dimension of the clearing itself. Merleau-Ponty calls this shift *generalization*, and uses this idea to give an alternative account of repression:

> Repression ... consists in the subject's entering upon a certain course of action—a love affair, a career, a piece of work—in his encountering on this course some barrier, and, since he has the strength neither to surmount the obstacle nor to abandon the enterprise, he remains imprisoned in the attempt and uses up his strength indefinitely renewing it. ... Time in its passage does not carry away with it these impossible projects; it does not close up on traumatic experience; the subject remains open to the same impossible future, if not in his explicit thoughts, then in his actual being. (Merleau-Ponty, 1962, p. 83)

Merleau-Ponty's prose is famous for its literary polish but hardly for its simplicity and clarity. He is saying that in a neurotic reaction to frustration and conflict the subject gets stuck in a certain way of having a clearing or sense of being, and so repeats his "solution" endlessly, thus generalizing it and taking it out of time.

This is, of course, a new version of the unconscious. Merleau-Ponty uses as an example of such a generalized unconscious the case of someone who relates to each person as if the issue were one of determining who is inferior and who is superior. In Merleau-Ponty's terms, inferior/superior, once an issue in the clearing, has become a dimension of the clearing. Merleau-Ponty uses the notion of context —this time called *atmosphere*—to explain why such a self-defeating stance is outside of the sufferer's awareness and control: "An inferiority complex ... means that I have committed myself to inferiority, that I have made it my abode, that this past, though not a fate, has at least a specific weight and is not a set of events over there, at a distance from me, but the atmosphere of my present" (Merleau-Ponty, 1962, p. 442).

Once such a way of taking people becomes a dimension of the background of all experience, a person is unlikely to experience anything that could cause him to change his one-sided way of relating to other people. Thus Merleau-Ponty arrives at an account of the static character of neurotic time, parallel to, but totally different from, Freud's notion of the timelessness of the unconscious:

One present among all presents thus acquires an exceptional value; it displaces the others and deprives them of their value as authentic presents. We continue to be the person who once entered on this adolescent affair, or the one who once lived in this parental universe. New perceptions, new emotions even, replace the old ones, but this process of renewal touches only the content of our experience and not its structure. Impersonal time continues its course, but personal time is arrested ... This fixation does not merge into memory; it even *excludes memory* in so far as the latter spreads out in front of us. ... whereas this past which remains our true present does not leave us but *remains constantly hidden behind our gaze instead of being displayed before it.* The traumatic experience does not survive as a *representation* in the mode of objective consciousness and as a 'dated' moment; it is of its essence to survive *only as a manner of being with a certain degree of generality.* (Merleau-Ponty, 1962, p. 83)

So far we have seen that Merleau-Ponty claims that if a child is faced with a particularly painful conflict the specific pattern already in place in the child's life gets generalized and becomes a dimension of the background upon which, from then on, persons and events show up. Merleau-Ponty does not tell us just why a conflict leads to the sort of ontological generalization that constitutes a character disorder, but using some ideas from Heidegger we can construct an account of how and why such a change might occur. To begin with, conflicts lead to strong emotions. Heidegger classifies emotions and moods as forms of what he calls *attunement* (*Befindlichkeit*), and he notes that attunements in his sense have an ontological capacity, i.e., they can color a whole world (Heidegger, 1962, sections 29 and 32).

Moods, for example, are always total. When one is in an elated mood everything is encountered as colorful and challenging, and, conversely, in depression everything shows up as drab and uninteresting. Emotions, unlike moods, are not always general. They can be quite specific, such as fear of a particular event, or anger at a particular person. Indeed, they normally are directed toward something specific that concerns some specific aspect of a person in some specific way. But emotions can flare up and come to color the child's whole world like a mood, as when a child's anger at how his father is treating him becomes anger at how his father *always* treats him, and even rage at how *everyone* has always treated him.

Now if we apply these ideas to the process of ontological generalization, we can see why emotion plays a central role. When the issues set up by the family lead to a crisis, the emotional reaction of the child not only magnifies and intensifies the crisis, but actually totalizes it, so that it engulfs the child's whole world.[1] Ordinarily, the emotion then subsides and the meaning it has carried out to the limits of the world again comes to be directed at the appropriate object in the world. But if, for any reason, the emotion is arrested in its course, then the local issue remains totalized and becomes an ontological dimension, or to put it in a way in keeping with Merleau-Ponty's emphasis on the body as correlative with the world, the body remains frozen in a certain stance which then distorts everything that shows up in its clearing.

On the hermeneutic account, a child comes to encounter all significant figures as superior, for example, not because the representations of specific threatening others make him anxious and are therefore repressed and return in disguised form as symptoms. An unconscious belief that he is inferior would not adequately account for the pervasive style of his behavior nor his imperviousness to counterarguments. A belief, or schema, is inadequate to account for a style of behavior because such mental representations do not explain how the person who has them behaves with the appropriate style in each particular case.[2] To see why a belief or schema cannot account for a style, take a concrete example. If our patient simply believes he is inferior or has a rule, e.g., whenever asked to do something claim one is not adequate for the job, he would not know just how to apply the rule to anomalous situations such as when his wife asks him to take out the garbage or when his boss congratulates him on work he has done. Yet it is clear that he will exhibit his unique style of inferiority behavior in each of these situations and indefinitely many others. According to Merleau-Ponty's account, the child's anger or shame about inferiority is sedimented into his posture and other body sets, which structures his world so that all significant persons show up as dominating and lead him to respond in a similar way to each new situation. We do not claim to know how a human body picks up a style of behavior, but it does seem clear that a cognitivist account in terms of beliefs and rules cannot explain precisely the unity of style across many types of situation that needs explaining.

Even after an issue *in* the world, e.g. who is superior, has become one of the dimensions of the clearing, however, a person's world is not completely static and one dimensional. There are still other dimensions people can show up on, e.g., as sexually attractive. To understand the last step to the closed world of pathology requires explication of one last ontological notion from Heidegger and Merleau-Ponty. Heidegger, in his later work, introduces the idea of a particular event in the clearing or Open, which focuses and stabilizes the cultural meanings already in the public practices. As Heidegger puts it: "There must always be some being in this Open ... in which the openness takes its stand and attains its constancy" (Heidegger, 1971, p. 61). He gives as an example the Greek temple that opens up and organizes a multidimensional world by highlighting crucial issues that then become the locus of conflicts of interpretation and the starting point of history. Heidegger's notion of an event that gives constancy to a cultural clearing might be called a cultural paradigm, for it has much in common with Thomas Kuhn's notion of a scientific paradigm, a particular experiment or explanation that serves as a model of good science and organizes the activities of researchers in a scientific community. Søren Kierkegaard emphasizes that a lover or a cause to which one is committed can serve the same function in an individual's life (Kierkegaard, 1983).

In his last book Merleau-Ponty introduces a similar idea concerning the role of particular objects or events in an individual's life. "It is necessary to have the ontological capacity ... to take *a* being as a representative of Being. ... The fixation of 'character' [takes place] by investment of the openness of Being in an entity—and, henceforth, takes place *through this entity*. Any entity can be *accentuated* as an emblem of Being" (Merleau-Ponty, 1968, p. 270). The emblem, as Merleau-Ponty calls the paradigmatic object, has the effect of reorganizing the background or clearing in which all contents appear. Thus, even though it is an object we actually confront, it performs the same function as the clearing.

Heidegger and Merleau-Ponty have noticed two closely related but antithetical kinds of ontological entities. Heidegger's notion of an event that gives constancy to a cultural clearing might be called a *positive paradigm*. Merleau-Ponty, on the other hand, is suggesting that there can also be negative paradigms—objects, persons, or events that focus a world not in opening it up but by closing it down, thus substituting timelessness for history.

As opposed to a positive paradigm, which determines what is important in a shared, many dimensional reality and so sets up conflicts of interpretation, the neurotic paradigm is a telling example that shows the hopeless way things are once and for all. A neurotic paradigm totalizes the world in advance so that all anomalies are either ignored or assumed to be assimilable to the reigning account. A healthy paradigm, on the other hand, allows anomalies to be revealed that can then be focused on as possibilities containing a truth that can challenge the old theory and may become central in a new one.

If psychopathology is the result of generalizing an issue until it becomes a dimension of experience and then focusing this dimension so that it colors all the others, then the cure must begin by showing the patient that his way of being-in-the-world has acquired a pervasive coloring. This is not to say that the patient must be given a new frame. The patient's problem is not merely that he has a disabling frame and needs a freer one. His problem is that a normal and sensible occasional issue, like the question of superiority, has become a frame. Any other specific issue that was treated as a frame would be just as disabling. So the problem for therapy is not changing frames, but putting some issue that has become a frame back into the patient's picture.

The patient cannot see that his clearing has a fixed and narrow content because he has nothing to contrast it with. So what can the therapist do? The therapist may try to lead the patient to experience the world before it became one dimensional by being focused by an emblematic event, or, even further back, to remember how things showed up before a specific issue in the family became one of the dimensions of his clearing. Of course, any ordinary memory will show the past as already colored by the current clearing, but perhaps there can be a kind of spontaneous recall, especially in dreams, in which past events are experienced as they were originally, not as they have been retroactively interpreted.

To get the patient to see he has a pervasive interpretation, the analyst can call attention to the pervasive and inappropriate style of the patient's behavior by making it difficult for the patient to fit the therapist into his world and calling attention to the anomalies that arise when he tries. Thus transference would be conceptualized differently in these two pure cases. Rather than following Freud in using transference primarily in dealing with specific resistances, one would work with transference, as most current therapists do anyway, as an occasion for showing the patient the inappropriate coloring or style of his world by pointing out that he is reacting to the therapist in a typical but inappropriate way. The therapist thus uses the fact that he inevitably becomes an emblematic focus for the one dimension through which the neurotic sees everything in his world to call attention to this dimension.

Even if the patient were thus led by contrast with the past to recognize the coloring of his present clearing, however, he would be likely to insist that at a certain time in the past he simply found out how things really are. Then the therapeutic strategy for turning the ontological back into the epistemological must undermine the patient's current sense of reality that the style or pattern of his life makes manifest. This is accomplished by working with the patient to piece together an account of how the patient's narrow version of reality developed through a series of accidental events, misunderstandings, and frozen emotions. Pointing out cognitive contradictions in the patient's view of reality will also help overcome the patient's conviction that reality must be the way he sees it.

Simultaneously the patient must be led to see the connection between his view of reality and his pain. The therapist thus tries to get the patient to see that what he takes to be unchangeable reality is really simply his particular and quirky story, and that this understanding has a high price. This "genealogy" will tend to undermine the patient's conviction that his way of seeing things is the way things are and have to be.

Also, since an issue *in* the world becomes a dimension when it is totalized by an emotion that is not allowed to subside in the normal way, the emotion that has been stuck in world expansion must be worked through so that the issue it has ontologized can shrink down to size. Only then will the patient be able to see the struggle for, say, superiority, only where it is appropriate—rather than as the central dimension of all human interactions.

Finally, resistance will be considered differently on the two views. Whereas Freud considered resistance to be the interpersonal manifestation of the patient's attempts to hide certain mental contents, and thus part of the pathological process, an ontological approach emphasizes that the patient is simply defending what to him is the real meaning of his experience. In other words resistance displays not merely pathology, but a form of integrity.

These techniques are not new to psychotherapy. The ontological view does not change what counts as pathology nor does it cast doubt on what have been successful ways of treating it. Rather, it conceptualizes both the pathology and the treatment in a new way. The issue that, as a dimension, has come to govern all possible ways of acting for the patient must once again become an object for him so that he can confront and deal with it freely as one issue among others in his world.

There are differences between the practices dictated by the two conceptualizations in their pure forms, however. These differences are not obvious in actual therapy since new ideas have entered therapy since Freud, and even Freud saw and did many things his model did not adequately explain. Nonetheless, one who thinks of neurosis as a pattern of behavior that has become generalized into an ontological dimension will tend to focus on character pathologies rather than symptoms. Furthermore, if Merleau-Ponty is right that a rigid reality is correlated with a rigid body stance, some kind of body work may be called for. Thus the kind of pathology that is taken as paradigmatic and the kind of therapy practiced begins to sound more like the Reich of *Character Analysis* than like Freud of the Dora case (Reich, 1972).

The idea of an ontological form of therapy based on Heidegger's work is not new. Both Ludwig Binswanger and Medard Boss are well-known existential or hermeneutic therapists. Both understand psychopathology as a distortion of the human clearing that makes it narrow and rigid. Binswanger distinguishes *my* world from *the* world and thinks of therapy as adjusting my world to the world. He was concerned with the style of a person's world. Thus, for example, he was not interested in the content of dreams but in the personal way of structuring space and time that dreams revealed. Binswanger also was concerned with constructing a narrative that captured the developing pattern of a person's life, but he was interested in the narrative as a way of clarifying and rendering consistent a patient's way of being-in-the-world, not as a way of undermining a patient's sense of reality. Thus, in "The Case of Ellen West," Binswanger tells how he helped his patient see that her desires were hopelessly contradictory, and so gave her the courage and insight to confront the nature of her own being-in-the-world (which in turn led her to commit suicide). In contrast, Medard Boss in his "Daseinanalysis" was committed to healing the patient by opening up his or her constricted world. He used the transference as a way of providing the love absent in a patient's childhood so as to enable the patient to develop a self that could open itself to more styles of relationship. Both Binswanger and Boss, however, get their basic conceptions from early Heidegger so they have no sense of the role of paradigms—introduced by later Heidegger—nor of the lived body introduced by Merleau-Ponty. Having only the idea of an empty clearing as in early Heidegger, both see psychopathology as a constriction of the patient's world, but neither sees this narrowing as the result of content becoming context by being focused in a paradigm and/or sedimented in a specific body stance correlated with specific expectations.

It is now time to consider briefly the relative merits of the epistemological and ontological views as conceptualizations of neurotic and character pathologies. Let us first take a look at a simple, very circumscribed symptom. In his *Introductory Lectures on Psychoanalysis*, Freud describes a man who, at odds with his wife, cannot find a book she gave him as a gift. When the couple is reconciled once more, he finds the book without difficulty. According to Freud a specific memory had been repressed.

Now, Merleau-Ponty holds that we never reject a specific memory in such a case. Rather, repression is always directed against a region of our experience, which includes a whole class of memories. Moreover, it is not the number of forgotten memories, but why the forgetting occurs at all that distinguishes Merleau-Ponty's view from

Freud's. About Freud's example, Merleau-Ponty says, "Everything connected with his wife had ceased to exist for him, he had shut it out from his life, and at one stroke, broken the circuit of all actions relating to her, and thus placed himself on the hither side of all knowledge and ignorance, assertion and negation, in so far as these were voluntary" (Merleau-Ponty, 1962, p. 162).

Merleau-Ponty is saying, somewhat hyberbolically, that this man had not merely shut out a group of memories, but he had shut out a space of possible relations with his wife, a dimension of experience. His coldness to her had become part of his background, and he now saw his wife differently, in fact was no longer capable of seeing or responding to her in a range of ways that had earlier been available to him. She has ceased to exist as the same sort of being she was before, for the man's space of possible actions, the "circuit" of actions, as Merleau-Ponty puts it, has been radically altered. This collapse of space of possibilities when we come to see someone differently suggests what Merleau-Ponty has in mind when he says that the man is now on the "hither side of knowledge and ignorance." The man's coldness began as a choice, a response to specific events within a relationship that contained many possibilities. But the coldness generalized so that open and warm feelings toward his wife are no longer a potential in his world. It is no longer the case that he could be warm or cold, but chooses to be cold. Rather, his field of possible choices has actually narrowed.

But how does the collapse of a set of possibilities for feeling and action toward his wife explain the man's inability to remember where he put his wife's gift? Merleau-Ponty's answer is, "In hysteria and repression, we may well overlook something although we know of it, because our memories and our body, instead of presenting them-selves to us in singular and determinate conscious acts, are enveloped in generality. . . . [M]emories are expressly grasped and recognized by us only in so far as they adhere generally to that area of our body and our life to which they are relevant" (Merleau-Ponty, 1962, p. 162). In other words generalization of some issue into the background pro-vides a new context or ground in which certain memories may not easily emerge. Generalization, then, sets bounds not only to the immediate availability of objects but to the availability of the past. The man's generalized issue with his wife has created a context where the memory of the gift does not easily come to mind.

Merleau-Ponty's account has the advantage that it attempts to explain how the symptom resulted from more general background issues. As a result it provides a built-in partial answer to the problem of the "choice of symptom" that has puzzled analytic theoreticians since Freud. On the other hand, Merleau-Ponty's explanation seems excessively convoluted, and goes far beyond the facts given in Freud's case vignette. In fact, the patient's wife did not "cease to exist" for him, and the degree of his shutting her out is unclear. There is no report of the loss of other memories concerned with her; in fact, it is the isolated nature of the amnesia that makes it so striking. In all, Freud's case does seem like one best explained at least initially as the repression of a specific memory. A deeper explanation might require some of Merleau-Ponty's machinery, especially if we wanted to explore why this man is the sort of man who would respond to marital disharmony in the way he did, but the epistemological level of explanation seems to have a rightful place here as the simplest explanation covering the known facts. In the case of other symptoms, the facts might warrant the opposite conclusion.

We turn now to the domain of character disorders. Character formation has always been a problematic area for traditional psychoanalytic explanation. A major impetus for dealing with character has been the desire to explain symptom choice, but once character is acknowledged to be involved, and in need of explanation itself, the overall explanatory situation seems to become worse rather than better. As David Shapiro says, "The view of symptomatic behavior as a reflection of how individuals characteristically think and see things is in certain ways not only different from but actually contrary to the traditional dynamic view" (Shapiro, 1981, pp. 3–4).

Freud himself appears to have been quite dissatisfied with his own attempts to give the representationalist mechanics of character formation. The classic position is stated in Freud's *Three Essays on Sexuality*: "What we describe as a person's 'character' is built up to a considerable extent from the material of sexual excitations and is composed of instincts that have been fixed since childhood, of constructions achieved by means of sublimation, and of other constructions" (Freud, 1905, p. 238). Yet character traits are so global that it seems hard to imagine their derivation from specific mental contents. Even in his most explicit attempts to account for traits, Freud acknowledged this essential mystery. In "Character and Anal Eroticism," he argues that an entire constellation of traits, including orderliness, stinginess, and obstinacy, derive from fixations in the anal stage of psychosexual development through the mechanisms of reaction formation and sublimation. Yet he acknowledges that "the intrinsic necessity for this connection is not clear, of course, even to myself" (Freud, 1908, p. 172), and that his explanations leave a residue of unintelligibility to the connection. When he confronts the relationship between character and symptom in his paper, "The Disposition to Obsessional Neurosis," he insists that "in the field of the development of *character* we are bound to meet with the same instinctual forces which we have found at work in the neuroses," and at the same time recognizes that "a sharp theoretical distinction between the two is necessitated by the single fact that the failure of repression and the return of the repressed ... are absent in the formation of character" (Freud, 1913, p. 323). But psychoanalysis is a process for exploiting failures of repression to bring forth the repressed, so Freud is forced to admit, "The processes of the formation of character are more obscure and less accessible to analysis than neurotic ones" (Freud, 1913, p. 323).

Later, in *The Ego and The Id*, Freud suggests identification as a central mechanism of character formation, along with sublimation. He describes identification as an alteration of the ego in which an object that has been lost is somehow replaced by a representation in the ego. This is as near as the representational view can get to the notion of an emblem. But without the notion of a clearing, how this process works, and especially how it brings about global stylistic changes in behavior, cannot be explained. Instead Freud admits, "The exact nature of this substitution is as yet unknown to us" (Freud, 1923, p. 29). Indeed, the two mechanisms Freud most often cites as possibly leading from specific representational states to global character traits, identification and sublimation, have in common that their natures are extremely vague and obscure compared to other defense strategies.

We feel that Freud's tentativeness was well-founded, and that there are intrinsic difficulties in explaining global character styles in terms of the workings of specific representational states. We cannot go through the entire argument here, nor is there likely to be a knockdown argument that complex webs of beliefs and desires, impulses, and defenses could never explain character. Again, it is a matter of plausibility and the smoothness of fit between theory and data. Character traits are notoriously difficult to change through the usual means of cognitive or depth approaches. They are not merely ego-syntonic, which might be explained by rationalization or very smoothly working defensive structures, but they are experienced as part of the essence and identity of the self. Rather than a person's style getting its meaning from specific mental contents, our intuition is that the direction of meaning—and hence of interpretation—should go the other way, with the global style giving meaning to the specific contents.

Contrary to the awkwardness of the epistemological approach, Merleau-Ponty's ontological view directly accounts for the extreme globalness, ego-syntonicity, and relative intractability to therapeutic efforts of character pathology. The context, or background, in which representational states appear will automatically have global implications for all areas of functioning, for it will determine the possible kinds of representations that can appear. Ontological generalization by its nature affects the whole of ego functioning at once. It is ego-syntonic because it is the structure of the ego, its source is not external hidden impulses nor particular introjects. And it is difficult to change in part because there is no easy target, such as an unconscious idea, to try to change. It is no less than the global structure of the patient's world, which is everywhere at once, that therapist and patient must attempt to alter.

Indeed, it is hard to see how therapy could succeed if every aspect of the patient's life had been infected by his one-dimensional view. For therapeutic, genealogical reconstruction of the arbitrariness of the patient's sense of reality then would be seen by the patient merely as showing the strange and idiosyncratic route he followed in arriving at the truth. Fortunately, however, this need not be his response. When a patient's world becomes totalized and one-dimensional, other ways of behaving from earlier days endure. These marginal stances, interpretations, and practices endure precisely because they are too fragmentary and trivial to be seen as important. The therapist must recover and focus the lost possibilities. Here transference has a positive role. Merleau-Ponty seems to be getting at this positive function of transference—the therapist as a positive paradigm—when he writes: "Psychoanalytical treatment does not bring about its cure by producing direct awareness of the past, but ... by binding the subject to his doctor through new existential relationships. ... It is a matter of reliving this or that as significant, and this the patient succeeds in doing only by seeing his past in the perspective of his co-existence with the doctor" (Merleau-Ponty, 1962, p. 445). Other ways of encountering things and people, which were once possible for the patient and are still present in his body and behavior but are dispersed, can be drawn together in the patient's relation to the therapist. The therapist can thus become for the patient a provisional paradigm that focuses and stabilizes an open and multidimensional world.

NOTES

—Both authors contributed equally to this chapter and to their rejoinder to Joel Kovel. Names are in alphabetical order.

1. Silvan S. Tompkins (1979) develops a similar idea in "Script Theory: Differential Magnification of Affects," but he only speaks of affects as amplifying and generalizing but not as totalizing.

2. See Michael A. Westerman, "Meaning and Psychotherapy: A Reconceptualization of the Value and Limitations of Insight-Oriented, Behavioral, and Strategic Approaches," presented at the American Psychological Association Convention, Montreal, September 1980.

REFERENCES

Freud, S. Three essays on the theory of sexuality. S.E., 1905, Vol. 7.

Freud, S. Character and anal erotism. S.E., 1908, Vol. 9.

Freud, S. The disposition to obsessional neurosis: A contribution to the problem of choice of neurosis. S.E., 1913, Vol. 12.

Freud, S. The ego and the id. S.E., 1923, Vol. 19.

Heidegger, Martin. *Being and Time* (Sections 29, 32). New York: Harper & Row, 1962.

Heidegger, Martin. The origin of the work of art. In *Poetry, language, thought*. New York: Harper & Row, 1971.

Kierkegaard, Søren. *Fear and trembling*. Princeton: Princeton University Press, 1983.

Merleau-Ponty, Maurice. *Phenomenology of perception*. New York: The Humanities Press, 1962.

Merleau-Ponty, Maurice. *The visible and the invisible*. Chicago: Northwestern University Press, 1968.

Reich, Wilhem. *Character analysis* (Part 1). New York: Simon and Schuster, 1972.

Shapiro, David. *Autonomy and rigid character*. New York: Basic Books, 1981.

Tomkins, S. S. Script theory: Differential magnifications of affects. In H. E. Howe, Jr., & R. A. Dienstbier (Eds.), *Nebraska symposium on motivation, 1978* (vol. 26). Lincoln: University of Nebraska Press, 1979.

Freud's Ontology—Agency and Desire: Commentary on Hubert L. Dreyfus and Jerome Wakefield

JOEL KOVEL

Hubert Dreyfus and Jerome Wakefield have widened the scope of clinical conceptualization by reopening the ontological dimension. Their essay is thus valuable both for its intrinsic usefulness as a contribution to clinical work and for its demonstration that philosophy—here, that of Heidegger and Merleau-Ponty—can make a practical difference. I am especially appreciative of the authors' nonchauvinistic attitude toward the subject: their recognition that every theory is less rich than the reality it tries to encompass, and the call that follows from this which is to work toward an integration of views, in this case, those of psychoanalysis and of existential-phenomenology.

As is so often the case, revisions of psychopathology and psychotherapy take Freud as their point of departure. Insofar as Freud remains the paradigmatic thinker of modern depth psychology, this is a quite sensible procedure, even if it sets aside the richness of post-Freudian psychoanalytic thought. However, it also runs the risk of using Freud reductively. There is no damage done in this so long as what is abstracted from Freud is heuristically useful; and to a considerable extent I find this to be the case here. Nevertheless, there is also a point past which some of the subtlety of Freud's thought is sacrificed in the interest of drawing a distinction between his medical-biological discourse and the philosophical approach of Heidegger and Merleau-Ponty—and it is to this that I would like to turn.

To be specific, I think it incorrect to identify Freud's original philosophy of mind as epistemological and not ontological. No doubt Freud was greatly influenced by Brentano, and it was from this point that representational thinking and intentionality—i.e., Cartesianism —entered psychoanalytic thought just as it led, through another branch from the same point, to Husserl, Heidegger, and all that followed. On the other hand, Freud had a very distinct ontology into which he synthesized Brentano's philosophy, and this led to a philosophy of mind that it would not be useful to call *epistemological* except in a superficial sense. I am not saying that this philosophy was unproblematic. Quite to the contrary, it was deeply problematic and its difficulties have not been surmounted to this day. But it was non-Cartesian in principle as well; indeed, Freud's break with Cartesianism's sharp mind-body distinction and assumption of a potent *cogito* as the steering mechanism of the psyche was in fact his central contribution. More, it deserves to be called *ontological* inasmuch as Freud was postulating a kind of human "being" that constructs intentional texts and narratives but can never know itself; a being, moreover, for whom the boundary between the mental and the somatic could never be sharply drawn. I would also hold that this ontology conferred a certain power on Freudian discourse that the alternate branch of non-Cartesian thought, leading from Heidegger through Merleau-Ponty, has not been able to appropriate.

The additional point of view in question is not readily summarized, but it can be briefly encapsulated as the incorporation of a Helmholtzian strand in Freud's thinking and its uneasy synthesis with Brentano's intentionality. Freud took from the great 19th-century natural scientist Helmholtz a conviction that the fundamental laws of nature must be obeyed by the psyche. This led to the naturalistic, protosymbolic, indeed, pre-epistemological root of Freud's ontology, epitomized in the conception of the Pleasure (and much later, Nirvana) Principle, that obeyed, in essence, the laws of the conservation of energy. The same kind of notion was expressed in chapter 7 of the *Interpretation of Dreams*, in which the "mental apparatus" (the choice of this term itself conveying Freud's protoepistemology) was constructed as a kind of reflex-arc.

The dilemmas to which this essentially physicalistic view of mind have led have been copiously documented as they devolve into the theory of the ego and the instinctual drives. Freud's post-Cartesian synthesis often breaks down on the level of clinical theory or concrete description, leaving the "force" (i.e., Helmholtzian) and "meaning"

(Brentanoian) terms to go their own way. On the other hand, the power afforded by the Pleasure Principle should also be observed, for it allows us to think of human beings as radically decentered creatures whose subjectivity fundamentally negates itself (in the words of Iago, "I am not what I am"). In other words it gave rein to the inclinations of Freud as "master of suspicion," to use the term of Ricoeur.

Two major implications may be briefly noted here. First, because of the tension between the pleasure and reality principles, the contents of the mind coexist with their opposites in a dialectic of subjectivity. Further, there is a material ground to the dialectic stemming from the organic source of negativity. This is the essential respect by which Freud surpassed Brentano, and it should be given prime recognition over the common ground with Brentano. After all, a thinker should be known by the way he advanced over his predecessors. In any case if such a viewpoint is epistemology, then it is first of all a negative epistemology, one in which the transparency of consciousness and the centeredness of the ego have been decisively undone.

Secondly, the theory gives space for desire, as the vectorial form taken by warded-off representations. Desire, which can never be caught in any net of positive signification, is antiepistemic through its very nature. Given the presence of desire, the mind can never be reduced to a set of representations, as such. And since desire is of nature, and spontaneous, it has to be unbound in the process of psychoanalytic therapy. The therapy must therefore be structured so as to let people speak freely. This measure introduces into the proceedings a moment of noninterference by the analyst as well as autonomy by the analysand. Finally, although it may seem only tangentially related to the matter at hand, I should add that Freud's ontology, aside from being antiepistemic, is also tragic in nature. That is to say, it confers upon subjectivity the qualities we associate with high tragic art (as in Freud's recognition of Oedipus and Hamlet). For this reason alone, which is but another side of the above observation about freedom and autonomy, Freud's ontology, for all its flaws, remains a decisive statement about the human condition —including psychopathology.

I would agree that the ontologies advanced by Heidegger and Merleau-Ponty amount to an improvement with respect to the reificatory potentials of the psychoanalytic view of the ego, and that they also constitute an especially favorable vantage point from which to engage the vexing problem of character. However, I do not think Dreyfus and Wakefield have given enough weight to some of the specific difficulties entailed in their position. For in contrast to Freud, we have here a view of subjectivity without negativity. In other words there is no notion of something like a pleasure principle to serve as a counterforce to the demands of reality. Consequently, there is no recognition of how the psyche can deceive and negate itself. We therefore get a view of subjectivity without object-seeking intentionality, but without desire as well. At least three serious implications follow.

First, there is no theoretical basis for illusion, self-deception, repression, and the whole panoply of devices by means of which false consciousness is inwardly installed. In the practical setting, there is no way not to take the patient's communications as transparent. One simply has to go with what one is told. For a pursuit the authors recognize as involving historical investigation, this poses a major difficulty. How is one to "go back with" the patient to such a point as when emotional blockage occurred in order to help him or her relive the pain? The rule in clinical work, whether with character problems or symptoms, is that the actual antecedents of psychopathology are not lying about ready at hand for investigation. They have instead to be painstakingly reconstructed, and there is no alternative, so far as I know, to the psychoanalytic method for this purpose.

Second, the concrete participation of the subject in his or her pathology is slighted. In fact, there is no mention by Dreyfus and Wakefield of any active engagement by the self in the emotional crises and blockages that are said to lead to character pathology. Without a notion of desire, no account can be taken of human agency. As a result the moral and tragic dimension of human existence becomes opaque. Things just happen to people, and all conflict occurs between the person and the outside world instead of including a moment within the self. Even Alfred Adler, who greatly foreshortened Freud's view of human nature, recognized that children have active strivings for superiority. Here, however, the child simply appears as victim. Moreover, the emotions, as described by the authors, take on an organic, desubjectivised quality. They just happen to people, like fevers that take their course, or intestinal blockages. Clearly, the authors do not intend any such interpretation. However, a purely ontological discourse, without intentionality in the form of desire, does not permit any alternative so far as I can see.

Third, the essentially static image of the subject offered by the ontological view implies a therapy that is either didactic or authoritarian in practice and whose outcome is dictated more by abreaction than by an unfolding of the self. Again, this would undoubtedly go against the inclinations of the authors. But I do not see how it can be avoided unless we invoke a more active, desiring, and nontransparent subject. According to this latter conception, the therapist can place the initiative and responsibility for the therapeutic process with the patient. Indeed, therapy can be envisioned as a liberating dialogical encounter (needless to add, this doesn't necessarily happen in real practice). The model suggested here, by contrast, denies to the subject active, intentional strivings, and therefore places him or her in a position of inertia against a wholly active therapist. The therapist in this model—and the examples in the text suggest just such tendencies—brings enlightenment to the patient through educational means. This is fine in its place and is undoubtedly necessary to some degree for all therapies. But the measure of a therapy is the degree to which its theory of subjectivity allows the transcendence of didacticism, and it is precisely this that I find missing here. Indeed, by invoking the figure of Reich and his character analysis—as well as by somewhat carelessly calling for "body work"—the authors reveal just how difficult it can be to link the ontological approach with practice. For whatever Reich's genius, his failing was to desubjectify the person. Reich was nothing if not consistent, and his practice of character analysis consisted, on this basis, of active, aggressive, and frankly authoritarian measures taken to break down character resistances through confrontation rather than by allowing the spontaneous emergence of subjectivity.

This is all by way of saying that we should have a genuine integration between ontological and epistemological approaches rather than a haphazard eclecticism, and that the path to such an integration may be fundamentally more difficult than suggested in the essay. It is not meant to imply, I repeat, that there is no value to the ontological approach, particularly in the study of character. Indeed, I think we need exactly such an insight as is given by Dreyfus and Wakefield into how generalization can occur in order not to get sidetracked in irrelevant hunts for the singular mental "pathogen" responsible for the way in which people become what they are. In this respect, though, I think we should widen the scope yet further, even if it complicates our task all the more. After all, the study of character cannot be divorced from history. A person's "way of being" is a measure of his or her participation in the totality of his or her time. The anal character referred to in the text (Freud's elucidation of which remains as one of his most brilliant insights) was, we should recall, specifically a product of capitalist social relations. Just so, and even more acutely important for the matter at hand, the shift in therapeutic practice from a focus on symptoms to one on character has not been in any sense an autonomous scientific development within the psychoanalytic profession. Rather was it forced upon the therapeutic world by the changing nature of neurotic experience and the ever-changing social relations of therapy itself. Thus the increased emphasis on character that animates this essay coincides with, and is in some measure identical to, the emergence of the narcissistic character type as the specific creature of late, or monopoly capitalism. No discourse on therapeutics can, it seems to me, afford to ignore this fact. In any case the authors' salutory closing statement, that it is the "global structure of the patient's world, which is everywhere at once," that must be altered, now takes on a new and enhanced significance.

Rejoinder to Joel Kovel

HUBERT L. DREYFUS and
JEROME WAKEFIELD

We are grateful for Joel Kovel's careful commentary. His remarks give us a chance to fill out some aspects of our account of pathology that we left undeveloped, and to correct a mistake that misled him and might mislead others.

To begin with, we need to reiterate a point we made at the beginning. The epistemic view of the mind does not equal the Cartesian view. By an epistemological account of human being we mean a theory in which all human directedness toward things in the world is based on representations such as beliefs and desires. As we noted, for Brentano, Husserl, and any Cartesian all representations are accessible to consciousness, but one can be an epistemological theorist and hold that some representations are not accessible to consciousness. So desires based on "warded off" representations are still fully epistemic in our sense.

Since we are not denying unconscious representation, we do not have to deny conflict. In fact, we can and do accept Kovel's account of some pathology in terms of conflict and repression—what he calls the negative moment in subjectivity. But our point is that this dynamic-representational approach is not sufficient to account for all pathologies. Whereas Kovel, like Freud, would use variations of the dynamical account to explain everything—an approach that, if it worked, would no doubt be elegant and parsimonious—our view is that different types of pathology may well need different types of explanations. Far from being "haphazard eclecticism," this seems to be the only way to deal with a reality as rich as that which psychotherapy tries to encompass.

Kovel claims that because we reject the generalization of the dynamic-representational account of character pathology, we cannot account for the role of human agency, choice, motivation, and conflict in pathology, and that we cannot account for the patient's illusions and the active participation of the patient in his or her therapy. The appropriate replies are of three sorts: We can use the traditional epistemological account to explain some aspects even of character pathology; in others our account of pathology specifically denies the need for epistemological factors; and in the third, and most interesting case, the ontological view has its own account of the phenomenon without recourse to epistemology.

Kovel says, "Without a notion of desire, no account can be taken of human agency." First, on our account some neurotic pathologies can be explained in terms of desires. Second, on the ontological view, although conflicts and the frustration of desires may be involved in the genesis of character pathology, we deny that character pathologies consist of an ongoing conflict. On the ontological account, once the world is distorted for whatever reason, no continuing cause is needed to support the distortion. The distortion is self-confirming and self-perpetuating. In these situations, we claim, human agency is not involved in the pathology.

This is a good point to correct an error that misled Kovel. We were clear that affects such as anger or rage, if not allowed to subside, could contribute to the formation of character distortions. We were not clear, however, that since emotions were not needed to actively sustain the distortion, abreacting them could play at best an indirect role in cure by its effect on the background sense of reality.

Kovel claims that if there are no repressed beliefs and desires the therapist has no ground for challenging the patient's own account of his situation. Remember that on the ontological account, generalization takes the place of repression. In most cases the patient is not aware of the pervasive pattern of his life, so the therapist's interpretation may well go beyond, and even contradict, the patient's own account of his situation. Furthermore, even if the patient is aware of his overall interpretation of reality, he is not aware of it as an interpretation. The therapist has to get the patient to see that what he takes to be the reality of human existence is a questionable and dysfunctional interpretation. Since the patient's interpretation is not a belief, the therapy cannot be merely didactic, although some discussion of the implausibility of the patient's understanding of reality might help to undermine it.

Kovel is mistaken in thinking that ontological therapy treats the patient as "inert" and puts the therapist in the authoritarian position of substituting his world interpretation for the patient's. To begin with, the patient is in therapy because he has sensed that in some way his life is dysfunctional. According to Merleau-Ponty, the person has inherent tendencies to form an optimal functional relationship to the environment. Whatever the patient's world view, there can be a sense of restriction and thus an opening for the possible restructuring of his background. Also, as mentioned, there is a tension or instability in a person's world view due to anomalous tendencies and experiences that he or she has difficulty integrating into an overall sense of reality. These anomalies are not like specific desires and beliefs that are repressed, but are a troubling sense of incompleteness in his or her world. The therapist does not impose his interpretation on the patient but helps the patient restructure his or her interpretation into a Gestalt that is experienced as more stable, complete, and satisfying.

As we said, the world view the patient brings to therapy and its instability are the result of how the patient has taken up from his family and culture an interpretation of reality. Thus we agree with Kovel that therapy must always take account of history, although we may well disagree with him about what history is.

Chapter 10

The Moral Topography of the Self

CHARLES TAYLOR

One of the things I want to try to bring out in this chapter is how our notion of the self is inextricably connected with our understanding of our moral predicament and moral agency. Our description of ourselves as selves is inseparable from our existing in a space of moral aspiration and assessment. Being a self is not like having some biologically given organs, say eyes, or faculty, like vision, which are there as part of our equipment regardless of how we understand them or interpret them. Being a self is existing in a space of issues, to do with how one ought to be, or how one measures up against what is good, what is right, what is really worth doing. It is being able to find one's standpoint in this space, being able to occupy, to be a perspective in it. This is what Heidegger was getting at in his famous formulation about Dasein that its being is "in question."[1]

Or anyway, that is what it has come to mean to us, in this age. Because there is, of course, more than one sense of the term *self*, not only in this age, but even more strikingly over history. Or better put, not every age refers to the human agent as a "self." In every language (permitting myself a wild reach beyond the evidence at my command), there will be reflexive expressions that will allow us to talk of directing our thoughts and actions toward ourselves. But this is not at all the same as making *self* into a noun, preceded by a definite or indefinite article, speaking of "the" self, or "a" self. Thus the Greeks were notoriously capable of formulating the injunction *gnothi seauton*—know thyself—but they did not speak of the human agent as *ho autos* (the self), or use the term in a context that we would translate with an indefinite article.[2]

I believe that this, at first sight innocent, difference of usage corresponds to a very important shift in self-understanding that has helped to constitute modern Western civilization. It is this that has both created our peculiar modern understanding of the self and has helped to obscure its historical origins, its dependence on the particular moral self-interpretations of our civilization, thus accrediting the illusion that we have selves as we have eyes, hearts, or livers. I would dearly like to explain this central but puzzling feature of modern culture, that it both generates a characteristic configuration of the sense of self and obscures its nature and its roots. As a result the real, interpretation-dependent nature of the self has to be perpetually recovered, by an effort of philosophical insight, against the grain of our thinking. I know I will not be able to give an adequate account of this here, but I want to throw some feeble light in this general direction.

My account will therefore not only have to say something about the modern Western sense of self, but also situate it in relation to other comparable senses that belong to other times and cultures. And this distinction, of course, supposes as background another: that between what belongs to human agency as such, in all times and places, and what is shaped differently in different cultures. Naturally, it is at best centuries premature to proffer anything like a structured theory on this latter issue. But it is also undeniable that we inescapably make hazy, provisional assumptions about those timeless features of human agency that hold across cultures whenever we try to define the historically specific sense of self of a given age, like our own. Provisionally, and to come a bit cleaner about my own assumptions, I believe that what we are as human agents is profoundly interpretation-dependent, that human beings in different cultures can be radically diverse, in keeping with their fundamentally different self-understandings. But I think that a constant is to be found in the shape of the questions that all cultures must address. This is all I feel able to say about this issue now, but it is enough to show how doing justice to these different considerations, both the constants and the historically specific interpretations, puts a number of different, and sometimes conflicting, demands on the following discussion, which I hope I can meet without hopelessly confusing you and myself.

My main thesis is: that the self exists essentially in moral space by means of a master image, a spatial one. And that is what I invoke as well in speaking of a "moral topography" of the self. This manner of speaking might seem fanciful or arbitrary, but it is not. At least, the image is not mine, but is anchored in moral consciousness itself. I mean by this not just that spatial images frequently occur in moral language—think of Plato describing the eye of the soul looking toward the Ideas, or of salvation as in heaven, or of the truth as "within" us—but that our most basic and inescapable languages of the self incorporate spatial terms, most centrally within / without and above / below, not to speak of the topographical construal of the unconscious, our sense of inner depths, the devaluing of some feelings as superficial, and so on. My thesis is that this inherent spatiality of the self is essentially linked to a moral topography, a sense of where moral sources lie.

Let me say a bit more about this notion of moral sources. Here I have to lay out some of the hazy background assumptions I'm making about human agency across the ages. Coming at it from the negative side, we can say that human beings, in addition to their other pains and frustrations—hunger, sexual frustration, ill-health, death, loneliness—and often woven into these, experience themselves betimes as spiritually out of joint. This is conceptually expressed in a host of ways: as being lost, or condemned, or exiled, or unintegrated, or without meaning, or insubstantial, or empty, to name some common categories .

Corresponding to each of these descriptions of breakdown is some notion of what it would be to overcome it, to have integration, or full being, to be justified, or found, or whatever. But more, there is a notion of 'where' this integration, fulness, etc., might come from, what might bring it about. This might be: communion with the cosmic order, or identity with Brahman, or unity with God, or harmony with nature, or the attainment of rational insight, or finding the strength to say "yes" to everything one is, or hearing the voice of nature within, or coming to accept finitude, or ... , again the list stretches on indefinitely.

Now when we speak, across this whole range of examples, of where we might go to attain *integration* (let this term now stand for the whole indefinite disjunctive list), the spatial metaphor is very weak. In some of the cases, our help is to be found in something imaged as a "place," e.g., in the order of Ideas, but in others the spatial metaphor seems strained, e.g., where we come to accept our finitude, or say "yes" to what we are. But it is still natural to speak of "where" we can go, because the spatial imagery of the self is so deeply rooted in our language. Thus the Platonists, and in a quite different way the theists, (at any rate believers in the God of Abraham), will see their strength as coming from outside them, in the order of Ideas they love, or in the God who gives them strength. But the one who sees the task as coming to accept his finitude may (there are many variants of this, including Judaeo-Christian ones) understand that the crucial resources lie "within" him and nowhere else. And "within" here may have more than one sense. For certain romantics one accepts finitude when one recovers contact with the voice of nature within, so that the image is of the moral agent as hearing or failing to hear another; there is a certain alterity within. But an austere naturalist might see this acceptance as something the reflecting agent does on his own, without benefit of interlocutor, in face of a silent universe and meaningless drives. In this case the resources are within him in a different sense, within him as a lone reasoning agency, not as a being whose impulses and desires reflect or express a deeper current with which he may commune.

In other words these different, often indefinite and tentative senses of what integration consists of incorporate notions of where it might be found, in the sense of where the strength lies, where the sources or resources are situated, which could bring integration, or fulness about. The sources may be found "without," in a wide variety of different senses; or "within," in a number of different ways. They may be related to us as something that we "see" (like the Ideas), or as something we "hear" (the "voice of nature"), or as something that comes upon us (the Holy Ghost). But always a certain topography, related to that of the self, plays a crucial part.

I don't think that it is unfair to say that the apparent exceptions to this simply prove the rule. There are a number of views that aim deliberately to overcome our most cherished topographical distinctions. For instance, Hindu strains of advaitism tell us that the distinction between inside and outside, between the "I" and Brahman, must be overcome. And Buddhism points to Nirvana, a "nowhere," as its goal. But these doctrines essentially draw on our topographies in order to define their destinations by the *via negativa*. This negation of our ordinary way of placing ourselves is not an optional extra, it is their essential mode of expression. This is because, I would claim, topography is essential to our language of the self, so that transcendence of the self is most naturally described in a language that negates topography.

Now a doctrine that tells us where our strength lies is what I want to call a doctrine of moral sources, or a *moral topography*. Needless to say, moral topographies are not just doctrines handed down by canonical guardians of traditions. They can also be rooted in moral phenomenology, i.e., our experience of our moral predicament. Indeed, they must be so rooted somewhere if they are to have any credence. Even the most disjointed life has moments when one feels at least closer than usual to moral integration or strength. Our conceptions of integration and the corresponding doctrines of sources articulate this experience.

This brings us to a first connection between moral topography and one of our most common senses of self. An understanding of moral sources involves a corresponding conception of what in us, what faculties, or levels, or aspects of our being, connects us to these sources—as reason (understood substantively, i.e., as vision of rational order) does to the Ideas, or reasoning (understood formally, i.e., as thinking according to rational canons and procedures) does to the austere naturalist's acceptance of finitude, or our uncorrupted first impulses do to the voice of nature, or the will does in turning us to or away from God, and so on. Our notion of moral sources connects, in other words, with languages of discrimination marking distinctions within us—body/soul, reason/desire, will/knowledge, deep natural impulse/superficial imposed responses—and these discriminate what is closer or more essential to our real being as agents from what is more peripheral, perhaps even to be repudiated altogether (as when the body is stigmatized as a "tomb," or instrumental reason declared quite perverse). Moral topographies provide the context in relation to which we can distinguish what we essentially are. They provide a principle of ordering the self. And in one very important sense of the term, where we consider the self to be what we truly are, our essence, they furnish the indispensable context for our having such a thing as a self at all.

This is, at any rate, what I want to claim. In the light of the above discussion, my thesis could take this form: a sense of self that is thus linked to essence and defined in relation to some understanding of moral sources is indispensable to us. It is inescapably part of our language of self-understanding, if we have a notion of the self at all, and where this term doesn't figure, some other expression for our essence or true being does.

There are two claims here: something about the general nature of human agency across cultures (as stated in the last clause of the preceding paragraph), which I put forward with trepidation, and a claim about how we use "self" today, about which I feel dogmatic and militant (but that may just hide my even greater inner uncertainties). Let me now try to say something to back this second claim.

The "self" is something we talk about a lot in our civilization. But it wasn't always so, as I argue above. Why is this expression so important for us? I think this is of a piece with our use of the "I" and the "ego" (our latinate translation of what for Freud was simply "*das Ich*"). We use this reflexive expression, or the term for self-reference, because this brings out what for us are the essential powers of human agency. These in our conception are connected to reflexivity or the first-person stance.

It may seem obvious that a human agent is one who can take a reflexive stance, can say "I". Other ages were as aware of this as we are. But that is not to say that they saw this stance as the locus of the defining human capacities. What this latter view involves takes some explaining, not because it is unfamiliar to us, but rather because it is so fundamental to our way of thinking that it escapes our attention.

A person's perspective concerning himself is different from that of an observer. This banality is central to human life. Things look different from the first-person perspective, and not just in this or that case, but systematically. The issue I am pointing to between modern and, e.g., ancient civilization concerns what you make of this. We make a lot of it because we have come to believe that the important human capacities can only be realized by cultivating this perspective, by focusing on and developing features which become salient only in this perspective. And this in more than one way. I want to examine two that I think are important to my main theme: self-control and self-exploration.

Self-control is a basic theme of our whole moral tradition. Plato (*Republic*) speaks of the good man as being "master of himself." He remarks himself how paradoxical this can sound. Mastery is a two-place relation. So mastery of oneself must mean that something higher in one controls the lower, in fact, that reason controls the desire. From Plato through the Stoics, into the Renaissance, and right to the modern day, this mastery of reason remains a recognizable ideal—even though it is contested in modern civilization in a way it doesn't seem to have been among the ancients.

But something very important happens to this tradition during the

17th century that alters it quite fundamentally. The understanding of what it is for reason to be master shifts. For Plato, reason in us is the capacity which enables us to see the order of things, to grasp the Ideas and their ordering for the best, which latter insight he captures with the famous image of the Idea of the Good. For reason to rule in us is for us to be moved by this vision, to want to imitate and realize the good it reveals to us; something that Plato thinks we cannot help but want once we see it. In a sense we are always moved by the Good. But when desire is on top, we have only a dim and confused perception of the Good. To be ruled by reason, in contrast, is to have a clear vision; it is to be ruled by that vision. One might almost say, that on this view one's action is under the hegemony of the order of things itself.

Reason, considered as a property of human thoughts and desires, is understood substantively. That is, our being rational just is our having the substantively correct vision of things. The latter is a criterion of the former. From Plato's point of view, it makes no sense to imagine a perfectly rational person who would nevertheless have quite erroneous views about the order of things or the moral good, for instance, who might believe in a kind of Democritan universe of accidentally concatenating atoms or might believe that the purpose of life was accumulating power or wealth.

The Stoics challenged many aspects of the Platonic philosophy, notably the prime importance it gives to the theoretic vision of the truth and its soul/body dualism. But they retain the view that the mastery of reason involves the mastery of a certain vision. What we are essentially, by nature, is reason; and for the Stoics that means above all practical reason. We have the power to direct our lives by deliberate choice, *proairesis* (to use Chrysippus' expression). All that truly matters to us is the fulfilment of this capacity, and (following an axiom shared among all the descendants of Socrates) this fulfilment must be in our power, for the proper form of life is self-sufficient. It follows that we should not care for all the merely external consummations that most men put great store by: power, wealth, success, even health and long life. The truly wise man is only really concerned about the state of his own moral capacity, what Epictetus called his *hegemonikon*, or ruling part.

Just as with Plato, the mastery of reason is understood by the Stoics as the mastery of a certain vision. Here it is a vision of the order of goods we can seek; it is one that concerns purely practical reason. Which is not to say that the grasp of a cosmic order did not also play an important role for the Stoics. The wise man sees all things as disposed by the Providence of God, and for that reason is perfectly consenting to the order of events however they fall out. But in the end, the key practical insights concern what is worth desiring and what is not. And just as with Plato, for reason to rule desire is for desire to be reshaped by the vision of order. As Plato says in the *Symposium*, the love that impels us toward perfection ceases to focus on imperfect copies of its real goal and comes to center on the unchanging and true. In the Stoic version, our passions disappear altogether because at base they are nothing but false opinions couched in affect, as it were, to the effect that things are to be loved and feared which reason shows to be worthless.

Now to show the contrast with the modern age, we can look at what Descartes did with a doctrine and language that was drawn from the Stoics. Descartes' conception of the mastery of reason, as he develops it in his correspondence with Elisabeth and his *Traité des Passions* (1649), is radically altered. It is not the hegemony of a certain vision, but the direct domination of one faculty over another: reason instrumentalizes the passions.

Thus Descartes gives a quite novel theory of the passions in his famous treatise. They are not understood in the Stoic way as opinions, but are explained purely functionally in terms of their role in the maintenance of the substantial union of the soul and body that God has designed for us. Rational mastery consists simply in our being able to control them so that they serve only these proper functions, so that they function in other words as instruments of our purposes as soul/body unions and do not escape from our power and subvert these ends. Rational mastery is instrumental control.

So Descartes (1645), in contrast to the Stoics, does not call on us to get rid of our passions. On the contrary he admires "les grandes âmes" who "ont des raisonnements si forts et si puissants que, bien qu'elles aient aussi des passions et même souvent de plus violentes que celles du commun, leur raison demeure néanmoins la maîtresse. ..."[4] The idea that our passions might not only be strong but even violent is not only unthinkable from a Stoic perspective, but shocking even for those other strands of traditional ethical thought that did not accept the extreme Stoic goal of a complete liberation from passion. But it makes sense from the new Cartesian perspective, where what matters is instrumental control. If this is what mastery means, then the strength of the subordinate element is no problem; indeed, the stronger it is the better, as long as it is properly steered by reason.

This new idea of the mastery of reason went along with a changed conception of reason itself. Descartes no longer accepts the substantive notion of Plato. Reason is now defined procedurally. The goal of theoretical reason is science, and science is defined by Descartes in terms of certainty. "Toute science est une connaissance certaine et évidente" is the opening sentence of the *Rules for the Direction of the Mind*. But certainty is generated by a certain procedure. We must organize our thoughts so as to achieve clarity and distinctness in our ideas.

The Platonic notion of an order of Ideas in the cosmos is utterly abandoned. It could not survive the Galilean revolution that Descartes espoused. But Descartes puts in its place, as it were, the goal of an order of representations in the mind. On the order of deployment of our ideas hangs their certainty and thus science. This order, however, is constructed. One of the instructions in the *Discours* tells us to conduct our thoughts so as to build from the simpler to the more complex, "et supposant même de l'ordre entre ceux qui ne se précèdent pas les uns les autres."[5]

Rationality is here being defined by a certain manner of thinking, regardless of the substantive beliefs that emerge from it. Of course, Descartes holds that this procedure will result in substantively true beliefs about the world. But this is something that has to be established. Indeed, it is one of the most important goals of Descartes' philosophy to establish it. We make the link between procedure and truth with the proof that we are the creatures of a veracious God. The procedure is not *defined* as the one that leads to substantive truth. It could have been leading us entirely astray if we had been victims of a malicious demon. Rationality is now an internal property of subjective thinking rather than consisting in its vision of reality. In making this shift, of course, Descartes is articulating what has become the standard modern view. In spite of the wide disagreements over the nature of the procedure, and despite all the scorn that has been heaped on him from the dominant empiricist trend in modern scientific culture, the conception of reason remains procedural.

Now this shift, at once in the conception of mastery and in that of reason, bespeaks a quite different notion of the human agent. And once more, what is involved comes out very clearly in Descartes. Reason and human excellence requires a stance of disengagement.

Disengagement here is a term of art, meaning a stance toward something that might otherwise serve to define our identity or purposes, whereby we separate ourselves from it by defining it as at best of instrumental significance.

In this sense Descartes calls on the enquiring mind to disengage from the cosmos. This can no longer be considered a meaningful order, in relation to which our paradigm purposes are to be defined, as with Plato. It is a neutral domain of mechanical movement, whose laws have to be adequately represented in the mind. But we have to disengage also from our own bodily nature, not just because the body is another part of the external universe, but also because in order to achieve the proper rational mastery, the soul must instrumentalize the passions, as we have seen. The proper stance to self and nature is one of disengagement.

Here again there is a sharp contrast to Plato within what seems like a close analogy. Both philosophers are notoriously dualist, distinguishing soul from body and calling on us to recognize and live in function of this distinction. One of the themes that emerges from Plato into neo-Platonism is the notion of the body as a "tomb" of the soul. But the nature of this dualism is radically different. Plato, for all the longing to escape the bodily that emerges in a dialogue like the *Phaedo*, has a conception of the corporeal as in some sense an embodiment of the Idea. The body can be an expression of the soul, and it makes sense to think of our love for bodily things as a confused mode of our aspiration for the eternal, as the doctrine of the *Symposium* sees it. This possibility is radically undercut in Descartes, with his embracing of mechanism. In that sense his dualism is more radical.

But in another sense, the place of the body is more salient in Descartes' philosophy. In the Platonic tradition, the soul turns away from the body and comes to its perfection by concerning itself with what is, like itself, immaterial. But for Descartes, the soul comes to itself by objectifying the bodily. It paradoxically needs the body in order to realize its distinctness and superiority over it. It climbs to its high status on the back of the body, so to speak. This is why Descartes is not unjustified in refusing what he thinks of as the Platonic image of the soul situated in the body like a pilot in a ship. In truth, his conception of the union is more intimate than that.

Descartes' disengaged subject, like his procedural notion of rationality, is not just an idiosyncratic conception. For all the challenges and disagreements to his dualism in modern thought, with the central idea of disengagement he was articulating one of the most important developments of the modern era. Recent research has shown the tremendous importance of the mode of thinking roughly designated "neo-Stoic" in the late 16th and early 17th centuries, associated with Justus Lipsius, and in France with Guillaume duVair. As the name implies, these thinkers were inspired by classical Stoicism, but with a number of important differences. These included not only soul/body dualism, but also an increasing emphasis on a model of self-mastery that prepares the Cartesian transposition to the model of instrumental control.

More significantly, neo-Stoicism was bound up with a broad movement among political and military élites toward a wider and more rigorous application of new forms of discipline in a host of fields: in first place the military, of course, as one sees with the reforms of William of Orange that had world-historical consequences in the Netherlands' revolt against Spain; but also later in various dimensions of the civil administration, which grew with the new aspirations and capacities of the "absolutist" state, regulating labor, health conditions, mores.[6] The rise and spread of these new forms of discipline have been described in very evocative terms by Michel Foucault in his *Surveiller et Punir*.

What one finds in common with all the aspects of this constellation, the new philosophy, the methods of administration and military organization, the new spirit of government, and methods of discipline is the growing ideal of a human agent who is able to remake himself by methodical and disciplined action. This calls for the ability to take an instrumental stance to one's given properties, desires, inclinations, tendencies, habits of thought and feeling, so that they can be *worked on*, doing away with some and strengthening others, until the desired specifications are met. My suggestion is that Descartes' picture of the disengaged subject articulates the understanding of agency that is most congenial to this whole movement, and that is part of the grounds for its great impact in his century and beyond.

Where it was heading beyond can perhaps be seen if we consider Locke's views as representing the next stage. Locke develops a view of the subject and his formation in which in principle everything is, as it were, up for grabs, susceptible in principle of being shaped in the direction desired. The mind is a tabula rasa. There are no innate ideas, not even an innate reality sense or tendency to assent to reality as truth.[7] We have to be shaped by education, and this means that we can also become, at least to a certain degree, self-shapers. The ideal stance of the rational subject is thus not to identify with any of the tendencies he finds in himself, which can only be the deposits of tradition and authority, but to be ready to break and remake these habitual responses according to his own goals, as far as this is possible.

The Lockean subject is in this respect something quite new, and deeply unsettling from a traditional perspective. He is essentially none of his properties. What defines him is the abstract power to remake these properties. There are empirical limits, of course, to this remaking in any given case, but there are none set by his identity. What does essentially define him is self-consciousness, and that is why Locke can define the issue of identity in the peculiar (but immensely influential) way he does, in terms of a person's awareness of his or her continuity (Tully, 1986).

Once again, many people have taken issue with Locke's philosophy, but this picture of what we might call the punctual subject has been of immense importance beyond the ranks of those Enlightenment reformers and their spiritual heirs who believe in the total malleability of man. Its strength comes from the central place of the disengaged, disciplinary stance to the self in our culture, so that even those who reject many of Locke's doctrines feel the power of this model. We can see it in one way in some contemporary discussions of identity (c.f., e.g., Parfit, 1984), and it is the basis, I believe, of the mature Freudian conception of the ego, which belongs to the "structural" model. This ego is in essence a pure steering mechanism, devoid of instinctual force of its own (though it must draw power from the id to function). Its job is to maneuver through the all-but-unnavigable obstacle course set by id, superego, and external reality. Its powers are incomparably less than Locke's punctual self, but like its ancestor it is fundamentally a disengaged agent of instrumental reason.

Thus, if we follow the theme of self-control through the vicissitudes of our Western tradition, we find a very profound transmutation all the way from the hegemony of reason as a vision of cosmic order to the notion of a punctual disengaged subject exercising instrumental control. And this helps to explain why we think of ourselves as "selves" today.

The crucial capacity for the great ancient moralists was that of seeing the order—in the cosmos (for Plato), or in the priority of human goals (for the Stoics). Introspection had no significance for the first and was not thought to be crucial for the second. The Stoics give us an argument about reason, nature, self-sufficiency to convince us that we should not put any store by ordinary satisfactions; they do not ask us to examine ourselves.

By contrast, the modern ideal of disengagement requires a reflexive stance. We have to turn inward and become aware of our own activity and of the processes that form us. We have to take charge of constructing our own representation of the world, which otherwise goes on without order and consequently without science; we have to take charge of the processes by which associations form and shape our character and outlook. Disengagement demands that we stop simply living in the body or within our traditions or habits, and by making them objects for us, subject them to radical scrutiny and remaking.

Of course, the great classical moralists also call on us to stop living in unreflecting habit and usage. But their reflection turns us toward an objective order. Modern disengagement by contrast calls us to a separation from ourselves through self-objectification. This is an operation that can only be carried out in the first-person perspective. It doesn't tell us, the way Stoicism does, to be aware of what is worth while for humans as such, or, like Plato, to focus on the properties of reason and desire and their relation to what we know about the happy life. It calls on me to be aware of my activity of thinking or my processes of habituation so as to disengage from them and objectify them. Indeed, the whole (strange and ultimately questionable) picture of myself as objectified nature that this modern turn has made familiar to us only became available through that special kind of reflexive stance I am calling disengagement. We had to be trained (and bullied) into making it, not only through imbibing doctrines, but through all the disciplines that have been inseparable from our modern way of life, the disciplines of self-control in the economic, moral, and sexual fields. This vision is the child of a peculiar reflexive stance, and that is why we who have been formed to understand and judge ourselves in its terms naturally describe ourselves with the reflexive expressions that belong to this stance: the "self", the "I", the "ego."

That at least is part of the story. Another is that this self, which emerges from the objectification of and separation from our given nature cannot be identified with anything in this given. It cannot be easily conceived as just another piece of the natural world. It is hard for us simply to list souls or minds alongside whatever else there is.

This is the source of a continuing philosophical discomfort in modern times for which there is naturally no analogue among the ancients. Various solutions have been tried: reductionism, "transcendental" theories, returns to dualism, but the unsolved problem continues to nag at us. I don't want to try to tackle this problem here. My point is that this ungrounded extra-worldly status of the objectifying subject accentuates the existing motivation to describe it as a self. All other appelations seem to place it somewhere in the roster of things, as one among others. The punctual agent seems to be nothing else but a "self", an "I."

Here we see the origin of one of the great paradoxes of modern philosophy. The philosophy of disengagement and objectification has helped to create a picture of man, at its most extreme in certain forms of materialism, from which the last vestiges of subjectivity seem to have been expelled. It is a picture of man from a completely third-person perspective. The paradox is that this severe outlook is connected with, indeed, based on giving a central place to the first-person stance. Radical objectivity is only intelligible and accessible through radical subjectivity. This paradox has, of course, been much commented on by Heidegger, for instance, in his critique of subjectivism, and by Merleau-Ponty. Modern naturalism can never be the same once one sees this connection, as both these philosophers argue. But for those who have not seen it, the problem of the "I" returns, like a repressed thought, as a seemingly insoluble puzzle (e.g., Hofstadter & Dennett, 1981).

Thus for us the subject is a self in a way he could not be for the ancients. To see the difference, we have to distinguish between ordinary reflexivity and a more radical kind. Ancient moralists frequently formulated the injunction, "Take care of yourself," as Foucault has recently reminded us.[8] And Epictetus reminds us that all that really matters is the state of our own *hegemonikon*, or ruling part, sometimes translated "mind," or "will." And, of course, what underlies all these admonitions is the basic fact that only I can cure my own soul, or bring myself to virtue.

But this reflexivity of concern was not radical, in the sense I want to use that word here. What we are called upon to take heed of, and concern ourselves with, is not those features of ourselves that are available only in the first-person perspective. The ancient call to take care of oneself is analogous to an appeal someone might make today in the same terms to a busy executive, to ask him to stop killing himself with overwork. The factors the addressee would have to heed to obey this injunction are all within the scope of a discipline, viz., medicine, which does not give any special place to the first-person perspective. Similarly, the lore that an ancient would have to turn to, if he wanted to obey the injunction addressed to him, would be wisdom about the soul, available in Plato, Aristotle, Chrysippus, without any special reliance on the first-person standpoint.

This is what makes the striking difference with the followers of Descartes, Locke, Kant, or just about anyone in the modern world. The turn to oneself is now also and inescapably a turn to oneself in the first-person perspective—a turn to the self as a self. That is what I mean by *radical reflexivity*. Because we are so deeply embedded in it, we cannot but reach for reflexive language.[9]

This portrait of the growth of the modern self has been meant to increase the credibility of my main thesis: that the self is intrinsically linked with moral topography. As we have seen, the modern disengaged self has arisen from a certain moral vision. It has been linked with a definite moral topography, one that has eschewed all external sources and seen our moral resources as inner. And in its more austere variants, these are not seen as in the impulses of nature within us, but in the power of rational disengagement itself. This goes along with a certain conception of human dignity. It is thought to reside in the power of disengaged freedom, and humans achieve their full stature when they realize this power integrally.[10]

But at the same time, and very paradoxically, this same notion of the self has made it difficult to see the link I am arguing for here. The modern disengaged self aspires after a kind of neutrality. Disengagement entails a kind of neutrality in relation to what is disengaged from. With Descartes or Kant, the connection of this neutrality with a moral ideal is clear enough. But once the drive to objectification becomes all-encompassing, as with modern naturalism, and is meant to account for the totality of human life, this connection becomes lost to view. We might even say that naturalism makes a point of losing it from view, in order to be true to its explanatory principles.

Then the disengaged subject appears like a natural fact. It appears like another fact about us that we have selves, or that we are endowed with egos as steering mechanisms, in the same way that we are possessed of heads or torsos. As with heads or torsos, the ego can be the object of moral judgments, the point of application of standards, but these are not essential to understanding its very nature. Neutralizing disengagement ends up including itself in its scope, and thus losing from sight what it is really all about.

Now the above discussion was meant to add to the conviction that something is indeed lost from sight, that there is an inescapable connection with a moral background. But just because the disengaged self is so much part of our modern identity, and because pushed to the limit it covers its own tracks and denies its own nature, one always needs to say more to convince people of this connection. And to this end a brief look at contemporary psychoanalytic theory might be of help. But before I turn to this, there is another facet of the development of the modern self that I announced above and about which I have said nothing so far. To leave this out would make an already unbalanced picture very distorted. So I will discuss it here: the theme I described above as "self-exploration."

We can get to the heart of this theme if we look at another important difference between our language and that of the ancients. Inwardness plays a big role for us. We think of people as having inner resources, or inner depths. We think of them as turning inward when they turn to themselves. We think of our thoughts as within us. This becomes so natural to us that we barely notice that other cultures don't always do the same, as seems to have been the case with the ancients. True, Plato speaks of our capacities as being "in" us. And the obvious distinction between thoughts and feelings that I express and those I keep to myself was carried in ancient cultures, as in most others, by the contrast inner/outer. But the suggestion that in turning away from bodily things to those of the soul we are turning inward seems to be absent. Plato doesn't speak that way.

In part this idea connects with a point made in the previous section: the fact that the lore of the soul gave no special status to the first-person perspective and that the moral sources were external. The turning is captured in the powerful image that Plato uses in the *Republic*, where the soul swivels around to direct its gaze toward the illuminated reality, the Ideas. It is not self-focus, but attention to true reality that makes for wisdom and justice.

The turn to a language of inwardness comes with Augustine. Although he shared much of the same metaphysical beliefs as Plato, he did constantly speak of turning inward. "Noli foras ire; in interiore homine habitat veritas."[11] Why this shift of language occurs is a difficult and deep question, but I believe it has much to do with the fact that Augustine found a crucial use for the first-person perspective.

Augustine holds that we discover God within ourselves. God is the "light which lighteth every man that cometh into the world," as he quotes from John's gospel (1:9). But what he means by "within" is that one encounters God in one's own presence to self. That is because God is not only the maker of heaven and earth whose work can be seen in the cosmos; he is also the power that continually sustains me as a spiritual being. He is at the foundation of my power to think, know, and love. God vivifies the soul, as the soul does the body.[12] But just as to see the evidence of God's creative work in the universe we have to turn our thoughts to the frame of the world, so to become aware of God as the foundation of our own powers we have to focus reflexively on these powers. We do not discover God through this route by considering human powers as such impersonally. Rather each in the awareness of his own can come to realize that he draws on a higher power. Radical reflexivity is essential to this path toward God.

And that is the point of saying that God is found within. He is found in the intimacy of self-presence. He is "intimior intimo meo et superior summo meo" (Augustine, *Confessiorum*, III. 6.11). That is why Augustine begins so many of his arguments for the existence of God with the *cogito*, anticipating Descartes. The *cogito* is the argument that essentially has to be made in the first-person perspective. It is an argument which only goes through (if it does) because it is about myself.[13]

Augustine's inward turn was tremendously influential in the West; at first in inaugurating a family of forms of Christian spirituality, which continued throughout the Middle Ages and flourished again in the Renaissance, and later when it took on secularized forms. We go inward, but not necessarily to find God; we go to discover or impart some order, or some meaning or justification to our lives. In retrospect we can see Augustine's *Confessions* as the first great work in a genre that includes Rousseau's work of the same title, Goethe's *Dichtung und Wahrheit*, Wordsworth's *Prelude*—except that the Bishop of Hippo antedates his followers by more than a millennium.

To the extent that this form of self-exploration becomes central to our culture, another stance of radical reflexivity becomes of crucial importance to us alongside that of disengagement. It is different from and in some ways antithetical to disengagement. Rather than objectifying our own nature, and hence classing it as irrelevant to our identity, it consists of exploring what we are in order to establish this identity because the assumption behind modern self-exploration is that we do not already know who we are.

There is a turning point here whose representative figure is perhaps Montaigne. There is some evidence that when he embarked on his reflections, he shared the traditional view that these should serve to recover contact with the permanent, stable, unchanging core of being in each of us. This is the virtually unanimous direction of ancient thought: beneath the changing and shifting desires in the unwise soul and over against the fluctuating fortunes of the external world, our true nature, reason, provides a foundation, unwavering and constant.

For someone who believes this, the modern problem of identity remains unintelligible. Our only search can be to discover within us the one universal human nature. But things didn't work out this way for Montaigne. There is some evidence that when he sat down to write and turned to himself, he experienced a terrifying inner instability. "Mon esprit ... faisant le cheval eschappé ... m'enfante tant de chiméres et monstres fantasques les uns sur les autres, sans ordre et sans propos."[14] His response was to observe and catalogue his thoughts, feelings, responses ("j'ai commencę de les mettre en rolle").[15] And from this emerged a quite different stand toward the impermanence and uncertainty of human life, an acceptance of limits, which drew on both Epicurean and Christian sources.

It is not that the aspiration to stability is altogether abandoned. Rather, Montaigne comes to a certain equilibrium even within the ever-changing by identifying and coming to terms with the patterns that represented his own particular way of living in flux. So although "nous n'avons aucune communication à l estre," Montaigne sought, and found some inner peace in, his "forme maistresse."[16] Self-knowledge is the indispensable key to self-acceptance. Coming to be at home within the limits of our condition presupposes that we grasp these limits, that we learn to draw their contours from within, as it were.

But self-knowledge cannot mean here just impersonal lore about human nature, as it could for Plato. Each of us has to discover his own form. We are not looking for the universal nature, but each for his own being. "Il n'est personne, s'il s'escoute, qui ne descouvre en soy une forme sienne, une forme maistresse. ..."[17] So Montaigne's study has to be essentially reflexive in a strong sense. "Le monde regarde tousjours vis à vis; moy, je replie ma veue au dedans, je la plante, je l'amuse là. Chacun regarde devant soy; moy, je regarde dedans moy. ...."[18]

The search for the self in order to come to terms with oneself, which Montaigne inaugurates, has become one of the fundamental themes of our modern culture; or so I would claim. His goal still resonates with us: "C'est une absolue perfection, et comme divine, de scavoir jouyr loiallement de son estre."[19] And this gives us another reason to think of ourselves in reflexive terms. There is a question about ourselves—which we roughly gesture at with the term *identity* —that cannot be sufficiently answered with any general doctrine of human nature. The search for identity can be seen as the search for what I essentially am. But this can no longer be sufficiently defined in terms of some universal description of human agency as such, as soul, or reason, or will. There still remains a question about me, and that is why I think of myself as a self. This word now circumscribes an area of questioning. It designates the kind of being of which this question of identity can be asked.

But it is clear that this shift, whereby the question first arises in our culture, is one that involves moral topography. No one ever doubted that there were individual differences, that one person differed from another. What is new in the modern era is that these have a specific kind of moral relevance. Although differences of endowment and temperament were thought to define relevant conditions for moral action, and hence required a refined kind of moral reasoning (Aristotelian phronesis, which was sensitive to the particular), nowhere before the modern era was the notion entertained that what was essential to us might be found in our particular being. But this is the assumption underlying the identity question.

This aspect of our modern sense of being selves is therefore in tension with the one based on self-control. We saw above how the disengaged self tends to occlude its connection with moral topography. We easily come to see our egos as neutral steering mechanisms, part of our de facto endowment, like our eyes or arterial systems. But when we come to consider our identity, it is evident that the question could not be asked at all in abstraction from moral considerations. Our identity not only presupposes points of moral reference in relation to which we define ourselves, but also itself constitutes a central moral issue. Whether one is true to one's identity can never be a neutral issue. If it makes sense to be neutral towards it, then it is no longer this issue.

And this brings me to the point about contemporary psychoanalysis that I mentioned above. Although the classical theory of Freud, and even the developments in ego psychology of his daughter, Anna, and Heinz Hartmann, relied on a theory of the ego as a neutral steering mechanism, in recent decades the issue of identity has been taking on increasing importance. This has led to a theory of the self,[20] but it is clear that the development of the self cannot be understood in abstraction from issues of moral topography. Winnicott's (1965) distinction between the "true" and "false" self itself defines such an issue. And Kohut (1977, chap. 4) holds that the self develops in relation to two poles: ambitions and ideals. These theories, in short, all recognize that the self only exists in a space of moral questions, that moral topography is not an external addition, an optional extra, but that the question of being or failing to be a self could not arise outside of this space.

Within the confines of psychoanalytic theory, therefore, the issue between the thesis I have been defending and its naturalistic negation comes down perhaps to this: Can we understand ourselves adequately just as egos, or does a satisfactory explanation of ontogeny and adult life require that we add the perspective in which we are selves? Put this way, the answer to the question seems to me obvious. But I recognize that many theorists still want to cling to the old, austere, naturalist formulations of the founder. To argue further here would take me too long (and also out of my depth). But perhaps the further development of psychoanalytic theory and practice will make the thesis I have been defending here increasingly plausible.

NOTES

1. Dasein is an entity (ein Seiendes), says Heidegger, that is "dadurch ontisch ausgezeichnet, dass es diesem Seienden in seinem Sein um dieses Sein selbst geht" (1927, p. 12).

2. Aristotle speaks of a friend as "another self" in a famous passage of the *Ethics*, but this does not have the same force as our present description of human agents as 'selves'.

3. Paul Tillich in his *The Courage to Be* (1952) rather bravely proposed a historical typology of such senses of spiritual loss, suggesting that an early phase in which the basic fear was of loss of being was followed by an era in which the greatest danger was condemnation (culminating in the time of the Reformation), which in turn has given way to the present epoch in

which our greatest dread is of meaninglessness. I believe that this tremendously ambitious scheme contains insights that would greatly repay further
working out.

4. "... those great souls whose reasoning is so strong and powerful that,
although they also have passions, and often even more violent passions than
the common sort, their reason remains nevertheless master" (Letter to
Elisabeth, May 18, 1645).

5. See also Descartes, who enjoins us to "l'observation constante de
l'order qui existe dans la chose elle-même, ou de celui qu'on a
ingénieusement imagine" (Regulae).

6. This whole development is very well described in Oestreich (1983).

7. I am indebted to James Tully's work (1986) for much of my understanding not only of Locke but of the whole movement of modern politics
and thought that starts with the neo-Stoics and lays the groundwork for
Locke.

8. "Epimeleia heautou." See Foucault, Le Souci de Soi.

9. Of course, ours is not the only civilization that has found a use for
reflexive words. Hindu-Buddhist thought also is concerned with the self, at
least if the majority of translations from Sanscrit, Pali, and other relevant
languages are not wholly misleading. And in relation to the fundamental
ideas of these religious traditions, this is perhaps understandable. If the aim
is to go beyond self, to take us beyond where we usually understand ourselves
to be in virtue of our having a first-person perspective, either by showing the
self to be illusory (Buddhism) or by looking for an identification of the 'I'
with some greater reality (as we see in at least some versions of Hinduism),
then plainly reflexive language is going to be indispensable. It defines here
what we are negating, and in the nature of things there is no alternative way
to say what we aspire to. It goes without saying, of course, that these terms
will be used in very different ways from the modern West.

10. Already Descartes had some proto-notion of dignity in his conception
of 'générosité'. I have discussed this at greater length in my "Humanismus
und Moderne Identität" (Taylor, 1985). See also the interesting paper by
Peter Berger, "On the Obsolescence of the Concept of Honour" (1983).

11. "Do not go outwards; return within yourself. In the inward man
dwells truth" (Augustine, De Vera Religione).

12. "ut vita carnis anima est, ita beata vita hominis Deus est" (Augustine,
De Civitate Dei). See also the Confessionum, VII.1.2, where God is described
as "vita vitae mei" (Augustine).

13. For Augustine's frequent invocations of the cogito argument, see E.
Gilson (1960, pp. 41–43). I have discussed the inward turn in Augustine at
greater length in my "Humanismus und Moderne Identität" (Taylor, 1985).

14. "My spirit ... playing the skittish and loose-broken jade ... begets in
me so many extravagant Chimeraes, and fantasticall monsters, so orderlesse,
and without any reason, one hudling upon an other. ..." (Montaigne, Essays).
I have drawn on the interesting discussion in M. Screech (1984).

15. "I have begun to keepe a register of them" (Montaigne, *Essays*).

16. "we have no communication with being"; "my Mistris forme" (Montaigne, *Essays*).

17. "There is no man (if he listen to himself) that doth not discover in himselfe a peculiar forme, a sawying forme" (Montaigne, *Essays*).

18. "The world lookes ever for-right, I turne my sight inward, there I fix it, there I ammuse it. Every man lookes before himselfe, I looke within my selfe. ..." (Montaigne, *Essays*).

19. "It is an absolute perfection, and as it were divine for a man to know how to enjoy his being loyally" (Montaigne, Essays).

20. The pioneering work is naturally that of Erik Erikson, e.g., in his *Childhood and Society* (1963). Among theorists of the self, I am thinking, for instance of D. W. Winnicott and Heinz Kohut.

REFERENCES

Aristotle. *Ethics.*

Augustine. *Confessionum.*

Augustine. *De civitate Dei.*

Augustine. *De vera religione.*

Berger, P. On the obsolescence of the concept of honour. In A. MacIntyre & S. Hauerwas (Eds.), *Revisions.* Notre Dame, Indiana: Notre Dame University Press, 1983.

Descartes, R. *Lettres sure la morale; Correspondance avec la Princesse Elisabeth, Chanut et la Reine Christine* (letter of May 18, 1645).

Descartes, R. *Discours de la Méthode.*

Descartes, R. *Regulae ad Directionem Ingenii.*

Descartes, R. *Traité des Passions*

Erikson, E. *Childhood and society.* New York: Norton, 1963.

Foucault, M. *Surveiller et Punir: Naissance de la Prison.* Paris: Gallimard, 1975.

Foucault, M. *Le Souci de Soi.* Paris: Gallimard, 1984.

Gilson, E. *The christian philosophy of Saint Augustine.* New York: Random House, 1960.

Heidegger, M. *Sein und Zeit.* Tubingen: Neomarius Verlag, 1927.

Hofstadter, D., & Dennett, D. *The mind's eye.* New York: Basic Books, 1981.

Kohut, H. *The restoration of the self.* New York: International Universities Press, 1977.

Montaigne. *The essays of Montaigne.*

Oestreich, G. *Neo-Stoicism and the early modern state.* Cambridge: Cambridge University Press, 1983.

Parfit, D. *Reasons and persons.* Oxford: Clarendon Press, 1984.

Plato. *Republic.*

Screech, M. *Montaigne and melancholy.* Selinsgrove, Pa:, Susquehanna University Press, 1984.

Taylor, C. Humanismus und moderne Identität. In K. Michalski (Ed.), *Der Mensch in den Modernen Wissenschaften.* Stuttgart: Klett Cotta, 1985.

Tillich, P. *The courage to be.* New Haven: Yale University Press, 1952.

Tully, J. Governing conduct. In E. Leites (Ed.), *Conscience and casuistry in early modern europe.* Cambridge: Cambridge University Press, 1986.

Winnicott, D. W. Ego distortion in terms of the true and false self. In *The maturational process and the facilitating environment.* New York: International Universities Press, 1965.

The Self in Contemporary Psychoanalysis: Commentary on Charles Taylor

LOUIS A. SASS

Charles Taylor has presented a compelling analysis of the intellectual background to a central predicament of modern life and thought —that of a self which both creates and imprisons itself through its own processes of self-control and self-examination. Like all things reflexive, this predicament is fraught with paradox and far from easy to describe. Taylor has pointed out some lived consequences associated with this great modern transmutation: a certain reification of and alienation from the self, as well as a felt separation from external sources of value and morality. Finding myself in essential agreement with him, I want to extend his cogent argument through an examination of recent psychoanalytic thought, where the self and its vicissitudes seem to have replaced the instincts as the central theoretical and therapeutic preoccupation.

Two schools of thought seem to provide particularly clear examples of the trends and paradoxes Taylor has described—the "self psychology" of Heinz Kohut and the "action language" of Roy Schafer. These two examples of what might be called the contemporary psychoanalytic avant-garde have in common an opposition to classical psychoanalytic theory and to ego psychology (the latter being the psychoanalytic school that places primary emphasis on the ego functions of adaptation and defense, and which, in the eyes of many, has come to be the psychoanalytic orthodoxy of today). Since both Kohut and Schafer reject certain of the reifying, objectivist, and instrumentalist tendencies of these earlier schools, they may seem to offer alternatives to the widespread modern tendency toward detachment and objectification of the self. Both Kohut and Schafer do, in fact, make such claims for the superiority of their theories. However, I will argue that, far from being exceptions, their positions are best understood as but the most recent and extreme heirs to the modern transmutation—in Kohut's case, to the self-exploratory tradition of Augustine and Montaigne; in Schafer's case, to the self-controlling tradition of Descartes. Both theories also illustrate a disturbing point that is implicit throughout Professor Taylor's discussion: the fact that, in addition to illuminating or reflecting experience, our psychological and philosophical theories also play a role in determining its nature.

HEINZ KOHUT

At the end of his paper, Taylor suggested that a psychology that concerns itself with the self rather than the ego (understood as a neutral steering mechanism) is more likely to accept "that the self only exists in a space of moral questions" and thus, presumably, that issues of psychological health, integration, or happiness are inseparable from those of the moral life. If I understand him correctly, he takes Kohut's statement that the self develops in relation to the "poles" of ambitions and ideals as an indication that self psychology is more inclined than other schools to look outward rather than inward in its search for moral sources. I must, however, disagree with Taylor's treatment of this example.

It is true that self psychology moves away from efficient functioning as the criterion of health and goal of treatment. But it does not, it seems to me, replace this with any greater concern for moral sources, and certainly not moral sources lying outside the self. Self psychology is, in fact, about as perfect an example as one can imagine of what Taylor called *radical reflexivity*—that turning to oneself which stresses the essentiality of the first person perspective.

This radical reflexivity is easiest to see in the technique of Kohutian therapy, which involves a hovering over the patient's private stream of experience in a way that seems bound to emphasize its innerness and uniqueness. The rationale for this treatment is that the fundamental source of psychopathology is the failure in child-hood to receive appropriate empathy, which results in a continued, often unconscious yearning for fulfillment of this need. Kohut defines empathy as *vicarious introspection*, and he describes the therapist's goal as to enter into the private world of the patient.

One must ask, it seems to me, whether such a theory and therapy might ultimately contribute to rather than diminish the patient's sense of isolation and inwardness. Outrageous as it may sound at first, we ought to ask how many patients might not, in a sense, really have *had* an inner life before they learned of it from their Kohutian therapist—and, perhaps, produced it for the therapist. By "inner life," I mean, of course, a life that the patient experiences as being in some essential sense inner, unique, private. Our humanistic tradition inclines us to assume that the inner life is both innate and precious, and that helping someone to recognize this life must necessarily be a good thing. It may be, however, that Kohut's increasingly popular views might encourage rather than cure the sense of inwardness and isolation. In this sense self psychology—at least as it is sometimes practiced—might be less a cure than a symptom of the narcissism of our times.

Now, a Kohutian critic might object that this is unfair—that such a therapy is exceptionally well-suited to many patients, and not because it panders to the patient's narcissism but because it provides a crucial transitional stage designed to lift the patient out of his or her inwardness. I would find this argument more convincing if self psychology and its therapy were, in fact, being applied in quite specific ways and primarily to certain kinds of malaise for which the approach may indeed be especially well suited. Actually, however, self psychology has become something rather more like a world view.

In spite of Kohut's claims to be theoretically pluralistic, his writings make it obvious that he regards all aspects of life and all forms of psychopathology as best understood in self-psychological terms, i.e., as resulting from failures of empathy. Further, he recommends essentially the same treatment for all forms of psychopathology other than psychosis—i.e., the provision of vicarious introspection. Kohut even interprets the curative effect of other aspects of treatment—e.g., the explanations and interpretations offered by the analyst—as curative not in themselves but because they are felt by the patient to show an empathic understanding of his inner world.

As with Freud's use of the concept *sexuality*, the Kohutian notion of self has obviously been stretched far beyond its original meaning. Just as adopting the traditional Freudian point of view can give to all aspects of life a certain erotic tinge, so the Kohutian view seems to give all of existence a certain quality of inwardness. This is apparent in Kohut's notion of what he calls *selfobjects*—those modes of experience in which others are essentially reflections or extensions of oneself. Kohut encourages an attitude of indulgence toward the patient's experience of selfobjects, and he even suggests, at times, that this is the essential quality of all our object relations. The effect, it seems to me, is to subtly undermine the feeling, or the sense of importance, of encountering a world felt as external.

ROY SCHAFER

The psychoanalyst Roy Schafer, inventor of action language, criticizes traditional psychoanalysis for its tendency to reify psychological processes, thereby treating these processes as events that happen to the patient rather than as actions the patient performs. The primary rule of action language is that all experiences and behaviors —including even dreaming, desiring, unconscious thinking, and the experience of emotion and bodily sensation—are to be regarded as actions and designated by active verbs.

Schafer regards action language as intrinsically therapeutic since it has the potential not just of translating but of transforming experience by encouraging in the patient an awareness of his or her own agency and "an enhanced and more rational sense of personal responsibility." This, in Schafer's view, is the defining characteristic of psychological maturity and health. It is clear that Schafer also regards action language as a truer way of describing human life, for, he claims, action language is innocent of the myth-like anthropomorphisms and reifiications he so harshly criticizes in traditional psychoanalytic theory. Further, it refers always to a unitary, active, and fully responsible ego, which for Schafer seems to be the only kind of ego it makes sense to imagine.

At first glance Schafer's protest against psychoanalytic reification may seem to place him squarely in opposition to the self-objectifying trends Professor Taylor has described. After all, instead of allowing the patient to treat his own experiences as thing-like objects of contemplation that exist and operate independently of the observing self, Schafer reminds us of the process-like nature of psychological events and of their intrinsic oneness with the acting subject. If we look more closely, however, we will find something more reminiscent of the Cartesian tradition.

Schafer does not overtly argue for the domination of the passions by reason, nor for disengagement from the self or detachment from external moral sources—the elements of the Cartesian project. However, his insistence on active over passive modes of experience and on admitting one's nearly hegemonic agency amounts to much the same thing. What, after all, is the effect of this relentless claiming of responsibility, this denial of the automaticity, natural inertia, or objective grounding of action and experience? Is it not something very close to the Cartesian project of self-mastery—a project that, as Taylor says, "demands that we stop simply living in the body or within our traditions or habits," and "calls on me to be aware of my activity of thinking or my processes of habituation," thus making my experiences into objects of scrutiny subject to potential remaking?

Schafer's vision is of a self in ultimate control, relentlessly claiming responsibility even for its dreams, desires, and emotional responses, and becoming explicitly aware of its own role as interpreter in all that it experiences. It is not clear, however, that actual increase in self-mastery is likely to come about from this semantic shift. How, for example, could action language make one in fact any less the witness and more the author of one's dreams? It does, however, seem that external reality might be subjectivized when so much emphasis is put on realizing the extent to which we are, as Schafer says, "authors of our own existence." Thus although Schafer, like Kohut, may seem to be offering a reunification of the self with itself and with the ambient world, his theory may, like Kohut's, actually encourage a further isolation and self-alienation, and a sense of the weightlessness of the external world.

Foucault has taught us that many an apparent liberation may involve a hidden but more intense form of oppression. One must ask whether action language brings about a truer and more salutary mode of existence or whether this particular prescription for well-being is likely to turn into a sort of Foucaultian nightmare—imposing a sense of total responsibility, accountability, and isolation combined with no actual increase in one's degree of autonomous control.

HEINZ KOHUT AND ROY SCHAFER

Both Kohut and Schafer are critical of what they see as the reduction-istic and reifying tendencies of classical psychoanalysis and its immediate successor, ego psychology. Both are uncomfortable with the postulating of elaborate metapsychological schemes onto which the lived events of the clinical encounter ought to be mapped. Both reject or downplay the role of universal, instinctual forces, especially aggression. Finally, both deemphasize extensive exploration of the deep unconscious or the distant past in favor of experiences that are more present and more conscious, "experience-near," in Kohut's phrase.

It is easy to sympathize with these epistemological moves, which have a natural appeal both to believers in Occam's Razor and to the devotees of empathy over explanation. But Taylor's discussion of the reflexive turn alerts us to another aspect that should give us pause. Though all of psychoanalysis is implicated in the predicament Taylor has described, there is something especially ominous about these recent developments, and this has to do with their greater emphasis on what he calls *radical reflexivity*—that quasi-solipsistic stress on the first-person perspective, on the feeling that this experience is my experience.

For Kohut, heir to the self-exploratory tradition of Montaigne, emphasis on the first-person quality of experience shows up in the importance accorded to the uniqueness and the innerness of experi-ence. These characteristics make the provision of empathy seem a most problematic act—not the natural coinciding of creatures who share a form of life but an exquisitely difficult, yet absolutely necessary, meeting of almost solipsistic universes. For Schafer, heir to the self-controlling tradition of Descartes, the first person quality of experience involves not innerness or uniqueness but agency—a sense of doing or having done. The visions of self psychology and action language are congruent in their tendency to aggrandize the self. For both schools the correct attitude—and the one held out as the source of psychological health—does not direct attention to ideals or realities outside the self but, rather, recommends a certain coinciding of the self with the self, through recognizing and height-ening the sense of innerness or agency.

But if one dispenses with, or deemphasizes, the past, the instincts, the unconscious, and the metapsychological apparatus—as do both Kohut and Schafer—what is there to motivate a therapeutic journey?

If one no longer moves outward toward a metapsychological scheme felt as real, nor backward toward a past felt as solid, nor downward toward the unconscious and the instincts, what is left as the goal of one's exploration?

What one critic has written of Rilke, Stevens, and Valéry—three great poets of our age—could as well be said of these modernist psychologies, from which all external reference points seem to have fallen away: "The most immediate datum of experience to be explored appears as an intransitive consciousness, unconcerned with outer objects except as counters in the game of positing the self" (Crasnow, 1976). One might say that, in psychologies like those of Kohut and Schafer, the shadow of the self has fallen upon the world.

NOTES

1. For further elaboration of this analysis, with discussion of Jacques Lacan and James Hillman as well as Kohut and Schafer, see Sass, "The Self and its vicissitudes." (in press)

REFERENCES

Crasnow, E. Poems and fictions: Stevens, Rilke, Valéry. In M. Bradbury, and J. McFarlane (Eds.), *Modernism, 1890–1930*. Penguin Books, New York, 1976.

Sass, L. The self and its vicissitudes: An "archaeological" study of the psychoanalytic avant-garde. Social Research (in press).

Is the Move toward Modernity So Simple? Commentary on Charles Taylor

SALVATORE R. MADDI

I have no quarrel with Charles Taylor's abiding theme that considerations of self are by their nature moral considerations. In such considerations it is quite possible to discern ideas of the good and processes of struggle to reach this. Indeed, it seems to me that psychological formulations are moral considerations in this sense even if they do not emphasize the self. Even in Skinner's insistent efforting after a value-free, atheoretical psychology there is a discernable ethic. This becomes abundantly apparent when Skinner (1948) potentiates his stimulus and reinforcement view into a relevant utopia, *Walden Two*. Written on every page of this remarkable document is the value of efficiency, that peculiarly American ethic.

I am more in a quandary concerning other conclusions reached by Taylor in his historical analysis of self-conceptions. He argues that the Greek view of the absolute order of things gave way to the modern emphasis on self and that self-as-controller emerged before self-exploration. Further, he contends that in neither self view is there a natural, absolute order to be discerned and used as a guide. Instead, self-as-controller defines the self in detachment from external and internal environments and finds its ethic in instrumentality. Inevitably, this rational emphasis gives way to radical subjectivity because the self-as-controller becomes the object of its own scrutiny. Presumably, self-exploration emerges from, and is even more modern than, self-as-controller. In self-exploration one turns within, formulating an identity from what is found. Individual differences are thereby given a paramount importance they did not have for the ancients.

If Taylor's analysis is accurate and complete enough, it should help us in understanding the conceptual and moral thrust of contemporary positions on personality and psychotherapy that rely on self formulations. Indeed, Taylor applies his analysis to Freudian psychoanalysis, where it seems to fit rather well. Early views of the ego qualify as self-as-controller in that the ego is a detached mediator between id and superego, without even any energy of its own. Taylor could have predicted that Winnicott and Kohut would emerge in the psychoanalytic movement, because self-as-controller must give way to self-exploration.

Is Taylor's position as useful in understanding other relevant positions? Consider, for example, Jungian psychoanalysis. Selfhood in that theory involves a dynamic blend of ego and collective unconscious. The ego, according to Jung, is the conscious mind, and it conforms well to Taylor's analysis of self-as-controller. Becoming mature in Jung's view (1933) involves supplementing or balancing ego with the sensitivity, intuition, and surrender that comes with opening oneself to the collective unconscious. At first glance it seems as if Taylor's analysis works here. But closer scrutiny reveals that the collective unconscious is no more within each of us than it is in the external environment. The collective unconscious is a universalistic order of things, and the archetypes are suspiciously like Platonic essences. In insisting that maturity lies in appreciating the wisdom inherent in the collective unconscious, Jung has provided us with a psychoanalytic view that does not seem very well illuminated by Taylor's analysis of modernity and the self. Appreciating the collective unconscious is not self-exploration as Taylor delineated it.

Even more problems emerge when one turns to the major contemporary self-theories of Carl R. Rogers, Abraham Maslow, and existential psychology. For Rogers, what is therapeutic is to turn inward in hopes of overcoming thereby the disengagment process he calls socialization. In turning inward one finds individuality, and this certainly underscores the importance of individual differences for Rogers. All this sounds like self-exploration, but there are aspects of it not covered by Taylor's definition. For Rogers, when one turns inward one finds the inherent potentialities. These are aspects of our nature that are not formulated so much as discovered. Further, beyond the individual differences involved lies universality at a higher level of abstraction. After all, Rogers (1961) details the aspects of the fully-functioning (or mature) self as openness to experience rather than defensiveness, spontaneity rather than planfulness, organismic trusting rather than social conditions of worth, and so forth. These aspects of functioning are present in all mature persons and absent in the immature. Maslow even adds to the list of criteria of the mature self democratic rather than authoritarian values, thereby clearly implying a social order to be consistent with the individual order. Indeed, Rogers has detailed the characteristics of interpersonal, familial, social, and international relations that well express the fully-functioning selves.

How far is all this from a universalistic view of the good? True, Rogers and Maslow advocate turning inward, but what is found there is not merely individuality but also that which is common to all persons and applies to all human contexts. Rogers is even against excessive self-absorption. The fully-functioning person is what he or she does, without the intervention of a brittle, evaluative self-consciousness. All in all, how different is this position from the Greek view regarded as ancient by Taylor?

Turning to existential psychology, we find the emphasis on being-in-the-world (e.g., Binswanger, 1963), or the relationship the self establishes with others, society, physical nature, and its own biology (Maddi, 1985). This involves neither turning inward nor outward, but both. Certainly there is no objective order, but does the subjective process lead only to radical subjectivity? Yes and no. There are, after all, some universals in the position. Given a person's past experience and current circumstances, there will always be facticity (e.g., Sartre, 1956) and possibility, and a value on optimizing the latter. Does the subjectivity of the process of making decisions lead to chaotic confrontations, a la Montaigne? Yes and no. Certainly there is no easy way, and there will be conflict and suffering. But there is an order imposed through the temporal accumulation of decisions. Witness Sartre's (1956) concept of the fundamental project that is there even though most of us are unable to apprehend it. One misses too much of the existential formulation of self by trying to typify it as the turning inward of self-exploration, or the detachment of self-as-controller.

So what are we to conclude regarding Charles Taylor's analysis of modernity and the emergence of self? Are the formulators of major contemporary positions on personality and psychotherapy too naive and confused to discern the inexorable march of modernity in views of the self? Or is Taylor's analysis too simplified and incomplete to help much in understanding what these practitioners are trying to accomplish? And if the rejoinder be that there have been many other influences upon such theoreticians as Rogers and the existential psychologists, then are we to understand that there are other themes of relevance to the self not explicated here by Professor Taylor? If so, we should attend more to the limits of applicability of his paper than he has.

REFERENCES

Binswanger, L. *Being-in-the-World: Selected papers of Ludwig Binswanger*, trans. J. Needleman. New York: Basic Books, 1963.

Jung, C. G. *Modern man in search of a soul*, trans. R. F. C. Hull. New York: Harcourt, Brace & World, 1933.

Maddi, S. R. Existential psychotherapy. In J. Garske & S. Lynn (Eds.), *Contemporary psychotherapy*. Englewood Cliffs, N. J.: Prentice-Hall, 1985.

Rogers, C. R. *On becoming a person*. Boston: Houghton Mifflin, 1961.

Sartre, J. P. *Being and nothingness*, trans. H. Barnes. New York: Philosophical Library, 1956.

Skinner, B. F. *Walden two*. New York: Macmillan, 1948.

CRITIQUE OF IDEOLOGY

Chapter 11

Missing Relations in Psychoanalysis: A Feminist Critique of Traditional and Contemporary Accounts of Analytic Theory and Practice

EVELYN FOX KELLER and
JANE FLAX

A principle goal set by feminist theory has been to explore the implications of the historical absence of women from our intellectual discourse. Out of that effort has come a broad-ranging critique of the role that socially constructed and culturally transmitted notions of gender have played in the organization of our inner and outer worlds. This analysis has led to the questioning of some of the deepest assumptions that have guided our thinking in virtually every intellectual endeavor of Western tradition; implicitly, if not explicitly, it has led to the demand that we rethink these basic assumptions. In our own work, on the relations between gender, science, and psychoanalysis, it has led to a number of questions that seem particularly pertinent to a volume on hermeneutics, psychological theory, and psychoanalysis. Like hermeneutics in general, feminist criticism requires attention to interpretation, to context; it demands an exploration of the relation between cultural practices and intellectual norms. Brought to bear on psychoanalysis in particular, it requires attention to the cultural context of the intellectual norms that cast psychoanalysis first as a science and, more recently, as a text. The issues we focus on here derive from some of the problems that inhere in either casting.

SCIENCE AND GENDER

Perhaps especially pertinent to the subject of hermeneutics and psychoanalysis is the observation of a set of parallel conflicts and confusions about both gender and science (and accordingly about psychoanalysis) that inhabit our collective consciousness. These conflicts are manifested in a number of ways—all variants of what we might call the one-two step.

The simplest case to be seen is in our thinking about gender—in particular, in our proclivity toward seeing gender as a product of either nature or culture, and in the facility with which we shift from one view to the other. In the first the human (and frequently nonhuman) world is seen as irrevocably divided in two; in the second it is seen as artifactually constructed out of an aboriginal unity. The ease and rapidity with which we move back and forth between the assumption of ontological duality on the one hand, and universality on the other, is perhaps most reminiscent of the perceptual puzzle of the invertible figure-ground diagram—suggesting, finally, that universality and duality are in some basic sense two sides of the same coin.

A similar facility in transition from conceptual unity to duality and back again is also indicated in a general problem, or paradox, that is latent in much of contemporary perceptions about science. Many people, including scientists themselves, seem to believe, at one and the same time, that "of course" the practice of science is not objective, and "of course" what distinguishes science, and accounts for its triumphs, is precisely its objectivity. The first of these beliefs owes a large debt to a pair of ideas emerging from the philosophy of science in the early sixties, and then rapidly rising to favor: One is that observation is theory laden, and the other, that theories are value laden. Half assimilated, these ideas coexist, more or less uncomfortably, with the continuing claim that the practice of science justifies itself by "progressive" discovery and successful prediction.

In other words the same kind of instability plagues our thinking about science that plagues our thinking about gender—both fixed, natural categories in one moment, and constructed, perhaps even indefinitely plastic, categories in another. Having no good way of mediating between these two sets of insights, we manage to slip readily from one to the other—back and forth between objective realism and relativism on the one hand, and between universality and duality on the other. An important question for us to ask, therefore, is how might we get past this impasse?

Keller (1985) has argued that a better understanding of the insights from both feminist theory and the social studies of science, and even more, an integration of these insights, points us in the direction of resolving these paradoxes—toward learning to count past two, and in the process toward a radically expanded meaning of what an examination of the interactions between gender and science might show. Such an endeavor should also prove useful in our thinking about psychoanalysis—particularly for the split between objectivism and relativism that continues to plague our discussions about the status of psychoanalysis. Feminist theory has brought home to us that gender is neither simply the manifestation of sex, nor simply an easily dispensible artifact of culture. It is, instead, what a culture makes of sex—it is the cultural transformation of male and female infants into adult men and women. All cultures do this, but they all do it somewhat differently. Invariably, how they do it—how they organize the spectrum of human attributes around sex—has a significant impact on their structuring of the world beyond sex as well; indeed, it permeates all aspects of their existence.

Similarly, science is neither a mirror of nature nor simply a reflection of culture. It is the name we give to a set of practices and a body of knowledge delineated by a community—constrained although certainly not contained by the exigencies of logical proof and experimental verification.

The relationship between gender and science is a pressing issue not simply because women have been historically excluded from science, but because of the deep interpenetration between our cultural construction of gender and our naming of science. The same cultural tradition that names rational, objective, and transcendent as male, and irrational, subjective, and immanent as female, also, and simultaneously, names the scientific mind as male, and maternal nature as female. Beginning with Francis Bacon and continuing into our own times, the same sexual division of emotional and intellectual labor that frames the maturation of male and female infants into adult men and women also, and simultaneously, divides the epistemological practices and bodies of knowledge we call science from those we call not-science. Modern science is constituted around a set of exclusionary oppositions in which that which is named feminine is excluded and that which is excluded—be it feeling, subjectivity, or nature—is named female. Actual human beings are of course never fully bound by stereotypes, and some men and some women—and some scientists—will always go beyond them. But at the same time, stereotypes are never idle. To a remarkable degree, to learn to be a scientist is to learn the attributes of what our culture calls masculinity. It is to learn how to perform in (or on) a (conceptual) world definitively cleft in two. Inevitably, psychoanalysis is caught on the same cleft stick by its own scientific aspirations.

Erikson, for example, notes that for Freud, "the dream itself may be a mother image," and that "the particular mode of [Freud's] approach impresses one as being intrusive, and thus somehow related to the phallic." Erikson goes on to suggest that this, in view of the strong maleness of the scientific approach cultivated by the bearded savants of his day and age, constituted an unfathomable division within the observer's self, a division of vague "feminine yielding" and persistent masculine precision (1954, p. 30).

This core observation—of the historic naming of science as male and nature as female, and of scientific as masculine, and unscientific as feminine—causes an immediate expansion of the subject of gender and science. It grows from the comparatively simple questions about women in science with which such analyses began, or even about the biology of women, into a much larger set of questions about how our ideas of gender have helped shape our construction of science, and how our ideas about science have influenced our construction of gender. In short, it becomes a study of the simultaneous making of men, women, and science. And it is to this study that much of Keller's own work—as well as that of a growing number of other feminist scholars—has been devoted.

By now, we have a considerable literature that has documented an extensive interpenetration between scientific, philosophical, and gender discourse. This literature has emerged in a critique of traditional notions of objectivity as deeply intertwined with traditional notions of masculinity. In that effort important aspects of the social, historical, and psychological dynamics of this intertwining have been illuminated. But in many ways, the question that must inevitably be of greatest interest to scientists—what difference does such a gendered discourse make to science (or to psychoanalysis)—has only begun to be addressed. It is easy enough to say, and to show, that the language of science is riddled with patriarchal imagery, but it is far more difficult to show—or even to think about—what effect a nonpatriarchal discourse would have had—or would now have (supposing, that is, that we could learn to ungender our discourse). This is, of course, part of the much larger question, namely, how does language mediate that representation of reality we call scientific? It is this question that defines the real task facing not only feminist critiques of science, but all of the history, philosophy, and sociology of science. Such a task derives much of its meaning from recent (and growing) recognition of the complex social, political, and psychological factors contributing to the actual processes by which first, science, and second, scientific objects, get named. Necessarily, it would seem, such an inquiry would have to begin with an examination of the process by which objectivity itself acquires definition, and it is this issue that has especially attracted the recent attention of feminist scholars. Our inquiry has particularly called into question two aspects of traditional meanings of objectivity: first, the dependence of that meaning on a radical division between subject and object, self and other; second, the casting of objectivity in opposition to subjectivity and the proclivity such a casting gives rise to of seeing fusion as the only alternative to division. Even Freud, who added so much modern credibility to the number three in his thinking about man, seemed himself only able to count to two in his thinking about relations between subject and object; Freud too seemed only able to think in terms either of objectivity or of what he called *oceanic oneness*.

In an effort to obtain some understanding of alternative possibilities in our conception (and construction) of science, it has proven useful to look to examples far from the ideological norm that have been provided to us by our own scientific history. In particular, Keller (1983) has found in Barbara McClintock, 1983 Nobel Laureate in physiology and medicine, an especially instructive guide.

What McClintock offers us in her vision and practice of science is in effect a philosophy of science in which difference rather than either division or unitarity constitutes the fundamental principle for ordering the world. Instead of aiming toward a cosmic unity of paired opposites—a unity typically excluding or subsuming one of the pair—she aims for an understanding in which respect for difference remains content with multiplicity as an end in itself.

Of particular interest in this world view is the fact that division between subject and object is not posited as a prerequisite for knowledge. For McClintock, the *sine qua non* of good research is "a feeling for the organism"—hence the title of the book (Keller, 1983). Respect for individual difference here invites a form of engagement and understanding not representable in conventional scientific discourse. What might look like privileged insight, and is readily misdescribed as a kind of mystical experience, is in fact a result of close, intimate attention and patient observation maintained over days, weeks, and even years.

McClintock's practice of science offers us a lesson in counting past two—it teaches us about a world in which self and other, mind and nature, survive neither in mutual alienation nor in symbiotic fusion, but in structural integrity. Here, objects can become subjects without a loss of self. McClintock's feeling for the organism need not be read either as sentimentalism or as mysticism: it is a mode of access— honored by time and human experience if not by prevailing conceptions of science—to the reliable knowledge of the world around us that all scientists seek. As such, it provides us with a lesson from which Freud himself might have profited.

But Freud did provide us with at least the rudiments of a framework for the more complex analysis that is needed. Object-relations theory offers an obvious framework for thinking about the interactions between the construction of objectivity and the construction of masculinity. More specifically, invoking psychoanalytic theory to analyze the scientific project allows us to see the historic labeling of nature as female and the scientific mind as male as constituting an invitation for (especially male) scientists to project onto nature unresolved conflicts about their own autonomy, particularly in relation to the first and primary others in their lives, namely their mothers. The argument goes on to suggest that the twofold disidentification required (or thought to be required) for the formation of a masculine identity provides critical support for an ongoing subjective association between masculinity and the aspiration of divorcing subject from object (see, e.g., Chodorow, 1978; Dinnerstein, 1976; and Keller 1978, 1985). The more serious problem that feminists have come to worry about, however, is the relation between objectivity and domination—a relation that object-relations theory also offers us at least a preliminary way of understanding. In particular, Keller has argued that the specific kinds of aggression expressed in scientific discourse reflect not simply the absence of a felt connection to the objects one studies but also the subjective feelings many children (and some adults) experience in attempting to secure a sense of self as separate from the more immediate "objects" of their emotional world (1985, pp. 124–125). The contest many scientists feel themselves engaged in, either with nature as a whole or with the particular objects they study, reflects the contest they feel themselves engaged in with human others. Similarly, the need to dominate nature is, in this view, a projection of the need to dominate other human beings; it arises not so much out of empowerment as out of anxiety about impotence. The feelings such domination causes are the same feelings that can be derived from subjecting others to one's will. In this sense, then, the dream of dominion over nature, shared by so many scientists, echoes the dream that the stereotypic son hopes to realize by identifying with the authority of his father. But such dreams are by their very nature self-limiting. They prevent the son from ever getting to know the real mother. And so, it could be argued, they similarly obstruct the scientist's efforts to know the "real" nature.

In all these efforts, however, it soon became evident that psychoanalytic theory—a theory hardly known for its gender neutrality—itself needed to be revised. In particular, if our concern was with an inability to perceive objects as subjects in nature, and if we linked this to our inability to see mothers as subjects, surely we could not help but notice the fact that mothers in particular, and others more generally, are in fact *called* objects (hence the name *object relations theory*). Furthermore, it soon became clear that not only are mothers "objects" in what is probably the best theory of subjectivity we have, but they are objects overwhelmingly perceived from the child's (especially the male child's) point of view—namely as never quite "good enough," frequently dangerous, with an apparently unlimited capacity to do damage. If scientists are bent on taming nature, in the implicit fear that, untamed, "she" would be overwhelming, so too, it seems, psychoanalysis is bent on taming mothers. Indeed, traditional psychoanalytic theory appears to have been caught in the very same antinomies as modern science: male vs. female, autonomy vs. intimacy, separation vs. connection, power vs. love. And object relations theory—even in its feminist revisions—remains itself at least partially plagued by this very same heritage.

For example, feminist revisionists of psychoanalytic theory (including ourselves) have invoked object relations theory to explain why we might expect women to privilege identification, relatedness, and caring in their relations with others—to be good at counting, if not *past* two, at least between one and two. Accordingly, many people have read the McClintock story as a story about a feminist science—by which they usually mean a feminine science. And, indeed, it is easy enough to see why. Virtually all of the aspects of McClintock's science that seem to be so distinctive—the value she places on feeling, intimacy, connection, and relatedness—all seem to confirm our most familiar stereotypes of women. And indeed, the antinomies between separation and connection, opposition and fusion, power and love, are hardly gender neutral. If men are prone to bring to science one set of commitments, then would not women be expected to bring the other? Without doubt, McClintock does bring to science precisely those attributes that have been traditionally devalued as feminine.

But there are many reasons why this simple schema will not work, neither for science in general nor for McClintock in particular. Put simply, the specifics of the McClintock story do not permit a reading that locates her distinctiveness in her femininity; instead, it forces a shift in our focus from the question of why McClintock was able to sustain and employ a feeling for the organism in her scientific work to the somewhat different question of why that capacity is so rare among most (male) scientists. It is to point away from the (perhaps necessarily) anomalous socialization of McClintock to the conventions of male socialization.

Looking, or relooking, at male socialization from a feminist perspective in turn, of course, requires a relooking at the conventions of female socialization. More importantly, perhaps it requires a re-visioning of theories of male and female socialization. In particular, it leads us to see that if the psychosocial development of men has been handicapped by an unhealthy set of gender prescriptions, so has that of women. As Keller has previously written,

> Just as the (stereotypic) son learns from his father a particular meaning of masculinity, so the (equally stereotypic) daughter learns submission as the flip side of domination—as a technique of female seduction. She seeks in love the means of vicariously sharing in her father's authority and simultaneously usurping and extending her mother's subterranean power. In short, she comes to internalize the spectre of the mother while at the same time retaining all its ambiguities. Domination and submission are thus twin ploys—both substitutes for real differentiation and for dynamic autonomy. In both, the net result is curiously the same. For children of both sexes, and for most of us as adults as well, the mythical power of the mother endures. (1985, p. 111)

Accordingly, neither daughters nor sons are well situated to ever know the mother in her own right.

In this entire process, psychoanalysis, both in theory and practice, has played a powerful, normative role that prescribes as it describes. It implies a model of parenting that has had far-reaching consequences for the ways in which mothers and fathers actually behave. In this, psychoanalysis itself is a player in the psychosocial dynamics that lend such force to the associations of love with female "impotence," and autonomy with male power. Freud's own deeply pessimistic view of human nature, his radical distrust of maternal influence, and his consequent idealization of "oedipal socialization" have effectively served to naturalize the psychology of his age. A feminist critique of the limitations of Freud's theories thus becomes imperative.

Briefly, this means bringing our attention to focus on the continuing absence of the mother as subject in psychoanalytic theory, on the use of psychoanalysis in the social construction of mothers and fathers, and on the tendency to characterize the psychoanalytic process in instrumentalist terms. At the same time, however, it is also important to note that, whatever the limitations of his age and his perspective, and whatever the limitations incurred by his attempts to cast psychoanalysis as a science, Freud was able to sustain a degree of recognition of others that is often lost in post-Freudian efforts at reading psychoanalysis solely as interpretation. If Freud's ability to see his patients as subjects was inadequate, at least he remained mindful of their presence. The risks of instrumentalism incurred by reading psychoanalysis as a science are thus countered by another kind of risk incurred in the hermeneutic reading. That is, in viewing the subject as a text reflecting the reader back onto himself or herself, the patient herself may get lost entirely. The reader becomes effectively more insulated and isolated, and other minds lose their reality altogether.

PSYCHOANALYSIS AND GENDER

Although we recognize the many contributions Freud has made to our understanding of gendered subjects, his treatment of gender remains extraordinarily complex and problematic. From a feminist perspective, one of the most paradoxical aspects of Freud's theories (as well as subsequent psychoanalytic work) is that it reveals the centrality of gender relations within individual and collective social life while at the same time exhibiting an extraordinary lack of consciousness of the role of gender and gender anxiety within the theories themselves. Contrary to the claims of Juliet Mitchell (1974, 1984), Freud's work cannot be neatly divided into those parts affected by his anxieties and biases about women, e.g., the essays on femininity (Freud, 1925, 1931, 1933), and those that are not. Rather, unexamined anxiety about gender and gender relations pervades and helps to structure the entire body of his work. The limitations of Freud's own self-consciousness are in turn echoed by a continuing lack of self-consciousness, indeed of repression, in the work of much psychoanalytic work that has followed.

The principal legacy of Freud's own "unhappy consciousness" (or perhaps, "happy unconsciousness") can be found in an enduring set of interlocking and gendered antinomies pervading virtually all psychoanalytic discourse. Among the most important and frequently recurrent of these are

nature vs. culture;

self vs. other, or, oedipal vs. preoedipal;

libido economics vs. object relations theory;

mind vs. body; and

analyst vs. patient.

In the remainder of this chapter, the gender structure of each of these antinomies will be examined in turn, showing how they function in Freud's writing. Developments since Freud's time have done little to soften these oppositions; if anything, they have become hardened in much of post-Freudian psychoanalytic writing—including even object relations and Lacanian theory. Indeed, at his best Freud struggled valiantly to do justice to the tensions he himself felt, and even though his theories remained plagued by all of the antinomies above, he also provided us with some of the tools necessary to recover the missing terrain between one and two. Through the following discussion, it will become clear that a crucial part of what is missing in psychoanalysis is a feminist consciousness of the power of gender in our social and intrapsychic lives as well as in our theories about them. Such a consciousness provides us with the means for bringing the psychoanalytic project to a kind of fruition, namely, its own self-analysis.

Nature/Culture, Female/Male

Freud believed that the process of acculturation is simultaneously and necessarily a process in which people are gendered. The polymorphous, perverse infant becomes (or at any rate is supposed to become) the heterosexual, genitally-oriented male or female adult. In this process part of one's "natural" sexuality is sacrificed. Similarly on the social level, as societies develop they require renunciation of instinct and the subordination of family ties to the demands of the larger group. The incest taboo is both the culmination of this process and its symbol.

The demands of women who represent the family and these natural ties come into opposition with the demands of culture, just as the natural desire of the son for the mother comes into conflict with the demands of the father and the culture.

In *Civilization and Its Discontents*, Freud says: "Women soon come into opposition to civilization and display their retarding and restraining influence—those very women who, in the beginning laid the foundations of civilization by the claims of their love. Women represent the interests of the family and of sexual life. The work of civilization has become increasingly the business of men, it confronts them with ever more difficult tasks and compels them to carry out instinctual sublimations of which women are little capable. Since a man does not have unlimited quantities of psychical energy at his disposal, he has to accomplish his tasks by making an expedient distribution of his libido. What he employs for cultural aims he to a great extent withdraws from women and sexual life. His constant association with men, and his dependence on his relations with them, even estrange him from his duties as a husband and father" (1930, pp. 103–4).

In this passage and others, Freud unconsciously replicated and accepted the gender-based division of labor that is pervasive in our society. This division of labor is organized in such a way that women have the primary responsibility of caring for young children. The organization of society is also predicated on a split between the realm of production in which instrumental relations are the norm and the realm of the family in which affective relations are to prevail. The affective realm is associated with the natural relations between parent and child, husband and wife, with sexuality and the satisfaction of bodily needs. In order to enter the instrumental realm, one must leave these affective ties behind. Furthermore, to succeed in this world, one must also learn to behave in nonfamilial ways—to treat others as objects, as means to an end, as competitors for scarce resources and rewards. What is in conflict here is not the demands of nature and culture. Rather, there is conflict between the (at least partially) culturally constituted demands of family life and those of society. The cultural roots of this conflict are obscured by the effects of gender on Freud's thinking. Familial relations are naturalized by equating them with the interests and activities of women. Since women can become pregnant and give birth, it seems natural that the childbearer should also be the childrearer. The family is thus seen as woman's world. As production occurs more and more outside the family, someone must leave it—the man. He must withdraw his energy from women/children/sexuality and associate with men who make very different and often conflicting demands on him.

In associating women and nature, Freud transformed a concrete product of social activity into an inevitable consequence of the evolution of civilization, inescapable as modernity itself. Freud's pessimism about the possibility of overcoming or transforming civilization's discontents was rooted in his assumption of the inevitability of the conflict between nature (drives) and culture. Once the (at least partially) social roots of this conflict are revealed, new questions emerge; how inevitable are these discontents? To what extent did Freud, while exposing aspects of bourgeois culture, provide another justifying myth or ideology for a patriarchal one?

From a feminist point of view, it appears that Freud was less interested in divulging the secrets of the fathers than in participating in them. Even more problematic is Freud's apparent desire to repeat rather than work through the fathers' wish: to protect themselves and their sons against the eruption of maternal secrets into consciousness. After all, as Freud himself tells us, part of the Oedipal drama lies in the conflict between the son's desire to identify with the father and to overthrow him. The successful resolution of the boy's Oedipal complex includes identification with the father and the abandonment of his wish to overthrow or displace the father (Freud, 1923). In a culture where gender is an exclusionary category, the son can only enter the masculine world by rejecting and devaluing the female world, including his own prior identification with his mother and his internalization of her (Chodorow, 1978; Dinnerstein, 1976; Flax, 1983).

Other/Self, Preoedipal/Oedipal, Female/Male

Freud admitted that the first "other" or object for the male or female child is the mother. Although Freud was eventually willing to acknowledge the importance of pre-Oedipal experience for the girl's development, he still insisted on the centrality of the Oedipal period for the boy, for psychoanalytic theory as a whole, and for the history and analysis of culture itself.

Despite his own admission that his theories do not include and cannot account for many of the most important aspects of women's experience, Freud nonetheless continued to claim authorship of a radically new understanding of human rather than male psychology (Freud, 1933). He remained consistently unwilling to consider the possibility that his most fundamental concepts were not universal but rather were gender specific (and gender bound) and hence must be delimited socially and historically.

Freud also failed to explore the extent to which the pre-Oedipal mother-child relationship affected not only women's psychological development but the very structure of masculinity itself. For example, Freud discussed the boy's earliest identification with his mother primarily in terms of its effect on the child's subsequent "choice of object." Thus even the earliest boy-mother relation was reconstructed backwards from its inevitable terminus in the Oedipal phase. The effects that this early relation had on the constitution of the boy's sense of self, ego defenses, and so forth, are rarely examined.

Freud even reversed the actual power relation between the mother and small child. By conceptualizing the woman/mother as "castrated" and in need of a son in order to acquire the longed-for penis, Freud made the mother dependent on her son for psychological fulfillment.

Such a fantasy reveals a rather high level of grandiosity about the son's significance to his mother, serving, at least in part, as a defense against acknowledging both his powerlessness vis-à-vis the mother and his fear of abandonment or injury by her. Perhaps Freud revealed more about his own fantasies than about those of women when he asserted, "Even a marriage is not made secure until the wife has succeeded in making her husband her child as well and in acting as a mother to him" (Freud, 1933, pp. 133-4).

To the extent that Freud discussed infantile helplessness, he did so in terms of the child's "longing for the father." Freud says, "I cannot think of any need in childhood as strong as the need for a father's protection" (Freud, 1930, p. 72). Here again it appears that Oedipal wishes are evoked in part as a defense against deeper terrors.

Not only are deeper terrors repressed, but also primary infantile longings, especially for fusion with the first caretaker (mother). Freud was very resistant to discussing this aspect of infantile experience, as can be seen by his treatment of "oceanic" feelings in the opening chapter of *Civilization and Its Discontents*. First he says, "I cannot discover this 'oceanic' feeling in myself" (Freud, 1930, p. 65). Then he tries to explain it as a consequence of primary narcissism: "Originally the ego includes everything, later it separates off an external world from itself. Our present ego-feeling is, therefore, only a shrunken residue of a much more inclusive—indeed, an all embracing—feeling which corresponded to a more intimate bond between the ego and the world about it" (Freud, 1930, p. 68).

Who was in the world about the ego? With whom was the ego enjoying a particularly intimate bond? Since Freud himself claimed the mother is the first love object of both boy and girl, we conclude that this oceanic feeling is derived from a re-experience of the early mother-child symbiosis when the mother is the child's world.

Even Freud's claim to have uncovered the most fundamental and hidden human terror—the dread of castration (arising of course in the Oedipal phase)—conceals the deeper, defensive gains of his own naming of the cornerstone of human psychology. In the light of subsequent psychoanalytic work, we must acknowledge that the dread of castration is in part a displacement of more primitive and deeply buried anxieties—fear of annihilation, of loss of love, of the fear also of our aggression and rage toward the mother for her autonomy and power over us and of our desire to take that power for ourselves (Klein, 1975).

Ironically, as is so often the case, Freud himself pointed the way to this reinterpretation when he discussed the "masculine protest." He warns us "not [to] be misled by the term 'masculine protest' into supposing that what the man repudiates is the *attitude* of passivity, or as we may say, the social aspect of femininity. Such a notion is speedily contradicted by the observation that the attitude such men display towards women is often masochistic or actually slavish. What they reject is not passivity in general but passivity in relation to *men*. That is to say, the 'masculine protest' is in fact nothing other than fear of castration" (Freud, 1937a, pp. 252–3).

As this passage reveals, what is feared in "castration" is to lack or lose a penis—that is, to become a female since in Freud's system what defines women is precisely this "lack." Such a lack also entails exclusion from the more privileged masculine world, from constant association with men, upon whom one is dependent to achieve any cultural aims. Access to power and social esteem would be denied once the "magic organ" disappeared. Of course to the extent that the work of (patriarchal) civilization really is "increasingly the business of men," the boy's fears and fantasies of returning to the "mother world" will be reinforced and intensified (Freud, 1930, p. 103).

It is indeed in the Oedipal struggle that the father and son become allies. The son's identification with the father becomes part of his fortification against the return of the repressed mother-world. By privileging the Oedipal phase and denying the power of the first object relation, Freud participates in and rationalizes an act of repression that is both typical of and necessary to the replication of patriarchal culture.

Libido Economics/Object Relations Theory, Female/Male

One way to bury the power of our relation to the pre-Oedipal mother is to simply deny that real interrelations between humans are possible at all. The mother cannot "get" us because whatever we feel is an internally generated fantasy. She and our relation to her are not really inside and inextricably part of us.

It is not surprising, therefore, that Freud's object relations theory centers on the internalization of the father, whereas pre-Oedipal psychosexual development basically remains conceptualized as endogenous and objectless. The split between object relations theory and the economic model is necessarily related to the other/self antinomy. The irresolvability of this split is partially grounded in Freud's own anxieties about female sexuality, his inability to imagine the mother (and mothering) as an actively sexual being (or relation from the mother's, not only the child's, point of view). Pre-Oedipal objects are female and their desire must be repressed. Once the sexuality of the object is repressed, Freud (and the child) is left with the solitary monad, not with an interrelated pair. The monad's sexuality then seems to unfold in a pregiven, drive-governed way.

Furthermore, Freud conceptualized this innate sexuality as male (not gender neutral). Freud's concept of desire as such was deeply affected by the equating of active and phallic sexuality. The expression of desire in its more mature phases depends upon possession of a penis—or in the girl's case the fantasy of having this magic organ.

Only "little men" can actively desire the mother. Hence Freud could only reconcile active sexuality and femaleness by calling the masturbating little girl a "little man." Freud named the phase of sexual exploration and desire, in which fantasies about an object first come into play, the *phallic period*: "With their entry into the phallic phase the differences between the sexes are completely eclipsed by their agreements. We are now obliged to recognize that the little girl is a little man" (Freud, 1933, p. 118). Here we see how a dualistic two is reduced to a gender-biased one. The little boy is never conceptualized as a little woman, despite the fact that his first object is a woman (mother).

Here we see also how gender and gender shifts are utilized to obscure potentially disturbing ideas in another way. The fact that the girl's first desired object is a female implies that therefore female homosexuality might be a psychosexual norm. Heterosexuality is rescued by changing the gender of one of the pair (mother/child).

Since Freud took heterosexuality for granted at least as a culturally enforced norm (if not a "natural" one; Freud, 1905), he also assumed that the girl must do more than renounce her phallic desire for the mother. In the Oedipal period, the "little man" must become a "little girl" and develop the kind of desire that is appropriate to girls/women—e.g., a passive (vaginal) receptivity to or indirectly expressed longing for an active male (penis). Since this transformed, now properly female, desire is more passive, girls do not have to completely renounce their Oedipal object (the father). (Of course, Freud did not mention that such desire is not a threat, indeed may be pleasing to, the father or the patriarchal order.) Girls remain partially attached to both their Oedipal and pre-Oedipal objects. Hence, the girl never completely resolves her Oedipal complex.

Body/Mind, Female/Male

Despite their sexual passivity, Freud believed that women are more determined by and subject to the body and its drives. Women represent the "interests of sexual life" (and nature); they are associated with unreason, feeling, and primary process. They favor family over culture, love over duty, feeling over thought. In addition, the powerful sense of lack produced by women's bodies (castration) determines the course of their lives to a much greater extent than men's castration anxiety determines theirs. Men can "master their castration anxiety"; women can merely learn to "accept without a trace of resentment" the "*fact*" of their castration (Freud, 1937a, p. 251).

The incomplete dissolution of the girl's Oedipal complex means that her superego is never as fully developed or powerful as the boy's.

Girls lack the mature conscience of post-Oedipal boys, because the superego is a precipitate and consequence of the resolution of the Oedipal struggle, including the (boy's) identification with the father. By identifying with the father the (boy) child also internalizes and makes his own the morality of his culture. Without a powerful superego, women will be "little capable" of carrying out the "instinctual sublimations" that civilization increasingly demands (Freud, 1930, p. 103).

Furthermore, because of the complex interrelations between the id, ego, and superego, the girl's (and woman's) ego and hence her capacity for rational thought will also be less powerful than the boy's. According to Freud the ego (which is the locus of reason) is a secondary formation. It is a precipitate of the id and develops as a result of the frustration the child encounters in trying to satisfy its drives, to sustain an internal equilibrium or even to preserve its own life, given the inability of the id to engage in reality checking. Although it is initially a precipitate of the id, in order for the ego to develop, it must attain a certain autonomy from the id and the drives. For example, through sublimation the ego can capture some of the id's libidinal energy for its own purposes. Although its demands may weaken the ego, to some extent the superego can also reinforce the ego's autonomy by requiring acts of (drive) sublimation or repression. Since women's superego is weaker than men's, it will be a less reliable or powerful ally against the id. Inasmuch as the capacity for rational thought arises at least in part from a sublimation of sexuality, to the extent that women are less capable of sublimation, they will also be less able to reason (Freud, 1923, 1938).

There is another reason why Freud believed that women are more associated with and determined by their bodies than men are. Freud believed that women suffer from a fundamental, irreversible wound to their narcissism — women are castrated not just in fantasy, but in fact, and the inevitable consequence of this castration is, as we know, penis envy. All but one of women's subsequent attempts to compensate for this narcissistic wound (e.g., their strivings for a career) are bound to fail. The only salve, but a partial one, for the wound of castration is pregnancy, and more particularly, the birth of a son. By giving birth to a son, a woman can utilize her "defect" (vagina/hole) to (at least temporarily) obtain the desired organ (the penis). Hence Freud claimed: "A mother is only brought unlimited satisfaction by her relation to a son; this is altogether the most perfect, the most free from ambivalence of all human relationships" (Freud, 1933, p. 133).

In Freud's discussion of women's bodily self and how he imagined we experience it, an important displacement occurs—the social construction of gender is fused (and confused) with biological sex (especially anatomical differences). Once again, as in the discussion of the conflict between nature and culture, biology is brought in to protect and more deeply conceal the riddle of sex. Anatomical differences immediately and without any social mediation become absolute determinants of women's lives. Anatomy does become destiny, but although the boy may rescue his penis and his self-esteem by entering culture, for women that same entrance into culture only ratifies their (anatomical) inferiority from which there is no escape. Freud says:

> We often feel that, when we have reached the wish for a penis and the masculine protest, we have penetrated all the psycholog-ical strata and reached "bedrock" and that our task is accom-plished. And this is probably correct, for in the psychical field the biological factor is really rock-bottom. The repudiation of femininity must surely be a biological fact, part of the great riddle of sex. (Freud, 1937a, p. 252)

With the split from one (precultural, phallic sexuality) to two (gender differentiation), the child recognizes not just a difference in bodies but a (social) hierarchy. The move from one to two for the child and Freud entails a realization that the two is less than the one; differentiation for the girl brings with it a feeling of loss and lack. Freud assumed that from the very first glimpse of a penis, the girl knows the boy's organ is superior to hers, that is, it can give the boy more pleasure than she could ever have from her stunted one. As good economists of the libido, both boy and girl have a biological reason for the repudiation of femininity—only the girl is stuck with it anyway. The girl quickly "extends her judgment of inferiority from her stunted penis to her whole self" (Freud, 1938, p. 193). Here again Freud argued that the girl's experience of her body determines the subsequent course of her psychological development. He assumed her biological equipment really is inferior and so there is no reason to explore possible social roots for her low self-esteem—or to treat her judgment of her self as problematic.

Freud also seemed to have assumed (as Lacan does subsequently) that the penis is superior in its ability to carry meaning. The little girl in Freud's account immediately assumes the penis is the "universal signifier" (Lacan 1985a; 1985b). Upon seeing the little boy's organ, she reconceptualizes her clitoris as a stunted penis, rather than considering the boy's penis as an enlarged and rather unwieldy clitoris. Like Freud, she assumes there is a "one," and that one is the penis. Difference is automatically conceptualized as negative variation from the (male) norm.

The avoidance and obscurantism integral to Freud's reductionistic moments is especially striking since he criticized others for adopting similar ideas. For example, Freud criticized Wilhelm Fleiss for his inclination "to regard the difference between the sexes as the true cause and original motive of repression. I can only repeat that I do not accept this view: I do not think we are justified in sexualizing repression in this way—that is to say, in explaining it on a biological instead of a purely psychological basis" (Freud, 1937a, p. 251).

Yet, the move from "purely biological" (sex/body) to "purely psychological" (mind/mental) is not a solution either; we just switch from privileging one element of the pair to the other, sustaining both dualism and the idea that one is always better than two. By conceptualizing differences as antinomies, Freud implied that there could be an undifferentiated whole, that wholeness or homeostatic equilibrium is the (desirable) norm. Here it seems the repressed and denied fantasy of symbiotic unity returns in a scientistic guise.

Whether Freud really favored the psychological/mental or biological/physical as the ultimate one is less important than his continual alternation between splitting mind/body into two and the wish for a final one. Freud did not seem to be able to sustain an idea of the bodily and mental facets of human experience as simultaneously different, related, and autonomous.

This alternation between dualistic and unitary views of the relationships between body/mind seems especially odd, since Freud's own notion of the unconscious points a way beyond it. The nature of the unconscious shows that there is something between one and two—in the unconscious and in unconscious actions the boundaries between mind and body blur. Without an absolute demarcation between mind and body, the relationship between the reasoning ego and the unreasoning id also becomes more complex.

Patient/Analyst, Female/Male

Freud's writings on the psychoanalytic situation are among his most complex and suggestive. All the contradictions and antinomies in his theories of self, knowledge, social relations, and gender are starkly present here. Freud's anxieties about gender enter both overtly and subtly into his accounts of the analytic process and the sorts of knowledge that can be gleaned from it. Some of the more subtle effects of gender can be found in Freud's persistent denial of the interrelatedness of the patient and analyst and in his repeated attempts to fit the analytic process within an empiricist model of scientific investigation and discovery.

The overt influence of gender on Freud's thinking about the analytic process is easier to see. He insisted that accepting his construction of the meaning of castration anxiety is one of the factors that determine the success of an analysis. Freud identified five factors that influence the outcome of any analysis: (1) constitutional factors such as the relative strength of libido, its mobility, the ability of the individual to change and the power of the aggressive drive; (2) the strength of the roots of the defensive mechanisms and how much the ego has been modified in the course of a person's life; (3) the quantity and quality of traumatic factors inflicted by the external world; (4) the personal characteristics of the analyst, including the success of her/his own analysis; (5) the "repudiation of femininity" (Freud 1937a, p. 250) and how successfully each person comes to terms with it.

As is well known, by the end of his life, Freud had grown much more pessimistic about the difficulties of the therapeutic relationship and the possibility of overcoming them. Given the extraordinary demands the analytic process makes on both analyst and the patient and the obdurate character of the unconscious, analysis takes on some of the simultaneously heroic and tragic nature of the *Odyssey*. Yet, one can also ask: To what extent are these difficulties self-imposed (as in any heroic tragedy)? Freud's writings on the psychoanalytic situation can tell as much about his theories, about epistemological problems in psychoanalysis and philosophy and, especially, about the obscuring effect of the riddle of sex.

Analyzing Analysis What did Freud think he was doing during all those hours in his consulting room? In some ways it is easier to say what Freud thought psychoanalysis is not, since a number of his writings on this subject are taken up with correcting what he believes to be misconceptions or malpractice of analysis. Freud's attempts to correct these misconceptions of the analytic situation are especially significant since many of these misunderstandings recur in contemporary writings on the subject.

For example, contrary to the views of some contemporary commentators such as Habermas (1971; 1979; Spence, 1982), Freud evidently did not believe that psychoanalysis is primarily a cognitive, linguistic, or narrative process. In a characteristic passage on analytic technique, Freud says: "The idea that a neurotic is suffering from a sort of ignorance, and that if one removes this ignorance by telling him facts ... he must recover, is an idea that has long been superceded and one derived from superficial appearances. The pathological factor is not his ignorance in itself, but the root of this ignorance in his *inner resistances*; it was they that first called this ignorance into being, and they still maintain it now. In combating these resistances lies the task of the therapy. Telling the patient what he does not know because he has repressed it, is only one of the necessary preliminaries in the therapy. If knowledge about his unconscious were as important for the patient as the inexperienced in psychoanalysis imagine, it would be sufficient to cure him for him to go to lectures or read books. Such measures, however, have as little effect on the symptoms of nervous disease as distributing menu-cards in time of famine has on people's hunger" (Freud, 1910, p. 225).

Contrary to Grünbaum's reconstruction of his argument, Freud believed that neither veridical insight nor the increased capacity for self-reflection are the determining factor in the therapeutic success of psychoanalysis (Grünbaum, 1979). The meaning and significance of "insight" cannot be understood outside of the context that gives it distinct connotations and status—the transference relation as experienced within the analytic situation. The capacity for veridical insight and self-reflection should increase within (and by accurate interpretation of) the transference relation. However, improving one's capacity for such insights and the analyst's interpretations of resistance to both insight and the transference are only aspects of a very complex analytic process.

If anything is definitive of the analytic process, it would be transference and resistance rather than veridical insight or the tally argument. Freud considered transference and resistance so definitive of psychoanalysis that he states: "Any line of investigation which recognizes these two facts and takes them as the starting point of its work has a right to call itself psychoanalysis, even though it arrives at results other than my own" (Freud, 1914, p. 16).

However, it is precisely on the crucial subject of the transference relation that Freud's ambivalences become most acute. His account of the nature of this relationship and the epistemological status of the data it produces is extremely contradictory and unclear (Gill, 1982). The language Freud used to describe the analytic situation and his treatment of the problem of suggestion reveal these contradictions most clearly.

Freud sometimes described the analytic process in the language of natural science or medicine, as if the analyst were a scientist confronting a piece of data or a surgeon who must insure that the operating theater is not contaminated (Freud, 1912a). He also described the analytic situation as an ongoing battle in which the analyst and patient are sometimes allies, sometimes enemies in a shifting constellation of forces (Freud, 1926). Frequently, Freud said somewhat ruefully, the "big battalions" seem to be on the patient's side (Freud, 1937a, p. 240).

Almost simultaneously, Freud discussed the need for the analyst to remain cold and distant and for there to exist a genuine positive alliance between analyst and patient, not merely a transference relation. Freud insisted upon the special character of the relationship between analyst and patient. This relationship must be based on the "love of truth, that is on the acknowledgement of reality ... it precludes any kind of sham or deception" (Freud, 1937a, p. 248). The practical form this love of truth takes in the analytic situation is adherence by both analyst and patient to the "analytic rule." For the patient this means trying to say whatever comes to mind without prior censorship (free association); for the analyst it means to listen with "evenly suspended attention" without prior assumptions about the relative importance of meaning for the patient of any of her/his associations (Freud, 1912a, p. 111).

Freud was also ambiguous (and ambivalent) about the role of suggestion in the analytic process and about the kind of truth that emerges in and through analysis. He both admitted and denied that the therapeutic efficacy of analysis depends upon the power of suggestion. He also claimed that what is recovered in analysis is the truth of what really (empirically) happened (the archaeological model) and a construction of what happened (Freud, 1937b, p. 259).

In the essay "Analytic Therapy," Freud admitted that psychoanalysis depends upon suggestion. However, unlike other practices that depend upon suggestion, he claimed that in analysis suggestion is traced back to its source in transference phenomena (Freud, 1917). Ultimately, for an analysis to be successful, transference, and with it the analyst's power of suggestion, must be dissolved. Transference is a necessary but reversible illness stimulated by the analytic situation but caused by the patient's own unconscious dynamics. As the transference is resolved, the contaminating influences of suggestion will also fall away; the data produced in the analytic situation will get "cleaned up" as the process procedes. Freud believed that a system of "conjectures and refutations" was an intrinsic aspect of the psychoanalytic situation.

This belief depends upon certain assumptions about the origins of the power of suggestion and about the nature of the analyst-patient relationship. According to Freud, the power of suggestion arises from unconscious sources; a present-day relationship becomes infused with the authority of and feelings about a past, usually parental, one. The continuing (but unconscious) power of the past renders an individual vulnerable to the present authority's judgment and susceptible to their influence. Transference material may emerge in a wide variety of relationships, including teacher/student, religious leader/follower, wife/husband, physician/patient.

However, only in analysis is transference made the object of investigation. The purpose of this investigation is twofold: to dissect transference in all the shapes in which it appears and ultimately to dissolve it. During the course of an analysis, resistances are transformed into or expressed through negative transferences. It is primarily by this means that inner conflict can become available for "working through." After all, Freud claimed, no one can be hanged *in absentia* (Freud, 1912b, p. 108). The success of analysis depends upon the establishing and resolving of the transference relation; to some extent interpretation, veridical insight, and the increased capacity for self-reflection are merely means to this end.

Previous acts of repression can be undone if the patient's attention can be drawn to the way they are enacted in the analytic situation (Freud, 1913). The role of interpretation in this process is to help the patient make sense (literally) out of transference experiences as well as out of dreams and slips of the tongue. As the analytic process proceeds, the ego is transformed; it gains more autonomy and becomes less rigid in response to unconscious demands. The unconscious compulsion to repeat is gradually replaced by a greater degree of conscious choice.

In discussing interpretation Freud says: "We do not pretend that an individual construction is anything more than a conjecture which awaits examination, confirmation or rejection. We claim no authority for it, we require no direct agreement from the patient, nor do we argue with him if at first he denies it. In short, we conduct ourselves upon the model of a familiar figure in one of Nestoy's farces—the manservant who has a single answer on his lips to every question or objection: 'It will all become clear in the course of future developments'" (Freud, 1937b, p. 265).

Whether any interpretation or insight was veridical can only be determined after transference is dissolved. Only then can we judge if success is due to suggestion or veridical insight. According to Freud whatever in the doctor's conjecture is inaccurate drops out in the course of the analysis; it has to be withdrawn and replaced by something more correct (Freud, 1917). This is so because the analyst's power is rooted in the patient's past, and in a successful analysis the past gradually loses its power over the patient.

The "objectivity" of clinical interpretations and veridical insight depends upon the capacity of both patient and analyst to become aware of the effects of the unconscious within themselves and on the relationship between them. The patient's neurosis and the analyst's countertransference material impede both the development of insight and a relationship in and through which such impediments can be experienced as problematic. Presumably, the closer any analysis approaches the ideal, the greater the probability that the "truth" about the patient's past, ego defenses, and fantasies will emerge.

Narcissism, Gender, and the Limits of Analysis Yet, what is this "truth"? What is its epistemological grounding and status? Why ought we or the patient accept any claims about the meaning of particular experiences, knowledge, or human nature based on material produced or evoked by the psychoanalytic process?

Freud's answers to these questions are complex and ultimately unsatisfactory. The answers depend upon several interconnected concepts, particularly the objectivity of the analyst and the purity of the transference relation. Underlying and grounding these concepts are the theory of narcissism and an empiricist notion of science and truth. Despite the evidence from his own clinical experience that such concepts are inadequate, Freud was unable to sufficiently revise or abandon them. This unfortunate situation can be explained in part by Freud's continuing defensive avoidance of penetrating more deeply into the riddle of sex. When Freud comes close to elucidating an essential element of the social construction of gender, he obscures it further by shifting to explanations on nature or biology.

In accepting the social construction of gender as a biological bedrock in human life, Freud transformed into a theory (narcissism) his own inability or unwillingness to undo the repression of pre-

Oedipal experience and the female (relational) aspects of his own practice. This defensive avoidance or denial has many debilitating consequences for Freud's (and subsequent analysts') work. These consequences include an inability to make full use of the richness of clinical experience in the development either of psychological theory or of an epistemology that is more appropriate to all the human sciences (and not only psychoanalysis).

Freud's theory of primary narcissism is intertwined with his drive theory, particularly the economics of the libido. As stated above drive theory is also deeply structured by Freud's anxieties about gender, especially by his need to deny the desire of and one's relatedness to the m/other.

According to drive theory, each person is born with a fixed amount of libido (Freud, 1938). Initially, all this energy is fixated upon the self. The goal of the human, like any organism, is the maintenance of internal (homeostatic) equilibrium. If somehow we could maintain such an equilibrium solely by our own efforts, we would have no innate need to relate to other persons (Freud, 1930). However, given the initial physical helplessness of the human infant and the inability of the id to engage in reality testing, such self-sufficiency is not possible.

Others come into being for us when we attach some of our own libidinal energy onto them; what we then experience is not another person as an independently existing self. The other person is literally our object and ceases to exist (for us) when we withdraw libidinal energy from them.

What we glorify as love is merely mutual self-gratification and a set of dual but solipsistic processes of cathecting one's own libido onto an object and reintrojecting it into one's self. In Freud's writings persons other than ourselves sometimes take on the characteristics of Kant's things in themselves. We know they must exist because otherwise certain psychic structures and life itself would not be possible. However, we can only know other persons as we ourselves construct them, never as they are in themselves apart from our fantasies and libidinal investments.

Since human relationships are merely mutual projection, if one of the partners could be abstinent, e.g., refrain from projection and from using the other as a means for self-gratification, the abstinent person would become as a blank facade or an empty movie screen. The patient's projections could bounce off that facade like light rays on glass. The patient's projections would shine so brightly in the mirror of the analytic process that she would be forced to acknowledge their existence (as projections). Since the patient is inherently a narcissist, and the analyst functions as a mirror, what the patient would see is herself, i.e., her own wishes and fantasies as wishes produced by her and not by the analyst as a person acting upon her or interacting with her. After all, it is her movie—acted, directed, produced, and projected by her alone. What she projects is derived solely from her own past experience. Like all neurotics that is the only script she knows.

Through an analysis of the transference relation, these wishes, once brought into the light, could be traced back to earlier psychosexual stages and/or object relations and the spell of the past can be broken. The analytic process will work and the accuracy of the patient's reflection in the mirror can be guaranteed only if the analyst remains neutral, that is if she abstains from projecting her own wishes and fantasies onto the patient. "The doctor should be opaque to his patients and, like a mirror, should show them nothing but what is shown to him" (Freud, 1912a, p. 118). The analyst must be as absent and unrelated as the child experiences the m/other in the initial stages of primary narcissism. The analyst's neutrality in turn depends upon the success of her own training analysis and her capacity for continual ruthless introspection, including a willingness to reenter analysis or supervision as necessary.

In this account the analytic situation seems like an empiricist's laboratory: it allows naturally occurring phenomena to be replicated in a controlled setting. If enough patients reenact more or less the same drama, we can begin to have some confidence in the theories we construct to account for the twistings and turnings of the psychoanalytic process. Furthermore, since neurosis is only an exaggeration of the physical processes of "normal" people (as can be seen by the fact that all of us dream and make slips of the tongue), clinical experience can be used to substantiate general claims about human nature and universally shared psychological processes.

Interrelatedness: Denial and Necessity The first and most obvious objection to this reconstruction of Freud's account of psychoanalysis is that it directly contradicts other aspects of his writings on the subject. In the same essay in which Freud likens psychoanalysis to an archaeological process and claims that "it depends only upon analytic techniques whether we shall succeed in bringing what is concealed completely to light" (Freud, 1937b, p. 260), he also says: "Quite often we do not succeed in bringing the patient to recollect what has been repressed. Instead of that, . . . we produce in him an assured conviction of the truth of the construction which achieves the same therapeutic result as a recaptured memory." Unfortunately, "the problem of what the circumstances are in which this occurs and of how it is possible that what appears to be an incomplete substitute should nevertheless produce a complete result" (Freud, 1937b, pp. 265–266), Freud leaves for a later and never completed inquiry.

It seems reasonable to assume that how an "assured conviction of the truth" can have the "same therapeutic result as a recaptured (actual) memory" may have something to do with the relationship between analyst and patient. But there we come up against one of the paradoxes of Freud's theories: how can someone who is fundamentally a narcissist have anything other than transference-like relationships? Presumably in the case of analysis, the patient eventually tires of trying to enlist the abstinent analyst into his delusory system and decides such a pursuit is a waste of libidinal energy. Presumably also the patient discovers through analysis which of her preexisting fantasies are ego-syntonic and puts her libidinal energy into maximizing gratification of the more promising ones. What does not seem possible, either in the analytic situation or in Freud's theory more generally, is that a drive-governed narcissist can also experience object love, much less the aspect of positive transference that arises neither from aggressive feelings nor erotic wishes.

Nonetheless, Freud claimed that in analysis it is possible to "raise the transference by making it conscious (;) we detach only these two components of the emotional relationship from the person of the physician; the conscious and unobjectionable component of it remains, and brings about the successful result in psychoanalysis as in all other remedial methods" (Freud, 1912b, p. 105).

What enables the patient to enter into a therapeutic alliance with the analyst? Why is this alliance the crucial factor in the remedial effects of psychoanalysis? Why and how does it work? What aspect(s) of the mind's structure and/or its dynamic processes make such an alliance possible at all, much less therapeutic? Freud seems to be unable to answer these questions. Thus, one can only conclude that he was unable to adequately solve the riddle of transference despite its centrality to his theory and practice.

Despite the contradictions and ambiguities in Freud's writings on this subject, there are also certain regularities. One of the most important of these regularities is his persistent denial of the interrelatedness of analyst and patient. Freud continually seemed to deny that the analyst and patient are engaged in a unique and intimate relationship. In this regard it is interesting to note his frequent use of the imagery of war to describe the analytic process. Surely war is one of the most objectifying and aggressive of all human practices.

Freud's continued use of metaphors for the analyst's role, like those of a surgeon, mirror, or general, is especially puzzling since we know that his actual clinical practice did not conform to his technical recommendations for the practice of psychoanalysis. According to accounts by Freud's patients, he expressed an active concern for their well-being. He loaned money to patients while they were in analysis with him. Freud was also far from silent or abstinent in the analytic situation. He even gave lectures to his patients during the analytic hour on the possible origins of artifacts in his consulting room and on the history of archaeology, ancient Egypt, and other topics (H.D., 1956; Ruitenbeck, 1973).

Gender, Epistemology, and Politics Although there are undoubtedly many reasons for Freud's denial of the interrelatedness of analyst and patient, two seem especially important. The first is Freud's attempt to make psychoanalysis a legitimate form of knowledge. In his time, and to a large degree in our own, truth claims must meet empiricist tests, and "science" and "reliable knowledge" are confounded. Despite his concern about the appropriateness of existing scientific theories and practices as models for psychoanalysis, Freud was deeply influenced by the scientism and mechanism of his time. If psychoanalysis was not a science, Freud believed, its claims to truth would not be taken seriously (even by him). Freud was not content to have psychoanalysis treated as one more "poetic narrative" of the human life story. Perhaps Freud also felt that he needed the legitimizing objectivity of science to counter the dismissal of psychoanalysis as a Jewish science.

Nonetheless, psychoanalysis cannot fit within an empiricist model of science or knowledge. In trying to make psychoanalysis conform to preexisting criteria for the practices of science, especially as these are posited (or "rationally reconstructed") by philosophers of science, analysts undercut the radicalness and power of their (potential) contributions to the philosophy of knowledge.

The data and methods of psychoanalysis are relational and intersubjective. The logic of discovery of psychoanalysis as it is practiced in the analytic situation directly conflicts with the empiricist's view of the self as separate from the object. It is inappropriate to dismiss the data generated within this situation as epistemologically contaminated because such a judgment presupposes exactly what psychoanalysis calls into question: psychoanalysis challenges the meaningfulness, possibility, or desirability of an absolute split between the subject and object in the search for reliable knowledge.

Psychoanalysis also calls into question the assumption that rational thought and the accumulation of reliable knowledge require suppression or control of subjective feeling. Psychoanalysis requires instead that analysts be in touch with and be able to use their own feelings and that they also be able to empathically experience the feeling of the patient. The feeling states of both patient and analyst provide important information about and insight into the patient's inner world as well as the relationship between the two members of the therapeutic alliance. The patient sometimes needs to make use of or be contained by the feeling states of the analyst (Bion, 1970). Rational insight alone is not an adequate basis for producing either analytic knowledge or a therapeutic success. Ultimately, reciprocity between the analyst and patient, not separation of subject and object, is the goal of analysis. Furthermore, the goal of analysis is to change its object (patient-subject) and its laws of causality, not simply to use or discover them as in empiricist natural science.

To give an account of the analytic subject or to evaluate the knowledge that results from analysis would require an epistemology that is simultaneously empirical, intersubjective, and process-oriented. Such an epistemology does not currently exist. If psychoanalysis were to give up its inappropriate attachment to the empiricist model of science, a disciplined reflection on the analytic situation could contribute much to the generation of such epistemologies.

The second reason Freud might have had for denying the interrelatedness of patient and analyst relates specifically to his anxieties about gender. We have discussed above some of the interconnections between an empiricist view of science that is grounded in and insists upon a rigid dichotomizing of subject and object and gender. Freud's attempts to retain that rigid dichotomy in the analytic situation must be examined as well. Despite the fact that his own clinical experience showed that such dichotomies were neither possible nor desirable, Freud retained a view of the analytic situation in which the analyst is the patient's object; the patient is the analyst's object, and each person can only be a subject separately from the object.

One of the relationships between this denial of relatedness and gender is that the possibility of such relatedness depends on what

Freud called "human prehistory," that is, on our capacity to be symbiotically attached to another person who is similarly attached to (yet separate from) us.

Freud was very resistent to discussing or reviving this aspect of infantile experience. In addition, given Freud's understanding of gender, culture, and knowledge, the reconceptualization of psychoanalysis as "relational work" would threaten both the social and scientific status of his creation. In a culture in which affective relations are seen as natural and female and work as instrumental, serious, and male, the very concept of "relational work" seems like an oxymoron. If we thought of the process of psychoanalysis as just establishing a relationship and then working this relationship through, who could take such work seriously, or even consider it work at all? Anyone could "mother"/relate if they so chose. There is nothing scientific or skilled about such practices at all. It is far better to present oneself as a heartless surgeon, an intrepid general, an emotionally unengaged scientist in the lab, or even an heroic and ruthless "deconstructor" of the illusions of bourgeois culture or the reader of a text.

The strongly felt need for fathers and sons (and to a lesser degree, daughters) to bond against the return of the repressed "mother-world" has not disappeared. Even in our postmodern culture, the gender splits between nature/culture, mind/body, subject/object, self/other, reason/unreason, and male/female recur. For example, in contemporary psychoanalysis diametrically opposed views of the relationship between self and others are posited. On one side Lacan and other writers deny that any genuine relatedness is possible between two selves. Lacan is so unnerved by his discovery of the desire of the m/other that his discovery results in the (theoretical) annihilation of the self. For Lacan the self cannot exist precisely because it comes into being in and through the desire of the m/other. The desire of the other for Lacan entails a loss (and permanent alienation) of the self. Thus Lacan merely inverts Freud's theory of primary narcissism. In Lacan's theory there are only others, never a self; even the self is an other to itself. Analysis can go no further than confronting the patient with this (ontological) estrangement. In contrast, object relations theory believes it is possible to be a true self, but only in and through a relationship with a "good enough" mother who exists (for the child and in the theory) as an object (Winnicott, 1971). Despite the centrality of the concept of reciprocity in object relations theory, the mother never appears as a complex person in her own right, with her own processes that are not isomorphic with those of the child.

In contemporary philosophy the split between reason/mind and empirical/contingent body still prevails. The concept of deconstruction, of the philosopher as a shatterer of "foundational illusion" (Rorty, 1979), implies that it is possible for the philosopher to break through and go outside the web of social relations and ideas into which he or she was born and through which he or she comes to be a person. Alternatively, philosophers still claim to investigate and present the logic of a disembodied, historical reason (or "speech act"). Philosophy is still presented as rationality's privileged protector, representative, and judge, as if each of these claims were relatively unproblematic or even self-evidently true.

In contemporary science anxieties about gender (and the split between nature and culture) are far from absent. Some researchers are busily trying to once again collapse gender into sex by positing that the origin of such "natural differences" (male/female) must lie in the "brain" and/or in our genes. Hence such differences are inevitable and their consequences are not amenable to transformation by human action (at least not without unacceptable risk). Alternatively, in fear that any discovery of difference would once again be utilized to justify hierarchy, other researchers want to insist that having a male or female body makes no difference at all, or that we should not even consider such questions.

Contemporary Western culture continues to express the (not so) archaic residues of pre-Oedipal experience. Any adequate theory of science, the subject, or culture needs to name and bring fully into the light that which exists before and despite the "Law of the Father." A more critical and feminist psychoanalysis has much to contribute to this therapeutic and edifying task.

REFERENCES

Bion, W. R. *Attention and interpretation.* London: Travistock, 1970.
Chodorow, N. *The reproduction of mothering: Psychoanalysis and the sociology of gender.* Berkeley: University of California Press, 1978.
Dinnerstein, D. *The mermaid and the minotaur.* New York: Harper & Row, 1976.

Erikson, E. The dream specimen of psychoanalysis. *Journal of the American Psychoanalytic Association*, 1954, 2, 5–56.

Flax, J. Political theory and the patriarchal unconscious: A psychoanalytic perspective on epistemology and metaphysics. In S. Harding and M. Hintikka (Eds.), *Discovering reality*. Dordrecht: D. Reidel, 1983.

Freud, S. Three essays on the theory of sexuality. S.E., 1905, Vol. 7.

Freud, S. Observations on 'wild' psycho-analysis. S.E., 1910, Vol. 11; quote from J. Riviere (Trans.) *Collected papers*, Vol. 2, New York: Basic Books, 1959, pp. 301–302.

Freud, S. Recommendations to physicians practicing psycho-analysis. S.E., 1912, Vol. 12.(a)

Freud, S. The dynamics of transference. S.E., 1912, Vol. 12; quote from J. Riviere (Trans.) *Collected papers*, Vol. 2, New York: Basic Books, 1959, p. 319.(b)

Freud, S. Further recommendations in the technique of psycho-analysis. S.E., 1913, Vol. 12.

Freud, S. On the history of the psycho-analytic movement. S.E., 1914, Vol. 14.

Freud, S. Introductory lectures on psycho-analysis. S.E., 1917, Vol. 16.

Freud, S. The ego and the id. S.E., 1923, Vol. 19.

Freud, S. Some psychological consequences of the anatomical distinction between the sexes. S.E., 1925, Vol. 19.

Freud, S. The question of lay analysis. S.E., 1926, Vol. 20.

Freud, S. Civilization and its discontents. S.E., 1930, Vol. 21.

Freud, S. Female sexuality. S.E., 1931, Vol. 21.

Freud, S. New introductory lectures on psycho-analysis. S.E., 1933, Vol. 22.

Freud, S. Analysis terminable and interminable. S.E., 1937, Vol. 23; quotes from J. Strachey (Ed.) *Collected papers*, Vol. 5, New York: Basic Books, 1959, pp. 351–352, 355–357.(a)

Freud, S. *Constructions in analysis*. S.E., 1937, Vol. 23.(b)

Freud, S. *An outline of psycho-analysis*. S.E., 1938, Vol. 23.

Gill, M. M. *Analysis of transference* (Vol. 1). New York: International Universities Press, 1982.

Grünbaum, A. Epistemological liabilities of the clinical appraisal of psychoanalytic theory. *Psychoanalysis and Contemporary Thought*, 1979, 2, 451–526.

Habermas, J. *Knowledge and human interests*. Boston: Beacon, 1971.

Habermas, J. *Communication and the evolution of society*. Boston: Beacon, 1979.

H.D. *Tribute to Freud*. New York: McGraw Hill, 1956.

Keller, E. F. Gender and science. *Psychoanalysis and Contemporary Thought*, 1978, 1, 409–433.

Keller, E. F. *A feeling for the organism: The life and work of Barbara McClintock*. New York: W. H. Freeman, 1983.

Keller, E. F. *Reflections on gender and science*. New Haven: Yale University Press, 1985.

Klein, M. *Love, guilt and reparation*. New York: Dell, 1975.

Lacan, J. The meaning of the phallus. In J. Mitchell and J. Rose (Eds.), *Feminine sexuality*. New York: W. W. Norton, 1985.(a)

Lacan, J. Seminar of 21 January 1975. In J. Mitchell and J. Rose (Eds.), *Feminine sexuality*. New York: W. W. Norton, 1985.(b)

Mitchell, J. *Psychoanalysis and feminism*. New York: Pantheon, 1974.

Mitchell, J. *Women: The longest revolution*. London: Virago Press, 1984.

Rorty, R. *Philosophy and the mirror of nature*. Princeton: Princeton University Press, 1979.

Ruitenbeck, H. *Freud as we knew him*. Detroit: Wayne State University Press, 1973.

Spence, D. *Narrative truth and historical truth: Meaning and interpretation in psychoanalysis*. New York: W. W. Norton, 1982.

Winnicott, D. W. *Playing and reality*. New York: Basic Books, 1971.

Is Science Really Masculine?: Commentary on Evelyn Fox Keller and Jane Flax

DONALD P. SPENCE

The subtitle for this paper might be taken as "Learning to Count Past Two," and I strongly support the authors in their dislike of either/or thinking. The problem of the excluded middle has become one of the subthemes of this conference, and it is clear that dislike of the middle path is connected in part with a deep-seated intolerance for ambiguity. "Is that a man or a woman?" we ask when we pass someone on the street with a punk hairdo, and it bothers us not to know. "Is that science or something else?" we ask of a piece of research; or more pejoratively, we might say, "Well, clearly whatever he's doing, it's not science." Case closed.

On the other hand—and here you see the either/or rule creeping in through the back door—on the other hand, or more accurately, from a slightly different point of view, I am not convinced that one aspect of the world—for example, gender—and the way this aspect is structured will necessarily have a bearing on how we structure a second aspect—for example, science. Nor am I convinced that the common stereotypes of masculinity and femininity are necessarily mapped onto those of science. In some settings to be a scientist means to act on an objective world in a roughly masculine manner. To *hunt* for correlations, to *manipulate* variables, to *analyze* the variance—these all seem to be masculine activities and to validate the masculine view of the world. But at other times, a scientist —even a male scientist—can be *in tune* with nature, can let ideas *come* to mind and be *sensitive* to layered meanings in the data, even though these sound like feminine traits. There is no clear distinction between action on the world and letting the world act on us; the good scientist will do both, and for this reason I wonder whether the authors are not perpetuating the very kind of either/or thinking they had come to dispute. When they say, "To learn to be a scientist is to learn the attributes of what our culture calls masculinity," it sounds to me like a way of extending the stereotype. Barbara McClintock, after all, was not the only investigator with a feeling for the organism.

Earlier I began a sentence with the words "on the other hand" and made a joke about the expression. But there is something we can learn from it as well. For many kinds of basic tasks, we have only two hands. If I am cutting down a tree, brushing my teeth, carrying a suitcase, or paddling a canoe, I have two and only two choices. This piece of body architecture is deeply rooted in our value system and carries a host of connotations, and I wonder whether right and left is not just as basic a dichotomy as masculine/feminine. What is more, I wonder whether the right/left split has not trained us to see the world in two's, one good, one bad, one right—in French, *right* is the word for law and we recognize the "right arm of the law"—and one left—in French, the word is *gauche*.

If this is true or partly true, we have another case of anatomy is destiny, but in a different sense than the one proposed by the authors. In other words the polarity cuts across sexes; the ultimate dichotomy is right vs. left, and this is mapped onto male vs. female or scientist vs. artist and, to a large extent, lies at the root of our adversary tradition in settling problems of right and wrong. I think it is no accident that justice is pictured as a blindfolded figure holding a scale with two balances—if one is up, the other must be down. Does the fact that we are born with only two hands explain some of our difficulty in learning to count past two?

Last of all, let me warmly endorse the authors' critique of psychoanalysis as a straightforward empiricist science. As they rightly point out, the data are almost never "out there," waiting to be counted; rather, the data represent an agreed-upon construction of what has emerged in the course of a continuing dialogue, parts of which will always remain implicit. It is partly for this reason that the transcript of a session so often seems empty and banal; the facts of the matter go far beyond the words spoken; indeed, some of the facts cannot be put into words. To separate subject from object is to lose the full force of the analytic instrument because it is as the analyst hears the materi-al—within his personal context and against the roles assigned to him by the patient—that it yields its full message. Some analysts can make this message clear; others simply practice. But the data are not the kind that can be stored away in an archive, a fact that becomes clear when we consider how few good specimens we have lying around.

I also support the authors in their claim that, at present, we have no satisfactory epistemology for the analytic process. To look only at the problem of what is called free-floating attention, it is clear, first of all, that no such thing exists; we are always listening from a certain point of view, trying to hear a certain theme. Part of this process has been captured by Gadamer in his concept of preunderstanding; this must be carefully distinguished from the grosser kinds of countertransference and studied as a necessary precondition for any kind of listening. The more conventional notion of free-floating attention, with the related myth of the innocent analyst, clearly belongs to an earlier time and place. If we take seriously the view that some kind of preunderstanding is always with us—that the listener hears the patient from within a particular horizon—then we can see that we have as many meanings as there are listeners, and we have to look skeptically at the idea—or myth—that there is a single thread running through any dream or any analytic hour, and our job is simply to find it.

But I differ with the authors in their efforts to explain this objective/subjective split. I am less sure than they are that Freud's anxiety about gender is the cause; rather, I would place the blame on the positivistic Zeitgeist of the early 20th century and on Freud's zeal—which the authors discuss—to make psychoanalysis into a science of the standard kind, else it would not be taken seriously. We now have a chance to undo some of the damage.

Chapter 12

On the Notion of Human Nature: A Contribution toward a Philosophical Anthropology

JOEL KOVEL

Of human nature it may be said that it is one of our most despised, used, and unexamined notions, surviving as unreflective prejudice and little else. As employed in everyday life, the idea of human nature is despicable in the crudity and inertia of its rationalization for the status quo. Nevertheless nobody, no matter how high or low in the social scale, can seem to negotiate a way through life without it. At the same time, the very commonness of the concept, its protean character and the manifestly ideological uses to which it is put, seem to defy any attempt at systematization, much less critique.

So shabby is the notion of human nature, so shot through with ideological contaminants, that one is tempted to give up the effort to define it right at the outset. Would it not be better to discard the whole idea and put in its place either a strong or a weak denial? That is, either we have no nature at all and are clay that can be molded by the environment, or—the weaker denial—we have a multipotential nature that can interact in any number of ways with the environment, and therefore it makes no sense to talk about human nature as an abstract essence.

Each of these maneuvers seems to skirt the conceptual swamp in which the notion of human nature is mired, either by abolishing the concept altogether or by putting it into a pluralistic context, thus diminishing the ideological contamination. As we might expect, such concepts of human nature appeal to liberals or progressives because they open a path to environmental influence and so to the possibilities of ameliorating our condition. By contrast, positive affirmations about human nature, particularly of a biologically grounded type, have classically been used as tools of political conservatism. To invoke a biological human nature as the basis for inequalities is to claim that such inequalities are universals and beyond human power to change in history.[1] On the other hand, if our nature is not fixed, then things can change us—and we can change things.

On closer inspection, however, we are not so sure that much has been gained by these strategems. Consider first the strong denial: human nature does not exist. Is this not but another positive statement about human nature, i.e., that human nature consists of "no human nature," in other words, that our nature consists of being infinitely open to the influence of the social environment? Setting aside this contradiction, it remains doubtful whether anybody could seriously agree with the proposition. To do so means denying that certain outcomes are either impossible or only infinitesimally likely as human types, for example, a race of people who would eat their children. We know that such groups have not appeared, and something tells us that they are not going to appear. This "something" can only be an intuition that human beings, "by nature," resist eating children. It does no good rejoining that in all practical or essential aspects the question is solved in the other way, through more or less countless demonstrations of the profound malleability of human beings and the enormous power of the environment to shape behavioral dispositions. Once any exceptions are admitted to the hypothesis that we are clay in society's hands, then the point at which resistance occurs is exactly what theory has to address—and also exactly what a strong denial of human nature is unequipped to address. Finally, one wonders whether the denial of human nature is really that liberating an idea. We can assert that there is nothing in us that causes our own oppression and degradation, thereby opening things up for historical transformation. But this creates a new problem elsewhere: for if we are completely malleable, then what can be postulated as the source of the drive toward freedom and the resistance to oppression?

The weak denial of human nature, that is, the notion that our nature is pluralistic, multipotential, and interactive with the environment, seems right away to be a better position altogether. In any event, none of the above strictures apply to it. The proposition is not self-contradictory; it is open to empirical experience and subtleties;

and it includes space for resistance to oppression. In fact, I rather like the whole idea and would subscribe to it and adopt it as my own, were it not for one thing, and that is its vacuity. What is a pluralistic nature? Can nature be divisible this way, or is it human value that introduces differences and distinctions? And now that we have toyed with the term a bit, what exactly is meant by "human nature," anyhow? The weak denial is fine, in other words, as long as one does not take the concept of human nature very seriously, or begin to look into the many intricate issues it raises.

However, I do think we should take the idea of human nature seriously. I would go so far as to say that there is no worthwhile inquiry into the human condition that does not clear a way through the problem of human nature. We are creatures who break with nature, but not absolutely, and our human nature expresses the partiality and the dialectic of this break. More, since I also think one's values should be squarely presented in ventures of this sort, I may add as well that I see the challenge posed by human nature as that of reclaiming emancipatory, as against conservative, possibilities in our relationship to nature. I particularly wish to reappropriate the notion within the tradition of Marxism, and to use it as a vantage point from which to continue an interrogation of the relations between Freud and Marx (Kovel, 1981). In sum, given the seriousness of the issues it raises, the notion that human nature is multiform and interactive means merely that it is a rather complex concept and that our work of investigation has just begun.

We may begin with the meaning of nature. In his *Keywords* Raymond Williams begins the entry on "Nature" with the observation that it "is perhaps the most complex word in the language" (1976, p. 184). He goes on to give three major meanings of the term, which I should like to draw upon as a way of entering the concept, as well as two others.

First, *nature* refers to the essential properties of a thing. This is obviously one of the main senses employed in the notion of human nature. In psychological parlance this sense of the term can be subsumed into the idea of character. However the usage can just as well be applied to the nonhuman world, as in, "it is the nature of diamonds to be very hard." It is this sense of the term that trips up the strong denial of human nature, referred to above. For to say that we have no natural disposition is to say that such is our essential property, hence, our nature.

Second, nature refers to the vital force animating the universe or any particular thing within it. This can be taken to refer to the spirit world, as it has been in many primitive and oriental religions; or it can be used to describe sexual drive, as it does in certain vernacular expressions. The sense of nature as animating force may be close to the original, archaic use of the term, and has been applied from the beginning of human history to one deity or another. The idea of human nature may be regarded as the remnant of this archaic sense, as the indwelling vital force, set apart from but somehow driving the person.

Third, nature refers to the whole external world, or whatever occupies space-time, whether or not it is an object of sense-perception. Whitehead says, "Nature is disclosed as a complex of entities whose mutual relations are expressible in thought without reference to mind" (1961, p. 200). This does not mean that nature is disjoined from mind, but only that nature is closed to mind (and, although it is not a claim he makes here, that mind is, or can be, closed to nature). Hence, "we can think about nature without thinking about thought," thereby making nature into the object of the so-called natural sciences. This in turn engages the issue of the boundary between the natural and human sciences, an especially acute problem for psychology. Clearly, the notion of human nature sits astride this boundary, either oxymoronically or dialectically, depending upon one's disposition. As oxymoron, human nature manifests an internal opposition: there is natural science on one side, building on extension and duration; and human or social science on the other, building on meaning and interpretation—and never the twain shall meet. As dialectic, on the other hand, human nature expresses the perplexing but compelling notion that we are part of nature even as we negate nature—that mind is part of nature even though nature is closed to mind. The yearning that people express for natural surroundings expresses this tension, which may be rendered as a feeling of being cut off from, but powerfully drawn to, the physical universe—or the meadow, or the park, or the flowerbox in one's window.

Closely related to this, but nevertheless distinct in that it does not arise immediately from any materialistic concept, is the fourth sense of nature: that which is anterior to civilization. Here nature always expresses what is past, and, correspondingly, what is transformed by historical action. It seems to be impossible to avoid projecting some degree of valence into nature so regarded, although the direction can oscillate wildly depending on the circumstances. Thus nature may be innocent and good, as Rousseau saw it, or as a perpetual state of war, in the version of Hobbes, with vastly different implications for social theory. Similarly, human nature, as the primordium of the self, is never divorced from value. Out of this conjuncture emerges the profound reflection concerning the essential goodness or badness of human nature. Once, this could be expressed as the problem of sinfulness, or to be more exact, original sin. Now, the same question is mystified under the technocratic rubric of "aggression."

The last sense in which nature is taken is the most obscure of all. It connects with the second and fourth senses and perhaps precedes them all. Here nature is regarded as the eternal feminine principle of the universe, the universal, archetypical mother.[2] The mediating term is the association between earth and the mother. It articulates the eternal dialectic between female-mother-earth-impulse-nature and male-father-reason-civilization. Nature is not only surpassed in the march of civilization, but the male is installed over the female. Around this notion lies the whole nexus of domination as it entangles women, nature, and, it should be added, darker races, who also represent nature and irrationality.[3] With respect to human nature, the notion surfaces in psychoanalysis in the debate over the primacy of Oedipal as against pre-Oedipal relations in the formation of personality. At a deeper level, it becomes metaphorically descriptive of the fundamental rationality or nonrationality of human beings. Freud's id, after all, is basically a representation of the primal mother, permanently established, like the Furies of Aeschylus' *Orestaia* in the underworld of the psyche.

From the above we may conclude that nature is no solitary external thing, passively yielding itself up for observation. It is, rather, the projection of human preoccupation, not of the individual brain but of the collective, social mind. It belongs, therefore, to history and undergoes historical development of its own (Collingwood, 1945). Here is the source of the difficulty inherent in the concept of nature, referred to above by Raymond Williams: the referent of the word *nature* is obdurately real and denotes the universe outside of thought or subjectivity; and yet "nature" can never be other than a human construction. As such we understand it to be a rich and complex ensemble of relations, reflecting our participation in the whole universe.

But a projection of what? Is there some unitary kind of relation that finds expression in the notion of nature, some basic preoccupation of which nature is the signifier? I think we can venture a tentative answer to this by abstracting the common features of the varying senses outlined above: of nature as essence, as vital force, as real material world, as past and as primal mother. From this angle, all the ideas of nature become variations on the theme of Otherness. They reflect a sense that our being is part of and yet distinct from the universe, as well as an attempt to comprehend the universe from the standpoint of our incomplete participation in it. The idea of nature, then, is at the other side of the sense of our incompleteness and our mortality. Only a creature who knows it must die would bother to construct a notion of nature. It is a mark of the self's nakedness—but also, as we shall observe, of its very existence.

FROM NATURE TO HUMAN NATURE

Human nature is about humanity in relation to nature, and whatever can be said of nature can also be said of human nature: that it refers to what is most essential about us; is a manifestation of vital force; reflects our participation in the real, material world; is what is below, before, or primal with respect to civilized behavior; and comes from the archaic mother, as was signified by Freud's id. Human nature stands or falls, so to speak, with nature itself. If we believe the latter a basic idea, then the former must be, too.

If nature refers to the sense of Otherness we experience about the universe, human nature refers to the Otherness we experience about ourselves—a being who is part of nature, yet capable of reflecting upon nature, including its own nature. The notion of human nature is the product of this reflection and emerges from the interpenetration of its two terms. Thus it is about the natural aspects of our humanity, and, no less significant if somewhat more obscure, the human aspects of nature. Human nature is therefore a statement about humanness. It is about what distinguishes us from other creatures while maintaining our participation in nature. Once we grasp this, then the vacuous and/or grossly ideological character of many propositions about human nature becomes starkly revealed.

As an example of vacuity, consider the proposition that human nature consists of an overriding need to eat. No doubt this is so, but it is also so for other creatures. The statement's claims, therefore, are directed at our generalized position as living beings (to be more exact, animals), not our specific position as human beings. The net it casts is too fine. It gathers in all creatures who need to eat in order to exist: protozoans, snails, and toads no less than persons. The need to eat is a statement about nature and the needs of animals to metabolize within nature, rather than human nature. And if this need is overriding, it simply means that human nature tends to subordinate itself to nature. Therefore if, for example, starving people on a raft resort to acts of cannibalism, we are not entitled to say that cannibalism is a part of human nature, as it would be, for example, part of the nature of a spider whose newly hatched offspring ate one another. Needless to say, the fact that this example is vacuous for the study of human nature does not make it unimportant as a motivation or value. People must eat, and this must be given priority in any structure of social policy.

The substitution of infrahuman for human qualities also encompasses, however, the most densely ideological distortions of the notion of human nature. Consider behaviorism. A behavioristic proposition inflated to the level of a statement about human nature (Skinner, 1971) might run along the following lines: the essential —i.e., natural in the first sense—feature of human psychology is the tendency of behavior to be shaped by environmental reward. Now there is no point in denying the great importance of environmental reward as a shaper of behavior. Anybody who has raised a child can testify to this. The problem arises, however, with the essentiality of this property. Is this what makes humans human? Or is it rather a common property of all beings whose nervous tissue enables them to store impressions received from the exterior and repeat those consequences that promote the welfare of the individual and/or species? Do we, in other words, give primacy to the behavioral infrastructure we share with pigeons (the way we share hearts and livers with pigeons), or do we look at what is specific for humans?

What makes humans human is what no rat or pigeon would ever do: consciously refuse the given environment at the behest of something else, which is in no sense immediately present, and certainly need not be rewarding. For example, the Sandinistas who eventually revolutionized Nicaragua in 1979 had to struggle for 17 years against often enormous odds and profound hardships before their goal was attained. For most of that time, their number could be totaled on one's fingers while they lived in the mountains or clandestinely, anticipating torture and death should they be caught (Cabezas, 1985). Similarly, Nelson Mandela has been sitting for 23 years in a South African jail, waiting for something he knows may never come and meanwhile resisting all sorts of "rewards" offered by his captors. Is this not specifically human, this refusal, this resistance? A fully developed theory of human nature would have to include this capacity as a leading feature. More concretely, it would have to concern itself with the drive toward freedom as an essential feature of humanness, and base it upon an elemental rejection of behavioral reward, insofar as this reward is tendered by other humans in the pursuit of their interests. Resistance is so quintessentially human, so unique among all forms of life, that it may be said that those humans who have become mature enough to have developed the capacity for freedom and yet deny it within themselves are actually violating their human nature. They are living, that is, at the level of infrahuman species, like pigeons in the experiment of a behaviorist, rather than humans who assert freedom through refusal. But we should remind ourselves, too, that the capacity to posit freedom is accompanied by the capacity to deny itself. It seems to be in human nature to retreat from its own implications and engage in self-violation. Therefore, a theory of human nature must comprehend not just freedom but also unfreedom and domination as specifically human forms of being (Fromm, 1941). These must also be understood, however, in a context of specific social conditions, forms of indoctrination and, indeed, reward. Thus if people behave like pigeons or rats in a maze, it is because their human nature has them live in a society and because that society is controlled by other people who exploit the capacity for unfreedom in their own drive toward domination.

The same considerations apply to the discourse of sociobiology, a more recently influential form of biological reduction. Here society itself is mystified through a comparison with the fascinating but irrelevant collective arrangements of infrahuman species (Wilson, 1975).[4] The key distinction inheres in the fact that ants evince no curiosity whatsoever about either their sociality or ours. This is not simply because they have a tiny brain, but because society is self-evident and without meaning so far as they are concerned, whereas for us it becomes an ineluctable problem. One might say that society does not exist for the mind of an ant, but only—incorrectly—in the mind of a sociobiologist, who does not understand that for society to exist there has to be history, which is to say, recollection, aspiration, struggle, and self-constitution—in other words, human nature, we being political animals, as Aristotle's famous remark stated. Sociobiology, by denying this, fulfills the same reactionary ideological role as behaviorism. It locks history into nature and denies its essential quality, which is struggle. If people can be persuaded—and a prestigious "Science" is a good way to induce persuasion—that they are as compliant as pigeons, as industrious and content as ants, and as satisfied as baboons with hierarchy, then things are so much the better for the commanders of society.

By reducing humanness to the common denominator of other forms of life, sociobiology and behaviorism render human nature naturalistically and downplay what is specifically human. But what is the "specifically human"? What is it that distinguishes us, as a species, from other forms of life? An answer, and it is a particularly influential one, seeks the human essence in our capacity to give meaning to reality. Dolphins notwithstanding, we are the only species to engage in symbolization. Further, the reason, broadly put, for the inadequacy of simple environmental reinforcement as a guide to human conduct is the varying and essentially unpredictable meanings given to events. Indeed, history would not take place were it not for the meaningful construction of reality. A nonsymbolizing creature lives in the world whereas a symbolizing creature is fated to transform reality—and to construct narratives and texts in the process. Therefore, a discourse that specifies meaning as the key to the human order and interpretation as its method has a clear claim to the status of a genuinely human science, or philosophical anthropology.[5]

Hermeneutics is just such a discourse, and because it regards the human situation from its most fully developed standpoint, has a great deal more of genuine interest to tell us than either behaviorism or sociobiology. By the same token, it plays a much more emancipatory role. Freedom depends upon the capacity to interpret reality differently from dominant groups. Whatever augments this capacity also empowers those who have been oppressed.

However, a philosophical anthropology must be able to comprehend human nature as an internal relation between what belongs to the human and to the natural worlds. We may wonder about the capacity of hermeneutics to play such a role. Symbolization and the creation of text and narrative are beyond doubt quintessentially human. But are they part of the ensemble of natural relations outlined above? or do they succeed in clarifying our relation to nature? Evidently not. The symbolic function is, shall we say, too much on the human side of the divide to express the sense of Otherness demanded of a proposition about nature. It fails to convey a sense of vital power; its relation to any material substratum is obscure when it is not tenuous; being a function of advancement, it cannot ipso facto be ascribed to what is past; nor does it tell us much about the archaic Mother and the surrounding cluster of themes. And so the symbolic construction of reality fails to convey the first sense of nature as well, that of being the essential property of a thing. As powerful and necessary as it may be, it is not comprehensive enough to be a description of human nature. By the same reasoning, hermeneutics can not be in itself an adequate basis for a full human science.

This is revealed by the fact that hermeneutic approaches, as they have been constituted, fail to come to grips with the polysemousness and negation at the core of texts.[6] Hermeneutics should not be confused with the deciphering of a code, where one meaning is smoothly mapped onto another. What makes human texts historically significant is the breakdown and decomposition undergone by meaning as it is subjected to ontologically disjunctive modes. This is the basis of the "suspicion," to use Ricoeur's term (1970), of which Freud was the master. That the texts of subjectivity are radically nontransparent and ambiguous is an insight that requires, as Ricoeur correctly recognized, an equivalently radical philosophical base. The problem haunts attempts to construe psychoanalysis as a pure hermeneutic (Kovel, 1978). What is excised in this operation is precisely the domain of nature—opaque to mind, as Whitehead divined, and so ontologically disjunctive from our efforts to interpret reality. It is the greatness of classical psychoanalytic theory, however flawed it may have been in other respects, to sense this ontological gap and try to fill it with the theory of instincts. Attempts to clarify psychoanalysis by putting it on the level of communicative discourses, e.g., that of Habermas (1971) or, from within the clinical field, that of Schafer (1976), end up, by contrast, in abolishing the negativity of the human situation, a negativity essential, one must add, in comprehending freedom (Adorno, 1973). There is a tendency in such a hermeneutic to regard the texts of subjectivity as something that can be purified in the direction of common sense, as though they could be distilled to remove contaminants and reveal the correct meaning underneath. Without any ontologic source of negativity, hermeneutics drifts toward an ultimately repressive and flattened view of human beings. Indeed, it more or less abolishes the notion of an unconscious, replacing it with blanks waiting to be filled in. To move in the direction of a fuller human science requires, therefore, breaking with both the transparency and sufficiency of verbalizable texts. Hermeneutics can then confront what is nameless within the human situation. But this requires an appropriation of human nature.

CONSIDERATIONS OF METHOD

The theoretical appropriation of human nature can be described as the development of a philosophical anthropology. But how is one to proceed with this? It would seem that the method for doing so has to satisfy a number of conditions. First, it should be logically consistent with the meanings of nature and human nature developed above and develop, on this basis, a sense of internal relation between the human and natural worlds. Second, we would ask of it that it be as parsimonious as possible, i.e., that it find the least number of concepts capable of expressing what human nature may be. And third, that it satisfy the condition of what may be called *transhistoricity*. By this we mean that for something to be a property of human nature it needs be manifest in all historical situations and wherever human beings have made their world (Kovel, 1981). Anything less, anything, that is, that is confined to particular historical locations (e.g., kingship, or vegetarianism) could not qualify as natural. On the other hand, the fact that something is transhistorical does not make it natural either, in a very informal sense, since the transhistorical is only manifest historically and so shaped decisively by particular social conditions, as we shall discuss below. But it does confer a degree of universality and essentiality. The class of transhistorical existents is too haphazard in itself to serve as an index of human nature. But it does provide raw material for a parsimonious refinement that can lead to human nature.

The set of transhistorical existents is very large and, so far as I know, has never been counted; indeed, it is hard to imagine that it ever could be counted. However, it is undoubtedly amusing and sometimes fascinating to gather in all those things that define us as a species. The vitality of the notion of human nature can be seen in the more or less uniform interest people evince in trying to figure out what humans have done as humans throughout the span of our existence as a species. Let us consider, then, some candidates for inclusion in the transhistorical: Humans bury their dead,

use tools,

prepare their food,

live in families,

have a sense of beauty,

use language,

adorn their bodies,

wonder about themselves,

take the differences between the sexes very seriously,

are subject to illusions,

and so forth. Now many questions spring to mind about this list—which has no pretensions to completeness, and was not made with any systematizing intention in mind. One may wonder first of all about its empirical validity. How can we tell whether these propositions are true? In fact, we cannot. On the other hand, the list is falsifiable. Perhaps, say, there are people somewhere who are not significantly prone to illusions, or who care not at all about why men are different from women, or who evince no more curiosity about themselves than a frog. If so, these categories would have to be dropped. I do not, however, expect that the list will turn out to be factually wrong because the major statements about human nature, as they manifest themselves in the transhistorical, have a compelling self-evidentiary character to them. Can we, after all, even conceive of human beings who do not use language or tools?

Next, one might wonder about errors of inclusiveness. Are not some of these properties also features of the infrahuman animal world—as was the case earlier in our argument with the question of eating? For example, intelligent apes have been noticed to use tools, as do certain birds in building their nests, and dolphins may well be capable of language.[7] In what sense, then, are we to claim that these functions are species-specific? In response, we can offer two thoughts. First, we should not repeat the error of behaviorism and sociobiology and mistake analogies for homologies. The point is not whether a certain kind of finch uses tools. It is rather whether it uses the tools in a fully human way, i.e., one consistent with human nature. This of course depends upon deriving an adequate notion of human nature, which both specifies what is human and relates it to nature.

And second, there is no chauvinism implied in our inquiry into human nature. Our record as a species does not entitle us to any arrogance on this account, and one might even wonder (it seems to be in human nature to wonder about foolishness of this sort) whether the "lesser" animals would feel embarrassed to be inducted into our ranks. In any event it is all the same to us if dolphins have language or chimps use sticks in a tool-like way. If another species does something in a human way, then this only means that they have some qualities of human nature—and if they did everything in a human way, then we would have to call them human beings and leave it at that. For us the category of a human being is defined not by genotype, but as a creature with human nature. In this respect it makes perfect sense for people to personify their pets. A loyal, loving dog is clearly entitled to at least partial membership in the human community. This is signified by the fact that it is given a name and that it recognizes its master and is recognized in turn as a unique individual. A being who can reciprocate this process to some degree has, to that same degree, human nature. The sign of reciprocity is recognition of the other as an individual, i.e., a person. This function is very close to the core of human nature. No animal incapable of individuation (consider, for example, the cockroach) should be entitled to any vestige of human nature, however dubious the boon. Not all pets, of course, are capable of personal recognition. In such cases, say, for example, rabbits or turtles, the human owner is simply engaging in a highly human form of illusion by projecting desire into another creature who happens to be incapable of reciprocation. In this respect even cockroaches could be made pets.

Now, however, we come upon a much more vexing theme. For it really is no more than a terminological point if a cockroach or pet cat has human nature or not. But it matters a great deal whether—and how—human nature includes qualities such as a capacity for love, for rationality, or for that most loaded of issues, the potentiality for violence, aggression, treachery, selfishness, or hatred—in other words, wickedness of one form or another. This is the point that draws the most attention. We might almost say that the entire meditation upon human nature is occasioned by a preoccupation with the problem of good and evil. In any case there is no adequate statement about human nature that does not place this problem at its center. And yet we do not find these categories listed with the transhistorical.

The reason for this is not that notions such as lovingness, wickedness, or rationality do not belong with the transhistorical. They may, or they may not, and it does matter in either case. But to tell whether this is so, we have to know what we are talking about; we have to be able to define these terms in such a way that the question of their transhistoricity can be addressed. This is no easy matter, to say the least. It is simple enough to determine that every society, at all times and places, has used tools or language. But been aggressive? or loving? or rational? What do these very words mean? The dilemma of human nature seems sedimented into them. The shakiness is not simply because these terms are so value-laden. This is so, of course, but as we have observed already, one must accept the value-laden character of any proposition about human nature. It is that the values embedded in these concepts are as tangled as the concepts themselves, so that it becomes most difficult to say anything coherent about them.

The difficulty forces us to take a harder look at the notion of the transhistorical itself. To be transhistorical means to be present in every historical setting—and determined by that setting. The transhistorical is not outside or beyond history. Quite the opposite. It is embedded within history and would not exist unless shaped by a specific historical formation. Tools are clearly transhistorical, as is language and the family. No one has been able to give evidence of people who live anywhere without them. But any actual tool, whether this be the boomerang or the thermonuclear missile, is an expression of the social formation in which it occurs. The same goes, obviously enough, for language and, less obviously, for the family. We are comfortable in saying that human nature must be such as to express itself in phenomena such as tools, languages, and families.

We must also emphasize, however, that transhistorical phenomena are produced historically. Practically speaking, this means that they emerge stamped with the form of the society and epoch that has made them. Consequently they do not present themselves as transparent and ready to use: they must instead be interpreted. In this respect a hermeneutic—one that is historical and critical—must be interposed in the method of philosophical anthropology, even if it is no substitute for that method, as we have seen. Now such interpretation is challenging in any case, but where the phenomena to be interpreted are both highly subjective and intensely ideological, the problem becomes critical indeed. And such is the case for "aggression," "love," and "rationality."

Take aggression, for example, perhaps the most confusing of all the categories by which human nature is apprehended. When we use terms of this sort, are we referring to activity as such, hostility, violence, cruelty, selfishness, or simply to what we don't like? Freud, for example, established one of the most famous of his concepts—the innate aggressivity of the human species—in *Civilization and Its Discontents*. So famous has this formulation become that the work in question is probably the piece by Freud most read in college. This seems, however, to have more to do with an ideological fit between *Civilization and Its Discontents* and the educational establishment than with the adequacy of its argument, which is essentially a slipshod presentation of bourgeois prejudice. For example, consider the following: "Human beings exhibit an inborn tendency to carelessness, irregularity and unreliability in their work, and ... a laborious training is needed before they learn to follow the example of their celestial models" (1930, p. 93). And his famous litany of evidence for the universality and necessity of human destructiveness concludes first with an unwarranted slander on wolves—*Homo homini lupu*—and then with the following methodological comment: "Who, in the face of all his experience of life and history, will have the courage to dispute this assertion?" (1930, p. 111).

One might reply that this is less a matter of courage than of being able to think critically and historically. For reflection tells us that a person's experience of life and history is itself within history and therefore subject to historical production. In the same manner, aggression, however transhistorical it may be, is also historical and therefore also produced historically. To make sense of these matters requires therefore at the least an objective grasp of history. Freud's notion is not based on any such sense; it is simply personal experience reflected back into history (and, with the wolves, nature) and thereby universalized. And this is little more than a subjective reading of Freud's place in the world—and his defense of that place. Freud's experience—anybody's experience—is itself within history; it is the product of a specific time, locale, and social class. When it employs terms such as *aggression* in an unreflective way, then the result is entirely caught within history. In this respect Freud's insight about the laziness of the masses becomes a complaint that the servants are not doing their job properly, or that the natives are restless. In propositions of this kind, nature becomes history, and history, nature. The transhistorical, however, cannot be collapsed into history. A dialectical space must remain—some function, of natural scope, that enters into history but remains to some extent outside of it as well.

Similar difficulties appear when we try to determine the transhistoricity of "love." Are we talking about *Ananke* and *Eros*, of chivalric love, romantic love, the "true love" of the pulp novels, the "intimacy" of the psychotherapeutic ethos, the love of Man for God, of a mother for her baby? (de Rougemont, 1956). The term is real enough, but so tied up in the way different social periods have constructed affectionate relations that we cannot immediately apply the criterion of transhistoricity.

Matters are even worse in the case of rationality, which is always embedded in the prevailing conceptions of a particular epoch. Thus modernity has imposed a certain stamp of rational behavior on the world. Psychologically epitomized in Freud's dichotomy between ego and id, this conception would have us believe that rational and nonrational are mutually exclusive categories. A person cannot, for example, be rational, i.e., submit to Freud's Reality Principle, and also believe in spirits or ghosts, or believe that the universe is alive. But people in all premodern social formations (including contemporary enclaves of premodernity, in which most of the world's population live as peasants) have believed just this. Are they to be consigned to irrationality—considering that they manage to order their affairs rather sensibly otherwise and have been capable of making the most brilliant inventions at a very low level of technological development? (Diamond, 1974). Is the ultimate in rationality to be the coldminded technocrat who has so separated fact from value that he can sit down with his computer and plot the annihilation of whole nations with nuclear weapons? The very notion of rationality changes so much according to the technical level at which it is assessed that we may justly despair of putting it to the test of transhistoricity.

We should not, however, draw back from the effort because of these difficulties, neither for rationality, love, nor the capacity for evil, all of which are palpably real and have some claim on universality. We may rather approach them as follows. Assume that we have enough already that is indubitable about the set of transhistorical existents to proceed with our second step of induction—the search for the most parsimonious notion capable of accounting for human nature. Let us see then what we can produce in this regard and use as a theoretical razor to approach the vexing triad. With this strategem we might be able to find a way around the conceptual difficulties outlined above.

PARSIMONY

We may now ask whether there is some unitary notion that underlies each manifestation of the transhistorical and that logically squares with the internal relations of human nature. There is, it seems to me, such a notion, the elements of which have been scattered about these remarks. It is not easy to put into words, but it runs something like this: that the core feature of human nature, its most central and essential aspect, is to create and express the self through transformation of the world.

A great deal is contained in these few words, and it will be necessary to dwell a bit upon what they mean—although it must be emphasized at the outset that an adequate exploration is beyond the present scope. We place the essence of human nature in the relation between self and world. In this proposition the self is said to be created and expressed and the world transformed. None of these key terms is self-evident or transparent, so we must next define what we mean by them.

When we speak of the *self*, we refer to the locus of humanness; and when we refer to the project of self-creation and expression, we intend to convey that the self is never given and never completed, and so never fully itself. It is thus human to be never fully human; or in the vernacular, to have weaknesses, "human" failings and, indeed, sin. And by the same token, it is human to have choices and to be never fully determined in the choosing—which is another way of arriving at the essential character of our capacity for freedom and morality.

The essential property of the self is subjectivity. By this, we mean to encompass two terms, or two poles within subjectivity: consciousness as such and a location of consciousness in a point of density, the 'I,' or representation of the person. Observe that we discover subjectivity to be differentiated and not homogeneous. In other words some element of consciousness is occupied with self and another with non-self, and there appears to be a more or less radical distinction between the elements such that self and non-self are at the least differentiated and, in some instances, split from each other. This is an important manifestation of the essential uncompletedness of the human condition. As for consciousness, people often speak of it as though it were a perfectly obvious entity. Nothing in fact could be further from the truth. Freud essentially abandoned his "Project for a Scientific Psychology" (1895), and embarked on the creation of psychoanalysis instead because he was unable to account for the properties of consciousness with natural science methodology. Psychoanalysis in general, and its core notion of the unconscious in particular, arose out of this need and became thereby a science whose specific object was consciousness—or rather, not consciousness in itself, but consciousness as deployed in the human being and under the terms of human nature, i.e., subjectivity. As the science of subjectivity, psychoanalysis has encountered many problems and difficulties, which it is not my purpose here to assay. However, it remains as true now as it did in 1895 that the naturalist methodology abandoned by Freud gets us nowhere in the study of subjectivity. One might as well try to study the oceans with the telescope on Mount Palomar. Psychoanalysis, flawed and in need of critique as it is, at least looks in the right direction: it studies not nature but human nature, manifest in subjectivity.

It did not take psychoanalysis to discover that whatever else consciousness may be in the rest of the natural universe, it takes the form of self-consciousness under the conditions of human nature. Such had been the elementary product of human reflection from the very beginning. What psychoanalysis was able to disclose empirically, however, was the actual contour of subjectivized consciousness——a topology created and constituted by the differentiation of the subject.

Essentially, psychoanalytic inquiry discovers this topology as desire. Desire is the transfiguration of subjectivity under the terms of the human condition. Because desire is a condition of consciousness and not an object of consciousness it becomes impossible to isolate and virtually impossible to define. This is not because of ideological contaminants (though these occur as well), but because of its essential nature. Desire is, we might say, the longing of a subjectivity that has not been completed for an object it cannot name; hence it always remains beyond the net of signification. Desire invests objects, so that these seem "the object of desire," and hence desire itself. But there is no "desire itself," only the topological transformation of the object world which renders that world into an occasion of continual longing.

We might say that this continual longing is the creation of, and makes itself known as, passion. Therefore we can add to our definition of desire that it refers to whatever is passionate in human experience, whether on the loving, longing side, or that of hating and wishing to annihilate. Desire is the wish as such, the experience of lack and impulsion, the want and not the need.

Desire cannot be analytically separated from the incompleteness of the self: it is, to put it metaphorically, the actual topology of that incompleteness, its way of being. Therefore desire includes among its relations a resisting of the distinction between subject and object. We become what we want, and want to become something other than what we are. In any case desire for the other is also desire for the self since in desire, other and self lose their discrete boundedness. In psychoanalytic lingo it is impossible to sharply distinguish narcissism and object love at deeper levels of the psyche. Distinctions that treat the one without the other are purely heuristic and arise because the verbal-syntactical mind that constructs psychoanalytic and other kinds of scientific propositions must repress its desire and see things in distinct and isolable form.

Although this is not the place to pursue the theme, I believe that all of the major propositions of psychoanalytic discourse can be placed on a sounder ontological footing through an appropriation of the concept of desire. Indeed, the notion is at the center of the psychoanalytic project, and the value of psychoanalysis is no more or less than its fidelity to desire, which touches upon whatever is considered worthwhile and beloved by human beings. This central role for desire, however, does not imply making a fetish of it, as if it were the alpha and omega of human existence. There is a kind of totalizing psychoanalysis that does this, interpreting everything of significance about life according to the deployment of desire—and forgetting that desire touches upon, but does not determine, everything essential to our life. Making a fetish of desire is romanticization, and this reminds us that desire is responsible for (we may say that it generates the transhistorical capacity for) the human proclivity to illusion and unreason of all kinds. Furthermore, as we have observed, desire is just as likely to end up in the sphere of hatred as that of love. There would be no racism without desire, no lust for power, no sexual cruelty, rape, and whatever else people do of a passionate nature to harm and divide one another. But however troublesome desire may be, it does remain central to human nature, and to displace it from the center of theory would only be another example of the proclivity to illusion (based on the desire to abolish desire).

Indeed, the human condition would be unthinkable in any other framework. No other notion so encompasses the senses of the term *nature* as this applies to human beings. Desire surely connotes the sense of vital power. As for its material quality, observe the intense corporeality of desire: its attachment to the body, its essential sensuousness. From this perspective desire now appears to be a reaching toward the material universe by a creature who has differentiated itself from that universe. It manifests our rootedness in the stuff of the world, our being as flesh. And since of course we were each quite definitely at one with the stuff of the world before we became conscious, and certainly before we became self-conscious, desire must be for this union, for the obliteration of differentness as such. Whatever exquisitely specific and individual form it may take, desire is also for a fusion with nature—and nature is the generic object of desire.

The remaining senses of nature also configure themselves readily about the notion of desire. It is evident that desire is primarily for the past—and the original human others who mean the past for us. Freud's recognition of the conservative quality of instincts and the compulsion to repeat epitomizes this insight. And if this is so, then fundamentally, desire is for the mother.

Here we should again be reminded of the need not to make a fetish of desire, i.e., to not be seduced into taking it out of history. Desire, too, is historically produced even as it rests upon its ontological foundation. Nor can desire be identical to the full meaning of human nature. If the symbolic function was too close to the human pole of human nature, desire is too close to the pole of nature, too ready to abolish the differentiation that is the hallmark of humanness. Desire expresses the distinctive quality of subjectivity, to be sure; but subjectivity is not the only feature of human nature. Human nature, recall, is the creation and expression of the self through transformation of the world. Desire expresses the essential backward-looking moment in this dialectic; the yearning for a nature lost in the process of self- and world-transformation. However desire may condition the goals, it cannot encompass what it is that accomplishes the transformation.

In other words there has to be a forward-looking moment if there is to be a backward-looking moment—or an organism capable of sustaining its dialectic. Nature would not exist for us as that which is lost unless we had the human-natural capacity to lose it. And this capacity, indeed, our existence as living beings, depends upon our active transformation of nature. We must have a practical dimension within human nature, a capacity for the engagement of praxis.

This notion formally engages the Marxist tradition in the discourse of human nature. As "historical materialism" Marxism is responsible for the insistence that everything transhistorical be revealed in its concrete historical setting. However, there is some doubt as to whether Marxists would agree that a transhistorical concept exists, inasmuch as Marxism is identified with the vigorous rejection of any human essence outside of social relations. The standard Marxist position is interpreted as that of humans producing themselves *in toto*, free from any biological or otherwise natural fetters. In a recently published and very thorough study, Norman Geras shows convincingly that Marx himself had a very definite and basic notion of human nature, and that it is this nature that is transformed and expressed in history.[8] Here, then, is another instance where Marx and Marxists do not agree (Miranda, 1980). Moreover, Marx's notion is formally quite similar to that of the transhistorical—with the significant difference of being much less interested in the subjective dimension. As I have discussed elsewhere, this downplaying of subjectivity is to the detriment of Marxism (Kovel, 1986).

If one idea can be termed primary in Marx, it is that consciousness mediates the relations between human and nature through the active transformation known as the labor process (which we are here terming *praxis*, in order to keep a distinction between the general human capacity for labor and its historical deformations, or alienation). Thus Marx is fully aware of the dialectic between humanity and nature, and he places subjectivity, i.e., consciousness, at its center. However, for Marx consciousness is purely active; it has no passive relation to nature, as is contained in the notion of desire. This is a serious deficiency—just as the Freudian downplaying of the active relation to nature is a serious deficiency. For both sides are needed in a full view of human nature.

Praxis, the conscious transformation of reality, completes the motion of human nature as it is dialectically intertwined with desire. Praxis enables us to eat, but also to prepare our food as we wish. Praxis is not, therefore, disengaged from desire, as severely rationalist conceptions of human nature might hold. And this is for the simple reason that the reality to be transformed—and the consciousness of that reality—contains desire. Desire is part of reality, and praxis transforms desire as much as it does the external world. From the standpoint of praxis there is no purely external world. Because of desire, the subject and the object world always contain aspects of each other: the external world contains the internal world, as the internal world contains the external world.

Thus the wise person makes no pretense of achieving positive and complete knowledge of reality, and true rationality consists of a recognition of the essential existence of the nonrational, or desire, in every human situation. By contrast, the rationalization that believes it can positively strip fact from value and attain fully objective knowledge of what is essentially human, is victim to a severe and potentially fatal illusion. It is an objectifier, not the creator of genuine objects. For the object includes the projection into it of subjective qualities, epitomized in the product of craft or art—the product made for individual use. However the objectification is stripped of individual quality: an indifferent thing suitable only for exchange and known only by its abstract numerical—i.e., cash— value.

It follows from the preceding discussion that the world is intensely differentiated according to the values projected upon it by desire and praxis. Inasmuch as the self is forever incomplete, it is forever seeking itself in the world. And inasmuch as desire is for the original others while praxis recognizes the mutual interdependence of pro- ducers, the world as it matters to us is the world populated with other humans: society. Thus to say that the self seeks its creation and expression through the transformation of the world is to claim nothing more or less than that the cardinal disposition of human nature is to make history. For history is the transformation of society through the transformation of nature. And so our human nature is to be historical, i.e., to transform itself. We are the creature that expresses its nature through the refusal of nature, that projects its being into the world and thereby makes itself.

RECURSION

Although it is beyond our present scope to do so, it should be possible to derive each of the transhistorical existents as a function of a human nature that creates itself through the transformation of the world. For some of our examples, say the property of wondering about ourselves or being subject to illusions, it can be seen, at least intuitively, how this may be. For others, such as language or sexual curiosity, a more elaborate derivation may be necessary and additional factors would have to be invoked. However, what about our vexing triad of rationality, aggression, and love, the discussion of which was suspended while we attempted to get at the core of human nature? Will the notions of self- and world-transformation, and of desire and praxis illuminate these phenomena?

Rationality, which should not be confused with intelligence, is the appropriation of reality by human intellective power. But our reality is saturated with subjectivity and desire. As a result we say the world is full of value. Value can be considered the form reality takes because of the demands placed on it by human nature. Therefore rationality consists of the appropriation of a humanized, value-filled reality—or what comes to the same thing, a reality that is both historical and transhistorical. Rationality must appropriate its own history, which means that it must be adequate to its time. In our time the form of rationality that appropriates history, value, and desire may be termed *critical*. It is known by its fidelity to depth, its refusal to accept the given (which is necessarily a product of the partial interests of the ruling groups) (Horkheimer, 1974). Critical rationality is marked by universal interest (hence the inclusion of value and desire), and may be opposed to instrumental forms of reason, which narrowly oppose means to end without accounting for the problem of value. Critical rationality must also be opposed to the kind of totalization that loses sight of the individual in the universal. It is the latter tendency that accounts for fanaticism and perverts the essential human capacity for refusal away from freedom and toward one form of destructivity or another. From another angle we have to oppose reason to rationalization, and since it is scarcely obvious in any given situation whether an intellectual operation belongs to the one or the other, we can understand on theoretical grounds why the category of rationality cannot be automatically ascribed to human beings.

Needless to add, one does not need theory for this judgment, since any glance at the world will confirm that reason and human nature sit uneasily together. In fact, it is easy enough to conclude that, for all our vaunted intelligence, unreason is the characteristic condition of our species, at least in the modern era. It is a much more difficult matter to decide the source of this unreason. Most people informally ascribe it to human nature, in the crude sense noted at the beginning of this chapter, specifically to our selfishness, aggression, or general badness. The vacuity of this argument should not blind us, however, to the fact that any statement about essential rationality is also a statement about virtue—which brings us to the matter of virtue or sin in light of philosophical anthropology.

If the essential feature of the self is its incompleteness, then it cannot also be claimed that people are by nature good, bad, or anything else. No enduring adjective clings to a formation as open as human nature. On the other hand, we are obliged—if we aspire to any serious view of the human situation—to account both for the capacity and the ubiquity of evil. Any attempts at denial or minimization can be immediately recognized as an idealistic illusion that simply flies in the face of what we see around us in the world. One such denial would be the proposition that malevolence is simply a reaction to bad circumstances. Obviously there is a truth to this— but just as obviously, it is a limited truth that denies human responsibility—and thereby denies human nature itself. If we do not have the capacity for evil, then we do not have the capacity for good; we are not human beings at all, but simply clay upon which the environment writes.

The notion of human nature contains within it an essential— albeit potential—space for choice, whether good or evil. The very fact that we express our nature by making history signifies that we have it in us to change the world. But first we have to refuse it. The inability of desire to name its objects creates the havoc of illusion, but it also ensures that no object will be sufficient. Thus, in a very fundamental way, we violate our nature by passively accepting the given state of affairs. This follows directly from the definition of human nature, since to acquiesce means to deny the full expression of our capacity for self-expression. On the other hand, to choose, express the self, and transform the world tells us nothing in itself about whether good or evil has been done. After all, Hitler expressed himself and transformed the world no less than Gandhi.

In any case, what is called evil in the real world cannot be encompassed in any calculus of aggression or any other naturalistic category. By the same token, we must ascribe a moral dimension to human nature, which is realized one way or another on the level at which human nature functions: history. This is not to deny the existence of aggression, but to understand its place. Aggression as such is simply the primordium of praxis—its basis in the need of every being to exist by negating other being: the breaking of eggs to make omelets. The farmer who breaks the soil is being aggressive, as was Jesus when he threw the money changers out of the temple.

Undoubtedly, John Brown used up more aggression in trying to free slaves than Adolph Eichmann did in routing Jews to extermination camps, but we would not call the one evil, or the other good, on this account.

Hatred is closer to the lineaments of evil than aggression, but it is not evil in itself. Consider again the comparison between John Brown and Eichmann, the one consumed with hate and rage, the other, placid and comfortable in his bureaucratic niche. Ontogenetically, hate begins in the matrix of bondedness, specifically, whenever desire transforms family relations in the direction of envy or jealousy. For practical purposes envy and jealousy are transhistorical inasmuch as they arise out of the ineluctable contradictions of infantile desire. They are way stations of a self in the process of creation and expression who happens to be small, dependent, and passionate—by nature—and who cannot attain its development unless it negates its infantility and undergoes loss.[9]

We cannot ascribe evil, however, to a small child. The category applies, rather, to grown persons with individuality and social agency. Once this position is reached, then the opportunity exists for the other to be recognized as a fully human being, and so to be denied that reciprocity, or to be dehumanized. It is only in this framework that the question of evil can be raised, not as a simple matter of destruction, hostility, or hatred, but as the violation of the other's human nature, that is, the suppression of another human being's capacity to freely express the self through world-transformation. We must emphasize the term *freely* to ensure that genuine reciprocity takes place. It cannot be evil to set oneself against another bent on fascism, reaction, obscurantism, and so forth.

Evil is a function, then, of the term connoted by *violation*: violence. More generally, it depends on domination, societally organized violations of human nature. It is the responsibility of those in power and rests in the configuration of the social order they establish, or are allowed to establish by the remainder of society. It is in this context that the real viciousness of human beings is mobilized. We may say then, using the terms developed here, that the capacity for evil is transhistorically grounded in human nature, and that social violence and domination are its general historical forms.

A parallel construction can be made for the virtues in general and the capacity for love in particular. In the same manner, this builds upon but is not directly constituted by any instinctual formation. As is common knowledge, love and hate, with their mutual origin in desire, have no real line between them, being only separated by love's intention to preserve the object's individual existence in the face of desire's tendency to obliterate this. Love is initiated by desire, but must transcend desire to become a full affirmation of the other's human nature: his or her capacity to express the self through transformation of the world. Only a fully developed human nature can begin to love, but only an adequate society can begin to develop human nature to this point.

Love so construed must of necessity take many forms beyond the elementary relations between two people. For a fully developed human nature is developed in relation to the actuality of its potential objects—and this is a matter of concrete historical deployment. The desire to fulfill the object's human nature may well take radical and even revolutionary forms when social domination imposes vast amounts of violence, suffering, and injustice. Great evil calls forth great good—as well as rationality—manifested as love for the oppressed and a willingness to take drastic measures on their behalf. Psychoanalytic reductionism can only see in such behavior a reaction formation against hostility. In doing so it forfeits its claim on rationality and sinks to the level of an instrumental justification for the ruling order. A fuller notion of human nature will see in these radical measures a fulfillment of being.

We referred above to a fully developed human nature. This is a contradiction in terms. By its own nature, human nature can never be fully developed since there is always an essential incompleteness to the self. But what do we mean by this? Desire helps us to describe the self's incompleteness, but it does not go far enough. For desire describes the self's looking beyond itself, but not its actual incompleteness, or emptiness. It is, so to speak, what the self wishes to fill this emptiness with.

To talk about the actual incompleteness of the self, we need another discourse entirely, one rather foreign to the technical establishment but quite well known to ordinary people of all times and places. And this would entail an understanding of that empty space within the self as a zone of potential spiritual development. Or to use another ancient term, the *soul*. We do not have any practical way of talking about the phenomena in this realm, but this should be no reason for neglecting something so manifestly crucial to human existence. If the discourse on human nature advanced here has any validity, then it must culminate in a recognition of the spiritual. Anything less would fail the test of rationality described above.

Spirit is no illusion, although it easily becomes illusory when grasped exclusively by desire. Then it devolves into infantile fantasy of rescue by or submission to the archaic parent, as Freud quite accurately pointed out in the critique of religion offered in *Future of an Illusion*, and indeed, throughout his life's work. However, in real human development, spirit actually breaks loose from desire. To deny spirit by collapsing it into desire—as Freud attempted to do—is an illusion born of the desire to repress the spirit, a common disturbance amongst the post-Enlightenment intelligentsia. We may suspect that Freud's hostility, or ambivalence, toward spirit was part of his desire to fawn on the patriarchal-technocratic establishment, involved then as now in the construction of a tough-minded medical discourse. Though beyond our scope to pursue, it may also be added that a close examination of Freud's work would reveal many genuinely spiritual elements peering out from the cage in which he trapped them.

I am not about to attempt here a "phenomenology of the spirit," but will confine myself to the following: we can distinguish between spirit and desire by the degree of transcendence contained in the former. Desire remains yoked to the self, seeking to complete the self through the appropriation of one object or another. Spirit, on the other hand, goes through and negates the self and becomes "selfless." It is experienced as a dissolution of the self and an emancipation from the craving for objects—this accompanied by a sense of union with what can only be called in a halting way, the universal. Freud felt he had disposed of this process in *Civilization and Its Discontents* by tracing it to the sense of "oceanic" union achieved by the infant at the mother's breast (1930). However, this model, which is essentially a depiction of the state of sleep, fails to account for the heightened and sharpened consciousness, i.e., the awakening of a spiritual state. By the same token, spiritual experience is not necessarily blissful, but can just as well be explosive, or engage the "dark night of the soul." Furthermore, the heights of spirituality are scarcely attained except through great struggle and discipline. All of this suggests that the transcendence of the self, or ego, is something that engages desire but radically surpasses it.[10]

If, however, the motion of human nature is to create and express the self, then spiritual development, which transcends the self, is both a transcendence of human nature and its fulfillment—a fulfillment in the sense of being the fullest and most expressive creation of the self. However, the self is neither created nor expressed without transformation of the world, a relation that must obtain for spiritual experience as well. This reminds us that spiritual development cannot be severed from material development: spirit transcends the isolated self, or ego, but not matter. It is not supernatural. At the same time, spirit, as a transhistorical existent, is also determined by particular historical conjunctures of the world. Indeed, the world remains to be transformed. How this is carried out becomes the decisive test for spirit. In order to fulfill itself as human nature, then, spirit must return to the world and invest reality with the same universalizing motion as was experienced in its own genesis. Otherwise, spirit is abandoned, leading to the soulless materialism that afflicts the modern age, or, turning inward, to the various deformations of narcissism, ranging between spiritual pride and psychosis. The fullest development of spirit, by contrast, seeks the compassionate reclamation of the material world on behalf of those beings whose nature—human or otherwise—has been violated.

But this is to recognize spirit as emancipatory and identical with the fully realized force of love, a notion common to all of the world's great religions. For it is love, too, that transcends desire and preserves it, along with its object, at the same time. Are we to conclude, then, by returning our philosophical anthropology with its scientific and rational claims to the spiritual traditions of humankind? As long as we do not lose sight of the many intricacies that lie in the path of this identification—in particular, the necessity for critical rationality and all this implies for the project of emancipation—such a return is long overdue. It would be, one might even venture to claim, part of the fulfillment of human nature.

NOTES

1. For an excellent discussion of this tendency as it has become embraced by the scientific establishment, see Lewontin, Rose, & Kamin (1984).

2. Major discussions of the theme can be found in de Beauvoir (1952), and Rich (1976).

3. The question of domination, scientific rationality, and women is taken up historically in Merchant (1980) and from the standpoint of the philosophy of science in Keller (1985). Each gives a particularly good sense of how nature is constructed by "man." For the question of race, see Kovel (1984).

4. For a review and critique, see Lewontin, Rose, & Kamin (1984).

5. It goes without saying that the space between such an anthropology and the academic discipline that bears the same name remains to be negotiated. Anthropology holds no privileged place among the existing human sciences, even if, in principle, its scope may be wider. And all of the established discourses have, as the theoretical reflex of their bureaucratic compartmentalization, an attenuated view of human nature.

6. Barratt (1984) develops this point most tellingly and combines it with a major critique of hermeneutics.

7. For example, W. H. Thorpe (1963, p.375) describes the Galapagos woodpecker-finch, which uses long cactus spines to dislodge insects from crevices in bark, as well as the satin bower bird, which uses fibrous material as a brush to paint its nest with a kind of dye. Many other instances could also be cited. See also MacIntyre (1974).

8. Geras (1983). See also Timpanero (1980) for an interpretation that stresses the remorseless biological limits against which human action must proceed. The whole field is opening up within Marxism, in part as a result of the nuclear and ecological crises and in another part because of the feminist movement, with respect to all of which Marxism had hitherto been somewhat obtuse. Perry Anderson writes that "the articulation of nature and history is ineludable," and that "the relations between nature and history bring us to the long overdue moment of socialist morality. Marxism will not complete its vocation as a critical theory unless and until it can adequately meet it" (Anderson 1983, pp. 83,84).

9. In my opinion Melanie Klein offers the deepest understanding of the transhistorical roots of hatred and rage (1948).

10. William James's description of the range of such states is still unsurpassed (1958).

REFERENCES

Adorno, T. W. *Negative dialectics.* New York: Seabury, 1973.

Anderson, P. *In the tracks of historical materialism.* London: Verso, 1983.

Barratt, B. *Psychic reality and psychoanalytic knowing.* Hillsdale, New Jersey: The Analytic Press, 1984.

Cabezas, O. *Fire from the mountain.* New York: Crown, 1985.

Collingwood, R. C. *The idea of Nature.* Oxford: Clarendon Press, 1945.

de Beauvoir, S. *The second sex.* New York: Knopf, 1952.

de Rougement, D. *Love in the western world.* New York: Pantheon, 1956.

Diamond, S. *In search of the primitive.* New Brunswick: Transaction, 1974.

Freud, S. Project for a scientific psychology. S.E., 1895, Vol. 1.

Freud, S. *Civilization and its discontents.* S.E., 1930, Vol. 21.

Fromm, E. *Escape from freedom.* New York: Farrar & Rinehart, 1941.

Geras, N. *Marx and human nature: Refutation of a legend*. London: Verso, 1983.

Habermas, J. *Knowledge and human interests*. Boston: Beacon, 1971.

Horkheimer, M. *Eclipse of reason*. New York: Seabury, 1974.

James, W. *The varieties of religious experience*. New York: New American Library, 1958.

Keller, E. Fox *Reflections on gender and science*. New Haven: Yale University Press, 1985.

Klein, M. *Contributions to psycho-analysis, 1921–1945*. London: Hogarth, 1948.

Kovel, J. Things and words. *Psychoanalysis and Contemporary Thought*, 1978, *1*, 21–88.

Kovel, J. *The age of desire*. New York: Pantheon, 1981.

Kovel, J. *White racism*. New York: Columbia University Press, 1984.

Kovel, J. Marx, Freud, and the problem of materialism. *Dialectical Anthropology*, 1986, *10*, 179–188.

Lewontin, R. C., Rose, S., & Kamin, L. *Not in our genes*. New York: Pantheon, 1984.

MacIntyre, J. *Mind in the waters*. New York: Scribners, 1974.

Merchant, C. *The death of nature*. San Francisco: Harper & Row, 1980.

Miranda, J. *Marx against the Marxists*. Maryknoll: Orbis, 1980.

Rich, A. *Of woman born*. New York: Norton, 1976.

Ricoeur, P. *Freud and philosophy*. New Haven: Yale University Press, 1970.

Schafer, R. *A new language for psychoanalysis*. New Haven: Yale University Press, 1976.

Skinner, B. F. *Beyond freedom and dignity*. New York: Random House, 1971.

Thorpe, W. H. *Learning and instinct in animals*. London: Methuen, 1963.

Timpanero, S. *On materialism*. London: Verso, 1980.

Whitehead, A. N. The concept of nature. In F. S. C. Northrop and M. Gross (Eds.), *Alfred North Whitehead, an anthology*. New York: Macmillan, 1961.

Williams, R. *Keywords*. New York: Oxford University Press, 1976.

Wilson, E. O. *Sociobiology: The new synthesis*. Cambridge: Harvard University Press, 1975.

The Pragmatics of Human Nature: Commentary on Joel Kovel

KENNETH J. GERGEN

It is refreshing to encounter a contemporary scholar willing to confront the problem of human nature in the bold, self-reflexive, and personally revealing manner that Joel Kovel has demonstrated. Most contemporary inquiry remains myopically fixed upon issues of localized significance; the implications for a full vision of human nature remain safely unarticulated. Thus, for example, most inquiry in the cognitive sciences provides a sophisticated elaboration of the metaphor of person as computational device while avoiding the question of what it would mean for the culture should this metaphor become the taken-for-granted or literal language for comprehending persons. Others conscientiously avoid the problem of human nature, because confronting it would threaten the rhetorical power invested in positions that now prove commonly acceptable. In his case, for example, those who claim that objective facts support their contentions often hold a position of power, for contemporary beliefs favor those who claim empirical support. Yet, if one were to elaborate the vision of human nature embedded within the empiricist position, objectivity as a warranting device would be sadly damaged. For how is one to separate subject from object, the knower from the known, consciousness from its contents, as one must presume if empiricism is to be justified?

Yet, how is one to regard statements about the nature of human nature; what status should be accorded to them in scientific, intellectual, or therapeutic communities? Of course, the immediate question that most would consider is that of verisimilitude: Is Kovel accurate in his assessment? Where has his portrait been misleading? Yet it is just this criterion of objectivity that we have just had reason to doubt. The concept of objectivity is warranted by an array of suppositions that are themselves without empirical justification and which themselves presume a vision of human nature. And Kovel's vision of human nature offers no alternative means of understanding the nature of knowledge (if this indeed can be presumed to be part of his vision), such that we could conclude that his contentions were knowledgeable. From his extensive experience with human beings Kovel has drawn inferences about underlying motives, needs, intentions, and the like. Yet, we have no means of understanding how Kovel could have gotten it right while all those in contention could have been so mistaken. Kovel claims that many of his conclusions are based on "palpable realities." However, this claim flies in the face of an immense body of hermeneutic analysis. As I have said in chapter 2, there is little apparent means by which any interlocutor can privilege any given interpretation for its superior accuracy.

So let us not ask whether Kovel is accurate in his portrayal; the answer to this question is principally indeterminate. Rather, I propose that we view Kovel's treatise as a move in an extended dance of which we the recipients are a part. That is, Kovel has offered a body of discourse, and if accepted or embraced, such discourse has consequences for what it is we may subsequently do or say. If we accepted the thesis, we would not be stepping properly if we were to then espouse a commitment to sociobiology or use the thesis to justify operant reinforcement experiments to determine the character of human nature. Kovel's treatise is an invitation to a dance of a particular sort; what remains unexplicated, however, is the remainder of the moves. What are the pragmatic implications of the thesis within social life?

The question of pragmatics is of no small consequence, for assumptions about human nature furnish the culture with the seemingly incorrigible bases with which the remainder of one's beliefs and actions should be consistent if one is to remain a participant in good standing. Such assumptions are particularly important within contemporary Western culture, as most expansions in the range of what we presume to be natural typically entail a reduction in what we take to be subject to moral choice. To the extent that human nature demands, requires, or imposes particular patterns of action, then the extent to which we grant choice to the individual is thereby diminished. Further, with each characteristic granted to human nature, patterns of justification within the culture are altered. Certain actions are "only natural," or intrinsic to our functioning, whereas others are to be delegated to a marginal status, possibly requiring treatment or punishment. And, too, statements about human nature often contain implications for matters of social control. They inform authorities of what to anticipate and what forms of sanction may be necessary. With these extensions of the dance in mind, let us explore more carefully the pragmatic implications of Kovel's valiant effort.

At the outset we find Kovel's picture of human nature a rich and variegated one. Although at its center is the assumption that individuals express themselves through the transformation of the world, we find many additional characteristics associated with or related to this central thrust. We learn that people by nature are self-alienated (experiencing themselves as dissociated from self and nature), dominating, self-violating (given to unfreedom), violent, prone to hatred and treachery, envious, jealous, and continuously in a state of unfulfilled (and principally unsatisfiable) desire. The portrait is surely a bleak one—more so than even Freud envisioned. Some compensation is furnished, however, as we learn that persons are also by nature rational, loving, oriented toward action, and possessing a spirit that, in its most advanced form, "seeks the compassionate reclamation of the material world on behalf of those beings whose nature ... has been violated."

As we immediately discern, this extensive list considerably diminishes the extent to which we would be justified in holding individuals responsible for their actions. Acts of violence and domination are not, on this account, matters of personal decision; by nature we are moved to such actions, and by nature we must put such impulses into practice. Further, and not without irony, we find that revolutionary actions are also natural. This stance is somewhat destructive to the cause that Kovel wishes to espouse, as such actions within the present account are bereft of moral significance. Revolutionary actions are no longer a matter of voluntary decision, for within the Western conception of morality, there is no morality without voluntary reflection. In these various ways Kovel echoes grounding assumptions located in many of Freud and Marx's writings: the inherent evil of the former and the revolutionary destiny of the latter.

Yet, although this conception of human nature militates against the rhetoric of individual morality, responsibility, guilt, duty, and obligation, there is a subtle reinstatement of such concepts on yet another level of Kovel's analysis. From his perspective single individuals cannot themselves be held responsible for their state of bondage, their hatreds, their lack of full rationality, or their callousness toward their fellow creatures. All of these tendencies are expressions of human nature. But when we inquire further into why patterns of domination, exploitation, hatred, and so on are more prevalent at some periods or in some persons to a greater extent than others, and when we inquire into the future potentials of humankind, we find that social conditions play a critical role. From Kovel's perspective social conditions are capable of eliciting or shaping the direction in which human nature expresses itself. When one lives under conditions of domination, then violence is a natural reaction; only when one lives in an "adequate society" can love for others flourish; contemporary social conditions now favor a "critical form of rationality," and so on. In sociological circles this line of thinking is generally termed *systems blame*. Rather than holding individuals responsible, it is to the social system that one turns. Such argument possesses a certain degree of legitimacy (surely on a par with individual blame). However, the next moves in this particular dance may be less favorable to Kovel's designs. This orientation has much in common with the environmental determinism of the Skinnerian behaviorist. In both cases the individual is considered more or less a pawn to environmental conditions. Further, when blame is cast upon the system it runs the risk of losing its value as a pragmatic wedge. When the system is to blame, responsibility is often diffused among participants; in such a way the moral force of the charge is dissipated.

Let us turn from the issue of morality to that of justification. As indicated, assumptions about human nature often serve as justificatory devices within the culture—favoring certain social institutions and militating against others. On these grounds there is much to applaud in Kovel's analysis. Most prevailing accounts of human nature continue to be influenced by the Darwinian emphasis on survival; optimal functioning of the organism is expressed through its adaptation to existing conditions. However, this orientation to human nature takes existing conditions for granted; it offers little justification for altering the status quo. In contrast, Kovel's analysis attempts to "reclaim emancipatory possibilities." The account of human nature posits that one's normal functioning should entail "transformations of the world." In effect, those who do not join together in defiance of the status quo are somewhat less than human (or at least, not fully expressing their full potential as humans). For those concerned with ridding the world of domination, oppression, and exploitation, Kovel's analysis is a very useful if not brilliant reconceptualization. It forms a powerful justification for revolutionary action.

Yet, although there is much to warrant this call to action in various corners of the world, would we be satisfied if such assumptions about humans were carried into every domain of human life? Many of us would applaud the application in El Salvador, Afghanistan, and South Africa. However, do we truly wish to see such calls to action extended to every other sphere—to Cuba, Nicaragua, or China? And would we wish close relationships to be continuously challenged because their very stability threatened human nature? If we truly believe that it is our natural calling to transform the world, then all forms of stability pose a threat. Stasis violates one's nature; remaining in a relationship, a job, a community, or any other form of long-term commitment suffocates or destroys one's fundamental being. I doubt that Kovel would wish to embrace such a conclusion. If not, however, more must be said about constraints over the drive for transformation.

It is this latter issue that usefully sets the context for our final consideration—that of social control. It is not simply that the Kovel analysis, if broadly credible, would invite an increase in the power of the state. After all, if existing powers believed their subjects to be naturally inclined toward revolution, they would surely increase expenditures for programs of surveillance and control—as opposed, for example, to programs of public welfare. (Prevailing assumptions concerning the chaos resulting from unchecked sexual passions can account for many restrictive laws and penalties in contemporary life.) Kovel's analysis also has problematic repercussions on the microsocial level of daily life. If I believe that my colleagues, neighbors, and family members are fundamentally moved toward domination, violence, treachery, and transformation, what kind of attitude is invited toward them? Yes, they may also possess capacities for rationality and love, but given the inventory of horrors that lies central to being, social existence would surely seem to be in precarious balance. Is there hope within this system for enduring trust or a sense of deep and genuine relatedness? It is surely not in immediate evidence. Kovel does offer the possibility for the emergence of a love, the fullest realization of which transcends desire and becomes a "full affirmation of the other's capacity to express the self through the transformation of the world." Yet even this love, which seems sadly lacking in critical ingredients, cannot take place without the future development of a more adequate society. In the meantime we are left with a deep sense of suspicion and doubt about our fellow creatures.

Yet, in spite of these various misgivings, I am pleased to see the Kovel analysis springing into existence. As we see, assumptions about human nature have a way of insinuating themselves into our institutions, strengthening some and debilitating others. Kovel's is a fresh alternative to the existing forms of justification. As such it offers fresh departures, a new voice, a state of refined consciousness. And with such conceptual tools one can build more effectively toward the kind of social equality that many of us believe to be just. However, my final hope is for an emendation of assumptions such that we might anticipate more from human relationships. We need not assume that human nature is a property of single, isolated individuals with relatedness a secondary and problematic byproduct. Invited is an analysis in which the individual is an emergent property of community—in which relationship precedes identity. If such were broadly realized, conflict might not be a necessary antecedent to communion.

Rejoinder to Kenneth J. Gergen

JOEL KOVEL

First, as to the "palpable reality" of the evidence on which to base a concept of human nature, one would have to agree that there are methodological and evidentiary problems here that I was unable to explore. But would anyone dispute that human beings, everywhere and at all times, have used language or tools or made much over the difference between the sexes? At the risk of sounding positivistic I must assert that these are facts, not hermeneutic problems. Of course, all facts have to be constituted by the knower and in this sense are interpreted from the moment of their inception. Some factual propositions about human beings are so subject to interpretation that we may fairly abandon hopes for any positive statement along the lines of "humans are such-and-such." I stated very clearly that propositions having to do with innate aggression and wickedness are of this sort, as are statements about the inherent virtue or rationality of the human species. On this account I must reject Kenneth Gergen's imputation that I see human beings as "by nature ... dominating ... violent, prone to hatred and treachery," and so forth, even if I would insist that we respect the realities of the human condition and not succumb to a Pollyanna-ish view of ourselves.

On the other hand, the universality of some facts about us—e.g., language, tools—cannot be gainsaid, for all that they too are interpreted. It is this set that I call the transhistorical and use as the raw material from which the notion of human nature can be derived. In this respect, though I would be the first to announce that what I am doing here has practical implications, namely, to rescue the notion of human nature, or essence, for radical discourse, I would also strongly oppose Gergen's wholesale relativizing. Whether or not the interpretation offered here is the proper one, I would hold that insofar as we are real beings, we have—like everything else in the universe—a nature that is discoverable and that determines certain conditions of our human existence.

But human beings are not "by nature" any one thing, whether good or bad. Human nature is necessarily a more abstract and synthetic concept. It is not identical with the transhistorical; it is rather what is necessary in order to explain the transhistorical. It was in this sense that I considered our human nature to be the creation of the self through the transformation of the world.

It must be said, however, that I do not recognize my view of human nature in Gergen's representation of it. For he seems to have the impression that I regard human nature as somehow antithetical to moral choice. His impression is not based on the ideas presented in the essay. What I was at pains to point out was that the human essence was, as I saw it, objectively centered about a moral and spiritual mode of being. Far from being opposed to morality, our nature is actually expressed in moral choice, and indeed, in all the relationships having to do with freedom. There is no reason to cite the passages in which this idea is developed; to do so would virtually require repeating the essay itself.

I also am at a loss to understand how he interprets my views on society. In any case let me insist that I have no intention of shifting the burden of responsibility to "society," abstractly opposed to an individual, and even less to the "environment," which to me is a term signifying mechanical and crudely material conditions. Social conditions indeed take the appearance, under capitalism particularly, of resembling laws of nature in that they seem to operate independently of human will or responsibility. But it is a superficial reading that stops at this point. In reality, things look this way only because of socially imposed alienation. Society is lived and made every day by every individual person. There is no real split between the individual and society, no matter how things may appear; the two constitute each other. To say therefore that "society is to blame" is to make a senseless statement. There is responsibility for what goes on in the human world, but it resides in the social action of persons, not the abstraction of society.

Nor do I have any objection to relatively steady-state social conditions. Primitives and peasants have lived so for aeons, and they have lived full human lives, transforming the world and creating themselves in a reasonable harmony with nature. After all, every time a farmer turns over the soil, every time a meal is cooked and eaten, human nature is expressed. Of course these people, being human, also expressed themselves by being foolish and tragic as well, as their legends will tell you.

Our fate is radically different, however. We have the fortune of living in a time that is in anything but a steady state, or a reasonable relation to nature. Simply put, the reason for this is that our wealth and "stability" have been extracted in an unequal exchange with the great mass of the world's peoples, specifically, the working classes and generally, the Third World. In conjunction with this, our society has dominated and befouled nature rather than lived in harmony with it. The result is a universal disorder against which one can only be shielded by retreating from reality. Our only choice is which way to transform the situation: to reproduce it in all its chaos and headlong drive to destruction, or to change it in a manner worthy of our human being.

Name Index

Achilles, 196
Adler, Alfred, 292
Adorno, Theodor, 21
Aeschylus, 374
Agamemnon, 196
Allport, Gordon, 225, 226
Anderson, Perry, 398n
Antigone, 195
Antonovsky, A., 198
Arendt, Hannah, 70
Aristotle, 312, 316, 317n, 377–378
Arkes, H. R., 127
Augustine, 313–314, 318n, 322
Austin, J. L., 45

Bacon, Francis, 336
Baier, Kurt, 151
Barratt, B., 398n
Bass, A., 105n
Beck, A., 123
Berkeley, George, 4
Bernard, Claude, 66
Bernstein, Richard J., 20–21, 39,
    109–113, 175–180
Betti, Emilio, 19–20, 38, 263n
Bhaskar, R., 65
Binswanger, Ludwig, 282–283
Bonner, Hubert, 225–226, 229,
    242–243, 245
Boss, Medard, 282–283
Bowers, K. W., 118
Brecht, Bertold, 88
Brenner, Charles, 67
Brentano, Franz, 273, 290–291,
    295
Brown, John, 394
Bugental, James, 225–227, 230
Bunker, Archie, 124
Burns, George, 157
Byron, Lord, 256

Chrysippus, 304, 312
Collingwood, R. G., 38
Comte, Auguste, 7
Creon, 195–196
Crocker, J., 125
Crusoe, Robinson, 253

Da Vinci, Leonardo, 90–94, 96, 102,
    105–106nn, 110
Davidson, Donald, 11
Derrida, Jacques, 88
Descartes, René, 4, 14, 19, 89,
    228–229, 256, 264–265n, 273,
    305–308, 312, 314, 318n, 322, 325,
    326
Dilthey, Wilhelm, 3, 6–8, 11, 12, 15,
    19, 20, 23, 24, 29, 38, 117, 125, 139,
    232, 234, 246, 250, 251–253,
    254–255, 264n, 266n
Dinnerstein, Dorothy, 212, 213
Dreyfus, Hubert, 12, 19, 142, 214n,
    264n, 265n, 289–294
Droysen, Johann Gustav, 8
duVair, Guillaume, 308

Eagle, Morris, 161
Edelson, Marshall, 63
Eichmann, Adolph, 394
Einstein, Albert, 177
Eissler, K. R., 106n
Epictetus, 304, 311
Erikson, Erik, 319n, 337

Farrell, B., 106n
Faulconer, J. E., 118
Fish, Stanley, 43
Flax, Jane, 24, 216–219, 367–369
Fleiss, Wilhelm, 92, 352
Folkman, S., 127
Follesdal, D., 264n

409

Subject Index

I, 243, 246, 303; narrow and
narcissistic, 244
Id, 375; female vs. male, 350
ideal speech, 23–24
idealism, transcendental, 265n
ideas, 141, 304, 306; embodiment of,
307
identity, problem of, 315
illusion, 391, 396; proclivity to, 388
Imagination: failure of, 193–197;
minimizing facticity through,
191–193
impressions, 5
individual experience source, 188, 189
individualism, 256; possessive, 257
individuality, 260
infantile helplessness, 346
infantile sexual experience, 106n
infantile sexuality theory, 91–92
inferiority complex, 277, 278–279
inferiority feelings, 194–195, 197–200;
pride and, 196
infrahuman species, 377; properties of,
380–381; qualities of, 376
in-itself, 234, 243
inkblot test, interpretation of, 128
inner events, 10–11
inner experience, 266n; impasse of,
30–40
innerness, 227, 253, 261; existence of,
52–58; of experience, 326; language
of, 313–316; value of, 231, 323
insight, 111, 354, 357
instincts, conservative quality of, 389
instinctual impulses, 273
intentional language, 45
intentionality, 134, 165–166, 273; in
human behavior, 160–162; Husserl's
concept of, 264n; meaning and,
162–163; See also motivation
internal dialogue, 123
internal dispositions, 42
internal perception, 37
interpersonal communication, 19
interpretation, 8–12; art and science of,
116–117; based on mistranslation,
90–97; biased vs. warranted
subjective, 88–90; cognate problem
of, 46–50; cognitive structures and,

125–126; context and, 117; of
dreams, 98–101; flexibility of,
120–121; Freud on, 356–357; goal of,
249–255; of human intention, 29–30;
impossibility of, 49; interdependent,
modifiable network of, 34–35;
knowledge derived from, 17; meaning
and, 145; vs. meaningful activity,
147n; multiple, 35–36; as
objectification, 20; objectivity of, 357;
problems of, 87–107; process of, 29;
relativity of, 38–39, 88–91; vs.
authenticity of, 59–61;
representational states and, 143–144;
restructuring of, 296–297; revision
of, 33–34; of self, 299–319; standards
or criteria for evaluating, 89;
symbolism and, 96–97; textual, 6–7;
transparency in, 39; truth of, 55–56;
ubiquity of, 85–86; uncertainty of,
20; validity of, 20–21, 39, 52–58,
60–61. See also hermeneutics,
psychoanalytic interpretation
Interpretation of Dreams, 290;
symbolism in, 97, 98–101
interpretative methodology, 140
interrelatedness, 359–361; Freud's
denial of, 360–363. See also
relationships
intimacy, 217–218; fear of, 212;
impossibility of, 49; possibility of, 43
Introductory Lectures (Freud), 99–100
introspection, 309–310; vicarious, 323
isolation, 217–218; introspection and,
323; self psychology and, 325

judgment: failure of, 193–197;
minimizing facticity through,
191–193
Jungian psychoanalysis, 329

Keywords, 372
Know-Nothing world view, 64–67,
74–75; in psychoanalytic
interpretation, 81–83
Knowing: Cartesian conception of, 16;
how, 47; that, 47
knowledge. *See also* understanding art
and, 17; atomistic conception of, 5;